2001

Regulating the Future

Recent Titles in
Contributions to the Study of Mass Media and Communications

The Press in Times of Crisis
Lloyd E. Chiasson, Jr.

Native Americans in the News: Images of Indians in the Twentieth Century Press
Mary Ann Weston

Rights vs. Responsibilities: The Supreme Court and the Media
Elizabeth Blanks Hindman

The Press on Trial: Crimes and Trials as Media Events
Lloyd Chiasson Jr., editor

Personalities and Products: A Historical Perspective on Advertising in America
Edd Applegate

Taking Their Political Place: Journalists and the Making of an Occupation
Patricia L. Dooley

Developing Sanity in Human Affairs
Susan Presby Kodish and Robert P. Holston, editors

The Significance of the Printed Word in Early America:
Colonists' Thoughts on the Role of the Press
Julie Hedgepeth Williams

Discovering Journalism
Warren G. Bovée

Covering McCarthyism: How the *Christian Science Monitor*
Handled Joseph R. McCarthy, 1950–1954
Lawrence N. Strout

Sexual Rhetoric: Media Perspectives on Sexuality, Gender, and Identity
Meta G. Carstarphen and Susan C. Zavoina, editors

Voices in the Wilderness: Indigenous Australians and the News Media
Michael Meadows

Regulating the Future

Broadcasting Technology and Governmental Control

W. A. KELLY HUFF

Foreword by Michael C. Keith

Contributions to the Study of Mass Media and Communications,
Number 61

GREENWOOD PRESS
Westport, Connecticut • London

Library of Congress Cataloging-in-Publication Data

Huff, W. A. Kelly, 1956–
    Regulating the future : broadcasting technology and governmental control /
    W.A. Kelly Huff ; foreword by Michael C. Keith.
      p. cm.—(Contributions to the study of mass media and communications,
      ISSN 0732–4456 ; no. 61)
    Includes bibliographical references and index.
    ISBN 0–313–31468–3 (alk. paper)
    1. Broadcasting—United States—History—20th century. 2. Broadcasting—Political
aspects—United States—20th century. I. Title. II. Series.
HE8689.8 .H84 2001
384.54′3—dc21   00–049497

British Library Cataloguing in Publication Data is available.

Copyright © 2001 by W. A. Kelly Huff

Library of Congress Catalog Card Number: 00–049497
ISBN: 0–313–31468–3
ISSN: 0732–4456

First published in 2001

Greenwood Press, 88 Post Road West, Westport, CT 06881
An imprint of Greenwood Publishing Group, Inc.
www.greenwood.com

Printed in the United States of America

The paper used in this book complies with the
Permanent Paper Standard issued by the National
Information Standards Organization (Z39.48–1984).

10 9 8 7 6 5 4 3 2 1

This book is dedicated to my beautiful wife, Rita, without whom I could not have done any of this. It is also dedicated to my two wonderful children, John and Laura, who patiently and impatiently put up with me while I did this book—all the while reminding me that my family was more important than this or any other endeavor.

Contents

Foreword *by Michael C. Keith*   ix

Preface   xi

Abbreviations   xv

Introduction   1

1. Learning from Broadcasting's Past   5

2. AM Stereo and the Marketplace   17

3. AM Stereo: The Wrath of Kahn   39

4. Digital Audio Broadcasting: A New Kind of Radio   67

5. Border-to-Border DAB   87

6. Advanced Television from HDTV to DTV   111

7. The Grand Alliance and the Introduction of DTV   145

8. The FCC's Changing Regulatory Role   185

Bibliography   197

Index   223

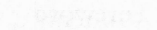

Foreword

One of the points that W.A. Kelly Huff raises in his book has to do with the age-old question of whether human beings are capable of learning enough from their past mistakes to avoid repeating them in the future. Like most reasonable and compassionate men, he is hopeful—if not certain—that this is the case. History would seem to suggest that we as a species are doomed to make the same blunders over and over again, and this sad pattern appears all the more likely to occur when big business and government constitute the elements of the alchemist's ladle. If you don't think this is true, just check your history books. Each faction (when business and government convene, it nearly always is factious) tenaciously and greedily clutches its cherished agenda as it sets out to apprehend a payoff that is more often than not at cross-purposes with the other faction, or so it seems. Invariably, the product of these ritualistic and futile machinations is a numbing standoff. One side objects to what the other side proposes, and vice versa, and the grand impasse begins. Mediators, lawyers, and regulators are called in, and the arterial clog congeals to a deadly density. Eons pass, the rest of the world moves on, but the original point (whatever that was) of contentious debate goes unresolved.

In the case of Amstereoization (as the author calls it), much of the preceding applies, but somewhat in reverse. In this particular situation the government's refusal to get in the way of manufacturers, to let them work things out for themselves, actually (and ironically) proved to be anathema to the timely development and full realization of stereo on the standard broadcast band. When broadcasters were given the much-coveted opportunity by the feds to decide for themselves (something that they had long sought), they could not do it. In fact, they were in profound discord as to which way to go, so they literally went nowhere, and the hope and dream of AM stereo faded like the theme music from an old radio melodrama.

When the FCC finally did get around to taking the bull (double entendre intended) by the horns and select an AM stereo standard, it was the proverbial case of doing "too little too late." By the mid-1990s the idea of two-channel sound on the AM band held little excitement for the listening public, especially those who had moved on to high-fidelity sound supplied by TV, VCRs, DVD, and so on. For those tuned to AM (about one in five radio listeners), it did not matter that the talk programs that they enjoyed could be split between a left and a right speaker. As one listener put it, "Who needs stereo on AM? All those talk guys speak with forked tongues anyway." Another listener questioned the virtue of two-speaker sound when all that was available on AM talk stations were "right"-wing speakers.

In *Regulating the Future,* Huff does an exceptionally good job of sorting out the whole lurid conundrum of broadcast technology and government control. All right, maybe lurid is not the best or most appropriate adjective to describe how the government and its unwitting (is self-serving and stupid too strong?) subjects can turn a grain of sand into a quasar—or black hole.

Several years ago, I assembled a symposium on the state of AM radio for the *Journal of Radio Studies.* One of the people I called upon to contribute to this effort was the author of this book. His grasp of the AM stereo question made him the resident academic expert on the subject. Now, nearly a decade later, he has produced a comprehensive, book-length study that adds further information and understanding to what has become one of the great sagas in the electronic media field, and he has aptly and appropriately applied the AM stereo model to other broadcasting technologies such as DAB and DTV.

Michael C. Keith

Preface

This book is about radio and television technologies and how they are regulated in the United States, but it is not a technical book per se, as it does little to describe how any of these technologies work. In writing this book, I have two broad objectives. The first is to put complicated technologies and issues into accessible terms to make them more widely understandable and approachable. The second is to explore what these technologies are, how they got started, and who's using them and then to examine their impact on the evolution of broadcast regulation. This book tells the stories of AM stereo, DAB, HDTV, and MTS (TV stereo) and compares them to each other and with other developments such as FM stereo and color TV.

Perhaps the most significant aspect of *Regulating the Future* is the examination of the change in governmental standard-setting policy for new technologies from the time of the FM stereo proceeding in the 1950s until the time of AM stereo in the 1970s, TV stereo in the 1980s, and DAB and HDTV in the 1990s and early twenty-first century. In the late 1950s the FCC tended to exert tremendous governmental control over broadcasting development. As a result, FM stereo was implemented smoothly and categorically. In 1980, however, AM stereo was caught in the middle of an FCC torn between governmental control and the marketplace that resulted from the FCC's deregulation of TV and radio. Prior to the infamous AM stereo marketplace decision of 1982, the marketplace method of FCC standard setting was unknown. Because of AM stereo, we now know what can happen to a technology when no standard system is selected, that is, Amstereoization. AM stereo has become the measuring stick for the success or failure of new radio-TV technologies. The histories of AM stereo, DAB, TV stereo, and DTV were marred by FCC indecision, which was prompted by complex technological gain and controversy over how to introduce new radio-TV technologies to the public realm in an era of deregulation.

Quests for aural and visual perfection have resulted in numerous technological advancements. In the radio industry, many broadcasters have tried to avoid improving sound quality by altering programming. An example would be switching from music-oriented formats to voice-only programming, such as news and talk shows. FM radio was created to free broadcasting from static but languished in the shadows of TV and AM for decades. The addition of stereo to FM was prompted by consumer acceptance of stereo recordings. Prior to FM stereo, there was no way to broadcast stereo recordings. Stereo enabled FM not only to catch AM but to reverse totally the audience in a 12-year period. AM broadcasters, until then content with sitting on their huge lead, were forced for the first time ever to fight from behind. AM broadcasters employed two general strategies: format changes and stereo.

Meanwhile, radio has been engaged in a long battle to compete with TV. TV itself was enough of a challenge to radio, but the introduction of color in the 1950s, stereo in the 1980s, and digital technology in the present and future has made radio less of a priority for the FCC. Radio survived TV's threat because it changed and adapted. By the early 1960s radio began to recover from the setbacks brought on by TV competition. Two reasons for radio's renewed vigor were portability of radio sets and localization of the medium. Portability was made possible by transistors that were cheaper and much more compact than previously used electronic tubes. The reduction in size of radios made it possible for listeners to carry the radio with little inconvenience. Because the radio could be used in an infinite number of places, such as beaches, bedrooms, ballparks, offices, cars, and so on, the changing and elusive audience could be reached more easily. By demographically defining the various audiences, formats could be targeted for maximum results. In turn, the specific audiences were sold more easily to advertisers.

In regard to cross-comparing technologies, a good example is seen in AM stereo and HDTV. AM stereo was seen as unnecessary by many, because it offered no apparent advantage over FM stereo. Likewise, there is sentiment that HDTV is not attractive to consumers. The problem with present-day TV, according to many critics, seems to lie more within content than within technology. It is believed that most consumers prefer better programming to a more detailed picture.

DAB may change radio, as we know it, forever, yet, outside industry trade magazines, little has been written about the technology and its impact. DTV receives much of the attention from the media and the FCC at present, but the TV industry and consumers continue to view the technology as a mystery. HDTV has been mired in a lengthy, ongoing proceeding that has been further delayed by the introduction of digital technology and the intervention of the computer industry. Because of rapid changes in technology, society, and culture, both radio and TV have found it necessary to evolve, and so has the FCC.

ACKNOWLEDGMENTS

The author wishes to give formal recognition to Michael C. Keith, a prolific author of approximately 20 books on broadcasting. For several years, Mike encouraged me to write this book, and I am honored that he wrote the Foreword. Special appreciation goes to my wife, Rita, who tirelessly read and edited the manuscript. I offer special thanks to Greenwood Publishing, acquisitions editor Pamela St. Clair, assistant production editor Leslie Billings, and assistant manager Leanne Small. I also express my appreciation to professors Jack Bridges, James Fletcher, Bruce Mims, and Jerry Donnelly for their support for both this book and myself.

Abbreviations

AAC	advanced audio coding
AAMSI	Association for AM Stereo, Inc.
ABC	American Broadcasting Company
ACATS	Advisory Committee on Advanced Television Service
ACTV	Advanced Compatible Television
AES	Audio Engineering Society
AIM	Promotion Association for Research and Development of Advanced Image Technology
AMRC	American Mobile Radio Corporation
AMSC	American Mobile Satellite Corporation
ASPEC	Adaptive Spectral Perceptual Entropy Coding
AT&T	American Telephone and Telegraph
ATRC	Advanced Television Research Consortium (the Grand Alliance)
ATS	FCC's Advanced Television Service
ATSC	Advanced Television Systems Committee
ATTC	Advanced Television Test Center
ATV	advanced television
BBC	British Broadcasting Corporation
BBI	Boston Broadcasters, Inc.
BSS	broadcast satellite service
BTA	Japan's Broadcast Technology Association
BTSC	Broadcast Television Systems Committee
CAB	Canadian Association of Broadcasters

CBA	Community Broadcasting Association
CBC	Canadian Broadcasting Company
CBO	Congressional Budget Office
CBS	Columbia Broadcasting System
CCIR	International Radio Consultative Committee
CD	compact disc
CDRB	Committee for Digital Radio Broadcasting
CEA	Consumer Electronics Association (formerly CEMA)
CEG	Consumer Electronics Group
CEMA	Consumer Electronics Manufacturers Association
CES	Consumer Electronics Show
CIRT	Mexico's Commission for New Radio and Television Technologies
COFDM	coded orthogonal frequency division multiplexing
CPB	Corporation for Public Broadcasting
C-QUAM	Motorola's compatible-quadrature amplitude modulation
CRTC	Canadian Radio-Television and Telecommunications Commission
DAB	digital audio broadcasting
DAR	digital audio radio
DARS	digital audio radio services
DBS	direct broadcast satellite
DCR	Digital Cable Radio
DOC	Canada's Department of Communications
DOJ	Department of Justice
DRAM	dynamic random access memory
DRB	digital radio broadcasting
DRE	Digital Radio Express Inc.
DRM	Digital Radio Mondiale
DRRI	Digital Radio Research Inc.
DSB	digital sound broadcasting
DSBC	Digital Satellite Broadcasting Corp.
DSP	digital signal processing
DSR	digital satellite radio
DTV	digital television
DVB	digital video broadcasting
DVD	digital versatile discs
EASE	Early Adopter Station Enhancement
EBU	European Broadcasting Union
EDTV	enhanced-definition television

EIA	Electronic Industries Association
8-VSB	8-level vestigial side-band
ENG	electronic news gathering
ETSI	European Telecommunication Standards Institute
FAA	Federal Aviation Administration
FBI	Federal Bureau of Investigation
FCC	Federal Communications Commission
FDA	Food and Drug Administration
FNOI	Further Notice of Inquiry
FNPRM	Further Notice of Proposed Rulemaking
FOB	FCC's Field Operations Bureau
FOIA	Freedom of Information Act
FOX	Fox Television Network
FPS	frames per second
FTC	Federal Trade Commission
GDP	Gross Domestic Product
GE	General Electric
GI	General Instrument
GM	General Motors
HDTV	high definition television
IBAC	in-band, adjacent channel
IBEW	International Brotherhood of Electrical Workers
IBOC	in-band, on-channel
IDTV	improved-definition television
IIS	Germany's Fraunhofer Institut für Integrierte Schaltungen
IRTS	International Radio and Television Society
ISM	independent sideband modulation system
ISO	International Standards Organization
ITU	International Telecommunications Union
IUEW	International Union of Electronics Workers
IWG-2	FCC's Informal Working Group 2
JPEG	Joint Photographic Experts Group
KCI	Kahn Communications, Inc.
LCD	liquid crystal display
LDR	Lucent Digital Radio
LMCC	Land Mobile Communications Council
LMS	Land Mobile Services
LP	long playing record

LPTV	low power television
MIT	Massachusetts Institute of Technology
MPAA	Motion Picture Association of America
MPEG	Moving Picture Experts Group
MSS	Multichannel Sound Subcommittee
MSTV	Association for Maximum Service Television
MTS	multichannel television sound (TV stereo)
MUSICAM	Masking pattern Universal Sub-band Integrated Coding And Multiplexing
MVPD	multichannel video programming distributors
NAB	National Association of Broadcasters
NAMSRC	National AM Stereophonic Radio Committee
NASA	National Aeronautics and Space Administration
NB	new band
NBC	National Broadcasting Company
NBMC	National Black Media Coalition
NCTA	National Cable Television Association
NFL	National Football League
NII	National Information Infrastructure
NOI	Notice of Inquiry
NPR	National Public Radio
NPRM	Notice of Proposed Rule Making
NRBA	National Radio Broadcasters Association
NRSC	National Radio Systems Committee
NSRC	National Stereophonic Radio Committee
NTIA	National Telecommunications Information Agency
NTSC	National Television System Committee
OET	FCC's Office of Engineering and Technology
OST	FCC's Office of Science and Technology
PAC	perceptual audio coding
PAL	phase alternation line
PBS	Public Broadcasting System
PCS	personal communications services
RadioSat	Radio Satellite Corp.
RDS	Radio Data System
RIAA	Record Industry Association of America
RMA	Radio Manufacturers Association
SB-ADPCM	Sub Band-Adaptive Pulse Code Modulation

SBE	Society of Broadcast Engineers
SCA	Subsidiary Communications Authorizations
SCI	Strother Communications Inc.
SDARS	satellite digital audio radio services
SDTV	standard definition television
SEC	Securities Exchange Commission
SECAM	séquential colour avec memorie, or sequential color with memory
Sirius	Sirius Satellite Radio Inc.
SMPTE	Society of Motion Picture and Television Engineers
TCI	Tele-Communications Inc.
UDTV	ultra-definition television
USADR	USA Digital Radio
USSB	U.S. Satellite Broadcasting
VCR	videocassette recorder
VOA	Voice of America
VTR	video tape recorder
WARC	World Administrative Radio Conference
XM	XM Satellite Radio Inc.

Introduction

Pohlmann (1992a) observed: "The future that lies before us is fascinatingly unpredictable until we experience it. Then it flies by us as the present and is transformed into the past, becoming something tedious we have to study in high school. Technology evolves similarly. No one can resist the promise of future technology. After it becomes reality it will be superseded and will inevitably become covered with dust. And our great-grandchildren may make a killing in the antiques market" (p. 62).

On October 25, 1993, the FCC adopted a *Report and Order* making Motorola's C-QUAM system the official standard for AM stereophonic broadcasting in the United States. The FCC was reluctant to make the decision and did so only because Congress forced it to finish what it originally initiated in its 1977 NOI. Section 214 of the *Telecommunications Authorization Act of 1992* required the Commission "to adopt a single AM broadcasting stereo transmission standard" and "to remove any remaining uncertainty among AM broadcasters as to which stereo system to use and thereby encourage the improvement and expansion of AM broadcast service." The FCC's (1993) decision was ordered into effect as of March 21, 1994.

Although the Commission opened its original AM stereo NOI in 1977, it neglected its responsibility with its 1982 decision to make no decision at all. AM stations were allowed to begin stereo broadcasting in 1982, but the FCC, in a state of flux concerning its regulatory role, chose to let the marketplace decide which system would best serve public interest. Five systems were approved to broadcast AM stereo: Kahn Communications, Inc./ Hazeltine Corporation (Kahn), Belar Electronics Laboratory, Inc. (Belar), Harris Corporation (Harris), Magnavox Electronics Company (Magnavox), and Motorola, Inc. (Motorola). Hazeltine Corporation owned exclusive licensing rights for Kahn's system. The systems were each engineered and designed differently, making any one of them incompatible with all the others. Each system required its own receiver, meaning that to hear each of the five signals would require five different receiving or decoding units.

Broadcasters, manufacturers, and consumers alike were left confused. AM managers did not know which system—if any—to buy and install. Receiver manufacturers were reluctant to build sets compatible with just one system for fear another system might eventually dominate the marketplace. Consumers could only wait and see what receivers might make it to retailers. Because of the confusion, three of the original five systems were withdrawn from the market by 1984. Just the systems of Motorola and Kahn remained. Over the next decade, Motorola built a tremendous lead in numbers of systems in use. By the time of the congressional mandate, the FCC had little choice but to select Motorola as the standard system. Unfortunately, the decision had not been made in 1982, when broadcasters appeared ready for stereo. With the passage of time, AM stereo lost its luster, in part, due to the emergence of other technologies, such as DAB, HDTV or DTV, MTS or TV stereo, and other technological advances.

AMSTEREOIZATION

Until the AM stereo decision, the FCC had set standards and exerted tremendous control over broadcast transmission, and most technologies were implemented smoothly and categorically. Ultimately, the importance of AM stereo is not the technology itself but how the FCC handled the standards proceeding leading to the marketplace decision. Montgomery (1999) wrote: "I always thought a great disservice was done to AM in the way stereo development was handled by the FCC, the inventors, receiver manufacturers, and even the broadcasters. It has been an opportunity lost, in my opinion" (p. 16).

Certainly, the technological opportunity was lost, but some good has come from the decision. The marketplace approach was previously unknown, so AM stereo illustrates what can happen to a technology relegated to it. Broadcasters rightfully feared the FCC's new direction and were concerned about how it would regulate the future of other technologies. Indeed, subsequent standards proceedings were subjected to Amstereoization, a syndrome representing the FCC's reluctance or refusal to set a system standard for broadcast transmission. The Commission elects to mandate and enforce operating parameters, allowing legal operation of any system meeting them. A chain of circumstances is set into motion resulting in a confused marketplace in which broadcasters, manufacturers, and consumers are uncertain how, if, or when to implement the technology.

Having been subjected to the marketplace, AM stereo became a barometer for other new broadcast technologies. MTS, DAB, and DTV have all been affected by the FCC's indecision over how to introduce them, and, as a result, broadcasters have begun to take a more active role in controlling their destinies. With DTV and MTS, broadcasters worked toward achieving a standard consensus in attempting to prevent Amstereoization. DAB has thus far seen less broadcaster cooperation and unity.

AM stereo was considered unnecessary by many, because it offered no apparent advantage over FM stereo. Therefore, it is entirely possible that the FCC may have sacrificed the technology to its new deregulatory direction. Likewise, there is sentiment that DTV may not be particularly attractive to consumers. Many critics believe that TV's ills lie more within programming content than within technology. To understand the FCC's regulatory shift, which began with the deregulation of radio (1979–81), it is important to understand how it handled other technologies—past and present. The purpose of the book is to examine and compare the FCC's standards proceedings from FM stereo and color TV approval in the 1950s until AM stereo in the 1970s, to MTS in the 1980s and DAB, HDTV, and DTV in the 1990s.

Carey (1989) said the study of history is important, because too often "there is a tendency to ignore lessons from the past or even to examine what occurred when earlier technologies were introduced" (p. 10). Carey explained the twofold purpose of employing a historical perspective: "First, there are many parallels between the introduction of new technologies or services . . . and the introduction of older technologies. . . . Second, a historical perspective can help us to view new technologies in a broader social framework. . . . It is helpful to examine how society dealt with the technologically disenfranchised in the past in order to develop policies about how we should deal with them today" (p. 10). Further, Carey said history is important in predicting the future of a technology's acceptance rate: "If our predictive skills in the past have been weak, we can at least try to benefit from an analysis of what actually happened and why. What are the patterns of adoption for new technologies by ordinary consumers? What lessons can we learn from the introduction of earlier technologies that may inform decisions about the development of new technologies" (p. 11)?

ORGANIZATION OF THE BOOK

In order to set a context for comparison to AM stereo, DAB, and DTV, Chapter 1 offers a brief overview of radio and TV history, including the onslaught of TV and the recovery of radio, with emphasis on FM stereo and color TV. Each had a significant impact on the future of broadcasting.

Chapter 2 begins an examination of AM stereo, from early attempts in 1925 through the wrangling that culminated in 1982's unprecedented marketplace decision, a decision that would have tremendous impact on the regulation of future technologies. The FCC was influenced by the reinterpretation of its regulatory role as exemplified in its *Deregulation of Radio* proceeding that coincided with AM stereo. Chapter 3 builds on Chapter 2, covering AM stereo's marketplace years and attempts to get the FCC to reconsider its decision. The FCC and broadcasters ultimately realized that stereo would make little difference without improving AM radio's overall technical state. The FCC eventually set an AM stereo standard, but it was too late to save the technology. Emphasis is placed on the marketplace battle between Leonard Kahn's small company and corporate giant Motorola.

Chapters 4 through 7 cover digital technologies for radio (DAB) and television (HDTV/DTV). Attention is also given to MTS. Both DAB and DTV have presented tremendous challenges in the selection of technical standards by the FCC. Unlike other broadcast enhancements, such as stereo or color, DTV and DAB radically alter traditional broadcasting. DTV has received the most attention from government, broadcasters, and consumers.

Chapter 8 compares the developments and standard-setting proceedings of FM stereo, AM stereo, color TV, MTS, DAB, and DTV in order to illustrate the FCC's changing regulatory role and the effects of Amstereoization. FM stereo was created as a means to broadcast stereo recordings and to enable FM to compete with AM. As the cycle progressed, AM stereo was invented to enable AM to compete with FM stereo. DAB, similarly to FM stereo, was inspired by digital CDs. MTS and DTV were introduced to keep pace with other technologies, such as VCRs and videodisc players featuring audio and video better than that of monophonic broadcast television. The cyclical nature of broadcast technologies in the United States is explored.

Chapter 1

⬧ ⬧

Learning from Broadcasting's Past

FCC PROCEDURE

In the United States, the FCC is charged with selecting broadcast transmission system standards. In typical proceedings, the FCC opens an NOI into the feasibility and necessity of a new technology, follows with at least one NPRM, and concludes with a final rule making. Petitions from broadcasters, interest groups, or manufacturers may prompt initial inquiries. The FCC solicits comments and reply comments as it examines proposed systems. In the final rule making, or *Report and Order*, the Commission announces its decision and the date when stations may implement the technology. Information is made available in FCC reports, but the industry gets its primary information from trade magazines publishing interpretations of the FCC's action. "Albeit passive," broadcast trade magazines can impact decisions and "non-decisions" and "often serve as a window on the 'real world' for regulators (and other readers)" (Brenner, 1992, p. 95). Setting standards is easier said than done. Wright (1997) explained: "Standards in the United States do not come about easily. Anyone who has ever participated in a standards organization will tell you that that comment is a gross understatement" (p. 7).

From 1977 to 1980, the FCC followed traditional procedure with AM stereo, attempting to select a transmission system standard from five systems proposed by Kahn, Belar, Harris, Magnavox, and Motorola. AM broadcasters, having lost 40 percent of their audience to FM in less than 20 years, hoped that stereo would remedy AM's ills. Various factions lobbied for the systems, and the FCC struggled over which would best serve the public interest.

In 1980 the FCC's tentative choice of Magnavox was leaked to the trades. Tremendous negative feedback ensued, prompting the FCC to resume its quest under increasing scrutiny of broadcasters and the trades. Simultaneously, the FCC questioned its regulatory role. A flustered Commission concluded in 1982 that it should authorize AM stereo but should not select a standard. Leaving the decision to the marketplace, the FCC would only police minimal technical operating requirements. In effect, it was like the government's saying, "We do not care what kind of car you drive, because we are not in the business of selling automobiles or picking one model as the automotive standard. But you must use unleaded gasoline and not exceed emissions standards. If the car does not meet technical operating requirements, we will take it off the road."

Regulation was initiated in the 1920s, when broadcasters asked for government intervention. From the *Communication Act of 1934* until AM stereo in 1982, the FCC always selected transmission systems, putting uncertainty to rest and holding firm to ensure stability for the industry and consumers. An exception was color television, for which the Commission withdrew its initial standard to set another. With AM stereo the FCC made a decision, reversed it, and ultimately did not pick a standard system, sparking far more uncertainty than was prevented.

Wright (1997) observed: "While standardization in and of itself does little to guarantee the success of a technology, it does provide one of the key factors required that can allow a technology to grow" (p. 7). Without a standard, most AM operators refused to gamble on one of five incompatible systems. To receive the signal of a system, a consumer needed a receiver specifically designed for that system. How was the consumer to know which receiver to buy to listen to a favorite station? If the wrong receiver was selected, would the consumer understand why the station could not be heard in AM stereo? If the system did not survive in the marketplace, thousands of dollars would be lost. The situation was much different from that of FM stereo and the second color television decision. With a standard, consumers could buy receivers confidently. Imagine consumer reaction if one's color TV set could pick up only CBS but not NBC or ABC. In fact, the original color standard did just that. CBS' color wheel system was incompatible with existing sets, and the FCC opted for another standard. How could the FCC expect the marketplace to filter out an AM stereo standard with so many unanswered questions? In a market in which vast numbers of consumers cannot set the clocks on their VCRs, much less program them, were these same people supposed to figure out which AM stereo system a station uses?

FM was created to rid radio of static, but it languished for decades in the shadows of TV and AM. When FM began its ascent in the 1960s, it trailed AM's audience by 80 to 20 percent. Since 1985 the figures have leveled at about 80 percent for FM and 20 percent for AM. Stereo and shrewd programming enabled FM to catch AM and to reverse the audience numbers. AM broadcasters, content with sitting on their huge lead, were forced for the first time to fight from behind. Many AM broadcasters avoided audio improvement by switching from music formats to voice-oriented ones like news and talk. AM broadcasters ultimately realized that their success depended on both format changes and improving technology.

At times it looked as if AM would not survive, but it has. If AM did not exist, there would probably be an urgency to invent it. AM sounds good if transmission and reception equipment is made well and properly maintained, but the quality went down as more stations crowded the band. Stereo was seen as AM's savior, but broadcasters eventually realized that adding stereo to poor technology was futile. AM needed improvement, and the FCC appointed the NRSC to help.

Beginning with the AM stereo marketplace decision, FCC standard setting changed drastically from tradition. Concluding that "the marketplace will correct whatever deficiencies may exist" (Ray, 1990, p. 170), the FCC's (1982) self-described "bold, new step" was final (p. 17). For the first time, the industry was forced to establish its own transmission standard. Some broadcasters believed that AM's situation was hopeless, but the FCC expressed confidence that the best system would prevail. AM broadcasters and receiver manufacturers did not share the optimism and were reluctant to align with one system that might eventually lose the marketplace fight. Few manufacturers built receivers, and few stations installed stereo. Thus, listeners were never given a reasonable opportunity to accept or reject the technology.

Two years after the decision, just Motorola and Kahn remained. Receivers capable of decoding all five systems emerged but were unsuccessful. Numerous petitions urged the FCC to reconsider, and although legally obligated to answer them, action was delayed purposely until 1988, when all were denied in one tidy proceeding. The FCC believed that the market was working. Citing Motorola's lead as evidence, the Commission declared it a de facto standard. Kahn refused to concede, leaving the AM stereo question unanswered until October 25, 1993. Section 214 of the Telecommunications Authorization Act of 1992 required the Commission "to adopt a single AM broadcasting stereo transmission standard" and "to remove any remaining uncertainty among AM broadcasters as to which stereo system to use and thereby encourage the improvement and expansion of AM broadcast service." The FCC's decision was ordered into effect as of March 21, 1994.

RADIO AND TV HISTORY

Radio broadcasting has always been affected by its own innovation and by social, technological, and economic change. Czitrom (1982) observed: "Radio broadcasting added a totally new dimension to modern communication by bringing the outside world into the individual home. The history of radio, however, was far more complex than the histories of previous media breakthroughs. The broadcasting industry tied together a bundle of technological and scientific threads that had been dangling for a generation" (p. 60).

Broadcasting profoundly influenced the generations that experienced electronic media's birth and development. Contributions of Guglielmo Marconi, Reginald Fessenden, Lee DeForest, David Sarnoff, and others are tremendous and without question. Broadcasting's early history is well documented, so there is no need to retrace it from the beginning. However, to understand AM radio's reversal of fortune, a contextual base is necessary.

Radio has seen numerous challenges, and although it has seen its ups and downs, it has remained a vital medium. *Radio World* opined: "Radio has not merely survived; it has thrived for 75 years, shaking off challenges from television, cable and digital satellite TV . . . even MTV's threat that video would 'Kill the Radio Star.' Radio has consistently ridden the waves of change and today enjoys the lion's share of media consumption; this kind of long-term success naturally attracts those looking for a piece of the action" (Take care of business, 1995, p. 5).

During the Great Depression, radio flourished while other businesses faltered. Radio provided inexpensive entertainment and an escape from harsh realities. Listeners were happy to have the medium and had little criticism for it. Prior to the 1930s radio signals were transmitted exclusively by AM, by which "information is encoded by varying the amplitude, or strength, of the carrier wave . . . the loudness of the sound would be encoded in terms of amount rather than the frequency" (Head & Sterling, 1982, p. 46). AM's chief advantage is its capability of covering great distances. Its main disadvantage is susceptibility to outside interference, often resulting in less than optimal sound quality. The listener hears natural or man-made electrical interference in the form of static.

David Sarnoff wanted static-free radio and shared his notion with Edwin H. Armstrong, who worked from 1922 to 1933 designing a system unaffected by outside electrical interference (Barnouw, 1968). The system was FM, which "keeps carrier wave amplitude constant, modulating its frequency," and "variations in amplitude caused by static can be clipped off the peaks of the waves without disturbing the information pattern" (Head & Sterling, 1982, p. 46).

Armstrong originated FM's first broadcast from New York's Empire State Building on June 16, 1934, some 28 years after the first successful AM broadcast. Sarnoff's employer, RCA, owned the antenna and station area. In 1935 RCA told Armstrong that more emphasis would be placed on the emerging medium of television. Armstrong was forced out of his experimental station but forged ahead with FM. In 1936 Armstrong (1948) tried unsuccessfully to gain official approval of FM, but the FCC was not convinced of its necessity. Finally, in 1940 the FCC admitted that FM offered many benefits. Although World War II (1938–45) further deterred FM's progress (Barnouw, 1968), AM's prosperity continued. Americans followed the events leading up to the war and grew to depend on radio for daily information. The number of legal stations nearly doubled during World War II and by 1946 totaled more than 1,000 (Head & Sterling, 1982).

After the war, FM remained in the shadow of television and AM. AM entered its postwar phase optimistically, truly becoming "the Fifth Estate, a factor in the life of the world without which no one can reckon" (Waller, 1946, p. 3). More homes had radios than telephones, and the audience knew no socioeconomic limitations. By 1948 television began to challenge radio with little effect, but during the 1950s it began to dominate AM radio.

FM Stereo

FM stereo's basic groundwork was laid in 1955, when the FCC (1955) allowed FM stations to initiate multiplexing, the act of one transmitter's sending out two simultaneous, but possibly different, signals. The method is not unlike one telephone line's handling several calls at one time (Sunier, 1960). Originally, the FCC's (1958) SCA were intended for nonbroadcast services, such as piped-in music often heard in medical facilities. The 1958 NOI was issued to discover if "additional uses are feasible, appropriate, and should be permitted in the FM broadcast band" (p. 5284). The FCC listed stereo as an SCA service, along with a host of others, including traffic light control, paging services, and operations directed toward specific interests.

Stereo created proponents and opponents. Advertising executives believed that stereo broadcasting went beyond the gimmicks and superficial attempts of the past. Pure stereo offered listeners an enjoyable sound and presented advertisers with "the opportunities of a whole new advertising medium" (Stereo broadcasting, 1958, p. 22). Many broadcasters believed that the average consumer was incapable of distinguishing stereo from nonstereo broadcasting. Little information or research about FM existed because little attention had been paid to it. There were mounds of opinions but a vacuum of research.

Under FCC supervision, the NSRC was formed in 1959 by W.R.G. Baker, organizer of monochrome TV and color TV standards committees. The FCC charged NSRC with setting stereo broadcasting standards for AM, FM, and TV (Stereo specs, 1959). The RIAA had already developed stereo standards for recordings (Stereo record standards, 1959). On March 11, 1959, the FCC (1959) adopted an FNOI to announce that the original notice was amended to separate FM stereo comments from other SCA authorization proceedings.

FM Stereo Systems. Fourteen systems vied to become the FM stereo industry standard. By January 1, 1960, NSRC narrowed them to seven: Crosby, Halstead, Calbest, Zenith, Electrical & Musical Industries, and two GE systems. RCA and CBS withheld their systems from NSRC scrutiny because the FCC refused to participate in testing. The FCC indicated that it could not become involved because of a backlog of other business. Therefore, NSRC was charged with recommending a system to the FCC (Stereocasting at crossroads, 1960). Some experts believed that stereo was ahead of its time technologically and feared that stereo would "not be making the big break-through for some time" (Emma & Wolff, 1960, p. 63).

Finally, the FCC issued completed regulations for multiplex nonbroadcast activities. The first NOI was issued in 1955. On May 4, 1960, the FCC (1960a) adopted two documents opening the door for FM stereo. The first allowed for "specified" activities on "multiplex basis," while the other called for engineering comments on seven FM stereo systems (p. 4257). Systems were numerically coded by the FCC and NSRC: 1—Crosby Laboratories; 2A—Calbest; 2B—Halstead; 3—Electric & Musical Industries; 4—Zenith; 5A and 5B—GE's systems. NSRC field testing was set for summer 1960 (Stereo tests on the way, 1960).

Testing materials, including tapes of experimental broadcasts from Pitts-burgh's KDKA, were completed and sent to the FCC in October 1960 (Elec-tronics newsletter: Stereo standards group, 1960). A decision was expected in early 1961. It was speculated the FM stereo standard might be a "hybrid" of at least two systems (Electronics newsletter: The question now, 1960). Some foreign authorities awaited the FCC's decision, hoping to base their standards on the results (Carroll, 1960).

On April 20, 1961, the FCC (1961) approved FM stereocasting via multi-plex and adopted an FM stereo system as the industry standard. It was a com-posite of Zenith's system and one of GE's two systems. In addition to meeting NSRC's standards, the system "impressed" the FCC with its "ap-parent lower cost" and other technical characteristics (p. 3533).

Broadcasters enthusiastically accepted the FCC's decision. Costs of adapt-ing stations to stereo were estimated between $2,000 and $4,000 (Stereo de-cision creates, 1961). H.H. Scott introduced the first receiver adapters for $99.95, while other manufacturers were to follow quickly (Carroll & Kolodin, 1961). The first station to broadcast FM stereo was WGFM, Sch-enectady, New York, at 12:01 A.M. EST, June 1, 1961 (Carroll, 1961). By the end of the year about 50 stations followed suit, with 185 making future plans to do so. At least 140 stations were now readying for stereo (Bruun, 1961).

Television

Television is a controversial medium. Critics have blamed it for many social ills since its inception, while defenders cite its potential. One thing is for cer-tain: TV has become part of the American way of life. Television is the result of technological developments of the nineteenth and early twentieth cen-turies. Vladimir Zworykin, a Westinghouse employee, in 1919 was given "permission to work on a new device that used electrons to detect and trans-mit pictures instantly" (Black, Bryant, & Thompson, 1998, pp. 112–113). Patented in 1923, the device was called "the iconoscope television pickup tube," becoming a prototype of television. Philo Farnsworth perfected the system. He and Zworykin are cocredited with fathering television.

RCA was experimenting with TV and in 1930 opened the first experimental TV station, W2XBS New York. As with FM's early days, the tower was on the Empire State Building. In 1935 RCA set aside $1 million for TV field testing. Home use was still not possible, but by 1936 receivers picked up TV signals from about one mile. That same year, the RMA formed a committee to recommend television broadcast system standards and technical operating parameters. RMA's recommendation to the FCC, which came in December 1937, was RCA's 343-line/30-frame system. RMA later evolved into the EIA (Whitaker, 1998b).

By 1937 TV sets were being promoted on New York City streets. In June 1938 a Broadway play (*Susan and God*) was televised from NBC's studios. The same year, David Sarnoff announced plans to market TV sets to the public. They were introduced in 1939 at the New York World's Fair. In 1940 the NTSC was created as a subcommittee of RMA (Whitaker, 1998b). In February 1940, the FCC was treated to shows televised from New York to Schenectady. NTSC submitted a report to the FCC on January 27, 1941, saying that it had formed a consensus with two exceptions. There was no agreement reached about scanning lines per frame or for synchronization signals. At a March 8, 1941, meeting NTSC settled on 525 scanning lines per frame and frequency modulation for synchronization. The recommendation was given to the FCC on March 20, 1941. Whitaker (1998b) explained: "Key elements of the standard included: the use of a 6 MHz RF channel with the picture carrier 1.25 MHz above the bottom of the channel and the sound carrier 4.5 MHz above the picture carrier; vestigial sideband modulation of the picture carrier with negative modulation and preservation of the DC component; frequency modulation of the sound carrier; 525 scanning lines per frame with 2:1 interlace at 30 frames (60 fields) per second; and 4:3 aspect ratio" (p. 156). The FCC followed NTSC's recommendations by authorizing the July 1941 construction of two commercial stations.

As with FM, TV's progress was hindered by World War II, when the FCC placed a 1942 wartime freeze on the issuance of station licenses. The FCC would issue no new licenses until an orderly development of television could be implemented. TV's growth was influenced by two major FCC decisions in the 1950s. The lifting of the TV license freeze on April 14, 1952, was the first. The second was the advent of color TV.

TV's Golden Age. The freeze on licenses did little to hinder TV's growth. From 1948 to 1952 TV growth was tremendous. From the beginning of the freeze until the end, U.S. homes with TV grew from 4 percent (172,000) to 34.2 percent (15.3 million) (Black, Bryant, & Thompson, 1998). The 1950s represent the golden age of television, when programs were presented live, and creativity and innovation dominated. TV was evolving as the United States was experiencing many post–World War II changes and challenges. Most Americans purchased TV sets for entertainment, but programming spanned a wide range of news, sporting events, music, drama, games, quizzes, humor, religion, and variety.

A primary influence on radio and TV was vaudeville. Many routines were adapted to radio, and the transition to TV was natural. Vaudeville stars such as Jack Benny and the Burns and Allen comedy team moved to radio and then TV. Others were less fortunate, as their radio routines did not translate visually. Radio also influenced TV's penchant for stars such as Bob Hope, Lucille Ball, Jackie Gleason, Milton Berle, and Jack Benny. Some shows featured ensembles, such as *Your Show of Shows*. Radio shows, such as the *Lone Ranger*, *Dragnet*, and *Gunsmoke*, were adapted to TV. Radio's influence on TV was also evident with soap operas and other daytime programs.

Broadcast networks originated on radio and established a model and foundation for television. NBC and CBS, the leading radio networks, made smooth transitions to television. David Sarnoff was the driving force for NBC TV as he was with radio. Sarnoff's principal rival, CBS' formidable William S. Paley, lured many NBC radio stars to CBS in the 1940s. Those same entertainers advanced the charge for Paley's television network. By the end of the 1950s Paley's direction helped CBS surpass NBC in advertising revenue. Among the legendary CBS entertainers were Jack Benny, George Burns and Gracie Allen, Red Skelton, Edgar Bergen, and the creators of *Amos and Andy*, Freeman Gosden and Charles Correll.

The earliest TV news shows appeared on CBS and NBC in 1948, and each was 15 minutes in length. TV news amounted to little more than an announcer's reading copy with some film footage added. Unlike radio news and its analysis, TV news was superficial and leaned more to entertainment than to information.

For the most part, live TV ended with the 1950s, and TV would never be the same. Despite the frequent accidents, flubbed lines, anxieties, and other problems, there was a magic that has never been recaptured. As TV matured, technology improved, but creativity suffered in the process. In the 1950s the FCC approved color television broadcasting, making the popular medium even more desirable among consumers. Many shows were shot in color, but it was comparatively expensive. Black-and-white programs were in evidence into the late 1960s.

Color TV. On July 3, 1928, John Logie Baird demonstrated color television. When field sequential color systems were demonstrated in 1929, the *Bell Laboratories Record* boasted of "Television in Colors." In 1940 an *Electronics* headline read: "Color Television Demonstrated by CBS engineers." In the 1940s both CBS and RCA developed color TV systems and competed to become the color system standard. Between Baird's demonstration and the first official color broadcast in 1954, most of the attention focused on the battle between those systems. In October 1950, to the chagrin of many broadcasters and consumers, the FCC approved CBS' field sequential (color filter wheel) color TV system developed by Dr. Peter Goldmark. Goldmark also invented the LP record for CBS, so his accomplishments were significant. Goldmark, who was inspired to develop a color TV system upon seeing *Gone with the Wind* on his 1940 honeymoon trip, wondered: "Why can't we have color television?" (Beacham, 1998b, p. 43). He laid out his system's basics in his honeymoon hotel room. It is important to note that Goldmark's system was not compatible with existing monochrome, or black-and-white, television. To create color, a disc spun in front of the picture tube.

CBS pledged 20 hours per week of color programming and produced its own receivers with a maximum screen size of 12.5 diagonal inches. Incompatibility was a terrific problem for CBS. When the network switched to color programming in New York City during certain hours of the day, the majority of its audience left for other networks because they could not receive the signal. Along with viewers, CBS lost advertising. CBS lost all its manufacturing investment (Cripps, 1997a). To escape the embarrassing dilemma, CBS is said to have convinced the U.S. government to stop color TV set manufacturing during the Korean War. Allegedly, CBS' factories were needed for military purposes (Beacham, 1998b). Almost 20,000 CBS color TV sets became obsolete within about four months of service.

Despite the FCC's approval of CBS' system, other companies continued developing color TV. All were compatible with monochrome systems. Among the competitors were RCA's tricolor delta-delta kinescope, Hazeltine's "shunted monochrome" system, GE's frequency interlaced system, and Philco's color system "composed of wideband luminance and two color-difference signals encoded by a quadrature-modulated subcarrier" (Whitaker, 1998b, pp. 156, 158).

In January 1950 RMA was reactivated to seek a solution. RCA's system, "employing the basic concepts of today's NTSC color system," was proposed to the FCC on July 22, 1953. The system was demonstrated on October 15, 1953. After a complicated legal battle, the FCC approved RCA's system on December 17, 1953. The system could carry both monochrome and color broadcasts. Color broadcasting was initiated on January 23, 1954 (Whitaker, 1998b).

Westinghouse introduced the first color TV set in March 1954, which sold for $1,295 and featured a 12-inch screen. That was "at a time when you could buy a new Ford for $1,195" (Schubin, 1998, p. 47). Even at that exorbitant cost, *Fortune* magazine prognosticated that 33 percent of American homes (18 million) would house color TV within five years. During the first month, however, 30 Westinghouse color TV sets were sold. Consumers were holding out for lower prices, bigger sets, and more programming. RCA also produced color TV sets, and the cost of its 15-inch model dropped from $1,000 to $495 by August 1954. In 1956 RCA's 21-inch set sold for the same price, before increasing by 10 percent the following year. Just 1 million color TV sets were sold by 1962.

NBC committed to airing 2,000 hours of color programming during 1963–64, but by January 1, 1964, only 1.4 million color sets had been sold.

Falling prices, combined with NBC's aggressive programming schedule, had a positive impact on the industry. By the end of 1964, the number of sets grew to 2.8 million. For two subsequent years, the numbers doubled. In 1965 there were 5.5 million color TVs, and in 1966 there were about 10.5 million. The exponential growth ended in 1968, when the number grew to just 15 million sets. In 1978 the number of color sets passed the number of monochrome sets. By 1981 color TV sets reached 85 percent of all TV sets (Schubin, 1998).

TV's Onslaught and Radio's Recovery

As television's popularity went up, radio's went down. TV replaced radio as the focal point of the family home, and from 1948 to 1956 the ratings for radio dropped more than 1,000 percent (Lichty & Topping, 1975). Radio fought back by reinventing itself. For the first time, automobile receivers outnumbered those in homes in 1951, and the trend has continued ever since. By the early 1960s radio began to recover from the setbacks brought on by TV. Two reasons for radio's renewed vigor were portability of the sets and localization. Portability was made possible by transistors, which were cheaper and much more compact than bulky electronic tubes. The reduction in radio set size made it possible to carry it with little inconvenience. In 1961 radio listenership increased by more than 14 percent, with much of the increase attributed to transistors. Because radio could be used in an infinite number of places, such as the seaside, bedrooms, ballparks, and offices, the audience could be reached more easily. By demographically defining its various audiences, radio formats could be targeted for maximum results. As a result, advertisers were attracted, and the radio business flourished.

Other changes in radio were to come. For almost three decades, FM languished in AM's shadow. In the late 1950s and early 1960s several factors initiated FM's slow ascent to prominence. It had become more difficult to obtain AM licenses. As spectrum filled, the FCC became stingier with allocations and all but stopped new AM licensing in 1962. By 1968 no AM licenses were being granted, and the FCC diverted applicants to FM.

Many FM stations in the 1960s were owned in tandem with AMs. Because FM was in little demand, most would simulcast AM programming. The FCC's action against duplication of programming in 1967 ultimately assisted FM. Owners were inclined to find alternative formats for FM affiliates to avoid direct competition with sister AM stations. FM's growth was fueled further by the development of improved musical recording techniques. This combination of factors contributed to a solid foundation for FM. The number of FM stations rose dramatically in the 1960s. Forty-six commercial FM stations were in operation during 1945. Between 1950 and 1960 FM stations increased from 691 to 741. Demand for FM operations nearly doubled by 1965, with a total of 1,343. More than 2,100 were broadcasting in 1970

(Lichty & Topping, 1975), and by the early 1980s more than 3,100 commercial FMs were in operation. Slightly fewer than 2,000 noncommercial FMs were on the air, bringing the total to about 5,000 FMs. The fragmentation of programming due to portable radios and nonduplication continued as the number of stations grew.

Radio since FM Stereo. The biggest boost for FM radio came when the FCC approved stereocasting in 1961. Already superior to AM's sound quality, FM also added to that supremacy. By 1965 approximately 98 percent of all homes had radio receivers, which was a 3 percent increase since 1950. In 1950, however, those receivers were AM. FM was contributing to the number by the mid-1960s. Ten years later, FM receivers totaled 40 percent, and about 25 percent of all new cars were equipped with FM receivers in addition to AM (Lichty & Topping, 1975).

An important change for radio came in the late 1970s and early 1980s, when FM ended AM's domination. FM gained near parity with AM in audience numbers by 1979 with 49 percent of the audience (FM: The great, 1979). AM had always commanded a vast majority of radio listeners, but with the momentum gained in 1979 FM reversed that trend. FM radio added to its lead and by 1984 garnered 70 percent of the audience, despite the fact that AM stations outnumbered FM stations (Rau, 1985).

By May 1985 FM led AM with 71 percent of the audience. Ninety-five percent of all teenagers listened to radio, with 91 percent tuning to FM. Adults 50 and older preferred AM to FM by 55 to 45 percent (FM share up, 1985). AM's appeal to the older audience meant that it still appealed somewhat to advertisers. Teenagers spent less money. The most serious problem for AM was that its audience was moving out of the buying-power range. FM's audience was growing into it. Although AM was losing massive audience numbers, its revenue had not dropped significantly. But in 1985 FM began to dominate in audience numbers and revenue. From 1984 to 1985 AM revenue shares dropped nationally from 43.1 percent to 40.1 percent as FM's profits rose "in an almost vertical line" (AM: Band on the run, 1985, p. 35).

The swing from AM to FM could be stopped successfully, according to many experts, if AM broadcasters employed proper strategies. A major problem for AM was that listeners 18 to 34 years old were considered lost forever, because they had grown up with FM. The chief solution, it was considered, lay in educating those people under 18 who had yet to develop firm radio habits. For the first time, AM radio faced a crossroads. Two approaches seemed obvious for successful AM broadcasting. One was alternative programming, banking that the audience would tune in if something were offered that could not be attained elsewhere. The second solution would be stereo and an attempt to attract a youthful audience as FM had done in the 1970s. The overriding imperative was to stop listener erosion without further damage.

AM operators saw their audience level off at about 20 percent by late 1985. Had the trend continued, AM was projected to lose its remaining listeners around 1995. AM executives could find little solace in a 20 percent share of the audience. Survival would depend on recapturing lost listeners. Such a goal seemed less than attainable given the formidable competition of FM. The best alternative seemed to be AM stereo, but stereo's implementation was much easier said than done.

Chapter 2

AM Stereo and
the Marketplace

AM STEREO'S ORIGINS

The concept of AM stereophonic broadcasting first arose as early as 1925, when WPAY, New Haven, Connecticut, crudely broadcast one channel of its sound on one frequency and another channel on a separate frequency, or AM-AM (Sunier, 1960). Other superficial stereocasting attempts were made over the years, using two separate transmitters, or stations: AM-FM, FM-FM, TV-FM (FCC, 1977a).

In the 1950s the FCC took its first serious look at stereo for AM, FM, and television (Stereo specs due this year, 1959), eventually deciding to allow stereocasting on FM but denying it for AM and television. Several reasons have been offered for the FM preference. Primarily, FM needed stereo to help it compete with AM. AM was considered technologically incapable to broadcast proper stereo (FCC, 1977a). Monophonic broadcasting involves transmitting a solitary audio signal to a receiving unit consisting of one speaker. With stereo, two signals are sent as one to a receiver that splits them apart "to afford the listener a sense of the spatial distribution of the original sound sources" (FCC, 1976, p. 69). Most audio engineers agree that FM stereo is much easier to accomplish than AM stereo because of the size of the audio channels. FM stereo employs multiplexing, in which two or more signals can be sent from one source. FM is much wider than AM, leaving more room for those two signals (What's all this about multiplex, 1961). Television was not permitted to use stereo because experts believed that the combination of stereo and TV's small screen would not satisfy viewers by distracting from the program (Feldman, 1984).

AM stereo is sent via two basic methods: (1) Kahn's ISM and (2) Motorola's C-QUAM. Both use two audio channels, but ISM transmits one channel above the frequency and another below it. C-QUAM is similar to FM multiplexing in that both channels are merged and then split by the receiver. The FCC combined the positive characteristics of multiple systems to yield one strong FM system, an impossibility with AM stereo (Shepler, 1985). That complication notwithstanding, the delay of stereo for AM or TV could not be blamed on technological complications. A more likely explanation may be that AM stereo and MTS were victims of circumstance. Initiating stereo proceedings for AM, FM, and TV was too great a task for the FCC to handle at one time, so stereo for AM and TV was postponed indefinitely (Stereo stimulates FM broadcasters, 1960).

Although AM stereo was denied, Leonard Kahn futilely petitioned the FCC in 1959 for approval of his transmission system (Graham, 1979). The FCC cited AM's poor fidelity and frequency response, susceptibility to static, and tendency for signal fading (Sterling, 1970). Although the FCC believed AM incapable of producing adequate sound quality, much less stereo sound, the basic stereo technology process for AM and FM differed little. Two audio channels are coded and sent as one signal, and a receiver decoder circuit splits them into two channels of audio—one for each speaker (Hawkins, 1980).

AM Broadcasters Want Stereo

Kahn again petitioned the FCC for action in 1977. The FCC (1977a) responded:

Kahn states that the technology for compatible stereophonic transmissions by AM broadcast stations has been fully developed and tested over the past 16-year period, and that permitting use of this technology would allow listeners to enjoy stereophonic reception with little or no additional investment in receiving equipment. Kahn claims that his system for AM stereophonic transmissions is completely compatible with existing station transmitting equipment and with monophonic receivers . . . and could provide high quality stereo with receivers designed for AM stereo reception. (p. 34910)

AM Stereo—The FCC's NOI. On June 22, 1977, the FCC (1977a) adopted its AM stereo NOI. The FCC stated that Kahn Communications and AAMSI had petitioned for a move toward AM stereo approval. AAMSI noted that "AM Stereo is an idea whose time has come" (p. 34910). The FCC said that AM needed a chance at technical parity with FM:

Although research has been conducted on both AM and FM single station systems of stereophonic transmissions, the primary attention was directed toward FM station stereophony because FM was considered to be a high-fidelity program service less subject to noise and interference, and stereophonic transmission could be more readily implemented in the developing FM broadcast service. At the present time, nearly 45%

of all radio broadcast stations are FM stations, and a large majority of those FM stations transmit stereophonic programming. For a number of years all music recordings . . . have been made in the stereophonic mode. A major segment of the electronics industry is involved in the supplying of equipment for reproducing stereophonic programs in homes and automobiles. The stereophonic recording, transmission, and reproduction of music and other programming has been fully developed and in use for some time, except in the AM and television broadcast services. (p. 34910)

The main objectives for the notice were to "determine if there was an interest and need for" AM stereo and to gather as much technical data as possible (FCC, 1977a). Kahn accused the FCC of delaying. In 1975 Kahn and Magnavox took advantage of an FCC authorization to experiment with on-air AM stereo testing. WFBR in Baltimore used Kahn's system, and WKDC in Elmhurst, Illinois, employed Magnavox. Kahn said that enough data had been amassed to make a decision, but the FCC called for additional information from NAMSRC, Kahn, and any other sources (FCC, 1977a).

AM Stereocasting NPRM. More than a year later, the FCC (1978a) adopted its AM stereo NPRM. The FCC received responses from more than 90 sources, including broadcasters, networks, manufacturers, and other parties writing in favor of AM stereo. The FCC (1978a) summarized:

Responses to the Notice of Inquiry express the view that FM stereophonic radio service is inadequate in automobiles and at fairly long distances from broadcasting stations. It is further noted that many small communities have only AM stations and thus are lacking local stereophonic radio service. Regarding the possible impact of AM stereo on the continuing development of FM broadcasting, it is reported that in many markets FM stations have already surpassed AM stations in audience and revenue. Many AM licensees claim that AM stereo is needed to keep their stations competitive. Additionally, it is claimed that the stereo performance of FM broadcasts in automobiles is poor due primarily to fading and multipath which should not be a problem with AM stereo. (p. 2)

In essence, the FCC acknowledged that the change in audience shares during the 1970s justified AM stereo. Flaws in FM broadcasting were highlighted, such as its range limitations. Respondents believed that AM stereo could achieve high fidelity, but FM would maintain favor among listeners interested in high fidelity. AM stereo was considered better than no stereo in communities without access to FM. The most relevant replies came from the five AM stereo system proponents, and all but Kahn contributed complete technical descriptions of their systems. The FCC (1960b) had substantial data on Kahn's system dating back to 1960. Nevertheless, Kahn submitted further comments.

The FCC (1978a) briefly described each AM stereo system, citing basic similarities in compatibility with mono AM equipment and in neutralizing poor AM fidelity and frequency response. However, each system transmitted stereo differently, making receiver incompatibility a major disadvantage. The only solution was to select one standard system or to develop a receiver that could decode all the systems. A single system selection would aid in rapid facilitation of AM stereo. The least desirable option was to leave that important decision to the broadcast marketplace.

Deregulation of Radio Inquiry

More than another year passed without FCC comment on AM stereo, because it was inundated with other business that would directly affect AM stereo: radio deregulation and FM's assault on AM's audience. On October 5, 1979, the FCC (1979) released its *Inquiry and Proposed Rulemaking; Deregulation of Radio*: "With this Notice, the Commission proposes to modify or eliminate certain rules applicable to commercial broadcast stations. The proposed deregulation encompasses limits on commercial matter, guidelines for the amount of non-entertainment programming, and formalized procedures for the ascertainment of community needs and interests" (p. 57636).

The FCC (1979) emphasized that radio deregulation did "not represent a sudden change in direction" (p. 57636). The move started in 1972 with a "re-regulation study" prompted by technological change: "The proceeding that we are instituting reflects the Commission's continuing concern that its rules and policies should be relevant to an industry and a technology characterized by dynamic and rapid change. It also reaffirms the Commission's commitment to fostering a broadcast system that maximizes the well-being of the consumers of broadcast programming" (p. 57636).

The FCC (1979) apparently made a great distinction between the terms "technical" and "technological." In paragraph 1 of the inquiry, the Commission stated that deregulation proposed only "rule and policy changes that would remove current requirements in nontechnical areas" (p. 57636). At various points in the docket, the Commission mentioned that deregulation would inspire new technologies. As would be emphasized in a future FCC (1982) docket, the Commission would encourage new technology while enforcing minimum "technical parameters" of "acceptable performance" (p. 17). In effect, the FCC's primary concern would be to ensure that any technological system must be of certain technical quality. New technology, then, would be encouraged but limited in minimum performance requirements. The FCC (1979) updated or deleted at least 800 rules and regulations between 1972 and 1979. The Commission said that presidential guidelines were being followed "to adopt procedures to improve existing and future regulations, including the deletion of unneeded ones" (p. 57636).

The Public Interest. Of vital importance to the FCC (1979) was that it had always operated in the public interest and would continue to do so. The Commission explained: "We have long been, and remain, committed to the principle that radio must serve the needs of the public. We have never, however, believed that radio is a static medium that requires the retention of every rule and policy once adopted. A regulation that was reasonable when adopted, and appropriate to meet a given problem, may be most inappropriate if retained once the problem ceases to exist" (p. 57636).

A large portion of the deregulation docket focused on the historical relationship between the FCC and broadcasting from the Radio Act of 1912 until the Communications Act of 1934. Despite vast change within the broadcast industry, the FCC said that its regulatory tradition had not evolved with it. After reviewing other events since 1934, the FCC (1979) reevaluated its "current regulatory approach in light of changed circumstances" (p. 57644). The Commission offered its own idea of the meaning of "public interest":

It was clear from the very beginning of broadcasting that radio was a rapidly developing medium. Accordingly, Congress' efforts to legislate in the area were complicated by the need to write a law at a fixed point in time that would be sufficiently flexible to allow for this quickly changing technology and industry. Therefore it couched the Commission's regulatory authority in terms of the public interest, convenience, and necessity. Thus, the Commission was given neither unfettered discretion to regulate all phases of radio nor an itemized list of specific manifestations that it could or should regulate. (p. 57644)

A major theme centered on the FCC's position as a content regulator. The new role was to be shifted from regulation of content to regulation of "structural vehicles" such as efficient use of the spectrum and increases in the "diversity of voices represented in broadcasting" (p. 57645).

The Commission acknowledged that FM had gained parity in audience numbers and noted the processes by which FM pulled even. These methods included reducing commercial time and capitalizing on superior sound technology (p. 57646). The FCC (1979) also acknowledged three problems that plagued the development of FM: (1) "relatively few radio receivers with FM capability," (2) "FM signals cannot be transmitted as far as AM signals," and (3) "the advent of television" (p. 57646). The FCC said that FM stations overcame many disadvantages to become "a viable and profitable competitive force" (p. 57646). If AM stations were to regain lost audience shares, they would have to be creatively responsive to these "strong competitive pressures" (p. 57646). Although FM had gained parity with AM, the FCC gave no indication of what would happen if FM totally reversed its fortunes to dominate as it had been dominated. The FCC admitted that stereo had helped FM (p. 57646), yet no mention was made of AM stereo in the inquiry—despite the ongoing proceeding.

The Commission concluded: "Alternatives that have not been set forth . . . may also be proposed" (p. 57667). Deadline for filing comments was set for January 25, 1980, and for replying to those comments the deadline was set for April 25, 1980 (p. 57667).

FM AND AM MOVE TOWARD PARITY

During the 1970s AM radio stations steadily lost ground to FM in cumulative number of listeners, primarily due to the superiority of FM's sound. The grim result for AM was loss of revenue. In 1979 several groups asked the FCC to expedite its authorization of AM stereo. It was evident that AM stereo authorization would happen eventually, but ABC officials, among others, felt there was an immediate need for it. ABC representatives stressed that both the listeners and broadcasters favored the advent of AM stereo. ABC believed that the listening public was used to stereo, having been exposed to it via FM and recordings. AM stereo would fill a void in areas without FM stereo. More stereo stations would mean more programming choices and a better competitive opportunity for AM (Not whether, 1979).

It was estimated in 1979 that 10 to 15 percent of the U.S. population could not receive FM stereo broadcasts. FM stereo needed stronger signal power than monophonic FM, and those few stations with the strength rarely broadcast a variety of formats. Due to the superiority of sound quality, FM stations relied primarily upon music programming. That left AM to concentrate on areas less dependent on clear sound quality, such as information (news, weather, sports), nostalgia, and call-in talk shows. Music became less a priority for AM stations.

Some startling figures began to appear in the late 1970s, adding considerably to the evidence that FM was making great strides to surpass AM's popularity. FM stations earned $418.2 million of a total $2,019.4 million of radio dollars in 1976 and $543.1 million of $2,274.5 million in 1977 (FCC, 1977b, 1978b), becoming only the second consecutive year that FMs had profited. In 1979 KBPI-FM in Denver sold for a record $6.7 million. The previous year, 16 stations sold for more than $1 million each. One reason for the huge prices was that FM's profits could average between 40 to 50 percent of gross revenues. A 29.8 percent revenue increase by all FM stations was realized in 1977 as compared to 1976. FM reached approximately 95 percent of all homes by 1979 yet lagged behind in automobile penetration. From 1974, when 24 percent of all cars were equipped with FM receivers, the number reached only 41 percent by 1979. FM's biggest gains were among teenaged listeners, increasing from 19 to 51 percent from 1973 to 1978. ABC's FM revenues tripled, and sales grew by 25 percent a year. CBS also reported 1978 as a record fiscal year for FM. FM broadcasters believed that AM stereo would have little, if any, impact upon deterring FM progress, particularly among listeners already committed to FM (FM: The great leaps, 1979). Although FM was quickly displacing AM with listeners, it did not necessarily mean that AM had suffered financial losses. As late as 1982, ABC reported that its AMs were grossing more than their FM stations (Josephson, 1982). By the close of 1979 FM listeners outnumbered those of AM for the first time ever with a 50.5 percent share (Radio 1979, 1979).

THE FCC'S "TENTATIVE" STANDARD

On March 31, 1980, trade magazine *Broadcasting* reported that an AM stereo announcement might be forthcoming. Information was leaked that the FCC might even pick as many as three of the systems. Such an option was not acceptable to the NAB and the NRBA. Four system manufacturers agreed. Only Kahn favored the multiple systems. If the information was accurate, a new and unexpected twist had developed. Previously, the FCC was expected to rule for all or for one. Those opposed to a multisystem approach believed that AM stereo would be put into such a chaotic state of affairs that no one would touch it. It was feared that the end result would be AM stereo's demise. Abe Voron, NRBA governmental relations VP, chastised the FCC for neglecting its responsibility to set technical mandates, believing that chaos would ensue. He could not have known at the time how prophetic he would be (Three's a crowd, 1980).

On April 9, 1980, the FCC announced its "tentative" single system decision, selecting the Magnavox system in a 4–2 vote. Chairman Charles Ferris, Joseph Fogarty, James Quello, and Abbott Washburn voted for Magnavox. Tyrone Brown and Anne Jones cast opposing votes. Robert Lee was absent and did not vote (FCC makes it Magnavox, 1980). Despite wanting a single system standard, Magnavox's four competitors were upset. Kahn, a marketplace proponent, predicted that the FCC's decision would delay AM stereo further. Kahn was uncertain what channels might be pursued to protest the decision but was intent on persuading the FCC to reverse its stance. Kahn recommended that the Commission convene a public hearing on the issue (There's only one, 1980).

The FCC said that it might reconsider if enough AM engineers filed complaints (The FCC on the firing line, 1980). Commissioner Lee admitted that a mistake might have been made. Harris, Motorola, and Kahn formally asked the FCC to release the results on which the choice was based (Bad vibes, 1980). By June 1980 the FCC confessed that an FNPRM would be issued. Apparently, the FCC was experiencing difficulty formulating an adequate defense for its decision. Stephen Lukasik, FCC chief scientist, said there was no question that the FCC hoped to set a single AM stereo system standard but was seeking ways to best accomplish that goal (FCC brings AM stereo, 1980).

Reconsideration of the Magnavox Decision

In its July 31, 1980, further notice the FCC (1980) rescinded its "tentative" Magnavox decision. The FCC's OST told the FCC that "the selection of Magnavox was not wholly defensible" (The final days, 1980, p. 23). The FCC initially considered the explanation unacceptable and considered forcing OST to defend the Magnavox decision. Instead, the FCC opted to spend more time studying all the systems. Brown and Jones, who originally voted against Magnavox, refused to adopt the further notice unless a compromise could be reached. They wanted to decide between governmental standard setting and the marketplace. Once the others agreed to include a call for comments on the marketplace idea and universal decoders, Brown and Jones agreed to support the FNPRM. Commissioner Washburn was embarrassed and said that the organization had taken "a step backwards" (p. 23). Not only had the FCC backed down on a standards decision, but it was possible that the decision would be passed on to the marketplace. Robert Lee agreed with the majority backing both the single system concept and Magnavox. Lee complained: "I don't know why we can't stick to our guns" (p. 23).

A Motorola spokesperson expressed the company's happiness and praised the FCC's retraction. Leonard Kahn said that multicoding receivers would make the decision a moot point. He indicated that multidecoders "would add only four to six percent to the cost of a receiver" and claimed that his contention was supported by an unspecified firm that he called "one of the largest . . . in the world" (The final days, 1980, p. 26). Kahn set no date for an announcement about multidecoders and the FCC offered no timetable for an AM stereo decision. Bill Streeter of Magnavox said that the FCC's FNPRM could not be interpreted as "good" or "bad." A Harris attorney was "generally pleased" (p. 26).

The FCC's AM Stereo Systems Ratings Matrices. In the notice, the FCC (1980) revealed the original ratings matrix that led to its selection of Magnavox. A revised matrix was also included, which apparently convinced the FCC to repeal its Magnavox decision. Although Magnavox may have been the best overall AM stereo system in the original consideration, Motorola clearly won round two.

Each matrix consisted of 11 ratings areas totaling 100 points with point values of 5, 10, and 15 assigned to each category. Magnavox led the pack on the original matrix with 73 points, and Belar (71) finished a close second. Motorola (64) and Harris (63) were virtually even, and Kahn (59) was last. The revised matrix results supported Motorola as the best AM stereo system. With a score of 67, Motorola finished ahead of second-place (tie) Magnavox and Kahn by 16 points. Harris (50) fell to fourth, and Belar dropped from a close second in the first matrix to last in the revised matrix.

Other than order of finish, the revised matrix differed from the original in that the FCC (1980) left three 20-point categories blank for all the systems. In addition, a 15-point category was left open for Magnavox, and two separate 10-point categories were not scored for Belar and Kahn. The FCC said that the categories could be scored if the companies provided evidence warranting a rating. The FCC encouraged all manufacturers, marketplace proponents, multisystem decoder advocates, and single system backers to provide information that might help in the final decision. In the event that no feedback was received, the FCC emphasized that a decision would be made anyway, which would benefit both broadcasters and citizens alike (It's official, 1980, p. 40).

Meanwhile, AM continued to lose ground to FM stations. Audience shares tipped in FM's favor for the first time in history, causing deep concern among AM broadcasters. Between 1970 and 1979 FM audience numbers increased by nearly 150 percent. Rick Sklar, ABC programming VP, compared AM operators to Custer—surrounded and fighting for survival. As stereo remained in limbo, AM broadcasters nervously experimented with various formats to try to stop FM's relentless progress. Efforts included talk, news emphasis, and attempts at reinforcing AM's tenuous hold on listeners in automobiles. Many AM officials hoped that FCC public service deregulation might free AM stations from predetermined obligations. None of the approaches seemed to curtail AM's audience erosion (Kirkeby, 1980).

Response to FNRPM. By mid-February 1981 the FCC received an enormous number of AM stereo comments. Only three system proponents provided new technical information. Kahn issued minuscule system information, choosing instead to lobby for the marketplace. Kahn believed that the best system would be publicly accepted—and, presumably, that system would be Kahn's. Kahn's lack of action was surprising in that the FCC specifically asked a question about a problem with the system's inability to reduce a sufficient amount of outside noise. No such questions had been asked of the other manufacturers. Kahn remained staunchly in favor of a marketplace decision and said that any single system decision would be the same as endorsing a monopoly.

Belar removed its system from the AM stereo battle, believing further effort to be futile. President Arno Meyer "didn't want to keep pouring money down the bottomless pit" (AM stereo gets, 1981, p. 84). Motorola officials, although confident with the outcome of the revised matrix, suggested several ways that the evaluation could be improved. They sent the FCC additional information, refuted some of the FCC findings, and clarified some of the FCC's terminology. Harris conceded that the FCC had enough positive data on the Motorola system to make it the AM stereo system standard. However, Harris and Kahn criticized the FCC's matrix, calling it an inadequate and flawed measuring stick for the purposes at hand. Harris contended that the matrix omitted other critical information and was laden with errors in data, comparative materials, and computation (p. 84).

Deregulation of Radio Docket

From September 1980 until March 1982 the FCC failed to act on AM stereo, but it was not inactive in other matters. The anticipated Deregulation of Radio docket was finally released on Tuesday, February 24, 1981, and was to take effect on April 3, 1981. The FCC (1981) primarily addressed reduction of paperwork and content regulations, which were raised in the 1979 notice. The FCC (1981) stated: "The Commission is eliminating its current processing guidelines relative to the amounts of nonentertainment programming which commercial radio stations should provide and the number of commercial minutes per hour which they should not exceed. Additionally, the Commission is eliminating its community ascertainment requirements and its program log keeping requirements for commercial radio stations. The action is being taken to reduce the paperwork and other burdens on commercial radio stations without having a substantial adverse impact upon the public interest" (p. 13888).

In regard to the development of AM stereo, perhaps the most critical words in the proceeding appeared in paragraph 15. The Commission acknowledged that "numerous" respondents to the initial deregulation docket were concerned about possible Commission attempts "to replace the statutory 'public interest' concept with the 'marketplace' concept" (FCC, 1981, p. 13890). The FCC (1981) defended its position:

We believe that this is an erroneous analysis of the proposals made in this proceeding. It is not the public interest standard that we proposed to eliminate. That standard is contained in the Communications Act of 1934, as amended, and could not be changed by us even if we wanted to. That is a job for Congress. Rather, since marketplace solutions can be consistent with public interest concerns, we sought to explore in the proceeding the question of whether or not in the context of radio the public interest can be met through the working of marketplace forces rather than by current Commission regulations. Again, that issue does not contemplate the elimination of the standard, only a debate over what the standard requires and what methods are best suited to meet that standard in the most efficient way and at least cost to the public. As discussed in the Notice, the public interest standard has never been regarded as a static concept and was utilized by Congress in enacting the Communications Act so as to provide the Commission with the maximum flexibility in dealing with a rapidly and dynamically changing technology and industry. (p. 13890)

The Commission had revealed a loophole that had existed since the Communications Act of 1934. For standards issues, the FCC had the legal right to set minimum technical requirements but could allow the marketplace to work within those parameters.

THE AM STEREO MARKETPLACE: A BOLD NEW STEP

After nearly two years of AM stereo standards deliberations, the FCC (1982), in effect, decided not to make a decision. On March 4, 1982, the FCC adopted a *Report and Order (Proceeding Terminated)*, which stated its intention to allow the marketplace to decide AM stereo's fate. Much of the document reviewed previous AM stereo notices, including the Magnavox decision. The Commission "received many comments from broadcast licensees objecting to its initial preference of the Magnavox system," especially in the area of technical problems with poor sound quality in the system (p. 5).

In response to the Commission's call for comments in the September 11, 1980, docket, there were "23 formal comments and 17 reply comments" from "33 parties" (FCC, 1982, p. 6). Many respondents addressed issues such as multisystem decoders, selection of a standard by government as opposed to the marketplace, and implementation of a lottery. Those who contacted the FCC generally supported one of those selection procedures.

Kahn, ABC, and NBC supported selection by marketplace. Each believed that AM stereo had experienced too many delays while the Commission mulled over a single system standard. GE advocated picking a standard and "was concerned the Commission did not explain how the marketplace would select the 'best' system" (pp. 6–7). GE believed that listeners would have little say in the selection process because "transmission" is a "necessary precedent to reception" (p. 7).

Many respondents supported multisystem receivers. Companies including Sony, Matsushita, National Semiconductor, and the EIA/CEG believed that multidecoders were impractical for two basic reasons: (1) high cost and (2) impracticality of developing switchers capable of automatically decoding the five systems. Respondents generally opposed a lottery. After weighing all the options, the Commission concluded: "After pouring this relatively large level of resources into this continued proceeding, the Commission finds that any decision for one AM stereo system would be highly tenuous. Of equal or greater importance, the Commission has reconsidered its earlier rejection of allowing a market determination of an AM stereo system or systems and is now persuaded that such a reliance on market forces in the present instance is the most prudent course to follow" (FCC, 1982, p. 9).

Defending the Marketplace Decision

The FCC (1982) included in its docket a third matrix of systems ratings. Before defending its AM stereo marketplace decision, the Commission discussed the work that had been done in assessing technical capabilities of the systems. The third matrix ranked the five systems: Magnavox (76), Harris (72), Motorola (71), Kahn (65), and Belar (58). The Commission listed and explained three reasons for its marketplace decision: "First, the data possessed by the Commission are incompatible in some instances since no uniform test procedures were employed. Second, the weights assigned to the various factors and the engineering judgements employed are subject to variance depending on the analyst. Finally, the results obtained are close even if the data and the methodological difficulties were absent. Thus, from the results in the evaluation table, no clear choice is apparent in any case" (pp. 13–14).

To support its reasoning, the FCC again emphasized the readiness of "two major broadcast networks," ABC and NBC, to place trust in the hands of the marketplace. The Commission admitted: "Private markets do not always function perfectly and with instantaneous speed; however, neither do government decision makers" (FCC, 1982, p. 14). In keeping with attitudes expressed in the radio deregulation dockets, the FCC reserved the right to set and enforce technical standards and to ensure that any AM system employed would not interfere with other spectrum services—domestic or foreign.

The Commission expected "benefits in three fundamental areas." First, private interests would be able to "assign their own value weights" to various technical aspects of the systems—possibly in disagreement with scores given by the FCC (FCC, 1982, p. 14). Second, the Commission believed that at least

three types of technological development are possible and are affected by this decision. The first type, which may be completely eliminated by the government mandating a single system, is development of new systems or products. . . . A second type of technological development concerns breakthroughs related to production processes which have cost reducing effects. Not only does free and open competition among manufacturers of the alternative systems permit exploration of ways to reduce the cost of existing systems, it provides a strong incentive for that development since each manufacturer will compete for adoption of his system. (p. 15)

The Commission listed the third kind of technological change as "improvement in the quality of existing systems" (p. 15).

The Commission argued that a major reason for eventually going with the marketplace was the creation of a monopoly by picking one system:

In addition to the costs on society by slowing or preventing technological change, there are costs to society resulting from a loss of competition on price among manufacturers of the systems. By selecting a particular system, the government would be giving an outright grant of monopoly to the manufacturer of choice albeit with the condition that he share part of his monopoly privileges to patent holders as a reward for their inventiveness. However, government removal from the market of other patented substitutes clearly enhances the value of the lone remaining patented system. Furthermore, society itself elects to pay a patentholder his higher prices in a free market in order to enjoy the benefits of his product. In the case of a government mandated system, it is government who decides that the public may only buy the products of a particular manufacturer at his monopoly prices rather than individuals making their own choices. (FCC, 1982, p. 15)

The FCC conceded that the marketplace would experience costs as well as benefits. The biggest drawback for AM stereo was the incompatibility of the five systems, but the Commission believed that broadcasters, listeners, and receiver manufacturers were capable of selecting a transmission system that would meet individual requirements.

Finally, the Commission predicted "several market outcomes" (FCC, 1982, p. 16). The most obvious might be the ultimate selection of one system. That system would be much improved within FCC technical parameters, particularly after competition with other improving systems. It was also possible that "no system would be chosen" (p. 16). In such case the FCC reckoned that it would be "obvious" that consumers felt no desire to employ stereo reception (p. 16). Still another possibility suggested that the competing systems may not be "adopted widely enough to sustain AM stereo in the market" (p. 16).

The FCC left open a vague possibility that a standard might be picked in the future, saying that "nothing appears to differentiate the AM radio market from most of the other markets in the U.S. economy" (FCC, 1982, p. 16). The Commission left itself an opening for reintervention into the selection process but stated: "A very strong case would have to be made in order to override the inherent benefits of consumers making their own choices rather than having their decisions made by government" (p. 16).

The Commission concluded by calling the AM stereo decision "a bold, new step for the Commission to take" (FCC, 1982, p. 17). Paragraph 62 of the *Report and Order* stated: "IT IS FURTHER ORDERED, That this proceeding is TERMINATED" (p. 17).

The bottom line is that the Commission itself became confused about its own mission and purpose. The FCC opted for the marketplace approach because of an internal uncertainty over its proper regulatory role. Sterling (1982) observed: "On the surface, the decision appeared to be a collective throwing up of hands, as the Commission staff admitted its inability to make a clear-cut choice among the systems, all of which were compatible with existing AM technology. Throughout the four-and-a-half years of the complex AM proceeding, a constantly recurring issue has been the proper role of the FCC in a time of dramatic technical, economic, and political change" (p. 137). Sterling further explained that "three interlocking" technical "trends" might have influenced the FCC's break with tradition (p. 139). The first was "the development of so many new potentially competitive delivery systems in a short space of time," such as basic and pay cable networks, subscription television, multipoint distribution systems, lower power television stations, direct broadcast satellites, and teletext-videotex (p. 139). Each of these is "unregulated (as they do not require spectrum) computer facilities allowing consumer choice of both material and time used" (p. 139).

Second, "prolonged economic downturn in the U.S." may have influenced the FCC (Sterling, 1982, p. 140). Because of limited budgeting, the FCC experienced decreases in manpower and research. Since standards setting "is a detailed and expensive process requiring prolonged effort by engineers and attorneys," the FCC may have faced "reduced . . . policy options" (p. 140). There was "the long-standing concern for the FCC's role: is it to be one of limiting, allowing, or actually promoting" new technologies? (p. 141). Upon examining the deregulation dockets, it appeared that the Commission might be open to new technologies as long as certain technical requirements were met. As for promotion of innovations, the FCC stated that it was not responsible for the success of AM stereo. The FCC (1982) declared: "[W]e do not believe that the Commission should undertake the obligation of warranting the success of one or more systems" (p. 16).

The Commissioners Respond. Commissioners Abbott Washburn and James Quello, believing that the FCC should have set a standard, predicted that AM stereo would face problems. The lone dissenting commissioner, Abbott Washburn, said that the FCC's responsibility was to select a system as it had with FM stereo. Although generally supportive of radio deregulation, Washburn believed that the FCC should set technical standards to "prevent needless delays and avoid the very significant waste of resources by broadcasters, manufacturers and consumers associated with marketplace determination" (Washburn: Proud, 1982, p. 67).

Washburn said that the Commission had selected technical standards "for over 50 years" (FCC, 1982, p. 45). He noted: "The data and analysis we need to set a standard in AM stereo are before us. I dissent to the majority's unwillingness to make the choice which would have assured a national standard" (p. 45). Because of system incompatibility, Washburn believed that public interest would be better served by picking a standard:

It is the proper function of government to lay down the guidelines for a single system that will result in AM stereo in every home at the lowest cost consistent with technical excellence and quality reception. I remain convinced that the Commission can choose with confidence a system which will meet the needs of broadcasters, manufacturers, and the public. To do so risks making the "wrong" choice. But with the five systems running a close race in their technical quality, that risk is minimal. And I continue to believe that it is in the public interest for the Commission to choose a single system. The risk in selecting a single system pales in comparison to the consequences of compelling multiple systems to fight it out in the marketplace. Specifically, the authorization of a single system will prevent needless delays and avoid the very significant waste of resources by broadcasters, manufacturers and consumers associated with marketplace determination. In addition, the benefits which would result from price and performance improvements due to competition within a single system, as well as from vigorous competition between AM and FM stereo services, would begin flowing to the public immediately. (pp. 44–45)

Quello said that his vote reflected embarrassment over the Commission's reluctance to stick with its first choice. With its credibility damaged, the

Commission was not in a position to stand behind any other choice. Quello believed that the marketplace possessed "very little competence to determine the relative merits of one technical standard versus another over the short term since its decisions are generally influenced by marketing efforts more than by technical superiority. To expect the American public to select a nationally compatible AM stereo system in a reasonable period of time from among even the five systems now before this Commission is sheer folly" (FCC, 1982, p. 42).

Quello emphasized his disappointment with the Commission. He said: "I am appalled that it has taken this Commission five years to decide that it cannot decide this issue. We have vacillated, temporized and rationalized this matter until I believe the Report and Order is correctly stating that a viable standard can no longer be set." He concluded: "Therefore, I concur in the result" (FCC, 1982, p. 42). Quello feared that broadcasters would be influenced more by "marketing efforts . . . than by technical superiority" of a system, leading to a choice based on guessing "which system will gain enough public acceptance over time to survive" (Quello: Worried, 1982, p. 124).

Commissioner James Fogarty voted for the marketplace because none of the systems appeared superior to the others, and it was "too close to call" (Fogarty, Favors, 1982, p. 69). Marketplace proponent Anne Jones disliked standards because future technological improvement would be discouraged. For example, both Sony and Sansui developed multisystem receivers capable of receiving all five systems. Although the decoders were unsuccessful, the marketplace gave them an opportunity (Jones: Staunchly backs, 1982).

Commissioner Henry Rivera explained that the FCC's methods of selection with AM stereo were inadequate. He agreed with Jones that the consumer should be allowed to make the decision on technology, unless it was certain that the FCC could make a better decision. He believed the marketplace would work better than governmental standard setting (Rivera: Pessimistic, 1982).

The Industry Responds. The reaction to the FCC's indecision was varied. Some analysts thought that even with AM stereo, a long time might pass before any progress could be made against FM. Many broadcasters adopted the attitude that AM stereo was a reality for better or worse. Others felt that the FCC "copped out" by not picking one AM stereo system, and "the ultimate loser in this comedy is the consumer" (Salsberg, 1982, p. 6).

Nevertheless, the FCC expressed confidence that the best system would emerge and emphasized that its major responsibility would lie in making sure that all systems being used complied with federal technical regulations. Stations were told that they could begin broadcasting AM stereo 60 days after the docket appeared in the *Federal Register* (FCC gives up, 1982). No matter the motives behind the FCC's shift in policy, the Commission stuck to its hands-off policy for 11 years.

In early April 1982 the four remaining AM stereo competitors gained their first major exposure after the marketplace decision. NAB's Dallas convention allowed companies to promote its systems. Each was optimistic that a number of stations would elect its respective AM stereo system (AM stereo: Big deal, 1982). However, optimism quickly turned into confusion. Broadcasters planned to pick a standard but were informed by legal counsel that any industry decision might be ruled an antitrust violation. Herbert Forrest, NAB attorney, said that two or more radio broadcasters could not jointly pick one AM stereo system. Any decision must be made independently by each AM station or group owner (AM stereo: The solution, 1982). As the convention wound down, no clear favorite was established, and it became more and more apparent that the marketplace would not provide quick relief to broadcasters interested in implementing AM stereo.

AM Stereo Debuts On-air

In the early 1920s, KDKA-AM in Pittsburgh debuted as, arguably, the first commercial radio station. On July 23, 1982, KDKA became the first AM stereo station by transmitting in stereo for approximately 10 minutes. The same day KTSA-AM in San Antonio, Texas, broadcast AM stereo for the first time, beginning about 11 minutes after KDKA's debut. KTSA officials contended that their station should be credited as the first, because KDKA only temporarily switched to stereo. KTSA continued broadcasting in stereo beyond July 23, 1982, while KDKA used stereo only on certain occasions. The solution probably meant placing an asterisk in the record books, making KDKA the first station to broadcast AM stereo and KTSA the first station to offer continuous AM stereo. Ultimately, the most important fact was that AM stereo had become a reality (AM stereo goes, 1982).

Several other AM stations followed suit, but the majority of AM stations declined to go stereo. Potential AM stereo receiver manufacturers were reluctant to begin production until some trend could be seen with individual stations' selections of stereo transmission equipment. Conversely, AM owners awaited information on which companies would enter the receiver market (Petras, 1982).

In mid-1982, GM's Delco division began testing procedures to determine which of the systems it would choose to be compatible with its receivers. Many broadcasters believed that Delco's choice would greatly influence AM stereo's outcome. Kahn agreed but said that Delco and other automobile receiver manufacturers would probably be swayed more by broadcaster influence than by test results (Abramson, 1982).

FM Surpasses AM. The situation was becoming more critical for AM in its battle with FM. During 1982, as AM broadcasters and receiver manufacturers waited, FM's audience share continued to climb. Between 1979, when FM first attained the major share of the audience, and 1982 the FM percentage grew from 52 to 63. Rather than implementing stereo, many AM broadcasters changed formats. Many were stalling and hoping that receiver manufacturers would break the deadlock (Josephson, 1982).

To expedite AM stereo's marketplace development, *Broadcasting* magazine invited the remaining four competitors to submit approximately 500 words to support "why AM broadcasters should adopt their system" (Four sides of the AM stereo coin, 1982, p. 50). Interestingly, each used different themes and strategies. For instance, Harris concentrated on the competition between FM and AM, Harris' compatibility with existing AM equipment, and Harris Corporation itself. On behalf of Harris, Roger Burns wrote, in part, that "broadcasters must look at the company they deal with in AM stereo. None of the other proponents, Magnavox, Motorola, Belar or Kahn, even remotely approaches Harris's 60-year stature in the broadcast industry. Harris's field forces in the broadcast industry are larger than the other four proponents combined. You certainly want to know that your investment in AM stereo will be protected, and only Harris can make that guarantee" (p. 50).

Leonard Kahn focused on the FCC's AM stereo marketplace decision. He did not refer to his or any other system. The only mention of AM stereo systems came when Kahn encouraged broadcasters to "follow good engineering procedures and evaluate all aspects of the situation" before selecting any particular system (Four sides of the AM stereo coin, 1982, p. 50).

Magnavox also discussed the marketplace but focused on the marketplace's players. In keeping with the idea that the marketplace allowed for improving the technology, Magnavox announced plans to introduce a 1983 system upgrade. Motorola chose to inform broadcasters of its prowess in the area of automobile radios. Motorola contended that AM stereo would make its most immediate impact in automobiles. Because of past success in the automotive sound industry, Motorola believed itself to be the best choice for broadcasters.

In August 1982, Chris Payne, NAB engineer, joined Motorola as AM stereo broadcast manager. Payne, considered NAB's AM stereo expert, said that he had watched the situation for six years and had become frustrated. He jumped to Motorola because it produced the best system (Chris Payne to Motorola, 1982). Delco engineers reported in September that they would soon conclude AM stereo system testing, but it was unknown whether those results would be made public. Apparently, Delco was unsure if endorsement of one system would constitute an antitrust violation. Likewise, other receiver manufacturers hesitated to pick a particular system, which probably had more to do with lack of an industry trend than with legal fears (Delco AM stereo, 1982).

NRBA released results of its 1982 AM stereo survey in December. Of 1,060 responses, 300 stations indicated plans to implement stereo as soon as possible. NRBA interpreted the results to mean that of more than 4,000 AM stations, probably 1,000 intended to carefully consider a move to stereo.

Only 40 stations were broadcasting in stereo at the time of the survey, but many industry insiders believed that Delco's much anticipated decision would influence more stations to convert (Holland, 1982).

Delco Chooses Motorola. As 1982 ended, there was still no industry AM stereo standard in sight, and audience shares continued to shift toward FM. During 1982 FM gained 4 percent more of the total radio audience to finish the year with 63 percent of all listeners (Fall RADAR study, 1982). Finally, Delco announced plans in December to recommend that Motorola-compatible receivers be included in future GM automobiles. Both Harris and Magnavox criticized Delco for being unobjective in the testing (Hall, 1982). Motorola's Chris Payne said in January 1983 that Delco's decision to build Motorola-only receivers had resulted in an estimated 300 percent increase in equipment orders. A Harris spokesperson countered Motorola's boasts, contending that the Delco move had not lessened the standing of Harris' system in the industry (AM stereo on parade, 1983). Harris believed that broadcasters would have more influence on AM stereo's outcome than would receiver manufacturers (Few visitors at booths, 1983).

Multisystem Decoders. Many proponents began to believe that AM stereo would not be successful. However, the mood changed somewhat with the unveiling of receivers capable of decoding signals of all AM stereo systems, a feat previously thought impossible (Walker, 1983). The next move was left to broadcasters and receiver manufacturers. Sony and Sansui AM stereo multi-decoders lent some credibility to the marketplace position taken by Commissioner Jones. Jones contended that technological standard setting eliminated incentive to improve technology. Had an AM stereo standard been set, manufacturers may never have been motivated to develop multidecoding receivers. Nonetheless, the battle was not over. Some broadcasters feared that Sony and Sansui would give up on AM stereo if multidecoders did not catch on quickly. To keep Sony and Sansui interested, it was suggested that station owners offer free airtime for promoting receivers and stations simultaneously. If Sony failed to jump-start AM stereo, other manufacturers could be deterred from producing receivers (Norberg, 1984). Kahn (1984) believed that the advent of multidecoders would enable broadcasters to "select the system that allows them to best serve the public because only multisystem AM stereo radios can survive in the free marketplace" (p. 26).

Harris, Magnavox, and Kahn were happy to have multidecoders on the market. Motorola was less enthusiastic, having already gained a marketplace advantage with Delco's decision to build Motorola-only receivers. Many industry officials were skeptical about multisystem receivers because the price was considerably higher than that for single system decoders. As a result, multidecoders were less attractive to consumers (Multisystem AM stereo receivers, 1983).

More than a year after the FCC's AM stereo marketplace proceeding, *Television/Radio Age* asked FCC chairman Mark Fowler if he had "second thoughts" about the commission's handling of the matter—particularly in light of the relative lack of progress in establishing a de facto standard. Fowler remarked:

Well if anyone thought that with AM stereo, you just snap your fingers and you instantly have AM stereo, they're very misguided. Even if the Commission had set standards, it would have taken several years for AM stereo to become a reality. Let's not kid ourselves. It probably will take a decade for AM stereo, in our view, to become something that would be of universal application. So with those critics one year after saying, "Well nothing's happened yet, we don't see a lot of AM stereo out there," that's just ludicrous. There's no such thing as instant gratification when you make those kinds of decisions. (In wake of TV, 1983, p. 68)

Fowler said that the FCC made "the right decision in terms of expediting AM stereo" and believed that a standards selection would have led to a lengthy losing effort in court (p. 68). He said that Sony's and Sansui's multidecoders proved the viability of the marketplace, although consumers "don't just automatically go out and buy a new radio set" (p. 68). He also confessed that the FCC was not proficient "at setting standards, knowing what's the right standard" and that "sometimes we set the wrong standard" (pp. 69–70). He cited NTSC's color TV standard as an example of a technology that was not as good as the European standard.

AM Stereo System Attrition

With little fanfare and no public announcement, Magnavox joined Belar as an AM stereo casualty. After two years in the marketplace, Magnavox had only six stations on the air. Reportedly, the company had ceased active promotion of its system. Both Kahn and Harris remained engaged in earnest competition with Motorola. Harris was deterred because of the FCC's order to withdraw the system. Prior to the withdrawal, Harris held an almost five-to-one advantage in system sales over second-place Motorola. Harris was later allowed to return to the market, but much damage had been done. Motorola, capitalizing on the problems of other manufacturers and with a great boost from Delco's decision to produce C-QUAM-only radios, began to forge a lead in the AM stereo race by the spring of 1984 (The AM stereo marketplace struggles, 1984). In addition, Chrysler decided to put Motorola-only radios in its cars (Motorola appears to be leading, 1984). Kahn ignored the other systems, focusing attention on Motorola. In March 1984 Kahn mailed audiotapes to almost all U.S. AM stations. The tapes compared broadcasts of the Kahn and Motorola systems. Kahn said the comparison would prove once and for all the superiority of its system, but Kahn was up against a hard-charging Motorola, which had pulled even with Harris and Kahn in numbers of systems in use. Motorola was far ahead of the others due to alignments with Delco and Chrysler, which had agreed to install the system in their automobiles (p. 94). No receivers were made to be compatible with just Harris or just Kahn systems. Ultimately, marketplace attention shifted away from a direct competition between the systems to a battle between Motorola-only or multisystem receivers (The AM stereo question, 1984).

By September 1984 automobile manufacturers were becoming even more receptive to AM stereo. GM put AM stereo receivers in automobiles for the first time, equipping 3,500 1984 Buick Century cars with Motorola. Delco announced that it was producing at least half a million AM stereo radios for 1985 cars. Chrysler ordered approximately 40,000 radios for 1984, with plans for obtaining 500,000 more in 1985. Ford also figured on equipping its vehicles with the product. Motorola's C-QUAM system was considered more complex than the other systems. Manufacturers declined to offer reasons for choosing C-QUAM, but more stations were broadcasting with C-QUAM. A Motorola spokesperson said that 175 stations were broadcasting with C-QUAM in 1984, 100 installed Harris, 90 chose Kahn, and only a minute number employed Magnavox's system, which had gone out of production (AM stereo makers, 1984). Motorola gained further ground in October 1984, when Pioneer, Marantz, and Concord announced that they would build only C-QUAM-capable receivers (Sweeney, 1984).

Early 1984 reports on AM stereo broadcast quality were favorable. AM stereo was considered by critics as equal to, or better than, FM stereo in many respects (Dreyfack, 1984). In contrast to FM stereo, which loses its stereo before the FM signal fades out totally, AM stereo could be received over greater distances (Greenleaf, 1984).

During October 1984 the Australian Department of Communications picked Motorola's C-QUAM as its single-system standard. Leonard Kahn voiced his disapproval but doubted he could do anything to change the results (Motorola gets Australian boost, 1984).

On August 17, 1983, the FCC had ordered Harris to take its system from the marketplace and instruct the 65 stations using the system to stop stereo broadcasting by September 1. The FCC charged and subsequently punished Harris for changing its system's equipment after gaining approval in 1982. Harris was considered to be winning the marketplace competition at the time of the FCC's action. Kahn was confident that all the Harris stations would convert to his system (FCC pulls plug, 1983). Harris cooperated with the FCC and proposed ways of correcting the problem. Harris' options consisted of resubmitting its original system for reapproval or asking the FCC to accept the modified version (Holland, 1983).

On November 26, 1984, Harris joined Belar and Magnavox as AM stereo marketplace casualties. Penalized on August 17, 1983, for changing its system after FCC approval, a temporary restraining order was placed on Harris (Holland, 1983). Harris was not allowed to sell its AM stereo equipment for a short period of time, and it lost valuable ground to Motorola. By the time that Harris announced its withdrawal, it had already implemented plans to alter existing Harris systems at stations so they could be received on C-QUAM systems (Two left in AM stereo, 1984). Kahn (1984) hinted that Harris and Motorola were in violation of antitrust laws (p. 26). He said that legal action was possible: "We are consulting with attorneys to determine what legal steps, if any, should be taken" (Harris throws, 1984, p. 109).

By the end of 1984 Motorola was the choice of an estimated 200 stations, and about 120 employed Kahn's. When combined with Harris systems, Motorola's total was expected to exceed 350. Harris officially joined Motorola in December 1984. In a December 17 news release, Harris V.P. Gene T. Whicker said: "We feel this agreement is in the best interest of all in making AM stereo thrive as a popular new broadcast technology and consumer medium. Harris' foremost interest is in providing AM broadcasters a high fidelity system comparable with FM stereo quality, and to develop transmission systems that will deliver the highest quality AM stereo to the listeners. We plan to concentrate our efforts on refining C-QUAM transmission hardware technology for the benefit of the broadcast industry" (Harris Corporation, 1984). Motorola senior vice president William G. Howard added: "The Harris-Motorola agreement underscores the acceptance and acceleration of the C-QUAM AM Stereo system as the marketplace AM stereo standard. There are now a large number of major manufacturers committed to the supply of broadcast equipment, integrated circuit decoders and stereo receivers for the C-QUAM AM stereo system" (p. 2).

Harris Corporation (n.d.) also issued an *AM Stereo Position* statement in which it reemphasized its support of AM stereo. Harris acknowledged AM's declining audience shares and the need to stop the erosion. The company explained the state of AM stereo and offered reasons for joining Motorola:

It was obvious to us at Harris that the many AM Stereo systems being offered were confusing to the industry and consumers alike, and the widespread utilization of AM stereo was in jeopardy. As a result of this confusion over the last three years, only 300 to 400 AM stations out of the some 4,900 stations licensed by the FCC have commenced stereo operation. Furthermore, the public has failed to purchase AM Stereo receivers in any significant quantities. It became clear to Harris that something had to be done to encourage a sufficient number of AM broadcasters to adopt AM Stereo and to reach a threshold level of acceptance or AM Stereo would fail. Therefore, Harris asked both Motorola and Kahn if they would be interested in entering into some type of licensing agreement whereby Harris could manufacture and market their systems. Kahn's response to our request was, "Unless you can offer us a very significant minimum yearly royalty income, we would not be in a position to license manufacture of our existing exciters to Harris."

Harris further explained that Motorola accepted an agreement involving no royalties or exclusivity. Similar arrangements had been made previously between Motorola and Delta, Broadcast Electronics, and TFT. Harris encouraged the manufacture and marketing of single system and multidecoder receivers.

With all the discussion of AM stereo in 1984, little attention seemed to focus on AM and FM audience shares. For the first time since the turn of the decade, AM lost no ground to FM. AM listenership remained stable throughout 1984 (Staying up, 1984).

Chapter 3

AM Stereo:
The Wrath of Kahn

In January 1985 Leonard Kahn issued a formal complaint to the FTC in regard to possible antitrust practices of Motorola, Harris, and other manufacturers. By March 1985 the FTC launched a formal, preliminary investigation but made no comment other than acknowledging it. The FTC was gathering information to determine if a full-blown investigation was warranted. Kahn's most egregious charge was Harris' December decision to drop its own system and adopt Motorola's. Kahn was upset that receiver manufacturers were not making consumers aware of AM stereo systems other than Motorola's. Kahn believed that if consumers knew about incompatibility, they would choose multidecoders. Kahn said: "The only way you can sell single-system radio is by sneaking it in" (FTC said, 1985, p. 42).

As April 1985 ended, Motorola's popularity continued climbing among broadcasters and manufacturers. Although all Harris equipment had not been changed to C-QUAM, Motorola's system was installed at 250 stations. Fewer than 100 remained with Kahn (AM broadcasters: Anxious, 1985). Major cornerstones in Kahn's camp, stations in Chicago, Los Angeles, Boston, and Toledo, changed to C-QUAM. All explained that listeners with AM stereo receivers such as Delco could not get their stereo broadcasts. By not understanding incompatibility problems, listeners considered the stations inferior. Many broadcasters believed that Kahn's system was better than Motorola's but were concerned about Motorola's lead and its alliance with major receiver manufacturers. It was difficult to promote AM stereo without a way to hear it (Ronaldi, 1985).

Weary of the fight, AM broadcasters wanted to focus on stopping FM. At the April 1985 NAB convention in Las Vegas, much discussion focused on AM unity and national stereo promotion. Manufacturers such as Harris, Continental, Broadcast Electronics, TFT, and Delta Electronics displayed C-QUAM equipment. With more than 16 major receiver companies in its camp, Motorola solidified its position as the future standard (NAB '85, 1985).

The numbers continued to build for Motorola in May with more than 300 stations reportedly using the system (AM stereo battle, 1985). The total grew to 400 by midsummer 1985 (Radio technology, 1985). In July NRBA released results from a 1984 survey indicating that AM stereo was gaining momentum. NRBA found that 13 percent of AM stations were broadcasting stereo, compared to 4 percent in 1983. Stations with news/talk, contemporary hits, religious, and big band formats showed little interest in stereo (Radio survey, 1985).

In August 1984 NAB (1984) surveyed 452 program directors to determine "the current and future status of AM stereo at their stations" (p. 1). In contrast to NRBA's results, only 13 (4.3 percent) of all respondents employed AM stereo. The survey revealed that AM stereo had "failed to reach anticipated adoption levels" for two reasons: (1) no standard AM stereo system and (2) expense of "updating transmitter equipment" (p. 7). While NRBA's survey produced different figures from those of the NAB concerning present use of AM stereo, inconsistent figures were also revealed for percentage of stations planning to add stereo. NRBA found that 11 percent of those surveyed planned to install AM stereo, and NAB discovered 16 percent.

AM stereo continued to receive high marks for quality. Critics continued to point out AM weaknesses, but proponents argued that FM also had problems. AM and AM stereo were arguably the best signals for those who listened in automobiles—if the listener's AM receiver was of good quality (Greenleaf, 1985). Because many AM broadcasters were unwilling to improve basic technology, both monophonic and stereophonic signals on some stations remained substandard. Poor technology and lack of a standard repelled many receiver companies from AM stereo. Lack of education among consumers became an even larger factor. Generally, receiver manufacturers hesitated because poor AM signals produced inadequate reception, and many buyers perceived the problem to be with the receiver. Other companies combated the problem of AM stereo ignorance. Sanyo and Sparkomatic utilized direct marketing strategies by taking receivers to shows and dealers. By doing so, the consumer could be exposed firsthand to AM stereo. Among those companies reluctant to add AM stereo, most indicated that they would build sets if AM technology was improved (Industry has AM stereo, 1985).

IMPROVING AM RADIO

The FCC should have improved AM long before considering stereo. Unless applied in conjunction with improved audio technology, AM stereo is not an impressive enhancement. Unfortunately, the perfect scenario did not occur. The FCC has been criticized, and justifiably so, for its blatant failure as regulator with AM, but much blame can also be placed squarely on the AM industry for its reluctance to improve its technology. AM was well entrenched as a medium for nearly two decades prior to FM's introduction. Thirty years later, FM still lagged pitifully behind AM in listeners. With such a huge audience, AM operators had little or no motivation to improve their product, to replace old equipment, or to upgrade basic AM technology. As FM stations and receivers began to proliferate, more listeners were exposed to its high-fidelity sound. In the 1970s FM's popularity grew exponentially, catching AM operators totally off guard. By 1980, when FM drew even in audience numbers for the first time, AM's troubles became frightfully apparent. Montgomery (1999) observed: "The critical situation AM finds itself in today is really a product of it being a successful broadcasting system. It can reproduce a broad range of audio frequencies approaching human hearing, and in the golden days of radio it was quite a medium" (p. 16).

Broadcasters, equipment manufacturers, NAB, and NRSC did not believe that AM and high fidelity had to be contradictory terms. In 1983 NAB proceeded with a long-term plan to bring back good AM radio. NAB's persistence eventually convinced the FCC to improve AM radio. Heavily criticized for its AM stereo marketplace decision, the FCC (1990a) appeared eager to help AM, saying that "we are dealing with no less an issue than the survival of the AM service" (p. 4381). The ultimate goal was to achieve a competitive quality sound equivalent to FM.

NAB and AM Improvement

To study AM's ills, the NAB formed its AM Improvement Subcommittee in 1983. By 1985 the committee evolved into the NRSC, which petitioned the FCC in October for formal AM improvement. Jim McKinney, FCC Mass Media Bureau chief, decided that something had to be done about AM radio's decline. For 10 years AM had lost at least 3 percent of its audience annually. McKinney believed AM would die by 1991 at that rate. McKinney's primary obstacle appeared to be the FCC's radio deregulation. Realizing that AM stereo had been left hanging by the Commission's marketplace decision, what could he do? He decided to be persistent and to argue that AM's survival was at stake.

The FCC had to do something to save AM, and it could not take the same tack as it had with AM stereo, which McKinney acknowledged was a mistake. McKinney believed that litigation over a standard would have taken less time than the marketplace in getting AM stereo off the ground. He said that the FCC could correct its mistakes by altering rules and allowing AM to compete on a more level playing field with FM. McKinney suggested that AM could temporarily compete with format experimentation and by updating and fine-tuning broadcast equipment, but he believed that AM's ills could be cured long-term only by selecting an AM stereo system standard.

McKinney ordinarily agreed with the FCC's hands-off policy, but AM radio needed intervention. It was broken and needed to be fixed (Fields, 1985).

Some observers attributed AM radio's decline more to poor programming than to poor technology (Reviving AM, 1985) and believed it mythical that listeners migrated to FM for stereo rather than programming. If innovative programming had not been employed, it was argued, listeners would not have stayed once they tried FM. AM radio could improve its technology considerably, but that did not mean that listeners would return without some other incentive. During 1985 a number of AM stations had tried new formats consisting of news, information, weather, traffic updates, country music, adult contemporary music, big band/nostalgia music, comedy, and even education (Format experimentation, 1985).

Many broadcasters agreed that format played some role in losing or winning listeners, but sound quality was a major factor, if not the major factor. *Broadcasting* reported:

The reversal of fortunes of AM and FM broadcasting, most agree, stems in large part from FM's greater fidelity, an advantage that was enhanced in 1961 when the FCC authorized FM stereo. About that time, FM licensees who had been taking advantage of the sound quality of their medium to broadcast classical music realized that it did as well for Elvis as for Bach. In the early 1970's, many radios in cars rolling off assembly lines were equipped to receive FM stereo as well as AM. Then there was the fact that FM stations traditionally, because of their music formats and out of necessity, interrupted their programming with commercials less often than their AM competitors. All of which helped generate FM's growth and AM's decline. (AM: Band on the Run, 1985, p. 46, 50)

McKinney pushed hard for AM rules changes, saying: "There is no other service for which such a review is more appropriate. AM broadcasting already is more than 60 years old, and while we have made great strides in updating the AM rules, some of the basic assumptions are little changed from the earliest days of the Commission" (McKinney's insight, 1986, p. 37).

The FCC promised changes but initially did nothing to improve AM's technology. The FCC released its much-anticipated AM report in April 1986. Much of the document consisted of ownership rules and technical requirements, which had little or nothing to do with AM stereo. Rather, the Commission focused on eliminating outdated licensing and regulatory constraints. One move was elimination of broadcasting's duopoly rules, which were implemented in the 1960s to help FM become competitive with AM. The rules banned AM/FM combinations from simulcasting programming. As a result, the FCC hoped to ensure programming diversity. Now the Commission proposed to allow simulcasting to help AM compete with FM. More precisely, it seemed that the Commission was lifting burdens from FM rather than assisting AM.

The "Print Model." FCC chairman Mark Fowler wanted to relax rules about same market ownership of stations and to regulate technical matters only minimally. Fowler said that the AM improvement report represented another development in a movement toward the print model of regulation. Fowler's legal assistant said that the "litmus test" for the print model "is whether a rule or policy would or could be imposed on newspapers, books, and magazines. If not, it must be eliminated" (Herwitz, 1985, p. 185). The spokesperson said that some broadcasting rules would always be necessary due to its technical nature and interference. Fowler (1982, 1984) preferred to discuss the print model in terms of American forefathers, contending that it was necessary because the federal government had strayed so far away from those who framed the Constitution. He believed that government should get completely out of content regulation.

NRSC and NTIA's AM Improvement Petition. Impatient with the FCC's lack of action, NRSC adopted its own voluntary AM broadcast frequency response standard in January 1987. As a private, industry organization, NRSC was not empowered to require compliance (Texar, 1987). NRSC, supported by NTIA, telecommunications policy division for the Executive Branch of the Commerce Department, petitioned the FCC on November 6, 1987, to make the voluntary preemphasis/de-emphasis standards mandatory. Preemphasis is the stabilization of the extent of boosting of audio highs—a common practice of AM stations, and de-emphasis is the resultant attenuation in the receiver in order to restore flat frequency response (AM uniformity, 1987). Al Sikes, then NTIA secretary and later FCC chairman, agreed with NRSC about the improvement, believing it to be far too supereminent to be left to voluntary industry compliance (Zavistovich, 1987b).

Having demonstrated minor success with 441 voluntary NRSC-equipped AM stations, attention shifted to receivers. Manufacturers were reluctant to design high-fidelity units without including AM stereo, which had no transmission standard (Zavistovich, 1987c, p. 3). Technological incompatibility compounded the situation. To receive stereo broadcasts, a multidecoder radio would be necessary. Stations' reluctance to gamble on a particular system resulted in receiver manufacturers perceiving a lack of interest for both AM and stereo.

NRSC-compliant stations grew to 523 by mid-January 1988 (Carter, 1988) and to 686 by the end of March (NAB radio, 1988); however, only a handful of companies, such as Delco, Sony, Sanyo, and Sansui, planned NRSC-compatible receivers (Zavistovich, 1988). Without receivers, AM's technological gains could not be demonstrated to consumers.

NRSC Proposed Rule Making and Industry Replies. The FCC (1988b) launched its NRSC proposed rulemaking proceeding on July 22, 1988, writing: "We agree [with NAB] that if the NRSC audio pre-emphasis is used at an otherwise properly adjusted and operating station, adjacent channel interference should be substantially reduced because the NRSC audio pre-emphasis standard would effectively limit the highest permissible audio frequency. . . . Use of the NRSC pre-emphasis characteristic may also aid

receiver manufacturers in designing better receivers . . . [and] could even
benefit reception on current receivers to a limited extent" (p. 5688). Despite
praising NRSC's proposals, the FCC said that a "better alternative" in improving AM could be addition of a receiver RF mask. The Commission said:
"This course of action would not only provide the benefit sought by NAB,
but would be compatible with voluntary use of the NRSC audio standard"
(p. 5689).

NRSC insisted on delaying additional mandatory standards until at least
1994 because of the financial burden placed on AM broadcasters. Urging the
FCC to relax its tentative stand, NAB argued that stations using NRSC voluntary standards demonstrated promise to comply with other enhancements
in the future. NTIA supported the FCC's alterations (NTIA likes, 1989).

The FCC seemed pleased with progress toward AM improvement. The
1982 AM stereo marketplace decision and the subsequent years of Commis-
sion-bashing convinced AM operators that the FCC wanted to destroy them.
Eager to counter the claims, FCC chairman Dennis Patrick praised the commitment to AM: "[F]or you skeptics out there . . . this [AM improvement
proceeding] suggests that the Commission will not shy away from the adoption of technical standards where it is demonstrated that we can advance the
public interest in a particular area doing so. We have by this item proposed a
technical standard which I think will go a long way toward improving the
quality of the AM signal if it is ultimately adopted. It's a good day for the AM
service" (FCC acts, 1988, p. 10).

NRSC-1 or NRSC-2? The FCC (1989) formally and unanimously voted to
require standards, dubbed NRSC-2, beginning June 30, 1990. Stations compliant with NRSC-1, the original voluntary standard, by June 30 would be allowed a four-year grace period for NRSC-2. NRSC considered NRSC-2 too
primitive and costly but with proper development would lend support (FCC
to include, 1988). NRSC-1 limited the boosting of the high frequencies in
audio and limited the bandwidth of audio to 10 kHz prior to modulation and
transmission, while NRSC-2 limited emissions during transmission. Simply
put, NRSC-1 reduces input interference, and NRSC-2 reduces output interference. The Commission presumed elimination of output interference would
cut input interference (FCC takes, 1989).

With NRSC-1 in place, stations would have time to study their needs, to
acquire equipment, and to make any corrections for complete compliance
with NRSC-2. Stations with NRSC-1 would obviously need less improvement than others. It appeared that NRSC, broadcasters, and the FCC met
their objectives. The Commission got full compliance with both NRSC-1 and
NRSC-2, and broadcasters and NRSC received a delay in total compliance
until 1994. The FCC (1989) cited six reasons for its decision:

By itself, the NRSC-1 audio standard will not be effective in alleviating interference
produced by overmodulation or transmission system anomalies; it requires the NRSC-

2 emission limitation to be fully effective; (2) the characteristics of the audio response intended to be produced by the NRSC-1 filter can be readily circumvented or abused by adjustments made to other audio processing equipment; moreover, to the extent NRSC-1 specifies a particular pre-emphasis of audio signals below 10 kHz, it limits licensees' flexibility in adjusting their audio processing equipment; (3) the NRSC-2 emission limitation alone provides effective control of interference due to emitted signals; thus, it renders NRSC-1 redundant; (4) very few transmitters will be unable to comply with NRSC-2; (5) the NRSC-2 emission limitation is readily enforceable through over-the-air monitoring techniques, whereas determining compliance with NRSC-1 would require an on-site inspection; (6) the cost to licensees of ensuring that a station conforms to NRSC-1 is the same as ensuring that it complies with NRSC-2. (pp. 19572–19573)

Broadcasters argued that NRSC-2 cost significantly more than NRSC-1. Depending on a station's needs, NRSC-1 cost $400 to $700, and NRSC-2 was $1,800 to $20,000 (FCC takes, 1989). Estimates were based on assumptions that some AM stations would require new transmitters to achieve NRSC-2 compliance. The FCC (1989) countered: "The record contains no evidence that any particular type of AM transmitter will be unable to meet the NRSC-2 emission limitation. To the contrary, it indicates that NRSC-2 was designed with current broadcast transmitters in mind and that cases requiring transmitter replacement should be few, if any" (p. 19573). The Commission added that "any additional time, effort or expense incurred to verify proper station operation will be the same for either NRSC-1 or NRSC-2" (p. 19573).

Even if broadcasters were correct about higher costs, the four-year grace period would relieve any immediate financial burden. Total AM overhaul would be accomplished within five years. Realizing that all AM stations would be NRSC-compliant by mid-1994, manufacturers had incentive and time to produce state-of-the-art receivers.

Slow Response to NRSC. An estimated 3,000 AM stations were not converted to either NRSC-1 or NRSC-2 by the end of January 1990 (On, 1990, p. 65). A month before the June 30, 1990, deadline, only an estimated half of all AMs had been upgraded. Because of slower than expected sales, it seemed inevitable that a number of stations would be delinquent on June 30. The Commission reported that it would not seek out noncompliant stations after the June 30 deadline but would depend on rival stations to turn in noncompliant competitors. If a station were found in violation, the FCC could impose fines from $25,000 to $250,000 for chronic offenders, and violators would be required to install immediately the more expensive NRSC-2 (Outside the law, 1990).

In an effort to educate consumers about NRSC standards and hopefully to stimulate sales, the NAB in late February 1990 asked member stations to air announcements urging listeners to buy NRSC-compliant receivers. Special certification marks authenticated them. NAB said that no particular make or model would be endorsed, but all NRSC receiver manufacturers would benefit from an estimated $50 million of publicity. Within days of NAB's request, nearly 700 stations agreed to run from 10 to 30 ads per week. NAB president Eddie Fritts believed that more receivers would spark interest in the AM improvement campaign. Stations would be more readily motivated to become compatible, and a positive cycle would ensue (Carter, 1990a).

NRSC Deadline. As the FCC's NRSC deadline approached, several hundred noncompliant stations remained. In a May release, the Commission announced that there would be no extensions or exceptions to the deadline and that violators would pay penalties for not serving the public interest. NRSC equipment distributors expected a late crush of orders (Taylor, 1990a). There was a large surge of orders, but manufacturers offered no exact figures on how many converters had been sold. In addition to its plans to depend on rival stations' blowing the whistle on each other, the FCC had "an ongoing broadcast inspection program" in place (Waiting, 1990, pp. 74–75).

Such a procedure was not unusual for the FCC during the first weeks after a major technical rule change. According to FOB chief Richard Smith, the NRSC standards were very important to the Commission. Smith said that enough notice was given stations to comply, and "after adequate public notice and education . . . everyone is aware of it" (Waiting, 1990, p. 75). He added: "The compliance effort is going in to see if some number of stations, as a sample, have installed the proper equipment or to see if their emissions are in compliance with the new standards" (p. 75).

The first audit for NRSC compliance by the FCC's FOB was taken from a sample of 374 AM stations, and 325 stations were found in compliance with NRSC-2 (87 percent). Upon further testing, the other 49 stations were found to be compliant with NRSC-1 emissions standards. Therefore, 100 percent of the sample stations met the deadline. Although an estimated 1,650 stations were believed to be delinquent, FOB's figures did not support the assumption (Looking good, 1990). Despite the FCC's finding of full compliance, a nationwide sample of 300 AM general managers two years later found less than universal compliance with NRSC-1 and NRSC-2 standards. In the survey, 43 (14.5 percent) managers reported that they had not made the NRSC-1 technical changes for improved sound quality. Another 42 GMs (14.1 percent) did not know or were not sure, having left technical changes to the station engineer. AM stations that simulcast, as well as those that were broadcasting in stereo, were more likely to have complied with the NRSC-1 requirements. Compliance with NRSC-2 standards was 27.8 percent, with 26.8 percent saying that they did not know, or were not sure, if their station was in compliance (Huff & Rosene, 1993–94).

Expanded AM Band. A major technical obstacle experienced by AM is interference from other AM stations. When World War II concluded, radio boomed along with many other industries. Many licenses were issued for stations in small communities, and the AM band became packed to the point that "receivers were no longer picking up clean signals free of whistles (heterodynes) and adjacent channel audio" (Montgomery, 1999, p. 16). To combat the problems, bandwidth was narrowed to the extent that "on the best receivers available, [AM radio] sounds like it is being received over a telephone line" (p. 16). Audio quality was sacrificed to cure the interference problem. In an effort to thin the band, the FCC (1990) proposed relocating some AM stations to an expanded band from 1605 to 1705 kHz. The FCC opened the spectrum in 1993 but did not know what to do since so many more stations applied to move than could. The FCC committed a false start in 1994 when it tried to move 79 stations, but broadcasters cited errors in the FCC's data, and the plans were scrapped. In March 1996 the Commission unveiled a new list and finally appeared ready to move 87 stations to new frequencies. Five petitions were filed asking the FCC to rethink its proposal, but by September 1996 the Commission believed that it had done its work thoroughly enough to move ahead (McConnell, 1996e). Two reconsideration petitions and a court case greeted the third plan in 1997, but the FCC would not be deterred a third time. From the beginning of the proceeding, the FCC said that it would give preference to stations promising to employ AM stereo, and about 95 percent of all applicants agreed to the stipulation. Applications were accepted from 67 of 88 stations that filed by a June 1997 deadline, and by September 1997 the Commission was issuing construction permits. Stations were given five years to make the transition before returning their old frequencies. The first station, WCMZ in Miami, was operating on the expanded band by the end of September 1997, but two stations got a two-year jump on the process with temporary licenses: KXBT in Vallejo, California, and WJDM in Elizabeth, New Jersey (Meadows, 1998).

NAB Super Radio—Featuring AMAX. It was no secret that much of AM radio's problem is not in transmission but in reception. Montgomery (1999) said: "AM transmission equipment is still capable of doing what it did 50 years ago. Most receivers are a shadow of their ancestors when it comes to reproducing the signal. The technology to improve fidelity exists, but most consumer receiver manufacturers fail to take action. In fact, many FM receivers don't approach the quality FM broadcasters are transmitting" (p. 16). With that in mind, NAB's Science & Technology team developed a "Super Radio" receiver called AMAX that featured C-QUAM AM stereo, AM noise blanking, FM sensitivity and selectivity, and automatic variable bandwidth (Butler, 1992). AMAX, NRSC's standard for AM radio, was an attempt to improve reception and to give manufacturers a model to follow when designing receivers. Audio receiver manufacturer Denon was commissioned to build the receiver, and its NAB TU-680 Super Tuner was unveiled at the NAB's New Orleans Radio Show in September 1992. Denon's Super Tuner was totally compatible with the standards set for AMAX AM. The Super Tuner was critically acclaimed for both its AM and FM performance, as well as for its many standard features (Feldman, 1992).

Under development for more than five years, AMAX receivers incorporated RDS technology, which was better received by the industry than AMAX. At 1993's Winter CES, just the Denon TU-680 NAB Super Tuner was on display. RDS would enable automobile radios to retune to a different station with the same format to which the consumer was listening. As the car leaves the coverage area of one station, it searches for another station employing the same format. RDS also could receive other information that a motorist might desire. RDS was installed in AMAX tuners due to a compromise between NAB and the EIA. Broadcasters were not opposed to its capability to search automatically for a similar format. The compromise was necessary because broadcasters were upset that NRSC, cosponsored by EIA and NAB, did not provide enough codes to represent a wide range of formats. Broadcasters also believed that EIA was too ambitious in its testing of DAB systems. EIA planned to begin testing on April 15, 1993, and broadcasters believed that was not enough time for system proponents to be ready. Further, broadcasters were not pleased with EIA's intention to test systems designed to operate in new radio bands (Sukow, 1992c).

In response to the lack of AMAX acceptance, EIA/NRSC lowered its standards to allow lesser receivers to carry the AMAX logo. However, that did not work either because there seemed to be little manufacturer interest in producing better AM radios.

AM has traditionally enjoyed better reception range and mobility than FM, but with NRSC technological upgrades, stereo enhancement, and improved receivers, AM can sound as good as FM (Trautmann, 1991). A proper blend of promotion, programming, and technology can give AM an opportunity to regain respectability with listeners and advertisers as a viable and valuable asset to society.

KAHN, MOTOROLA, AND THE
AM STEREO MARKETPLACE

Leonard Kahn, president of Kahn Communications, Inc. (1985a, 1985b, 1985c), launched an assault on the AM stereo issue on July 3, 1985, mailing a package of information to AM broadcasters. An enclosed letter was addressed to "The Best AM Stereo stations in the world 'the Eagles.'" In the letter Kahn (1985) quoted from an article that documented some of the complaints leveled at AM stereo by receiver manufacturers. Kahn said: "Broadcasters did not push Motorola stereo, it was the receiver people." Kahn continued: "Isn't it interesting . . . [*sic*] Motorola radio manufacturers think AM Stereo sounds bad because of the broadcasters. But you never heard Sony, Sansui or Advanced Design, badmouth the sound of AM Stereo. Indeed, one of Motorola's strongest supporters told me recently that when their radio falses, and works on our stations, our stations SOUND BETTER THAN THE MOTOROLA STATIONS EVEN WITH THE MOTOROLA DECODER."

Kahn offered AM stations employing his system some advice on how to cope with the criticisms of AM stereo. First, stations must let "listeners know that you broadcast QUALITY AM STEREO and if they don't receive quality stereo to blame their radio not your station." He added: "You must be vocal about it or you will be tarnished just as if you weren't an 'Eagle.' " Second, he said: "Assist your friends. Right now your best friends, (except for KCI) are the receiver manufacturers who make multi-system quality radios—Sony, Sansui and Advanced Design. If you have any ideas in helping promote QUALITY AM STEREO RADIOS, please write to me with your permission to share your letter with receiver manufacturers and other Eagles." Kahn said that his suggestions "will give me added strength in our campaign for the multi-system quality AM Stereo radios."

In his mailer, Kahn also included a brochure, various letters, and several information sheets. For the most part, Kahn focused on the advantages of his system and the disadvantages of Motorola's system. Kahn Communications, Inc. (1985a) called the state of AM stereo "an 'Eagle and Egg' situation." He explained: "Broadcasting, like a number of other industries, is subject to the well-known 'chicken and egg' economic theory. For example, manufacturers were unable to sell Color TV receivers until broadcasters accepted a system and initiated color broadcasting. In the case of AM Stereo, where there are now two basic systems, the situation is a step beyond the "chicken and egg," it is more like an "Eagle and Egg" situation." Kahn suggested broadcasters should pick the best AM stereo system—in his opinion, the Kahn—and promote multisystem receivers. He called it "exercising your veto." Kahn urged AM broadcasters to "Join the Eagles protecting AM Stereo and AM radio."

Despite Kahn's strategies, the number of Motorola stations grew to about 225 between 1984 and 1985. An additional 80 to 85 stations used Harris equipment modified to be Motorola-compatible. Almost 400 stations used one AM stereo system or another. Motorola contended that it had sold 3.2 million stereo integrated circuit decoders for use in C-QUAM receivers and that nearly half of those were already in radios. By contrast, Sony and Sansui reportedly had sold only 50,000 multidecoding receivers. Motorola said that while its system's sales continued to rise, Kahn's had leveled out (Radio technology coming of age, 1985).

In August 1985 Leonard Kahn continued his attack on the Harris and Motorola arrangement. He contended that someone had "pressured" Harris-equipped stations into Motorola-compatibility rather than offering a refund. Harris officials reiterated that the move was done in the best interest of AM stereo and was an attempt to break the deadlock that was taking shape. Harris officials said the decision was based on helping broadcasters and was not motivated by economic reasons (Kahn fights, 1985).

August 1985 also brought another AM stereo movement to the forefront when the Connecticut Department of Consumer Protection proposed that mandatory labels or tags be attached to receivers and advertisements by manufacturers and sellers to identify AM stereo radios and compatibility. The problem was not new, but Connecticut offered the first viable solution. Consumers, in most instances, had no idea of the AM stereo compatibility dilemma. The regulation would, however, need approval by other state agencies before taking effect. No immediate action was announced. In June Utah's Division of Consumer Protection issued a similar tag warning buyers that there were multidecoders available but that not all receivers could decode all AM stereo signals. Both Utah and Connecticut officials hoped to help buyers make informed decisions about radio receivers. Naturally, multidecoder proponent Leonard Kahn was happy with the action in both Connecticut and Utah. Motorola's reaction was split. Motorola's Chris Payne contended that Connecticut's legislation would raise an unnecessary warning flag, which would further confuse consumers by creating misunderstandings. As a result, Payne said, sellers of receivers and dealers of AM stereo-equipped cars would shy away from stereo products. Payne said that Motorola favored Utah's consumer alert because the company supported understanding of the AM stereo situation among consumers (Connecticut weighs, 1985).

On October 22, 1985, Connecticut's Regulatory Review Committee acted on the matter. The committee was charged with examining proposals before they were sent to the full legislature. The committee returned the proposal to Connecticut's Department of Consumer Protection, which had the option of shelving, rewriting, or resubmitting it (Hughes, 1985b). It was shelved due to intense resistance from receiver manufacturers who believed that the labels would confuse consumers. It was suggested that a more effective strategy might have been for broadcasters to tell listeners which AM stereo system was being used (Promote AM stereo, 1985). Connecticut's receiver-tagging proposal was refiled with the state's Legislative Regulation Review Committee in early 1986, but it was rejected (Hughes, 1986b).

Because of the confusion over AM stereo and incompatibility with receivers, NRBA launched an examination into the feasibility of asking Congress to require AM stereo multidecoders as a standard component of all radios. NRBA's Chester Coleman said the purpose was to make AM stereo's quality equal to FM stereo's. Coleman alluded to precedent agreed upon by the FCC and Congress in which all televisions were required to include UHF as well as VHF (Hughes, 1985a). In view of the FCC's position on technical standard setting in the 1980s, the prospect of any such requirement looked slim. After all, what would be the point? The FCC already had refused to pick an AM stereo transmission system, so why reverse itself to pick a receiver standard?

Another proposal offered by NAB engineer Mike Rau contained more promise. Rau suggested a continuous tuning radio, an innovation on par with television's VHF/UHF situation. Such a tuner would require no switching from AM to FM but would do the job automatically. It was not known if any manufacturers were making plans for one of the receivers (Hughes, 1985a).

In December the FCC's James McKinney suggested that Motorola and Kahn could ask the DOJ and FTC for antitrust immunity so that one might buy out the other. McKinney said that attempting such a move could not hurt. McKinney believed that AM stations should forge ahead and transmit stereo so listeners would have an incentive to buy receivers (More hope from McKinney, 1985). McKinney maintained his stance that the FCC should have set a standard whether it was the best system or not. He also encouraged manufacturers of receivers to produce better products, especially for automobiles (Hughes, 1986a).

During December 1985 the NBMC approached the FCC about reconsidering its AM stereo decision, primarily because of marketplace failure. NBMC believed that valuable time had been squandered while awaiting movement in a stalemated marketplace. The prolonged deadlock was hindering both consumers and broadcasters. NBMC contended that there was no economic motivation for AM stations to stand behind one stereo system. As a result, stations already using AM stereo would be unwilling to give up an installed system in favor of another (Hughes, 1985c).

With no comment, the FTC ended its nearly yearlong investigation of Motorola on December 1, 1985. The investigation had started in March 1985 at the urging of Leonard Kahn, who charged Motorola with committing potential anticompetitive activities in its quest to become the AM stereo standard. Kahn was disappointed with the outcome but indicated that he still might file a civil antitrust suit against Motorola (Scratch one, 1986).

For the second time in two years, a country selected Motorola as its AM stereo standard. Australia selected it in October 1984, and Brazil followed suit on January 29, 1986. Motorola officials hoped that the move would prompt other South American countries to select C-QUAM (Brazil chooses C-QUAM, 1986).

The CAB, originally charged by the CRTC to select an AM stereo system standard by April 1, 1986, requested a one-year extension. CRTC is Canada's equivalent to the FCC. CAB was to recommend a single system to CRTC but did not have broadcasters' full support of any one system. CAB encountered many of the same obstacles as U.S. broadcasters. Canadian broadcasters were torn between a single standard and the marketplace. With the availability of multidecoding receivers, some broadcasters believed that there was room in Canada for both Motorola and Kahn (Wytkind, 1986a).

AM Stereo Promotion

Following Brazil's selection of its AM stereo system, Motorola officials began marketing plans for the country. Motorola executives were enthusiastic because AM was Brazil's dominant medium with at least 1,000 stations (Wytkind, 1986b). Canada was urged to follow the lead of Brazil and Australia in order to avoid the United States' marketplace mistake (Canada: Avoid, 1986).

U.S. AM stereo was receiving a lot of negative response, but there were success stories. Several stations benefited by utilizing stereo, promotion, and format experimentation. Many stations chose Motorola's C-QUAM, and others decided on Kahn's system, but there was little doubt that stereo was an improvement over mono. Some stations remained with news/talk or informational programming, while others were more music-oriented. Classical music, in particular, seemed to enjoy resurgence on AM.

Regardless of the type of programming, promotion appeared to be the key to AM stereo's success. A good example was Norman Communications' WZKY in Albemarle, North Carolina. President Bill Norman (1986) noticed that AM stations in nearby Charlotte did not appear to be promoting stereo. Norman decided to be aggressive and successfully accomplished his campaign in two basic ways. He formed listening outposts and held an open house. Listening outposts were audio equipment stores and automobile dealerships featuring AM stereo receivers tuned to WZKY. WZKY profited, and so did retailers as customer interest was piqued. The local Dodge/Chrysler/Plymouth dealer ordered only AM stereo/FM stereo in all his new vehicles. Norman's open house featured a comparison test between WZKY, a monophonic AM, and an FM stereo station, so listeners could hear for themselves. Norman provided refreshments and gave away products with WZKY's AM stereo logo.

Kahn Presses Onward

Leonard Kahn continued his assault on Motorola in April 1986, complaining to the FCC that Motorola and three of its licensees violated FCC rule 73.44. The rule covered adjacent channel interference and how spectrum was to be used. Kahn received the information from an unnamed radio engineer who had taken measurements of Motorola transmissions. Motorola said there was no basis for the charge (C-QUAM violations, 1986). All of Kahn's allegations had gone for naught, and Motorola Inc. (1986a) offered an assessment in the company's quarterly bulletin:

Once again, we see a continuation of the clear pattern of Kahn making potentially damaging accusations concerning the C-QUAM AM stereo system to a government agency, widely publicizing it during its consideration, and then having it soundly rejected. We are finding more and more broadcasters disgusted with the behavior of Leonard Kahn and his version of "the marketplace." Surely there is no doubt now that the standard for AM stereo is the Motorola C-QUAM system. There is also little disagreement that AM stereo is a vary desirable asset for AM radio and that it should by [*sic*] implemented as quickly as possible by both receiver manufacturers and broadcasters. But attempts by Kahn to slow the momentum of the C-QUAM program causes damage far greater than simply delaying the ultimate establishment of an AM stereo standard. The damage is to an opportunity for revival of the AM broadcasting industry itself. (p. 2)

Kahn may not have stopped Motorola, but reports showed that Motorola's progress was slowed somewhat. Four years into the battle, only 288 (6 percent) stations installed Motorola AM stereo equipment. By contrast, 86 stations used Kahn's system. Kahn's chief advantage was major market infiltration. The greatest disadvantage was that no manufacturers built Kahn-compatible receivers. Just Sony and Sansui marketed multidecoders. At least 24 companies produced Motorola receivers, with about 4 million sets "in the hands of consumers or in the distribution pipeline" (The AM stereo fight, 1986, p. 68).

Motorola and many broadcasters were tired of the marketplace struggle, and Kahn did not help by filing charges, "beating on a dead horse," and "clouding the issue and stunting sales" (Wytkind, 1986c, p. 4). Rumors circulated that one company might buy out the AM stereo interest of the other, but both sides said that it would never happen. Motorola's Chris Payne said: "Write this down. Ha, ha, ha, ha, ha" (p. 70). When asked if Kahn had ever made overtures about buying Motorola out, no comment was offered. Payne contended that if Kahn would buckle under, 100 million AM stereo receivers would exist to boost AM audience shares to a competitive level with FM (p. 68). Kahn stated: "I'm not interested in selling out because I'd be selling out the industry" (p. 70).

In May, Kahn announced that a Japanese firm would market and distribute his AM stereo transmission system. No comment or details were offered concerning the arrangement with Tohtsu Co. Motorola was affiliated with four other companies: Harris Corporation, Delta Electronics, Broadcast Electronics, and TFT, Inc. (Wytkind, 1986d). Motorola Inc. (1986a) also boasted the number one station in 11 markets. Two Houston, Texas stations switched from Kahn to C-QUAM.

FCC Dismisses Kahn's Complaint. On July 18, 1986, the FCC formally dismissed Kahn's complaint against Motorola (FCC dismisses Kahn complaint, 1986). The letter was brief. Of seven total paragraphs, just four addressed Kahn's latest complaint against Motorola. The remaining three paragraphs contained background on previous Kahn complaints (Stanley, 1986). Just four days later, on July 22, 1996, Kahn filed an FOIA request with the FCC's FOB to acquire results of the FCC's field tests. Kahn released a statement asking why the FCC had not released its findings without being forced to do so by the FOIA request. In addition, Kahn questioned several of the FCC's technical testing procedures. One complaint focused on the FCC's use of field, rather than laboratory, tests. Kahn contended that the FCC neglected to observe specific Commission rules in reaching its decision based on tests that were "unscientific" and "subjective" (Hughes, 1986d, p. 3). The FCC said that Kahn's charges of on-air interference warranted the use of field testing, because laboratory testing would not have properly addressed the technical issues raised by Kahn. Kahn also accused the FCC of alerting the test stations prior to observation, which could have caused distorted measurements. In September the FCC released the results but revealed that in addition to testing 23 stations using Motorola's system, Kahn stations were also examined. Both systems were found to be barely above required "emissions limitations" at two separate stations in the Washington, D.C., market (Hughes, 1986e, p. 3).

In spite of Kahn's persistent allegations, Motorola again began to flex its muscles. Between March and August 1986, 10 more companies were licensed to build C-QUAM-compatible receivers—raising the number from 30 to 40. As of August Motorola also reported increases in the number of C-QUAM stations: United States, 315; Australia, 58; Canada, 38; and 10 in other countries. Motorola (1986b, 1986c) boasted 421 total stations on the air worldwide.

THE TEXAR PETITION

Midsummer 1986 was most interesting in regard to AM stereo. First, the FCC cleared Motorola concerning Kahn's allegations. In a July 18, 1986, letter, the FCC told both Motorola and Kahn that none of the reported violations existed. The Commission's testing results were not released (FCC acquits C-QUAM, 1986). Second, Texar Inc. of Pennsylvania announced plans to petition the FCC to select an AM stereo standard. Texar president Glen Clark acknowledged the FCC's intent to filter out a de facto standard through the workings of the marketplace but believed that both Kahn and Motorola had the financial backing to compete indefinitely. Texar, an audio equipment manufacturer, stepped in to help save AM stereo. Clark said that only about 10 percent of all AM stations broadcast in stereo. Because of the small percentage, manufacturers had quit marketing AM stereo receivers. Sony, Pioneer, and other receiver manufacturers admitted that their decisions to discontinue or never even to enter the market were not based on lack of a standard but on lack of demand. It could be argued, however, that a shortage of demand might be attributed to no standard and the obvious side effect of unawareness of the product. The companies said that only rudimentary interest had been generated. Clark added: "It's not enough for some stations to do well with AM stereo. The truth is that everybody's got to do it. It's got to be a national effort" (Hughes, 1986c, pp. 1, 4).

Texar intervened in an attempt to inject new life into AM stereo, which had "degenerated into a battle that no longer represents a measure of the effectiveness" of the FCC's marketplace (AM stereo support eroding, 1986, p. 5). Texar was scheduled to file in the middle of July but delayed in order to work out details.

Texar officials believed that it was time for the FCC to step back into the picture. AM stereo was trapped in a seemingly endless nightmare. Texar argued in its petition that the FCC's self-envisioned "worst case scenario" had come to pass. The time had come, Dave Van Allen observed, for the commissioners to earn their pay and reinvolve themselves in AM stereo. At least one very important FCC staffer, James McKinney, appeared in agreement with Texar that something should be done to save both AM and AM stereo. McKinney openly criticized the FCC's reluctance to pick either the Kahn or Motorola system as the standard. McKinney believed that the FCC could correct its "mistakes" through altering rules and allowing AM to return to "a competitive level" (Fields, 1985, p. 95).

Texar Inc. still had not filed its petition in early September. But, in a September 4, 1986, phone interview with the author, Texar Inc.'s senior design engineer Dave Van Allen explained: "Texar plans to vigorously pursue all avenues of the petition and anything, you know, related to the petition." Van Allen spoke candidly about Texar's involvement and what Texar hoped to accomplish by petitioning the FCC. He said: "We're not advocating either system as being better or worse than either of the systems, than one another. What we are asking for is that the petition, or the Commission, act immediately and without delay on the petition and pick an AM stereo standard based on the fact that the Commission has sufficient technical information on both of the systems already available and needs not to ask for more technical information." Van Allen said it was critical that the FCC involve broadcasters in their decision:

[The FCC] should rely on the broadcasters, the broadcast industry as a universe, and their opinions and feelings as to which system is making the most inroads, being implemented the most, has the most future, so on and so forth. And, if they were looking for a de facto standard, in my personal opinion I believe they have it. The Motorola system has proven to be the de facto standard based on the fact that it has a five to one penetration over the Kahn system, that there are 30 receiver manufacturers building for it, that there are four second sources of the IC chips, that there are five second sources for the C-QUAM transmission gear, and that there are a number of broadcast companies out there supporting it from a seller of equipment standpoint. I feel, you know, that it would be real easy to make a decision, and it's got to be done now because of the mass confusion aspect that AM is going through. If we don't do something with AM stereo, we're already starting to see receivers drop off the market. Pioneer and Sony have both released the product from their, their allocation table. And, we have spoken to nearly all the receiver manufacturers and have very good reason to believe that there are going to be more dropping off very, very shortly. In fact, if anything, the petition has held that at abeyance for a while. So, it's something that is positively necessary. It's got to be done. The Commission has got to make an action on this. And, if they don't make an action on this and decide to continue to push along with the marketplace decision, Texar has full intentions and capabilities of taking it to appellate court. . . . We had five [systems] originally. . . . At that point in time if you looked at the, at the situation, there was so much argument over even what was going on that making a decision at that time probably would've led to years and years of court battle and it wouldn't have been very smart. So, I advocate the original marketplace decision. I think that it has done exactly what it was supposed to do. And, it has effectively removed [three of the] systems. Now, we're down to two. But, the problem is that we have two companies that are both strongheaded, both appear to have financial inclination to go about this thing with vim and vigor and don't appear to be relaxing their intentions at all. All that's doing is creating an extremely confused marketplace. Based on that, the marketplace decision has stopped working. So, as all good things change, it's time for a change and that's what we're out to get.

Interestingly, in the 1920s broadcasters asked for regulation. With AM stereo, it was interesting to see that many broadcasters of the 1970s wanted to deregulate, or "unregulate," as FCC chair Mark Fowler has said. Broadcast history seemed to be coming full circle. Yet, Van Allen believed that regulation was not the issue:

Well, this isn't a regulation, a regulation/unregulation issue. This is a compatibility issue. We're trying to take an entity, the broadcast industry, and upon let's say, well, hypothesizing for a second. Let's say a thousand people need to make a decision. Well, a thousand people with all different thoughts and egos and so on and so forth cannot possibly sit down and make a decision, because they can't have all the facts. . . . a lot of people think, it's just so easy to build both receivers until you start really looking at a receiver manufacturer's problems. Just to put out a product. Just to put out a receiver, costs millions and millions of dollars in tooling alone and years of development. And, when you have a bad radio, here's a Delco statistic for you, one in every 17 radios that comes back because of a defect blows the profit on the 16 other radios. That's a serious scenario there. The decisions on bandwidth and the decisions on how to implement the equipment have got to be carefully scrutinized. Or, you end up losing a lot of money, and never recouping or recovering your costs. So, the only way to make a valid decision is to elect a body of individuals like the FCC who can dictate the law. We, as broadcasters, cannot dictate the law. We cannot as a group get together and say what we're going to do is we we're all going to band together and vote on Kahn because Motorola could file an antitrust and infringement suits against us. But, the Commission cannot be sued like that. No matter what they say, they cannot be sued for antitrust in making a standards decision. So, it is time for the Commission to pump a little iron. This is where the Commission needs to be. If they're not going to be here for standardization, for something that affects the entire country, and potentially the entire broadcast entity in the world, then why are they there in the first place? This is their job. As far as doing program logs this week, whether we have to do a proof next week, okay, these are things that can now be relaxed if they feel that that's necessary. Imagine the chaos if they were to all of a sudden go out and say, "Okay, what I think what we're going to do here is we're going to change the color signal equation today. And, we're going to make it an amplitude-modulated subcarrier. And, everybody right now start to rebuild!" I mean the place would be chaos. You know, or you're not allowed to transmit with this method any more. That's why we have elected and paid commissioners and staff at the FCC. And, this is a responsibility that they're slacking off and ignoring. And, they're trying to head it under unregulation, as you said the famous Fowler quote: deregulation as it really should be. They're taking it way too far. As far as I am concerned they can pick a standard for stereo and then they can relax all rules and can say, "Well, I don't care if there are any kind of separation figures, or whatever." They have got to pick an equation for transmission. And, if they don't pick an equation for transmission we're going to end up with a disaster. We're already into what I call the 10-year cycle. The 10-year cycle started three years ago. We've got seven years left. Three years ago AM radio was destined in 10 years to be paging taxicabs and not an entertainment medium. Now, whether it stays in taxicabs or being a cellular radio type entity or some sort of an information service, that's another thing. But, it's not going to be an entertainment medium in seven years. And, if we do not do something now to reverse that trend, we are going to lose a historical and valuable chunk of spectrum that used to be entertainment, which will now be, you know, like I said, taxicab. And, that's where it is.

Texar Files Its Petition

On September 26, 1986, Van Allen and Texar president Glen Clark personally delivered the petition to the FCC. NTIA was readying an AM stereo report of its own. The FCC's James McKinney admitted that Texar's petition would have been denied immediately without NTIA's intervention. As a result, the FCC placed Texar's petition on hold until release of NTIA's findings (FCC asked to choose, 1986).

Texar's petition began with some of the history behind AM stereo since the 1982 marketplace decision. Texar then assessed the state of AM stereo after almost five years under the marketplace philosophy. Basically, Texar attempted to establish a rationale for formulating and filing the petition. The most passionate appeals for government intervention appeared in Texar's conclusion. In the first paragraph of the conclusion of the 75-page document, Texar pointed out a possible loophole in the FCC's 1982 *Report and Order*:

Immediate intervention by the Commission to establish a single AM stereo technical standard is warranted and justified, and will best serve the public interest. The Commission itself acknowledged in its *Report and Order* that it envisioned some chance that the marketplace decision would fail to work to completion, calling it the "worst case scenario." Four and one-half years after the *Report and Order* was released, the worst case scenario has materialized and the AM stereo marketplace is hopelessly deadlocked. The Commission also admitted that the actions (or lack thereof) chosen in the *Report and Order* were not suited to resolving its worst case scenario, should it arise, but were tailored for "the more likely outcomes" which it expected. (Baraff & Peltzman, 1986, p. 71)

Texar quoted from paragraph 55 of the FCC's 1982 *Report and Order* and concluded:

The public and AM broadcasters can no longer be whipsawed by the ongoing, parochial actions of the remaining system proponents. The lessons learned from four and one-half years of uncertainty in no way indicate that anything constructive will be gained by extending the period. On the other hand, the establishment of an AM stereo standard will provide an environment conducive to investment and will result in the wide availability of an improved service to the listening public. It will also put an end to the very real danger of losing the existing valuable service which AM provides. The present conditions and future dangers are not imaginary. *AM radio is in serious trouble*. If AM radio is to be saved, the Commission must intercede now. (p. 75)

Reaction to Texar's petition was mixed. Motorola officials were happy with the idea. Should the FCC decide to set a standard, Motorola would not support the move without details of how the proceeding would be conducted. Motorola officials feared that the FCC would take action anyway. Leonard Kahn was not pleased with Texar, calling the filing "very irresponsible" (FCC asked to choose, 1986, p. 35). Kahn added: "The only thing this will do is give Texar a little publicity. It won't do anything else" (p. 35). NTIA's Al Sikes also considered petitioning the FCC to set an AM stereo standard but preferred conducting a study. He said that a study might be more worthwhile to AM stereo's cause by speeding up the marketplace's progress. Sikes (1986) explained NTIA's plans:

NTIA is going to take the responsibility to revisit the AM stereo question. Specifically, what we intend to do is to try to begin to answer questions that are being asked daily, and that you pick up in trade publications and read about so frequently. There are claims; there are charges; there are counterclaims; there are countercharges. How many receivers are out there? Which systems are those receivers capable of receiving? Is there a de facto standard or not? What we intend to do and intend to release before year's end is a study on the state of the AM stereo market, and we intend to answer questions like those just asked. We intend to look at this in the international sense—because we no longer live in a simply domestic market. We live in an international marketplace. (p. 24)

Sikes was certain that AM would work if NTIA could show that broadcasters were positive about AM stereo. He emphasized NTIA's commitment to do all that it could for AM stereo. Sikes gave no indication of whether NTIA would support one of the AM stereo systems but said that FCC intervention would probably be out of the question. Primarily, the NTIA's purpose was to answer questions for the benefit of the broadcast industry.

In a strange twist of events, GM agreed to give the state of New York's Attorney General's Office $10,000 to cover costs incurred during an investigation of GM. Apparently, the attorney general believed that GM had not adequately informed customers that its C-QUAM-equipped Delco receivers would not pick up all AM stereo transmissions. A GM spokesperson said that the company offered to pay the money voluntarily, but the exchange should not be construed as a confession of guilt or innocence. GM also promised to give the following warning in all future Delco AM stereo receiver advertising: "Receives C-QUAM AM stereo broadcasts. Most AM stereo stations across the country broadcast in C-QUAM but some do not. Check with your local stations for compatibility in your area" (Hughes, 1986f, p. 1).

Group W/Westinghouse Broadcasting announced in October 1986 that all seven of its AM stations would install C-QUAM AM stereo by December 31, 1986. Even more importantly to Motorola, all the stations were in major markets: New York, Philadelphia, Pittsburgh, Boston, Denver, Los Angeles, and Phoenix. Interestingly, three of the stations featured all-news, two combined news and talk, and the others were unknown. The group's engineering manager, Glen Walden, said that it would be intriguing to discover how news and talk would go over in stereo.

On October 3, 1986, the CAB adopted Motorola's C-QUAM as the national AM stereo standard for Canada. CAB's move had no official status, because the DOC was the only body with the authority to make such a standard official. DOC hoped to make a decision by April 1987, more than a year after it had originally scheduled to set the standard. CAB's influence, however, could affect DOC's decision. CAB officials explained that the decision was based on C-QUAM's large shares in the marketplace, not on technical aspects (CAB advises government pick C-QUAM, 1986). CAB's stance figured to have minimal, if any, effect on any future decisions by the FCC.

As November approached, Texar and the broadcast industry were still awaiting the FCC's response to the AM stereo petition. Texar president Glen Clark said that the real responsibility of AM stereo rested with broadcasters. He explained that the more response given to the FCC, the more it became likely that the FCC would act. Bill Hassinger, an assistant to the FCC's James McKinney, said that the FCC was obligated to respond to Texar's petition. He said that one of three things would probably happen. The Commission could refuse the petition, ask for comments within a designated time frame, or implement rule-making procedures. Texar's Clark indicated that he had communicated about the AM stereo situation with Leonard Kahn, who intended to continue his support of the AM stereo marketplace. Motorola, on the other hand, was pleased with the intervention of Texar and NTIA. Motorola officials were convinced that C-QUAM would emerge as the national AM stereo standard one way or another. Motorola said Texar's petition could provide an impetus to assess the current state of AM stereo (Hughes, 1986g).

In November 1986 it was rumored that CBS would convert all seven of its stations to C-QUAM. Initially, CBS implemented C-QUAM broadcasting at KNX in Los Angeles but denied that all the network's stations would install any AM stereo transmitter. CBS officials did concede favoring C-QUAM but said that no decisions had been made. If CBS were to choose Motorola, its bid to become the de facto standard would be greatly enhanced. Three of the network's stations were in the major markets of Philadelphia, New York, and St. Louis. Motorola said that two New York stations were converting to C-QUAM. By mid-December 1986, CBS finally admitted that it would install stereo in all its stations but maintained that it had not settled on a specific system. Rumors held steady, however, that CBS would select Motorola's system.

Press Broadcasting's Multimode Receiver Petition

Press Broadcasting, parent company of C-QUAM station WJLK in Asbury Park, New Jersey, filed its own petition with the FCC in November 1986. Press Broadcasting asked the FCC to mandate that all AM stereo receivers be multidecoder units. Robert McAllan, Press Broadcasting VP, figured that setting a receiver standard would be an easier route to getting AM stereo off the ground than waiting for a transmission standard. Press acknowledged many of the same points made previously in Texar's petition and emphasized the detrimental effects of the continuing battle between Kahn and Motorola. The FCC was powerless in setting a standard for receivers, because such a ruling would need congressional support. The FCC's responsibility lay primarily in regulating receiver interference standards. A parallel was drawn between AM receivers and all-channel TV in the 1960s. Congress, not the FCC, had to intervene in the requirement of including both UHF and VHF channels on TV sets. Bruce Franca, an FCC engineer, admitted that the Commission could possibly take some action with receiver manufacturers but would open itself to a challenge of authority. Motorola spokesperson Frank Hilbert said that the petition was a positive move for AM stereo, but he doubted that anything would come of it all since only 2 percent of existing AM receivers were multicoders. Leonard Kahn had not commented on the Press Broadcasting petition, but he was expected to support the idea (Hughes, 1986h).

In terms of economics, Press Broadcasting failed to consider the costs of requiring AM stereo receiver manufacturers to install multimode chips. The actual cost of a multidecoder chip might be minimal, but licensing of chips from two transmitter companies would result in doubling the royalties paid— one payment to Motorola and another to Kahn. Extra royalty payments would increase the cost of the product for consumers. In the end, many AM stereo receiver manufacturers would probably choose to step out of the market (Single standard needed, 1986).

In a late December 1986 announcement, Japanese broadcasters and manufacturers said that they were already two months into a scheduled two-year testing procedure to determine the best AM stereo system to adopt for a national standard. Japanese researchers began testing all five of the original AM stereo systems in October 1986. Plans called for Japan's BTA to recommend the best system to the Japanese Post and Telecommunications Ministry, a group similar to the United States' FCC. BTA comprised 15 receiver manufacturers and 17 AM stations (Japan testing five, 1987).

NTIA's Marketplace Report

NTIA said that it would not finish its AM stereo status report until at least January or February 1987. Originally, the report was planned for a late 1986 release. NTIA hoped to determine if a de facto AM stereo standard existed and if the FCC should intervene in the process (Hughes, 1987). The FCC was not expected to react publicly to Texar's petition until after NTIA's report could be examined. AM stereo was at another crossroads and was at the mercy of others. A lot would depend on NTIA's findings and the FCC's response. Would the Commission intervene in the marketplace, or would it maintain its hands-off policy? The only chance for AM stereo rested in the hope that one system would win out as quickly as possible over the other. As 1987 began, broadcasters anxiously awaited the results of NTIA's study. Should the NTIA determine that a de facto standard existed, the marketplace might finally support one solitary system.

NTIA finally released its report in early 1987, but it resolved neither issue. NTIA concluded that the marketplace was stalemated and proposed mandatory multidecoders for all receivers. NTIA also urged AM stations to install stereo in order to accomplish mass promotion (Zavistovich, 1987a). It was also decided that a second study should be done. In its second report, NTIA drew three important conclusions—all of which contradicted its first study. NTIA declared Motorola's system a de facto standard, found multisystem receivers economically unfeasible, and suggested FCC intervention to protect Motorola's stereo pilot tones. Pilot tones are signals that light the stereo indicators of receivers. The pilot tone was controversial because stations could falsely light indicators in incompatible receivers. The listener then unwittingly believed an AM stereo broadcast was being received. With FCC protection, such abuse could be eliminated. Motorola's pilot tone was protected over Kahn's because of Motorola's considerably greater penetration in the marketplace. Kahn called the report a "blow" to his system's chances. NTIA found a definite market preference for C-QUAM AM stereo and discovered that a single system standard was greatly preferred to a multisystem environment. Interestingly and contrary to earlier industry beliefs, NTIA concluded that multisystem receivers cost no more to produce than single system units. NTIA also urged AM stations to install stereo systems as soon as practicable (NTIA wants C-QUAM protected, 1987).

Despite NTIA's suggestions, AM operators had little reaction. Total Motorola systems in use reached 500 by September 1987, and Kahn systems languished well below 100. Interestingly, total numbers of systems in use differed little from those of FM stereo two decades earlier, and some in the industry began to draw comparisons. Stereo FM was launched with the benefit of having a single system standard, yet FM broadcasters did not readily accept the technology. For a decade or more, FM stereo was not a factor until FM stereo receivers began to saturate the market. Certainly, it would take a long time for AM stereo to catch on, but it would not happen at all unless AM stations would install stereo (Likely candidates, 1987).

FCC Denies All AM Stereo Petitions

The FCC delayed answering the Texar and Press petitions until January 14, 1988. It issued a blanket denial for all petitions to protect Motorola's C-QUAM pilot tone, to require all receivers to be multidecoders, to select a standard, and to proclaim Motorola the de facto AM stereo standard. The FCC (1988a) succinctly stated: "Petitioner's arguments and presentations do not convince us that Commission intervention at this late date would prove beneficial to the public. Rather, while only ten percent of all AM stations have installed stereo capability, the market is working towards the selection of an industry standard. . . . the field of competitors has narrowed and the majority of stations now choosing to broadcast in stereo seem to be selecting one particular technical system" (p. 404).

In regard to pilot tone protection, the FCC (1988a) simply did not want to open another rule-making proceeding. The Commission said that "uncertainty and delay of further proceedings could thus discourage broadcasters, manufacturers, and listeners from investing in AM stereo in the interim, thereby hindering its development" (p. 405). Further, the FCC found "no compelling need" to require all receivers to be multisystem decoders, which is "consistent with our general policy of limiting our regulatory role regarding broadcast service enhancements" (p. 405).

The FCC officially refused to declare Motorola the de facto AM stereo standard but unofficially declared the system a de facto standard (FCC holds the line, 1988). (In 1982 the number of FCC Commissioners was reduced from seven to five members. At the time of the AM stereo petition review, two seats were empty.) The FCC (1988a) defended the marketplace, particularly in view of the vast numbers of supporters of one system and a clear industry preference "towards establishing a de facto standard" (p. 404). Responding to claims that the marketplace negatively affected AM stereo, the Commission stated: "[W]e conclude that the rate at which broadcasters have chosen to install AM stereo capability cannot be attributed to our decision" (p. 404).

After years of hope that the FCC would pick a standard, the rejection of all petitions appeared to place the AM stereo decision forever into the hands of broadcasters. After the 1982 marketplace decision, many in the industry continued to believe, or at least hope, that the FCC would eventually pick a standard.

On April 29, 1988, Kahn sued GM for patent infringement on compatible AM stereophonic receivers. Kahn sought royalties and requested a jury trial (Kahn files lawsuit, 1988). On May 27, 1988, Motorola countered with a declaratory judgment filing against Kahn asking "the court to stop . . . Kahn from making claim on the patent against Motorola, GM or any other Motorola customers" (Motorola files for AM stereo, 1988, p. 14).

Motorola's numbers grew as manufacturers demonstrated slow, but increased, confidence in C-QUAM. Most new Ford and GM automobiles featured AM stereo receivers as standard equipment, and Chrysler planned to equip all its 1989 models with C-QUAM. Indeed, "28 percent of all foreign and domestic new cars" came with C-QUAM AM stereo; 30 manufacturers produced about 50 different C-QUAM receiver models; and at least 16 million C-QUAM AM stereo receivers were sold (Motorola Inc., 1986d).

Still, 1989 came and went with more AM stereo questions than answers. With a lock on the receiver industry, it appeared that AM operators adding stereo would have little option other than Motorola (Huff, 1992b). In effect, Motorola was the de facto standard. Was it too late to save AM stereo?

AM STEREO REVISITED: THE 1993 SYSTEM STANDARD DECISION

From 1989 until 1992 nothing of import occurred as the AM stereo marketplace remained stalemated and stagnant. In February 1992 Japan launched AM stereo, and it was received enthusiastically. Motorola was chosen as the standard system, and 13 stations broadcast stereo right away. Receiver manufacturers responded by producing numerous AM stereo sets. Among the makers were: Aiwa, Sony, Hitachi, Sanyo, Sharp, Pioneer, Kenwood, Sansui, Onkyo, Nippon, Columbia, and Clarion (Carter, 1993). Unfortunately, the Japanese receivers were not seriously marketed in the United States. European interest in AM stereo seemed to wane as it had in the United States, with most of the attention turning to DAB. Funds that would have been spent on AM stereo research were considered better spent on DAB.

Congress, convinced that an AM stereo system standard was needed, intervened with Section 214 of the *Telecommunications Authorization Act of 1992*. The act mandated that the Commission "adopt a single AM broadcasting stereo transmission standard" and "remove any remaining uncertainty among AM broadcasters as to which stereo system to use and thereby encourage the improvement and expansion of AM broadcast service."

As might be guessed, Kahn was not pleased with the decision and would not go away without one last fight. Kahn asked for an extension on the deadline for comments to the FCC's proposed *Report and Order* but was denied, yet there appeared to be no one listening anymore despite the fact that Kahn again threatened legal action. What chance was there, given that there was a congressional mandate and that there were fewer than 20 stations employing the Kahn system?

To satisfy its obligation to Congress, the FCC adopted a *Report and Order* on October 25, 1993, making Motorola's C-QUAM system the official standard for AM stereophonic broadcasting in the United States. The FCC (1993) ordered its decision into effect as of March 21, 1994. The FCC (1993), left with little alternative but to select Motorola, explained:

[The] system appears to have become the de facto choice of the market. We observed that this system has become by far the predominant choice of AM stations choosing to convert to stereo, there are large numbers of existing receivers capable of decoding only C-QUAM and receivers for other systems are generally unavailable. We also noted that the Motorola system has been adopted as the national standard in six other countries, while none had adopted the Kahn system, the only other system for which transmitting equipment is still available.

The Commission believed that to select a system other than Motorola, such as Kahn or some new candidate, "would set back the clock on the implementation of AM stereo service" (FCC, 1993). Nonetheless, the FCC allowed proponents of other systems to submit their alternatives. Among other reasons for choosing Motorola, the FCC cited technical acceptability in providing stereo, quality at an affordable price, and tremendous market penetration. Though a majority of responding parties supported the Motorola selection, there were many in opposition. Interestingly, engineers have historically favored the Kahn system. While the Commission did not dismiss their claims of Motorola's "technical deficiencies," it did "reject the premise . . . the decision . . . should be based solely on technical performance, particularly at this relatively late stage of the implementation of AM stereo." The FCC (1993) explained:

We believe it is entirely appropriate that we take into account that strong preference demonstrated in the market place for the Motorola system. We note that the market place takes into account not only technical parameters, but also other factors such as subjective performance, costs of broadcaster's initial conversion to stereo, reliability, service, ease of receiver design and performance, etc. We also believe it is incumbent upon us to consider the sunk costs in existing stereo transmission equipment, compatibility with millions of existing envelope detector receivers, and availability of compatible stereo receivers, as well as the potential for obsoleting the public's investment in existing stereo receivers. In this regard, we find that selection of a system other than Motorola's would result in substantial costs to broadcasters and consumers, and thus would be detrimental to the expansion of AM stereo service.

Further, the Commission did not see any valid reason to consider seriously any systems other than Motorola and Kahn. The FCC (1993) wrote: "To do so would introduce significant delay and confusion without any assurance that a significantly better alternative could or would be forthcoming." The FCC opined that AM stereo had been in the hands of the marketplace long enough for any and all interested parties to have made their comparisons between the existing systems:

We believe that the past nearly twelve years of unrestricted competition between the systems has given the public and the broadcast and receiver industries the opportunity to weigh the known technical performance considerations against other factors and to make appropriate personal and business decisions. We find that there has indeed been a convergence in the marketplace during these years toward the Motorola C-QUAM system. Based on the overwhelming marketplace preference for the Motorola C-QUAM system, and the long history of tests of this system, we believe the Motorola system will provide excellent AM stereo service. Accordingly, we conclude that the public interest is best served by adopting the Motorola C-QUAM system as the AM stereo standard.

In regard to the congressional mandate to select a single system standard, the Commission found it necessary to order "stations that employ alternative systems for stereo operation to discontinue such operation as of one year from the effective date of these rules." However, the FCC allowed "stations currently employing the Harris system [which] were sufficiently compatible with C-QUAM to continue using the Harris system indefinitely." Further, the Commission stipulated that Motorola must "license its patents to other parties under fair and reasonable terms."

Finally! There was a single system AM stereo standard. The FCC's marketplace decision was always difficult for the broadcasting industry to swallow, primarily because it was an unwelcome break with tradition. But, even when it was over, the marketplace remained difficult to understand and accept. Perhaps the best that could be hoped was that something could be learned from the experience.

In the final analysis, the success or failure of AM stereo was placed firmly in the grasp of AM owners and operators in 1993. Seven years after the standard was finally set, it has become evident that AM stereo has not worked out as many had hoped. There are approximately 300 AM stations employing stereo, and many engineers continue to believe that the technology can help AM. The biggest hurdle remains the lack of good stereo receivers on the market, but AM stereo is available on the Internet. Additionally, there are AM stereo aficionados who steadfastly believe in the technology and who continue its promotion by using the Internet. At least three sites list receivers that are currently available and out of production, stations broadcasting in AM stereo, and more current AM stereo information than is available elsewhere. See, for example:

http://www.stereoam.com

http://ourworld.compuserve.com/homepages/kevtronics/radio.htm

Chapter 4

❖ ❖

Digital Audio Broadcasting: A New Kind of Radio

On August 1, 1990, the FCC (1990b) initiated an NOI into DAB development and implementation. The United States became interested in DAB in the late 1980s after learning that the EBU was developing a system called Eureka-147. The purpose of Eureka-147 was to start a new European terrestrial radio system. But American broadcasters did not want to give up their spectrum for a new band. Initially, NAB favored a new U.S. radio system—one that would give AM and FM equal footing—and supported L-band and Eureka-147. Tremendous outcries from broadcasters convinced NAB to change its stance and to support IBOC DAB. Shapiro (1993) observed: "Other than high definition television, nothing can draw quite as much emotion from electronics manufacturers and broadcasters as digital audio radio. If you need proof, look no further than the various trade magazines—including this one [*Radio World*]" (p. 42).

By 1991 Americans responded with USADR, a partnership established by CBS, Westinghouse Electric Corporation, and Gannett Co., Inc. to develop IBOC DAB for AM and FM. USADR declared its commitment to a universal DAB technology and was supported by Xetron Corporation, Shively Labs, BittWare Research Systems, and Germany's Fraunhofer IIS. USADR (1998d) cited radio's "critical role in everyday life" and said that "the vast majority of Americans across the country will be impacted in one form or another by digital radio broadcasting."

DAB offers improved sound and greater fidelity than analog AM and FM broadcasting. Analog is a physical quantity (or data) characterized by being continuously variable rather than discrete. Acoustical waveforms are analog. With digital, stereo separation is improved considerably over analog, and interference and signal fading are reduced to minimal levels (Gatski, 1990b). DAB is considered CD quality, the new buzzword replacing FM-quality as the measure for audio excellence.

Other than superior audio, DAB offers other advantages over analog and presents U.S. broadcasters the greatest opportunity since the invention of radio itself by offering the "next plateau of audio performance" (Pai, 1997, p. 14). DAB produces "increased bandwidth, higher dynamic range, and less susceptibility to noise and interference than analog signals" (Hartup, Alley, & Goldston, 1998, p. 64). In addition, digital provides data transmission delivery, giving consumers a variety of information via a mobile receiver, such as station ID, program-related information, traffic and weather information, and emergency alerts.

USADR (1999a) preferred IBOC over other terrestrial methods of delivery because it was "designed to permit stations to use their current radio spectrum to transmit existing AM and FM analog simultaneously with new high-quality digital signals which eliminate multipath, noise, and reduce interference." Therefore, USADR "provided a unique opportunity for broadcasters and listeners to convert from analog to digital radio without service disruption while maintaining current dial positions of existing stations." Most interference experienced during mobile reception is caused by multipath reception, a radio signal's susceptibility to interference from other signals bouncing around the airwaves. A directly received signal and parts of signals reflected from buildings and hills overlap each other to cause frequency-dependent interference. Direct and reflected signal components arrive at the receiver at different times. Unlike analog broadcasting, when multipath occurs with digital signals, the receiver responds to the better of the two signals, reflected or direct. The bits for digital transmission are sent as groups, or symbols. With multipath reception, interference between symbols occurs when symbols adjacent in time overlap each other due to different signal content arriving at different times. To alleviate the problem, the symbol duration is lengthened by a protective interval at the transmitter, supplying the receiver with a clean symbol since it delays using the signal until the interference caused by overlaps has concluded (WorldDAB Forum, n.d. b).

Other proposals and system proponents soon emerged, hoping to implement IBOC, IBAC, and SDARS. IBAC differs little from IBOC but would broadcast DAB in blank spaces between existing frequencies (Mitchell, 1993). Satellite DAB was an entirely different matter, bypassing terrestrial broadcasters entirely by sending direct signals to consumers and possibly making traditional radio obsolete.

Radio has responded to many challenges and has reinvented itself many times. DAB is just another step in radio's evolution. Radio faced a dilemma in the 1950s when hi-fi stereo recordings prompted consumer interest in stereo broadcasting. Stereo records were available, but there was nowhere to broadcast them until FM stereo was approved in 1961. Likewise, digital CDs emerged in 1981, but there was no way to hear their full impact on analog broadcasts. Both radio and TV were forced to improve because of competition from technology afforded to consumers by other means. Many stations were equipped with digital production equipment, but that did little good when the signal needed conversion from analog for transmission. Digital was brought to the forefront of consumers' minds because of the home computer market. Forrest (1994) observed: "[Since then,] there has been a relentless move toward digital audio, radio, and television. CDs were the most obvious manifestation of digital technology as far as the public was concerned, bringing a real benefit in sound quality and durability of the recording" (p. 5).

Digital Perceptions

The word "digital" is used and even abused, and it "clearly has been positioned in our modern technological language to define the zenith of audio" (Hahn, 1994, p. 27). Therefore, "people expect to pay a premium for audio software or hardware if it is 'digital,' " even if it is not "any better than other versions previously available" (p. 27). True digital offers benefits over analog delivery. In reality, "'digital' is no more than a promotional buzzword, regularly misapplied and misunderstood in a marketplace where an accelerated rate of change works against mass comprehension" (Nelson, 1993, p. 94). Many consumers believe that "anything with digital properties automatically offers some kind of superior quality, particularly when applied to electronic devices in which older analog components are being overrun by smarter, faster, cheaper digital parts" (p. 94).

Is digital really an improvement that consumers want, or is it the desire to have something different? Hirsch (1992) observed: "A never-ending drive for improvement of our lives seems to be an intrinsic part of human nature" (p. 26). Some consumers are "future junkies" who are always "clamoring for next year's products," yet living in "fear that our cherished gear will grow obsolete" (Pohlmann, 1992a, p. 62). With digital, that perception may be reality. Rare is the electronics ad that does not proclaim products that are digitally encoded, digitally enhanced, digitally processed, digitally synthesized, digitally altered, or digitally remastered. Hahn (1994) confessed: "I'm 'in the business' and I don't know what some of these things really are or mean or how they might improve or affect performance. I do know they affect price" (p. 27). How, then, would the average consumer understand the digital difference? Digital has varying degrees of quality, but like analog "there are 'high-end' performers, 'low-end,' and many in between" (p. 54). Haber (1996) questioned the necessity of digital transition: "An industry observer who wished to remain anonymous questioned whether people who listen to radio could tell the difference 'between a radio station that's doing digital broadcasting and a radio station that's broadcasting in analog.' The source said, 'we keep forgetting that John Q. Public is a non-educated, non-informed listener. Most people couldn't tell you that the radio station they're listening to plays compact discs or (is) running analog tape'" (p. 63). Whether digital is necessary seems to be beside the point. Diamond and Sneegas (1992) investigated the impact of labeling and image on the selection of audio by conducting their version of the cola taste comparison test—only with a twist. Using the same product packaged under three different labels, they consistently found that audio labeled AM, although exactly the same as the other products, evoked the most negative listener reaction. To eliminate the AM and FM analog system might have a more positive impact on consumers than IBOC DAB. Canada wanted a fresh start on L-band and was intent on replacing traditional AM and FM radio with a new terrestrial DAB system. The strategy might have merit. Basically, would American consumers hear a digital difference if broadcast on the traditional AM and FM frequencies? As Diamond and Sneegas (1992) observed: "The central issue is not whether we can or cannot, or whether we should or should not, but whether the consumer wants, and will purchase, the new technology. The cost to broadcasters to compete in the arena of emerging technologies is high. The cost not to compete is even higher" (p. 20).

Like DTV and AM stereo, DAB has critics who question its necessity. The problem with radio, some say, is not audio quality but the state of programming. Dorsey (1992) believed: "Unless stations start distinguishing themselves from the rest of the market by playing different music, I don't see any great hope for DAB. Ten thousand channels with identical 200-song playlists, all distinguished only by their varying processing schemes—now that just doesn't sound like my idea of a vast improvement" (p. 5). Eddie Fritts, NAB head, agreed: "People don't listen for digital sound. They listen for programming. They listen for their favorite music, for their favorite announcers, for their favorite station that is a mix of all of the above. So they listen to programming. They don't necessarily listen for quality, per se. If you can combine the two, you have the best of both worlds" (NAB poised, 1996, p. 55).

The DAB Challenge. DAB presents a tremendous challenge in the selection of transmission standards by the FCC. Unlike previous analog enhancements, such as stereo or color, DAB may radically alter radio. Still, it "must meet the needs of consumers, broadcasters and government regulatory agencies" (Hartup et al., 1998, p. 64). DAB can be accomplished by one of three methods: (1) IBOC or IBAC via existing AM and/or FM frequencies; (2) terrestrially over another broadcast band (S-band in the United States and L-band in other parts of the world); and/or, (3) SDARS. U.S. broadcasters want IBOC DAB, the "Holy Grail solution because it preserves station independence as well as existing regulatory statures, allows easy transition from analog to digital, and requires no new bandwidth" (Pohlmann, 1997c, p. 26). Further, "signals are simulcast over existing equipment" with low "start-up costs" (p. 26). Europe, Canada, and much of the world opted for terrestrial delivery using L-band and Eureka-147. The United States reserved L-band for aeronautical use and assigned S-band for SDARS. Either terrestrial method differs little from traditional radio delivery. Stations may be moved to another band such as L-band, as has been the case in Canada and Europe, but even then the most noticeable change for listeners and operators is the improvement in sound quality. Terrestrial DAB is transmitted from towers like traditional radio, but the main difference is in the economical use of spectrum. A powerful analog signal can use 100,000 watts, but digital delivery can reduce that to 1,000 watts (Pohlmann, 1992a, p. 64).

Originally, DAB put the United States squarely in a position to regain its world leadership role in setting technological transmission systems standards. The United States lost its standing in an era of deregulation, as exemplified by AM stereo, in which the world waited for the FCC's decision that never came. Countries previously dependent on United States decision making reluctantly established their own AM stereo standards. Canadian broadcasting officials have said that the United States's unreliability and unpredictability in dealing with new technologies have befuddled them. Ron Strother, SCI president, agreed: "The United States is no longer leading in research and development. While we have done marvelous things through our universities and the Defense Department, we seem to have a very hard time getting technology to the marketplace" (HDTV, DAB, 1990, p. 67). A 1992 *Radio World* editorial opined that visions of world leadership should not deter broadcasters from proceeding "as planned" and should "not succumb to pressure from our neighbors to make such an important decision in haste" (DAB: Stay, 1992, p. 5).

Is there enough consumer interest in DAB to justify the changes? Will the difference in sound quality be enough to sell DAB? That remains to be seen. Some experts are "unconvinced that the consumer will go out and buy special equipment to receive digital quality when an alternative is available to them in FM stereo" because it is not the same as color TV and black and white (Looking into, 1992, p. 50). Eddie Fritts, NAB head, believed that DAB would be consumer-driven, but it is possible that United States consumers could reject DAB. He stated: "I think that's the threshold question. The United States and North America clearly is the largest marketplace in the world. It has been and will be. The automobile manufacturers are the largest producers of radios in the world, in spite of other interests" (NAB poised, 1996, p. 55).

SDARS implementation means that local radio could be forced to compete with national and regional stations. DSR has been available for years but should not be confused with SDARS. DSR is not broadcast and is not mobile or portable. DSR, developed in Germany, is a subscription service received like satellite television via a dish aimed at the orbiting satellite (Willis, 1992). Another alternative is DCR distributed through cable TV systems. DCR is not limited to subscription music channels, as some local radio stations are available. DAB could utilize DSR services, but the signal would be received by a radio station and then broadcast to consumers. Radio's advantage over TV has been its mobility, and cable cannot compete with that. Automobile audio manufacturers took heed. Ford audio sales account for about $1 billion per year. While most homes are dominated by video, it is "possible to surmise that cars will become the high-fidelity listening places of the future" (Pohlmann, 1992b, p. 33). An early 1993 $20 million deal struck by DCR with Time Warner Cable and Sony Software Corporation/Warner Music Group ensured that cable radio would be a force in home entertainment. DCR gained funding to assist in foreign expansion and planned to double its 28 channels to 56 channels by May 1993. As of February 1993 DCR was available to approximately 5 million cable homes and expected to gain another 3 million homes because of the deal. However, only an estimated 50,000 homes actually subscribed for DCR at $10 per month (Brown, 1993).

DAB Systems

Three companies proposing DAB delivery systems petitioned the FCC to open its 1990 NOI. CD Radio and SCI suggested a combination of terrestrial and satellite delivery. However, RadioSat sought exclusive satellite delivery. Over time, other proposed systems joined the DAB battle. One was the European Eureka-147 terrestrial system proposed by a consortium of organizations from France, Germany, Great Britain, and the Netherlands. By 1992 at least nine DAB systems were proposed: USADR (Project Acorn), AT&T/Bell Labs, Digital Planet, Kintel Technologies, Mercury Digital Communications, GI, SCI/Lincom, Thomson Consumer Electronics (United States representative for Eureka-147), and American Digital Radio.

CD Radio asked the FCC to find and allocate new frequencies for both satellite and terrestrial distribution. Satellite transponder feeds would be sold on a noncommon carrier basis to AMs and FMs. Stations would receive or send satellite programming. In some cases, stations could broadcast locally to traditional radio audiences and provide subscription programming nationally or regionally. Radio "superstations," similar to television's WTBS in Atlanta and WGN in Chicago, would be created. Local viewers receive over-the-air signals, but national viewers get satellite feeds relayed to homes through cable.

CD Radio's original plan called for dividing the continental United States into three regions, distributing 66 national channels and 34 local stations to each region. GM supported CD Radio's position, but radio broadcasters were staunchly against any threat to localism. CD Radio eventually decided to act as carrier only of the winning system. The company would implement 10 satellite DAB channels and make them available via subscription or through a program provider, such as a radio station. Martin Rothblatt, CD Radio president, believed that USADR would win but said his company was "prepared to carry any system for which DAB radios are made in the United States, as long as they meet the basic specifications of our system" (Gross, 1992, p. 7). Rothblatt's position was an attempt to prevent Amstereoization by helping the FCC move ahead with DAB. SCI also requested additional spectrum but suggested that AM and FM broadcasters be given priority. Instead of relaying satellite signals, the feed would go directly to the consumer (Strother, 1990).

RadioSat planned to build an earth station and transmit DAB exclusively through a satellite licensed to AMSC. RadioSat would sell noncommon carrier satellite capacity to radio stations and common carrier signals to anyone willing to pay for them.

USADR was considered to have the best chance for success among IBOC proponents, and its Project Acorn system generated tremendous industry interest because it required no additional spectrum (Crowley, 1991). Project Acorn was predicted to produce CD-quality audio within both the AM and FM bands.

Broadcasters Respond to DAB

Radio has primarily been a local endeavor for the vast majority. Proposals for DAB satellites, superstations, and other nontraditional delivery systems have clearly disturbed broadcasters. Nearly two months before the FCC's notice, uneasy radio engineers pressured NAB to lobby for terrestrial delivery. NAB formed an eight-member technical advisory group to "raise awareness of the broadcasting industry on the challenges and opportunities of DAB" and to "promote and coordinate radio broadcast industry consensus" (DAB: Radio's, 1990, p. 79). The task force was also asked to examine political, legal, and technical aspects of DAB and to "fully investigate the challenges and opportunities a potential terrestrial service would have on the nation's 12,000 radio stations and their listening audience" (Taylor, 1990b, p. 10). NAB opposed satellite delivery, which RadioSat called "a pure anticompetitive response" (Carter, 1990b, p. 8).

The FCC's inquiry asked broadcasters to comment on DAB. Replies were mixed. Overall, there was excitement about DAB, but there were concerns about the threat from satellite delivery. Capital Cities/ABC responded: "The substantial time and investment stations have made over long years to the needs of their local communities qualifies them to introduce digital audio service to the public" (Broadcasters, 1991, p. 34).

GM favored a combination of direct satellite and IBOC delivery. Although conceding many listeners' desires for local and regional programming, GM believed that many travelers grew weary from constant station-seeking: "Even in many areas with good radio service, long distance drivers must continually change radio stations as they enter and leave the coverage area of particular stations" (p. 34). SDARS reception did not require large parabolic dishes like television. Small, omnidirectional, patchlike antennae the size of a silver dollar mounted atop automobiles or carried on one's person received signals. In early 1994 CD Radio announced that it had developed SDARS that would provide 30 noncommercial channels to automobiles and homes across the

United States. Cost was five dollars a month for the service that would not interfere with normal AM and FM radio (Satellite radio, 1994).

Parties lobbying for localized terrestrial IBOC DAB or another band asked the FCC to devote liberal time to its decision making. NAB, obviously concerned over the FCC's tendency to abandon its regulatory authority, wanted the Commission to make its intentions known. NAB wrote: "Like a giant ocean liner, the DAB ship is underway in the United States. The question is who is steering and where are we going" (DAB strategy, 1991, p. 53).

Although the United States was just beginning its DAB debate, Canada had successfully tested Eureka-147. A CBC official boasted: "We got it first, because we got our act together ahead of the Americans" (Careless, 1990, p. 14). Canada planned to simulcast DAB on AM and FM stations until all of them could be moved to another band. Canadians were uneasy with the United States' slow pace, because they wanted a strong ally at the 1992 WARC. Canadian officials believed that the United States was more interested in HDTV than DAB (p. 14).

NAB's "Preemptive Strike." In early 1991 NAB attempted to avoid duplicating the AM stereo marketplace. An NAB VP explained: "The principal lesson we have learned is that a single broadcast standard must be adopted by the government. But the government should not be the initial decision-maker; industry must make the first decisions, and make a strong representation to the FCC. We need to determine our own futures" (NAB goes, 1991, p. 15). NAB threw its support behind Eureka-147 and L-band—a region of spectrum at 1500 MHz (1.5 GHz) used for military testing of aeronautical devices. NAB sought co-primary status for satellite and terrestrial DAB on L-band, meaning that "both satellite and terrestrial interests would need to be accommodated whatever the amount of spectrum allocated" (Gross, 1991a, p. 9). To better facilitate DAB's transition, NAB wanted preference for AM and FM stations on L-band. *Broadcasting* called NAB's move "a preemptive strike in favor of terrestrial DAB" (NAB's preemptive, 1991, p. 66). NAB's decision followed the leads of CD Radio and SCI as outlined in their petitions to the FCC. Both envisioned DAB's maximum benefits to be realized at national and local levels. NAB recognized DAB's inevitability and, rather than stubbornly risk the welfare of thousands of radio stations, believed it better to compromise.

Broadcasters and DAB system proponents were not pleased with NAB's Eureka alignment. Ron Strother, SCI president, wondered if NAB was "going to perpetuate a move into foreign technology by further allowing other" EBU members "to also profit from this move" (Operators, 1991, p. 44). The United States Air Force and Secretary of Defense Dick Cheney also opposed reassignment of L-band, arguing that it was necessary for development and testing of weapons systems, such as the next generations of Patriot and Tomahawk cruise missiles (Cole, 1991b). L-band was highly coveted because its very high frequencies do a good job of eliminating multipath interference of the signal. Although it is line-of-sight transmission like FM, L-band tends to penetrate obstacles, such as buildings, that cause problems for FM and many other signals (Masters, 1997).

The FCC received a number of letters opposing NAB's position and questioning the abandonment of occupied AM and FM spectrum in favor of a new band that would precipitate the obsolescence of about 500 million radio receivers. NAB flooded its members with faxes and letters defending its position and promised to consider IBOC on an equal footing with Eureka-147. NAB also asked Eureka to develop an IBOC system (Gross, 1991b).

L-band, S-Band, or Both? With WARC on the horizon, the FCC's IWG-2 identified seven possible DAB bands. Reallocation would create problems because each band was already assigned to services such as fixed and land-mobile radio, UHF-TV, NASA, the military, the FAA, microwave communications, Departments of Agriculture, Treasury, and Justice, and instructional TV (DAB looks, 1990).

Despite its own researchers' recommendations and realizing that its decision would spark controversy, the FCC proposed three bands to be presented at WARC. HDTV advocates were especially incensed over the inclusion of 728-788 MHz, or UHF channels 57–66, because it was considered crucial space. The Commission admitted that it was purposely provoking opposition to inspire broadcasters to conduct expensive research (FCC offers, 1990). With 96 stations occupying the channels, the economics of relocating even some to other frequencies could be counterproductive. Costs for transmitters, antennae, and other miscellaneous items could easily surpass tens of millions of dollars (No, 1990).

IWG-2 believed that L-band was best for terrestrial and satellite DAB and urged the FCC to support it at WARC 1992 (Working, 1991). The FCC wanted spectrum at both L-band (1500 MHz, 1.5 GHz) and S-band (2300 MHz, 2.3 GHz) but eventually bowed to pressure from the military and Bush administration (Broadcasters, military, 1991). NTIA refused to allocate L-band for United States domestic use. NAB also relinquished its support of L-band and Eureka, bowing to the United States's preference for S-band (Jessell, 1992a).

At WARC 1992, world DAB allocations were made regionally in three bands. The United States was given unofficial permission to use 50 MHz of S-band. China, Russia, Japan, India, Pakistan, and other Asian countries were issued 2.535 to 2.655 GHz, and 40 MHz (two times the available FM spectrum) of L-band was allocated for the rest of the world (Leinwoll, 1993). NAB believed that pressure from Mexico, Canada, and receiver manufacturers would eventually persuade the United States to switch to L-band. With two different DAB bands, it would be impossible to build compatible broadcast receivers. In early 1992 Canada researchers found that L-band was effective for DAB. NAB believed that L-band was a moot point, because the FCC was more concerned about protecting its spectrum entente with the

Department of Defense than about technical appropriateness (Careless, 1992). FCC chairman Sikes acknowledged that DAB progress would be slowed but noted that HDTV had overcome similar difficulties: "Keep in mind that some years ago you couldn't possibly do HDTV in 6mhz. Today we're not only looking at the possibility, or the probability, of doing HDTV in 6 MHz, but also going from an analog to a digital system. It's my guess there will be some very important technological developments in the next year or so with regard to in-band" (Debriefing, 1992, p. 54).

Due to terrestrial distribution limitations, S-band implementation greatly increased IBOC's odds. S-band operates at a higher frequency than L-band, costs two to three times more, and is more susceptible to interference from physical obstacles, such as buildings and mountains (Sukow, 1991). Despite S-band's drawbacks, SDARS proponents were satisfied.

NAB and many broadcasters believed that DAB's future was IBOC, but which system would emerge as the standard? Since Eureka was designed for L-band, did the S-band decision eliminate it? An NAB executive VP did not think so: "Just because something works out-of-band doesn't mean it won't work in-band" (Bunzel, 1991, p. 52). A Eureka scientist said that redesign of Eureka-147 for IBOC was unlikely because European DAB was a priority (Eureka's Plenge, 1991).

To expedite DAB progress, EIA formed a Digital Audio Radio Subcommittee to define industry goals. A successful catalyst in FM/MTS standards proceedings, EIA recognized the importance of centralizing lab and field tests, funding, industry liaisons, and other objectives. EIA represented manufacturers, and broadcasters demanded more input and representation by NRSC (Gatski, 1992b). NAB's DAB Technical Advisory Group scheduled a January 23–24, 1992, meeting in which proponents would demonstrate their systems. SCI and American Digital Radio balked because they were perturbed about the makeup of the task force, which included among its members supporters of USADR's IBOC system, Gannett's Paul Donahue and CBS Radio's Tony Masiello. The advisory group promised that these individuals would dismiss themselves during competitors' presentations, but American Digital Radio and SCI were not appeased, stating: "Groups formed to objectively evaluate and test DAB technology should not appoint proponents to their membership" (Gatski, 1992a, p. 3).

IBOC DAB

USADR predicted in April 1992 that IBOC would be ready by April 1993. NAB's Michael Rau applauded USADR but did not think that broadcasters shared his optimism: "I think broadcasters have a wait-and-see attitude; there does not appear to be a rush to embrace any DAB technology" (Lambert, 1992b, p. 32). Steve Kuh of SCI agreed: "We're not seeing any support from broadcasters" (pp. 32–33).

Fallout from WARC '92 was very negative, resulting in lack of IBOC development funding. HDTV's hoopla deterred DAB, and the HDTV World Exposition, held concurrently with NAB's 1992 Las Vegas meeting, was evidence (Sukow, 1992a). DAB's American momentum was declining due to broadcasters' frustration over delays. NAB's Eddie Fritts said that broadcasters needed "some evidence of meaningful progress," and he promised to "actively seek" updates from system proponents (Zavistovich, 1992a, p. 3).

Zavistovich (1992b) believed that broadcasters should have required a good new system and should not have demanded IBOC to fit into the old system. Bob Botik (1992), a broadcaster, said that Zavistovich was "missing the point," because "what is under debate here is not what is logical or simple or in the best interest of all, but what is best for America's current owners and operators, screw the rest of the world" (p. 5). Botik added: "We are not talking about what is logical or what is good technology" (p. 5). Zavistovich (1992b) replied: "I have to disagree with you that 'good' technology (to use your term) will win out over technology based on non-technical considerations. If that were the case, we would now have an uncontested AM stereo standard. . . . We live in a society blanketed by layers of politics, and compromise has always been the name of the game, even in technical matters. That is no less true for DAB" (p. 4). NAB's John Abel commented: "The only thing I can say with any certainty about DAB is that the future seems uncertain" (Carter, 1992, p. 1).

Contributing to DAB's uncertainty, CD Radio withdrew its system from the experimental licensing process in August 1992. CD Radio's license was for a complete DAB system, and company chairman Martin Rothblatt did not believe that his company's proposal would be accepted. CD Radio did not give up on SDARS, just the broadcast portion. NAB was happy with the withdrawal. In September 1992 American Digital Radio withdrew its system, citing inadequate developmental funding. American Digital Radio officials appeared more worried about DAB in general than for its system, fearing that no IBOC system in development would beat Eureka-147's L-band system. Nonetheless, the United States maintained its united front against an international movement toward L-band and stuck to its guns (Zavistovich, 1992c).

On August 26, 1992, USADR successfully delivered DAB on AM's expanded band at 1660 kHz in Cincinnati and planned to test FM IBOC DAB over WILL-FM at 90.9, a station licensed by the University of Illinois (DAB in-band wagon, 1992). USADR tested its Project Acorn system in 1993 in Chicago over CBS' WBBM-FM and Gannett's WGCI-AM. At the September 9–12 NAB Radio Show in New Orleans, USADR demonstrated its system using WNOE-AM and NPR affiliate WWNO-FM. USADR wanted Mexico and Canada to delay their L-band plans because forging ahead could prevent worldwide standardization. USADR's strategy was not working. In October 1992 NAB accused Canada of poor-mouthing IBOC to other countries. Michel Tremblay, CAB VP, denied any underhandedness. Although crediting

USADR's efforts, Tremblay believed that it was "very far away from what Eureka has achieved" and was "not convinced that in-band will work" (Gatski, 1992d, p. 8).

At the September 1992 NAB Radio Show in New Orleans, broadcasters continued voicing their displeasure with EIA, even though it was conducting DAB business much as it had MTS. Although happy with that outcome, broadcasters wanted more input into the DAB process. Of 12 votes that would decide the system of choice, broadcasters had but two votes. Receiver manufacturers were given four votes, and satellite interests, the software industry, and the semiconductor industry were allocated one vote each. Broadcasters' unrest focused on the 10 votes of nonbroadcast interests that were EIA members. NAB's Michael Rau was optimistic: "The more we talk with EIA, the better EIA understands NAB's concerns" (Gatski, 1992c, pp. 1, 10).

The FCC began its SDARS spectrum allocation process on October 8 with an NPRM. The Commission set a November 13, 1992, deadline for industry comments, December 1 for replies, and December 15 for responses. The FCC established a December 15 deadline for proposals from companies other than CD Radio. CD Radio hoped to implement a 30-channel direct broadcast radio subscription service and asked for a 50 MHz chunk of S-band spectrum from 2310 to 2360 MHz previously assigned for mobile radio services. S-band was ill suited for terrestrial purposes. As a pay service, CD Radio posed no threat of luring advertisers from commercial stations but could attract some of their audience (Jessell, 1992b). Robert Briskman, CD Radio president, said that marketers of recorded media such as compact discs and cassettes should be more worried about satellite radio subscription services than broadcasters: "When you get in your car to go to work, you'll tune in the local AM or FM stations for the news, weather and traffic reports. Then at some point as you're slogging your way down Route 66, you'll hit the satellite button and pick a channel. People are doing that now, except they're popping in CD's or cassettes" (Jessell, 1992c, p. 12). NAB was not happy with the FCC's proposal, saying: "The FCC seems to be rushing to judgment on satellite DAB, and the prospect that satellite development might be placed ahead of terrestrial DAB is troubling" (p. 12). Despite concerns, the FCC issued a terrestrial DAB FNOI. The FCC speculated that a satellite system could be in place by the end of the century, but a terrestrial system would not be introduced until after 2000. The FCC also said that DAB would apply to terrestrial delivery and that DARS would refer to both satellite and terrestrial DAB. DAB had become a headache with all its acronyms. EIA preferred DAR, which should not be confused with DARS. DRB was contributed by CDRB. Another acronym from an unknown source was BSS. Many observers wondered what was wrong with plain DAB (Zavistovich, 1992d).

Although American Digital Radio withdrew its system from consideration, there was no shortage of systems. By November 1992 a new proposal jointly produced by NASA and VOA brought the total of DAB system proponents to 11. The updated list included AT&T/Amati Communications Corp., AT&T/Bell Labs, Digital Planet, GI Kintel Technologies, Mercury Digital Communications, MIT, NASA/VOA, SCI/Lincom, Thomson Consumer Electronics, and USADR. The number of systems jeopardized EIA's December 1993 testing deadline (Gatski, 1992e).

SDARS Comments. Industry comments to the FCC's NOI regarding CD Radio's request for spectrum were received by the November 13, 1992, deadline. Broadcasters strongly opposed allocation of spectrum for SDARS, citing the negative impact on AM/FM broadcasting. Yet, 60 percent of all respondents supported CD Radio's request, typically noting advantages not provided by AM/FM radio. Minnesota Public Radio responded: "It would allow delivery of specialized, well-targeted programing [*sic*] to national audiences in an inexpensive manner" (Sukow, 1992d, p. 42). Reply comments were due by December 1, and responses to replies were expected by December 15.

Replies and responses to the FCC's NOI regarding CD Radio's petition were mixed. As expected, SDARS license applicants supported S-band allocation. Six respondents wanted a delay, if not total rejection, of all applications. NAB said it was too "premature" for the FCC to "be granting applications for digital services when they haven't even begun to establish the ground rules for DAB" (Viles, 1992, p. 33). SBE found technical reasons to reject applications by Primosphere, CD Radio, and Sky-Highway, which wanted space at 7 GHz. SBE believed interference would be compounded by the introduction of HDTV but was satisfied with proposals from AMRC and DSBC asking for space at 6 GHz. Why couldn't the other three systems accomplish delivery at 6 GHz as well? NPR was disappointed that applicants had not accommodated its request that about a quarter of the SDARS allocations be assigned to it. NAB asked for complete rejection of the applications, arguing that SDARS could not offer the benefits of the free terrestrial broadcasting already in place (Scully, 1993a). Broadcasters were concerned about threats to radio's localism.

Because one of SDARS' shortcomings was lack of mobility, DSBC designed and developed a six-inch-diameter automobile antenna. DSBC, Primosphere Limited Partnership, AMRC, Sky-Highway Radio Corp., and Loral Aerospace Holdings (formerly Ford Aerospace) wanted FCC approval to launch a service that would provide as many as 500 digital channels. By April 1993 Loral withdrew its system in order to join forces with CD Radio and to build its satellite (Holland, 1993). By mid-1994, Sky-Highway sold its interests to CD Radio for $2 million (Stern, 1994).

United States broadcasters were concerned about protecting their interests, while manufacturers set their sights on the global digital arena. NAB was adamantly opposed to EIA's efforts and wanted any standards decision made by its own DAB Task Force and NRSC. EIA's deadline was April 15, but by December 1992 five systems had been submitted: AT&T/Bell Laboratories, AT&T/Amati Communications Corp., Thomson Consumer Electronics

(Eureka-147), Jerrold Division of GI, and NASA/VOA. USADR refused to submit its IBOC system for testing, because it did not want to alienate broadcasters who believed that EIA was not seeking their input (Lambert, 1993a).

Digital Compression

As with DTV, compression was introduced into the DAB equation. AT&T/Bell Labs, which later merged with Lucent Technologies to form LDR, was a late entrant in the DAB derby but, with seemingly unlimited resources was catching up quickly. LDR (1998b) developed a compression scheme called PAC that "uses psychoacoustic modeling—that is, a mathematical model of how the human auditory system hears sound—to filter out irrelevant information in an audio signal" for "better signal compression ratios, greatly simplifying transmission." Project Acorn and Eureka-147 employed MUSICAM compression, which was expected to become the de facto compression standard. MUSICAM is an implementation of the Layer II coding algorithm, which ISO and MPEG determined was the best overall compression system. The main principle of the MUSICAM ISO MPEG Layer II algorithm is "the reduction of redundant and irrelevant information in the audio signal," resulting "in a lower bit rate without perceived degradation of the audio" (MUSICAM USA-CCS Europe, 2000). MUSICAM facilitates the transmission and reception of CD-quality stereo.

Compression, also known as DSP, data reduction, or the squeezing down of data, is applied to audio and video signals in order to save storage space. Digital transmissions could then work within limited bandwidth for both satellite and terrestrial delivery. Bandwidth is the range between the upper and lower limiting frequencies and the width of a band of frequencies and is the maximum amount of digital data capable of transmission or storage. A compressed signal uses minimal spectrum space, conserves bandwidth, and allows use of multiple audio and video services within the available spectrum space (Hoffner, 1994). With DTV and DAB, many broadcasters wanted to use extra space to generate revenue via other services. There was a downside to compression. Because "large portions of the audio signal can be discarded as irrelevant to the ears," and "while not readily apparent at first listen," quality degradation can "be detected down the line" (Treasure, 1992, p. 5). To study audio compression, the CCIR task group TG-10/2 conducted "listening tests in February [1992] with the mandate to recommend standards for several radio applications" (McVicker, 1992, p. 8). TG-10/2, comprising engineers from the United Kingdom, Canada, Australia, and France, invited participation from compression algorithm proponents, including ASPEC, Dolby AC-2, Aware System, SB-ADPCM from Switzerland, a Japanese system, and MUSICAM (p. 5). Testing confirmed the worst, that digital audio can withstand only "so many compression schemes before compact-disc quality becomes sub-broadcast quality" (Compressing business, 1993, p. 5). With further compression, serious degradation of audio would occur. Experts believed not only that there would be no DAB compression standard, but that there could not be one. Several methods are used to compress audio, but tests revealed that different compression schemes used in combination caused tremendous audio degradation. NAB believed that the best solution lay in teaching broadcasters how to cope with multiple compression schemes, because domestic groups NRSC and AES, as well as international groups CCIR and ISO/MPEG, were involved in determining compression standards (Gatski, 1993f). Some experts believed that even with compression, AM's 20 kHz signal would not be a large enough carrier for DAB. AM's signal is only about one-fifth the size of FM's 100 kHz signal. However, even at 20 kHz digitized AM figured to be of better quality than analog FM (Scully, 1993f).

Democrat Bill Clinton was elected president of the United States in November 1992, and regulatory change was expected after his January 1993 inauguration. Typically, Democrats favor regulation, and Republicans tend to deregulate. Some hoped that the new administration would reregulate and move away from the marketplace approach initiated under Reagan's administration. Not surprisingly, Republican FCC chairman Al Sikes announced that he would resign on January 19, the day before Clinton's inauguration. Sikes' regulatory philosophy was in tune with that of Reagan and Bush. Longtime FCC commissioner James Quello served as interim chair until Reed Hundt's 1993 appointment. However, prognosticators were wrong about the FCC's direction. Upon his appointment, Hundt said that he would continue the deregulatory work that had begun with Chairman Mark Fowler. The FCC had a string of marketplace proponents as chair, including Fowler, Dennis Patrick, and Al Sikes. The biggest enigma of them all was Hundt, who was notorious for changing his position from the beginning of a speech to the end.

IBOC Endorsed. Very early in 1993 NAB's DAB Task Force officially endorsed IBOC DAB. The task force believed IBOC to be less expensive to implement, especially since the FCC would not allocate alternative spectrum for DAB. Receiver manufacturers criticized NAB's stance. EIA said that no system should be selected until all types of systems were tested. Robert Heiblim, president of Denon, said: "We're not the enemy. We just want to make radios" (Gatski, 1993b, p. 6). At its January board meeting, NAB decided that it would support only testing done by NRSC (West, 1993). At the minimum, NAB wanted IBOC DAB to have priority over SDARS.

By March NAB and EIA compromised. NAB would not "consider systems other than IBOC unless IBOC systems are shown to not substantially meet the requirements for terrestrial DAR" (Flint, 1993, p. 51). EIA would test SDARS and IBOC systems, but NRSC would guide the IBOC tests and evaluations. NAB and EIA would jointly fund the initiative (DAB truce, 1993). Deadline for finishing IBOC testing was June 30, 1994, but USADR had not agreed to avail its system.

Many industry types compared EIA's DAB work with its 1984 MTS standard. Gary Shapiro, VP of EIA's CEMA, said that no comparison could be made because, unlike DAB, the MTS decision was not between terrestrial and satellite delivery. Shapiro explained: "What happened with TV stereo was that there was an interest by all industries to come up with the best system. And it was just a matter of testing and recommending that. Here, we don't have an interest in all industries coming up with the best system. I think the FCC will act in the best interests of the country. The best interests of the country is not necessarily one system or the other" (Gatski, 1993c, p. 12). NAB believed that relations between NAB and EIA were improving, but "there are going to be some rough spots along the way" (p. 12). Five DAB systems would be tested: NASA/VOA (satellite), Eureka-147 (NB), AT&T/Amati Communications Corp. (IBOC), AT&T Bell Laboratories (IBAC), and GI (IBAC).

In a speech at NAB 1993, interim FCC chairman Quello cautioned broadcasters about stubbornness and taking excessive time in finding a DAB solution. Quello urged broadcasters to produce terrestrial DAB standards expeditiously. He wanted priority given to IBOC but intimated that satellite DAB proponents were aggressive and would not stand by idly. Quello admitted that the FCC needed to help radio, and one way was to freeze licenses until DAB was finalized. Quello proffered: "What would be the effect on local radio service if we had 30 to 50 new radio voices from a satellite in every community? It seems we've already flooded the market in the name of competition and diversity" (Sukow, 1993b, p. 8).

The rest of the FCC showed little desire to expedite DAB. While the rest of the world appeared convinced that L-band was the best DAB spectrum, the FCC supported S-band. Most experts agreed that S-band was more expensive and less effective than L-band. As a result of the S-band decision, United States DAB would have to be IBOC- and/or satellite-delivered, causing incompatibility with the rest of the world. Nearly three years into deliberation, DAB was experiencing Amstereoization.

NAB's preemptive strike was intended to unite radio broadcasters and spur the FCC to action. The initiative failed, and progress was delayed due to NAB's waffling between Eureka-147 and IBOC. NAB had become almost as indecisive and unpredictable as the FCC, and both were "divided on key decisions not only between themselves, but within themselves" (Taylor, 1993, p. 15). Many feared that DAB interest would disappear as happened with AM stereo.

In June 1993 results were released from the first study determining that the costs of station conversion to DAB. Digital consultant Skip Pizzi determined IBOC would be cheaper to implement than IBAC and NB DAB. Estimated costs were $60,000 to $65,000 for IBOC-FM, $55,000 to $75,000 for IBAC, and $66,000 to 141,000 for NB. NB cost more because totally new transmission systems would be necessary (Gatski, 1993d).

EIA twice postponed its DAB testing deadline because USADR's IBOC-AM system was not ready for testing. The original July 1, 1993, deadline was changed to October 1993 and then December 31. Other DAB systems were ready for testing: Amati Communications/AT&T (IBOC and IBAC), Eureka/Thomson Consumer Electronics (L-band terrestrial), and NASA/VOA (S-band, SDARS). Each agreed to the deadline extension but believed that the process could not be delayed beyond December 31 without detrimental affects (Sukow, 1993c). However, the deadline was not met.

Germany Balks. Germany, where DAB originated, decided to delay introduction of Eureka-147 until 1997, causing uneasiness in Europe. Reportedly, there were financial constraints and frequency allocation problems, but the decision was not expected to affect progress in other countries such as Sweden, Canada, Mexico, France, or Great Britain. USADR saw Germany's postponement as an opportunity to gain a European foothold for IBOC (Gatski, 1993e). Ultimately, Germany's process resumed full stride in 1994, and worldwide DAB interest seemed to be rekindled.

Perhaps because of Germany's decision, EBU decided to invite global input about Eureka-147. Pioneer, a Japanese receiver manufacturer, announced plans in January 1994 to build an L-band DAB radio receiver, becoming the first non-European company to answer EBU's global call. Canadians believed that Pioneer's plans validated terrestrial L-band delivery of DAB (Careless, 1994). Pioneer's receivers were not expected for several years, giving time for development of IBOC receivers. Without receivers, DAB transmission would not matter. Manufacturers built AM stereo receivers, but without a transmission system standard few were sold. By April 1994 at least eight other companies expressed interest in developing DAB receivers: Thomson, Telefunken, Philips, Grundig, Pioneer, Sony, Kenwood, and Delco (Taylor, 1994).

Certainly, DAB would offer improvement over traditional broadcasting in sound and audio quality, but it was becoming an egotistical tug-of-war between the United States and the rest of the world. The strongest tugs seemed to come from Europe, Canada, and Mexico. United States broadcasters wanted to work with deliberate speed, but others saw DAB as an opportunity to assert themselves as technological leaders. McLeod (1994) observed: "While DAB shines technically, it is clear that there is a political imperative to beat United States technical proposals. . . . Although U.S. work is at a much earlier stage of development than Eureka, IBOC has such strong attractions for established broadcasters that if they do prove viable, Eureka will almost certainly be eclipsed. So there is a rush bordering on desperation to have Eureka accepted and up and running before IBOC has the chance to prove itself one way or the other" (p. 161).

During January 1994 five DAB system proponents had nearly completed installation of their systems at the NASA Lewis Research Center in Cleveland, Ohio. Although the December 31, 1993, deadline was unmet, there was no date set for completion and no timetable scheduled for field testing. EIA and NRSC hoped to release preliminary laboratory results at the April 1994 NAB meeting but remained behind schedule on DAB laboratory testing and predicted an August 1994 conclusion (Sukow, 1994a, 1994c). Perhaps "a third of the way through" with lab tests, EIA and NRSC delayed field testing until at least 1995 (Gatski, 1994, p. 1).

Digital Radio on Cable. DCR announced in March 1994 that it had struck a deal with DirecTV, a division of GM's Hughes Electronics, to initiate SDARS in April. DCR's Music Choice service was not a cable exclusive service. NAB said DCR's announcement "will shock the broadcasting industry" as "the guys coming in from Japan with inexpensive cars in the 1960s . . . shocked the automotive industry" (Beacham, 1994a, p. 1). Music Choice would be programmed like the cable service with 30 channels of varying formats. DirecTV planned to make Music Choice a part of its basic DBS service. DCR made little progress in distributing its signal to automobiles. SDARS was progressing, but until it gained mobility, it would not totally jeopardize broadcasters. DCR differed from the service proposed by CD Radio, which sought to use space on S-band. DCR would be distributed via an approved DBS provider. NAB was trying to circumvent CD Radio but could do little about DCR.

Michael Bloomberg, owner of WBBR-AM in New York, wasted no time taking advantage of DCR. Bloomberg contracted to transmit his station's business news format via DirecTV beginning in May 1994. Bloomberg, a businessperson and not a broadcaster, was critical of broadcasters' approach to new technologies. He stated: "I don't know much about radio stations and the people in them but they don't look like they accept new ideas easily. And it's funny because it's an easy business to get into" (Beacham, 1994b, p. 1). He added: "I went to an NAB convention a year and quarter ago in New Orleans. What struck me was there wasn't a good idea since 1929. When you talk to people their whole thought process was how do we do well within the constraints of what we've been doing. Nobody ever looked at the forests. These were tree people" (p. 3). Bloomberg was not alone in his position. NAB's John Abel told broadcasters that they did not "have a clue" about technology, and none challenged his statement (Tough talk, 1994, p. 5).

Huff and Rosene (1993–94) queried 300 AM station owners and managers about DAB in 1992, finding many respondents viewing it as the next step in technical development. FM was considered more threatening to AM than DAB. Interestingly, most AM managers had no DAB opinion, which seemed to support criticism leveled at broadcasters by Bloomberg and Abel. Perhaps broadcasters had insulated themselves so much that they did not understand the gravity of the situation. Owners and managers were inconsistent in their responses. While retrospectively wishing that the FCC had imposed mandatory AM improvement prior to initiating stereo, many of the same executives wanted no part of future FCC-mandated improvements. AM general managers serve many roles, and the researchers presumed that they were salespersons at heart or in practice. Many served as sales managers and may have used the survey to sell the researchers on AM. A good salesperson would naturally believe in his or her product or service. AM managers may have been unrealistic or uninformed, or perhaps selective perception may have been at work. Businesspersons, such as Bloomberg, say that American business has been guilty of not looking to the future by avoiding long-term planning, focusing only on immediate profits. AM broadcasters may be guilty as well.

Egon Meier-Engelen, Eureka-147 project coordinator, believed that the United States would never implement DAB, bluntly stating that NAB "wants to kill DAB," and IBOC "was put forward simply as a way to eventually kill it" (Homer, 1994, p. 59). He doubted that United States broadcasters carried enough influence to prevent SDARS implementation. FCC chairman Hundt acknowledged the impact of NAB's lobbying against SDARS but admitted that the FCC was unsure about its role in an era of tremendous technological development. Hundt scolded broadcasters attending an industry luncheon, saying: "A year ago conferences like these were filled with the rhetoric of removing government from the communications revolution. It turned out you were kidding. You didn't mean it. You keep asking us to do things" (Pear, 1994, p. 3).

Worldwide DAB? In December 1994 the ITU working party recommended that DAB be accomplished worldwide using Eureka-147 for both SDARS and terrestrial to vehicular, portable, and fixed receivers in VHF/UHF range. The ETSI adopted the European Standard ETS 300401 of the Eureka-147 DAB system. Eureka-147 could carry services other than audio, such as program-associated and independent data services compatible with RDS. It was capable of expanding radio broadcasting to the future multimedia services and the information highway infrastructure (WorldDAB Forum, 1997). Despite ITU's action, no one needed to look beyond AM stereo to understand that there was a huge difference between recommendations and standards, but USADR believed that ITU's recommendation would lead to worldwide standardization.

Great Britain became the first country to establish Eureka-147 as its DAB standard on September 27, 1995, when BBC launched four stereo channels and one high-quality mono channel (Tait, 1995). Germany, which in 1993 had announced a delay of DAB implementation from 1995 until 1997, met its original deadline by beginning DAB broadcasting on October 17, 1995. To jump-start DAB, the Bavarian government planned to distribute 4,000 receivers to dignitaries, politicians, and researchers (DAB launched by Germany, 1995). But, no receivers existed. Although Grundig was commissioned to produce receivers, a prototype had not been developed (DAB receivers delayed, 1996).

Despite broadcasters' pleas, the FCC expected to open an SDARS rulemaking proceeding as early as January 12, 1995. NAB asked: "Why risk the financial stability of 11,000 radio stations in the United States in order to offer new services?" (Stern and McConnell, 1995, p. 10). NAB's Eddie Fritts said: "The fact that the FCC has waited three years since WARC to allocate spectrum is in itself an indication of the uncertainty about the need for satellite radio in the United States" (Haber, 1995b, p. 12). SDARS proponents claimed that their service would have little impact on broadcasters. The FCC ultimately voted to allocate 50 MHz of S-band spectrum (2310-2360) for DARS, but plenty of hurdles remained. The FCC still needed to set rules, policies, and guidelines for DARS, known by the industry as SDARS. NAB vowed to continue its fight, and the FCC planned to study SDARS' impact on broadcasters. Commissioner Andrew Barrett was "concerned about [SDARS'] potential adverse impact on localism and the possible economic harm to these broadcasters" (McConnell, 1995b, p. 28). Commissioner Rachelle Chong believed that there was room for terrestrial and SDARS. Commissioner Susan Ness viewed SDARS as a way "to maximize the new and unique benefits" of the service (p. 28) and hoped that SDARS would "expedite the radio broadcasting industry's move to digital technologies" (Haber, 1995a, p. 1).

Commissioner Quello wanted to protect broadcasters' interests but believed that they should be moving toward DAB. Quello explained:

We are doing everything to tell them that they have at least three years to develop terrestrial broadcasting. Remember, pure satellite transmission does not provide for a local service, and radio's biggest value is local news, local emergency alerting, local traffic reports. We are telling radio, if you can, get some kind of terrestrial (digital) service. They have some proposals. You cannot roll back advances in technology, and DBS does represent advanced technology. On the other hand, you don't want to regulate something or deregulate it just for the sake of advanced technology. The number one thing we always have to keep in mind is: "What best serves the public?" That is where the public interest lies. So if it appears to me that we can serve the public by delaying it (digital satellite broadcasting) just a little bit, I might even do that. (Quello: You cannot, 1995, p. 60)

SDARS proponents were ready to implement their services and wanted a piece of the radio revenue pie, which exceeded $10 billion in 1994. Europe was rallying around Eureka-147. DAB was inevitable, but how would it be implemented in the United States? Even Quello, broadcasters' staunchest supporter, would wait only so long before relenting. Quello said: "The role of the commission today actually should be the orderly, compatible implementation of the advanced technology services of everything—computing, fiber optics, DBS, DAB, HDTV, BCS, cellular—practical implementation of all these services, and it is a complex job. I've always said that the rate and extent of the development will be decided pretty much by consumer acceptance and consumer appointability" (p. 60).

Chapter 5

Border-to-Border DAB

One of the bigger tests for DAB was along the U.S.–Canadian border, where interference was inevitable. One area of particular concern was Vancouver, British Columbia, and Seattle, Washington. Seattle-based aircraft manufacturer Boeing used L-band for testing. With Vancouver stations occupying L-band, there could be overlap. There would also be competitive situations in other cross-border adjacent cities such as Windsor, Ontario, and Detroit, Michigan. U.S. citizens could easily obtain DAB L-band receivers, so comparisons could be made between Eureka-147 and IBOC. Given a choice, would Canadians and Americans prefer IBOC or L-band?

A similar situation was brewing along the Mexican border. Mexico's CIRT was divided in its opinion. Many broadcasters favored L-band and Eureka-147, but border stations preferred IBOC due to dependence on income from U.S. listeners and advertisers. The dilemma eventually led to a third possibility of implementing a combination of L-band and IBOC services (Plata, 1995).

At NAB's April convention in Las Vegas, USADR introduced broadcasters to its IBOC system by offering bus rides every half hour featuring broadcasts over KUNV-FM. All FCC commissioners except Hundt took advantage of the demonstration and were impressed. Hundt's absence did not endear him to broadcasters, and he harmed himself further by asking how much new spectrum IBOC would require. Broadcasters were flabbergasted that the FCC chairman did not know that IBOC meant in-band and on-channel via existing AM/FM frequencies (Taylor, 1995). USADR proved IBOC was more fully developed than any system other than Eureka-147. Canadian representatives were not impressed, but given the competitive circumstances, it was difficult to know whether their opinions were legitimate or prejudiced.

In June EBU held the first meeting of its EuroDab Forum, created in October 1995 when EBU invited global input about Eureka-147. At the meeting, it was decided that all parties would be grouped under the EuroDab moniker rather than continuing with separate categories. American input was limited to manufacturers. EuroDab, an international, nongovernmental organization claiming more than 100 members, later evolved into WorldDAB Forum. WorldDAB's (n.d. a) purpose was "to promote, harmonize and co-ordinate the implementation of Digital Radio services based on the Eureka-147 DAB system" and was "dedicated to encouraging international co-operation and co-ordination between sound and data broadcasters, network providers, manufacturers, governments and official bodies, thus gaining consensus for the smooth introduction of DAB."

The FCC's DARS NPRM

The FCC issued its DARS NPRM on June 14, 1995, and sought comments on a range of matters, including number of licenses to be issued, how much spectrum a licensee could have, regulation of the service, and non-DARS service uses. Would the FCC allow new DARS applicants into the process, or would it be limited to only those already proposed? Commissioner Ness hoped to limit DARS to subscription services. She and Quello were concerned about the impact of DARS on terrestrial broadcasting. Chong wanted to consider all options. The FCC set the deadlines for comments at September 15 and replies at October 13 (FCC seeks comments on DARS, 1995). Chairman Hundt leaned toward allowing new DARS applications, saying: "We should let DARS compete with terrestrial. Every instinct tells me that the results of that competition will be better radio service for the American public" (FCC chairman wants to reopen, 1995, p. 8). Hundt said that even though a company had invested in DARS and had filed an application, that fact did not mean that the company would get a license. Hundt wanted DARS providers to pay for spectrum. SDARS was complicated by Canada's complaint that use of S-band would interfere with its aeronautical telemetry. Conversely, Canada's L-band use would interfere with the United States' aeronautical telemetry (McConnell, 1996a).

Although USADR was well into development and testing of IBOC, there was little progress with IBAC. AT&T tested its IBAC system over a New Orleans station concurrent with the September 6–9 meeting of the World Media Expo. Listeners were impressed, making it a serious threat to IBOC and Eureka-147. Glynn Walden, Group W engineer, declared: "This is very damaging to Eureka because this is a replacement for their L-band system. It's an 'any-band' system" (Carter, 1995, p. 1). The main criticism of AT&T's system was that it had to fit into already overcrowded AM/FM bands. AT&T officials admitted that the New Orleans test was not a true test since it was done over a frequency unaffected by other stations. The real test would come in San Francisco with the EIA and NRSC conducting field tests in a crowded FM environment (p. 14).

EIA and NRSC tested DAB systems for more than a year before making laboratory results public. It was concluded that IBOC DAB worked, but not to what extent. EIA cautioned that the report was preliminary and that further results would be unavailable until field testing was finished. Eureka-147 received extremely high marks from EIA, as the organization reported:

The independent test results provided by the EIA confirm that the digital radio concept that Canada has developed (Eureka-147 in a new band at 1452-1492 MHz) will indeed provide the highest quality DAB service. The tests showed the Eureka system to be far superior technically to any other proponent system and confirm the extensive evaluations conducted in Canada and Europe since 1990. Moreover, as Eureka-147 will operate in a new band, it automatically avoids any impairments caused to, or suffered from, existing analog services. The In-Band systems showed particularly badly with respect to the key attribute their proponents have always touted—their ability to co-exist in the AM/FM bands without causing interference to analog services. Demonstrations in carefully controlled environments may have produced promising results previously. But the independent lab tests show that IBOC fails when it is operated using simulations of real-world impairments, such as multipath and adjacent-channel interference. (Digital Radio Research Inc., 1995)

EIA added: "FM IBOC system performance and interference impairment worsens significantly in the presence of multipath. Of the IBOC systems, the AT&T/Amati system performed best in a multipath environment, although failures still occurred under certain conditions. The USA Digital FM-1 and FM-2 systems generally produced degraded performance (or failed completely) whenever multipath was added to the signal."

There was controversy over some of the testing procedures, particularly the methods used for multipath simulation (Cobo, 1995). USADR responded by withdrawing its system from field testing. USADR objected to the testing of NB systems, was not clear about the testing criteria, and disputed the testing contract. A *Radio World* editorial charged EIA with "stacking the deck in favor of Eureka-147" (In-band: The only choice, 1995, p. 5). The editorial continued: "EIA's stance of serving the interests of United States receiver manufacturers does not hold up this time. Two of Eureka-147's driving partners are Europe-based Thomson and Philips—both members of the EIA" (p. 5). *Radio World* urged NAB to accelerate its endeavors on behalf of U.S. broadcasters and to seize an aggressive lead in testing. The editorial observed: "This is a joint project through the NRSC; make it equal, too" (p. 5). *Radio World* was incensed because field testing was delayed to allow Eureka-147 to modify its system and believed that too much emphasis was placed on testing an NB system rather than IBOC. The FCC was advised "to realize that those making a recommendation on the choice of DAB implementation in this country have too many vested interests in seeing a certain system succeed" (Too many vested interests, 1995, p. 5). To IBOC and IBAC supporters, it was disappointing to learn that TIA and the Aerospace & Flight Test Radio Coordinating Council granted the EIA approval to use L-band spectrum at 1452-1492 MHz to test Eureka-147. The allocation for testing would last until the end of April 1996 (DAB tests get, 1996).

The FCC received many comments by the September 15 deadline about its DARS NPRM. Unsurprisingly, broadcasters remained against SDARS for fear it would hurt their business. SDARS proponents argued that there would be no harm and that impact on broadcasters would be minimal. NAB said: "Even losing only some audience some of the time, a local station without a critical mass of audience and already operating on a modest profit margin may fall quickly into unprofitability" (McConnell, 1995g, p. 54). The original four SDARS applicants continued their argument against opening S-band spectrum (2310-2360 MHz) to new applicants. Primosphere, CD Radio, DSBC, and AMRC wanted the entire allotment. NAB requested reopening the application process and that the FCC approve SDARS as a subscription-only service as opposed to broadcasting (p. 54). Reply comments received by October 13, 1995, varied little from the comments.

SDARS and Pioneer's Preference

In regard to DARS, the FCC's International Bureau proposed dividing 50 MHz of S-band allotted for DARS into three parts. CD Radio, the original SDARS proponent, would get a "pioneer's preference" allotment at 12.5 MHz. On September 1, 1995, the FCC issued a waiver to CD Radio to build an SDARS satellite over which CD Radio would deliver 30 music and 20 news/information channels to small mobile antennae. Three other SDARS proponents would bid for a second 12.5 MHz allotment. The remaining 25 MHz would be auctioned for other purposes, meaning that only two SDARS providers could compete for listeners with broadcasters (McConnell, 1996b). Congressmen Thomas Bliley (R-VA) and John Dingell (D-MI) asked the FCC to postpone the plan and to study the possibility of auctioning off the entire spectrum, including what may have been given to CD Radio. Dingell, in particular, questioned why CD Radio should be given pioneer's preference and wanted to hear evidence to support the claim, especially since DSBC and Primosphere also sought "pioneer's preference." Dingell said that he "was underwhelmed by the description of the procedures used by the FCC" (Meadows, 1996c, p. 6).

SDARS' situation was based on economics and was not intended to delay DARS. But delay it did, as the FCC had no idea when the proceeding would resume. In response to congressional concerns, the FCC asked NTIA to form a peer review panel, comprising representatives from other government agencies, to audit its findings. Dingell appeared unmoved. Cole (1996) observed that DARS is "kind of like the big storm that all the weather forecasters say is on the way. You look out and, sure enough, the sky is getting really dark. You can pretty much safely assume that the storm is going to arrive, although you might not be sure just when" (p. 42).

Pioneer's Preference Denied. Ultimately, CD radio was not given the coveted pioneer's preference for SDARS, as the peer review panel concluded that the applicants did not prove that they could provide a locally "'seamless' service" (McConnell, 1996g, p. 18). With seamless service an SDARS signal would be received directly by dish and then passed along through transmitters to give listeners uninterrupted service. CD Radio was disappointed, but NAB's Fritts was elated: "We believe that local stations best serve local audiences and that any fragmentation by SDARS undermines the principle of localism" (p. 18).

Originally, the FCC allocated 2310–2360 MHz on S-band for satellite distribution. In the 1997 Appropriations Act, Congress obligated the Commission to reserve spectrum at 2305–2320 and 2345–2360 MHz for use by wireless services. The FCC sought to develop a Wireless Communications Service and to allow it to use that spectrum as it saw fit. Some of that spectrum fell within 2310–2360 MHz. With the peer review panel's decision, just two of four companies could implement DARS on just 25 MHz of the allocated spectrum. The FCC had not decided if the spectrum would be auctioned to the two highest bidders or allocated in some other manner. In the 1997 Appropriations Act, Congress mandated that the FCC auction the spectrum and to initiate the process by April 15, 1997, with completion by September 30, 1997. NAB supported the measure because it would limit the number of DARS providers but expressed concern about the impact of DARS on broadcasters. NAB asked that DARS services not be allowed to use terrestrial technology to relay signals once they were received on the ground, which it argued would be no different from terrestrial broadcasting (Spangler, 1997a).

On August 29, 1997, the FCC (1997k) discontinued its pioneer's preference practice in response to congressional legislation and to President Clinton's signing into law the Balanced Budget Act of 1997 on August 5. The act amended the Communications Act to terminate the FCC's power in giving preferential status in licensing procedures for pioneers, which was instituted in 1991 for parties that the FCC believed "made significant contributions to the development of a new spectrum-using service, or to the development of a new technology that substantially enhanced an existing spectrum-using service." Although about 140 applications had been made for pioneer's preferences, just five requests were ever granted. By terminating pioneer's preference, the FCC (1997k) dismissed all 13 pending requests.

As of June 1996 USADR continued to withhold its IBOC system from EIA field testing. Since laboratory testing, USADR had been upset over procedures and contracts. USADR wanted specific, written details and definitions about the field tests and indicated that it might contract for testing with another organization. USADR said: "The EIA isn't the only sanctioned testing body" (Meadows, 1996a, p. 11). Presumably, USADR referred to NRSC, but where was the FCC during the situation? The FCC apparently wanted no part in the DAB standards process, preferring to await an industry recommendation to rubber-stamp. The Commission had taken a similar approach with almost every proceeding since MTS in 1984. DAB's problem was that no one seemed to be in charge. EIA and NAB struggled for leadership, a job that should have been done by the FCC.

Canadian DAB and Amstereoization

On October 29, 1995, Canada officially followed Great Britain and Germany into the digital age. The CRTC said that it would begin issuing DAB licenses forthwith. CRTC cited Eureka-147's anticipated selection as Canada's standard and said that there were no technical obstacles to prevent issuing licenses. Since the process was ongoing, the first license would be transitional to accommodate any DAB policy changes (Careless, 1995). Although group owners seemed pleased, small station owners were not as positive. Nick Frost, who owned SILK-FM in British Columbia, was very skeptical, believing that DAB could be another AM stereo-like debacle because consumers would not hear a distinct difference between DAB and FM. He said: "It is the consumer who drives technology, not the guys who invent it" (Careless, 1996a, p. 14). Frost, like many others, was leery of implementing a DAB system inconsistent with the United States standard.

Canada and other countries soon began to experience Amstereoization of DAB. Stations were reluctant to convert to DAB without receivers on the market, and manufacturers were hesitant to produce receivers without DAB on the air. Although Canada began granting licenses on October 29, 1995, no DAB stations were on the air by June 1996. DAB receivers were not available or expected until at least mid-1997. As with AM stereo, chicken-and-egg references were surfacing. Eureka-147 had gained global support, but it was not making the breakthrough that many had predicted. Could it be the world was looking to the United States for leadership?

Finally, Canada began DAB frequency allocations in August 1996. The DRB Allotment Plan was not intended to promote competition between L-band and IBOC, because Canada planned to implement NB. Canada planned to divide L-band frequencies from 1452 to 1492 MHz into 23 channels of 1.5 MHz. Careless (1996b) explained: "Under Eureka-147 DAB technology, adopted as the Canadian standard, each channel carries five services. This means AM and FM stations will find themselves grouped together with competitors, on centralized transmitter 'pods.' . . . Deciding who should be on which pod, and where, was a major concern of the architects of the plan. In the end, the emphasis was placed on cooperation, letting the broadcasters themselves decide which stations should be on which DRB transmitting pod" (p. 8).

DAB Field Testing

DAB field testing began in San Francisco in July 1996. San Francisco was selected as the site because of its numerous hills, tall buildings, and electrical transportation systems. It was believed that if DAB worked in San Francisco with all its potential interference, it would work almost anywhere. Many broadcasters believed that the tests were moot without USADR's three IBOC systems (two FM and one AM). Because NAB supported IBOC and because USADR was one of only two IBOC systems, there seemed to be little point in testing. Fritts said that NAB still supported the testing because "a deal is a deal" (Meadows, 1996b, p. 13). NAB appeared unconcerned about how Eureka-147 and other systems performed, but some broadcasters were interested. EIA's Gary Shapiro urged broadcasters not to be too worried: "Digital radio is going along swimmingly well. The only comparison where it is disappointing is to Europe where because of their less than democratic structure, they've managed to implement it quicker than we did here. I like our democratic institutions and I like the separation between broadcasters and government that we have, so that is a trade-off" (Radio should look ahead, 1996, p. 15).

NAB was growing weary of the lengthy DAB process—especially testing. NAB was uncomfortable with the situation and maintained concerns about EIA's voting makeup. Fritts was displeased with EIA's control over testing despite the presence of NRSC, claiming that "criteria changed as the testing took place" and that Eureka-147 was given "certain advantages" over other systems (NAB poised, 1996, p. 55). Fritts did not "know why they changed, but it was an internal decision by EIA for them to change" (p. 55).

In September 1996 AT&T/Lucent Technologies/Amati also withdrew its system from EIA's San Francisco field testing. AT&T/Lucent Technologies/Amati's system was not completed to the satisfaction of company engineers. NAB, which had decided to do its own IBOC testing, said it was ready to begin whenever notified.

In January 1997 EIA completed DAB field testing. Despite the withdrawal of both IBOC systems, data were included in the report from earlier laboratory tests. Some confusion surfaced concerning IBOC's performance, but USADR said that its FM system operated successfully. Opponents suggested that USADR was unrealistic, because it would not believe that IBOC interfered with the host FM signal. Eventually, USADR confessed some problems but was working to correct and enhance the system. Given IBOC's ongoing evolution, NAB said that all previous EIA lab test results should be discarded in favor of a fresh start (Meadows, 1997). There were criticism and disagreement, and there was disdain for EIA's praise of Eureka-147. What did it all mean? Simply, DAB was a long way from a U.S. standard.

A corporate merger slowed development of USADR's three IBOC systems. USADR was a consortium primarily sponsored by Westinghouse, which purchased CBS and planned to buy Infinity Broadcasting. There was concern that IBOC would be lost in the shuffle. In October 1996 Westinghouse said: "USADR's work over the past five years has yielded a great deal of information on the AM and FM bands and on working in-band DAB systems. While this work has also raised a series of difficult challenges, USADR is now proceeding with a revised technical design of its DAB system" (USADR proceeds, 1996, p. 12). Westinghouse assured NAB that it would work toward practical DAB implementation.

DAB's saga took another turn in March 1997, when CEMA petitioned the FCC to forgo SDARS spectrum auctions and to allocate that portion of S-band for terrestrial DAB. CEMA also endorsed Eureka-147. NAB's Fritts was incensed: "CEMA is a partner with NAB in a number of projects and they didn't even have the courtesy of giving us the heads-up on their underhanded proposal. If CEMA's looking for a fight, they damn sure found one" (Spangler, 1997b, pp. 1, 6). CEMA, claiming DAB would not work on S-band, IBOC, or IBAC, asked the Commission to reconsider its S-band allocation in favor of L-band where DAB's potential could best be realized. CD Radio and Primosphere, SDARS proponents, were not happy with CEMA's stance.

Despite CEMA's protests, the FCC planned to auction S-band spectrum on April 1. Chairman Hundt wanted the auction opened to other parties, but all other commissioners opposed him, deciding that only CD Radio, AMRC, Primosphere, and DSBC would be allowed to participate in the auction. Commissioner Chong explained: "These applicants have been the victims of regulatory delay, and that delay should not continue" (McConnell, 1997a, p. 21). The winners were CD Radio, which paid $83 million, and AMRC, which spent $89 million. With a mid-1999 target, CD Radio planned to distribute 30 music and 20 news/information channels. AMRC released no timetable for implementation. SDARS promised to enable a person to drive coast to coast without interruption of service or intervention of commercials. NAB maintained concern about SDARS' seamless delivery, because potentially, thousands of terrestrial repeaters would be necessary for seamless, uninterrupted service (Spangler, 1997c). SDARS implementation was still a long way off, because satellites needed to be built for the service.

DARS Reply Comments

On March 3, 1997, the FCC released reply comments to the NPRM along with its DARS *Report and Order*, which would make SDARS a reality. Initially, the Commission asked for comments on the *Report and Order* by

May 15. NAB charged that SDARS proponents had not answered questions raised as early as 1995 and asked the FCC to extend the comments date to June 13 and reply comments to June 27. The FCC obliged. The NPRM contained two major issues. The first was the use of terrestrial repeaters, and the second was that those repeaters would not be allowed to transmit local programming. All commenters agreed with the second issue, but the first ignited controversy. Respondents took issue with repeaters, aka signal gap fillers. The winning SDARS providers cited a need for the repeaters, but NAB maintained that repeaters were actually terrestrial DAB delivery. NAB believed that repeaters, or transmitters, would provide localized service, meaning that SDARS would compete directly with broadcasters. In regard to NAB's assertion that SDARS proponents had not provided solicited information, CD Radio and AMRC disagreed. One of NAB's complaints focused on interference to terrestrial broadcasting by SDARS. CD Radio and AMRC responded: "Additional information is unnecessary because the Commission's rules for SDARS licenses already restrict out-of-band interference and are applicable fully to terrestrial devices" (Spangler, 1997d, p. 14).

In May 1998 AMRC paid Hughes Space and Communications International more than $400 million for the construction and launch of two satellites to carry its SDARS signal. Both satellites would be put into orbit in 2000. CD Radio contracted with Space Systems/Loral for three satellites. Two would be primary carriers, and the third would be a spare. Launch was planned for some time in 1999. Interestingly, AMRC and CD Radio were collaborating on a receiver that would be compatible with either company's S-band signals. Each planned to provide 50 channels of music and news/talk/information (AMRC closer, 1998).

WorldDAB, previously known as EuroDab, supported Eureka-147 as the standard DAB system. WorldSpace was a partner in the WorldDAB consortium, and the company had tried to develop a system compatible with Eureka-147. However, WorldSpace believed that its efforts had yielded a better SDARS system and wanted it to be employed in Europe and elsewhere. WorldSpace cited Eureka-147's DARS limitations, which ultimately led the company to decide that its own system should be chosen. WorldSpace's decision did not sit well with WorldDAB. As a result, WorldSpace changed its system's moniker from satellite DAB to DSB. WorldDAB was most upset in the timing of the conflict, since there was concern about the manufacturers' hesitance to produce receivers. DAB development was fragile, and negative information could cause major problems (Cohen, 1997). WorldSpace planned to provide SDARS in 1999 to an estimated 4.6 billion people worldwide—except for the United States. Panasonic, Sanyo, Hitachi, and JVC contracted to build compatible receivers for WorldSpace. Pohlmann (1999) pondered: "The United States is generally agreed to be the world's leader in digital technology, so wouldn't it be ironic if Africa, the Middle East, Asia, Latin America, and the Caribbean got digital radio before us?" (p. 16).

Although Europe was ahead of the United States in DAB development, receivers remained unavailable to consumers in November 1997. Receivers were demonstrated at consumer electronics shows but were not being mass-produced. Despite their de facto Eureka-147 system standard, Europeans were experiencing a problem similar to that for AM stereo—lack of receivers and consumer acceptance. There was uncertainty over how to interest consumers in DAB. Thomas Rohde of manufacturer Fujitsu Ten Europe said: "We need to find an easy way to market and explain the product so that the consumer is not intimidated and seeks more information" (Clark, 1997, p. 6). Similarly to AM stereo, there were rumblings that multimodal DAB receivers were being developed that would receive both analog and digital signals. Consumers rejected multidecoding AM stereo receivers.

A *Radio World* editorial, evoking Amstereoization in the United States, believed that a DAB decision should be made and adhered to for the sake of DAB:

Our industry is prone to this kind of second guessing. But the time to pick a direction and stick to it is here. Indeed, it may have passed. Let's not be slowed, once again, by hesitation and doubt. You need only mention the words "AM stereo" in a room full of radio managers and engineers to hear the moans and chuckles start. That technology failed to reach its potential, not because it was poorly designed, but because the industry failed to embrace it and to make swift, sure decisions about its implementation. We have no qualm with observers who debate the technical merits of any improvements to the U.S. a radio system. But the ground rules have been established: Any successful digital radio system must provide notable improvement to the listener, meet the needs of the existing broadcast community and recognize the realities of available spectrum. IBOC meets the second and third conditions; we expect it will prove itself on the first point. (Stay the Course, 1998, p. 5)

Some broadcasters were concerned about the cost factor of DAB conversion, which would depend on how much upgrading had been done over time. Regularly upgraded stations that had replaced worn analog equipment with digital would spend less than stations that had not kept pace with technology. Some stations would require only a DAB exciter costing from $15,000 to $35,000. A total upgrade, including transmitter, could cost $150,000 or more. Some smaller stations would not survive the transition.

System Mergers and Splits. In May 1997 USADR and Lucent Technologies (formerly AT&T) agreed to work jointly on IBOC, prompting optimism from broadcasters about DAB. NAB, an IBOC supporter, had not endorsed any particular system. Consolidation of the only two IBOC systems freed NAB to support one system and hopefully to expedite DAB. In a surprising February 1998 announcement, however, DRE announced that it was developing an AM/FM IBOC system. Derek Kumar, who had previously been associated with USADR partner National Semiconductor, founded DRE. A noted digital researcher, Kumar left the company in 1995 to pursue his Ph.D.

With 12 employees, DRE was not a big company (McGinley, 1999). USADR was backed by big business, and LDR was created from a merger that included telecommunication giant AT&T. Was it possible that a small company could shape DAB's destiny as Kahn did with AM stereo? Kahn pushed Motorola to its limit, giving DRE a model to follow.

NRSC deactivated its DAB Subcommittee in September 1996 but later reactivated it because DAB had developed enough to warrant further investigation. Thirty-four broadcast representatives were present for DRE's announcement. Why had no one heard of the system beforehand? DRE president Norman Miller explained: "We didn't want to go public in announcing our systems until we had hardware and lab data that gave us a high probability for success" (Stimson, 1998a, p. 8). USADR declined to participate in testing proposed by DRE. CBS' Glynn Walden, a USADR cofounder, responded: "We have our plans underway and are not interested in changing them" (p. 8).

DRE allied with semiconductor manufacturer TriTech Microelectronics and was in negotiations with Telos Systems, a company that produced exciters and a compression algorithm device with MPEG-2 AAC. As a component of the USADR and Lucent Technologies deal, Lucent provided the PAC algorithm for USADR's IBOC system. PAC replaced MUSICAM, USADR's original compression device (Peterson, 1997). DRE obtained an experimental license from the FCC to allow testing in San Francisco, where EIA conducted DAB testing.

After 10 months, USADR and Lucent Technologies ended their alliance on February 28, 1998. LDR (1998a, 1998c) said that its "mission is to develop technology and to ensure successful and rapid market adoption of IBOC. As the technology developer, we see it as our responsibility to build consensus amongst the key constituencies that will partake in the deployment of IBOC AM and FM technology." Constituencies were identified as small and large radio broadcasters in urban and rural markets, equipment and receiver manufacturers, and regulatory and standards bodies. LDR said that its primary "objective is to deliver a working IBOC system in the year 2000" and to take IBOC global.

A potential conflict surrounded the PAC compression algorithm owned by LDR and employed by USADR. LDR planned to implement PAC in its own IBOC system (Stimson, 1998b). USADR officially welcomed LDR's competition but did not rule out legal action. Robert Struble, USADR president, said that the split validated the importance and potential for IBOC (USADR, 1998a).

USADR and DRE would license IBOC technology to transmitter and receiver manufacturers, but neither would build equipment. USADR predicted that the transition from analog to DAB would begin in 2000 and continue at least until 2010. USADR believed that station owners and consumers would not differ in terms of acceptance, with some adopting early and others waiting for trends to develop and prices to drop (Stimson & Barnes, 1998).

USADR'S RULE-MAKING PETITION

USADR (1998c) took the proverbial bull by the horns in October 1998, petitioning the FCC for a rule-making proceeding to make its system the DAB standard. Further, USADR applied for trademark status with the United States Patent and Trademark Office, claiming that it coined much of the terminology used in describing digital audio broadcasting, including IBOC, IBOC DAB, In-Band, On-Channel, IBOC2000R, and IBOC2000E. USADR contended that ownership of the names would help alleviate confusion about DAB within the industry. USADR wanted to prevent competitors from using DAB terminology that had become commonplace. If approved, "IBOC DAB" could no longer be used generically. Eventually, USADR decided to call its technology iDAB.

USADR (1998b) asked for a 12-year transition period to allow analog broadcasting to be phased out, disrupting consumers and stations as little as possible. If IBOC worked as promised, CEMA believed that it was possible that DAB would be implemented within two or three years. Otherwise, governmental intervention could delay DAB for years. There was tremendous potential for Amstereoization of DAB. LDR and DRE were not happy with USADR's premature filing (Anderson, 1998b). On November 6, 1998, the FCC called for comments by December 23 from broadcasters and other interested parties. Robert J. Struble, USADR president, was "gratified that the FCC is moving quickly to develop rules and procedures for implementing DAB" (USADR, 1998d).

Despite USADR's aggressive move, some people were not as enthusiastic. There were broadcasters who never wanted full digital, preferring a hybrid analog/digital system. McLane (1998) explained: "The logic: most listeners own multiple radios—in their living room, bedroom, bathroom, workshop, car and office. When we replace radio with a digital-only system, those receivers will be obsolete. Consumers might buy one new digital receiver, but they are unlikely to buy four or five. Once the listener gets accustomed to not having radio in the bathroom or garage, the argument goes, they might not come back. Other media will serve them, and radio loses ground" (p. 4). Arnold (1999) added: "There has been a feeling, not just in broadcasting, but throughout the entire nation that anything that is more than a few years old is bad. Well, sorry guys—that isn't so. Will there continue to be digital improvements? Undoubtedly. But there's no reason to 'throw the baby out with the bath water' " (p. 5). Without regard to making analog TV sets obsolete, the FCC did set a deadline for DTV conversion. Why should radio be different? As with radio receivers, consumers have multiple TV sets. The only difference is that TV sets cost more to replace than radio receivers. Twelve years appeared to be a sufficient transition period and was twice the time given for DTV conversion.

NRSC's DAB Subcommittee released its laboratory *System Test Guidelines*, consisting of more than 60 pages, on December 3, 1998. The DAB Subcommittee was also devising guidelines for field testing. Testing would not be comparative, as the systems of USADR, DRE, and LDR would be evaluated and results released. Upon release of the information, anyone could compare the results and draw his or her own conclusions. The FCC, for example, would probably compare the data before making a decision. Milford "Smitty" Smith, Greater Media Inc. radio engineering VP and DAB Subcommittee head, said that testing was purely voluntary. Any proponent could participate or send its own data to the FCC, which was not necessarily dependent on the NRSC's DAB work. Smith thought that "the commission would welcome the NRSC ultimately recommending a system or systems to it, although we have not decided to do that yet" ("Smitty": A radio career, 1999, p. 14). As with DTV and MTS, Smith believed that the FCC wanted a standard IBOC DAB system recommended to it. However, he did not foresee a situation, at least in the near future, like DTV's Grand Alliance, in which proponents worked together on one system. Some thought that would happen when USADR and Lucent joined forces. Smith stated: "The real question here is not what system is the best, but are any of them good enough. . . . The goals and objectives of the DAB subcommittee is that this should be something that is demonstratively better than the existing AM and FM service. At the same time it (should) not cause undue degradation or interference of the existing analog service. That is really the big hurdle" (p. 16).

As 1998 ended, there was still no DAB solution in the United States. In Europe and Canada, there was a de facto DAB system in place, but there were few receivers and even less consumer clamor. Although USADR had petitioned the FCC to begin a rule-making proceeding, no action had been taken. Both DRE and LDR also planned petitions but believed that USADR's was premature. SDARS was preparing for its launch, so its impact on the broadcast industry remained unknown. Lucent Technologies' Suren Pai believed that the next important step for IBOC was not in development but in government approval. He said: "The question is how quickly the regulatory process moves along to get a standard established and put in place . . . because ultimately, standards are a key gating factor in the deployment of IBOC" (Stimson, 1999d, p. 8).

USADR Incorporates

In January 1999 a number of large U.S. radio groups invested in USADR to make it a corporation. No specific dollar figure for the deal was given, but USADR president Robert Struble said it was in the "tens of millions of dollars" (Stimson, 1999a, p. 1). Originally initiated in 1991 as a partnership of CBS, Westinghouse Electric, and Gannett, the new list of USADR owners included Emmis Communications, Clear Channel Communications, Cox Radio, Cumulus Media, Heftel Broadcasting, Entercom Communications, Chancellor Media, Jacor Communications, Citadel Communications, Radio One, Sinclair Broadcast Group, and Chase Capital Partners (investment firm). Among the 12 companies were nine of the top 10 U.S. broadcasting groups, which accounted for 1,628 stations taking in about $5.4 billion per year. They covered 207 million listeners in 192 of 267 Arbitron-rated markets, including 49 of the top 50 (USADR, 1999a). The new corporate status of USADR was important in showing that the U.S. broadcasting elite believed in IBOC DAB. As a result, other broadcasters and electronics manufacturers were expected to fall into line. With AM stereo, a number of broadcasters proposed banding together to support one of the five competing systems but were not allowed because it would violate antitrust laws. USADR was not a company like Magnavox, Harris, Belar, Motorola, or Kahn but was a corporation of investors working to produce a DAB system and not merely to promote one manufacturer's system.

USADR (1999b) announced its Board of Directors on March 11, 1999. They were James E. de Castro, president, Chancellor Media Radio Group; Daniel S. Ehrman Jr., VP, Gannett Co., Inc.; Mel Karmazin, president and CEO, CBS Corporation and Infinity Broadcasting Corp.; Al Kenyon, VP, engineering, Jacor Communications; Alfred C. Liggins III, president and CEO, Radio One, Inc.; Robert J. Struble, president, CEO, and chairman, USADR; and Farid Suleman, executive, Infinity Broadcasting Corporation. USADR said that the Board of Directors would provide strategic direction in development, field testing, and implementation of IBOC technology.

Responses to USADR's Petition

The Commission received a mixed bag of replies to USADR's DAB petition. Broadcasters as a whole did not embrace IBOC, believing that it may interfere with existing signals. Some supported IBOC but urged the FCC to delay selection of a standard system. Others opposed use of AM/FM spectrum for DAB and supported Eureka-147. DRE and LDR compared their systems to USADR's, citing the superiority of their own. NPR said that "there is no basis for concluding at this time that IBOC, as opposed to some other system of digital audio broadcasting, is in the public interest" (Stimson, 1999b, p. 3). USADR's support came primarily from its investors. Bonneville International Corp. reminded the FCC about the perils of Amstereoization: "The commission's prior experience with AM stereo reflects that a more open-ended approach will delay rather than expedite the introduction of digital radio technology in local markets. In addition, a unified terrestrial DAB standard is necessary to provide consumers and equipment manufacturers with the certainty required to encourage marketplace acceptance" (p. 14). CEMA agreed with USADR that terrestrial DAB was in the public interest but, as a supporter of Eureka-147, believed that terrestrial service should not be IBOC (p. 14).

Asked about their preferences for DAB delivery, receiver manufacturers attending the 1999 CES in Las Vegas wanted a single system standard approved for terrestrial DAB and SDARS (Stimson, 1999c). Without standards, consumers would be left in confusion, as with AM stereo. In an age when many—if not most—consumers still have trouble setting clocks and programming for VCRs, how would they be expected to select a DAB receiver on their own?

AM and FM radio faced formidable competition from more than DAB or DARS. Automobile receivers, long associated with radio-only reception and tape or CD players, were being designed to do far more. Navigation systems and DVD players were already available, although not yet built into receiver units. Computers and Internet connections, along with graphics, were being planned. One car stereo with the capability for downloading music from the Internet was shipped to retailers in March 1999. The Empeg receiver and recorder carried a suggested retail price of $999. As with computers, the consumer could purchase units with more memory for higher prices. The FM-only receiver was not capable of connecting to the Internet from the car but could be pulled from the vehicle and plugged into a PC for loading music (Techweek, 1999).

In March 1999 LDR began testing its IBOC system over two New Jersey stations: WPST-FM in Trenton and WBJB-FM at Brookdale Community College in Lincroft. The sites were convenient, since LDR was based in nearby Warren, New Jersey. Tony Gervasi, WPST-FM engineering VP, saw DAB "as high-definition radio." He said: "High-definition TV has revolutionized what a TV station is going to be able to do. Radio should have the same capabilities" (Stimson, 1999e, p. 10). Gervasi believed that DAB had to offer more than "CD-quality radio," because "if the only thing we're going to do is take them from FM quality to CD quality, we're wasting our signal" (p. 10).

DAB "Grand Alliance"? At NAB's annual Las Vegas meeting in April 1999, some broadcasters and manufacturers called for a "Grand Alliance" like DTV's. USADR, LDR, and DRE agreed to set a voluntary deadline for submitting lab and field-test data to the NRSC by December 15, 1999. Derek Kumar, DRE VP for engineering, said that his company would support a Grand Alliance: "We support anything that brings IBOC to a conclusion faster. If that's a contribution on behalf of all the proponents through a single melting pot . . . if that makes the reality that everybody can sign up for as opposed to one segment of the industry, or somebody in a market-leading position, then I think it's a good thing" (Stimson, 1999f, p. 8). LDR's Suren Pai said his company wanted a single standard, but "there are multiple ways to approach a standard" because "a standard essentially means there's going to be one technology that you will adopt" (p. 8). USADR's Robert Struble accurately stated that as a coalition from the beginning, USADR was the Grand Alliance (p. 8).

To expedite IBOC, USADR (1999c) announced on April 19, 1999, its EASE program to help smaller broadcasters have access to DAB technical and business expertise. USADR would assess and advise stations about what equipment and preparations would be needed for conversion. There was no charge, but USADR's objective was clearly to give immediate access of its system to participants. In June USADR reached an agreement with Kenwood Corp. to develop IBOC broadcast receivers. Kenwood said that its receivers would be on the market within about one year of the setting of an IBOC DAB standard.

In mid-1999 Mexican officials entered negotiations with the FCC in regard to S-band. Both Mexico and the United States planned to use portions of S-band at 2310 MHz to 2360 MHz. At the heart of the negotiations was elimination of interference. Mexico planned to use S-band in lieu of L-band to reach remote areas. Further, it meant an opportunity for United States satellite interests to sell subscription services in Mexico, which by law permitted foreign infrastructure investments of up to 49 percent (Plata, 1999).

SDARS: Sirius and XM

In 1999 CD Radio, Inc. changed its name to Sirius Satellite Radio (Sirius). Ira Bahr, marketing VP, said: "As we approach the consumer launch of our service we recognized there was an opportunity to create a stronger, clearer brand name. The old name had some confusing and limiting aspects to it. The new name and logo will be enduring, valuable and distinctive" (New name for CD Radio, 1999, p. 8). A year earlier, SDARS proponent AMRC changed its name to XM Satellite Radio (XM). Hugh Panero, president and CEO, explained: "First there was AM, then FM and now XM Satellite Radio. Our new name represents the next band of radio and the future of the industry" (p. 8). Both organizations, which planned to begin service in 2001, were busy signing SDARS licensing agreements with receiver manufacturers. GM and Ford planned to install SDARS receivers in automobiles in 2001. GM aligned with XM to produce AM/FM/XM receivers, and Ford signed with Sirius to make AM/FM/CD radios. Other Sirius receiver manufacturers were Recoton, Jensen, and Delphi-Delco. Clear Channel Communications Inc., a major investor in USADR, invested $75 million in XM, while GM invested $50 million. XM had other receiver alignments with Pioneer, Alpine, Sharp, and Delphi-Delco (Stimson, 1999g).

Both XM and Sirius licensed LDR's PAC compression scheme. It was a step toward achieving interoperability between XM and Sirius receivers. The companies began to work cooperatively, and both set their sights on competing with traditional radio. They were particularly interested in targeting commuters, truckers, and travelers.

XM and Sirius expected to begin services in 2001. AM/FM/Satellite receiver costs were estimated at about $200. Subscriptions would cost $9.95 per month. XM's Lee Abrams observed: "In 1970, most radios were AM.

Then FM started getting some decent programming on it, with rock formats and beautiful music, and by 1974 you couldn't find an AM radio. Everything was AM and FM. I see the same pattern happening now" (McLane, 2000, p. 4). There was a difference, however, in that FM was free. It remained to be seen if consumers would pay for SDARS. Sirius and XM would offer about 100 channels each for about $10 per month.

Canadian SDARS Concerns. Pioneer Electronics, which was producing digital receivers for Canada, was concerned about the rapid development of SDARS in the United States. Pioneer was most upset about the lack of DAB progress in Canada and was concerned that the slow rollout would allow SDARS to gain a foothold with Canadian consumers. Pioneer's Peter Cos believed that DAB was going to turn out like satellite television. It was illegal for U.S. SDARS to vend in Canada, but with satellite TV, in excess of 200,000 Canadians found a way to get DirecTV illegally.

Canadian DAB was certainly in the throes of Amstereoization. Canadian broadcasters had not forgotten how badly AM stereo failed in their country, and they were not eager to repeat the experience with DAB. Also like AM stereo, Canadians knew nothing about DAB. It was the chicken and egg all over again, as broadcasters would not implement DAB without receivers, and manufacturers would not produce receivers without DAB transmission. Pioneer, as the most aggressive marketer of DAB in Canada, had invested a lot in the technology. Other DAB receiver manufacturers included Kenwood, Grundig, Bosch, and Sony, but none were pushing the technology like Pioneer. Pioneer's competitors were watching the situation closely (Careless, 1999).

Noting discrepancies in test results, LDR called for NRSC to conduct common testing of its system and those of USADR and DRE. DAB testing was primarily being conducted by the companies and at different sites. Common testing meant using the same labs and stations for testing. There were no common standards being applied. Further, direct comparisons were not being made between systems, but between digital and analog. NRSC's DAB Subcommittee planned to take common testing under consideration, but some quarters accused LDR of delaying an extremely tardy process. Meanwhile, each of the IBOC proponents continued its own separate testing procedures to meet the December 15 NRSC deadline agreed upon by all three companies. Upon evaluation of the results, NRSC would make a recommendation to the FCC. However, it was not certain that LDR would submit data without a common testing agreement (Stimson, 1999h).

The DAB NPRM

On November 1, 1999, the FCC (1999b) opened its NPRM for DAB, writing, "DAB technology has the potential to significantly enhance the American radio broadcast service." The purpose for the NPRM was "to consider

alternative approaches to introducing DAB service to the American public."
The FCC acknowledged that it was motivated to open the proceeding due to
"the progress" of IBOC, which is "designed to allow the simultaneous broadcast of analog and digital radio signals in the AM and FM bands without disrupting existing analog service."

The FCC (1999b) cautioned: "IBOC DAB systems have not been conclu-
sively proven to be technically viable at this point in time, yet great strides
have been made and the systems certainly hold real promise. It is helpful for
the Commission to determine whether an IBOC model and/or a model utilizing new radio spectrum would be the best means of promptly introducing
DAB service in the United States. By initiating this proceeding now, we can
foster the further development of IBOC systems, as well as new-spectrum
DAB alternatives, help DAB system proponents identify design issues of public interest dimension and, where possible, encourage modifications that advance these policy objectives." The FCC (1999b) promised "to be in a
position to act expeditiously when the time is ripe." Of course, the Commission had promised the exact same thing in 1990.

The FCC (1999b) maintained its belief in IBOC's great promise and how
it "may be able to facilitate a seamless transition to an all-digital radio broadcast environment by affording all broadcasters a concurrent digital and analog broadcast opportunity." The FCC cautioned: "Nevertheless, this Notice
should not be construed as the start of an IBOC rulemaking."

As typical, the FCC (1999b) documented DAB's background, referring
back to its initial proceeding in 1990. Although the Commission did not believe that IBOC was feasible at the time, it recognized that "existing radio
broadcasters can and should have the opportunity to take advantage of new
digital radio technologies." The FCC wanted to preserve localism but also
wanted to facilitate satellite DAB. Despite broadcasters' protests, the Commission "concluded that 'the record does not demonstrate that licensing
satellite DARS would have such a strong adverse impact that it threatens the
provision of local radio service.'" The FCC acknowledged that terrestrial and
satellite DAB "would compete to some extent," but "it found that the new
satellite DARS would complement existing, local radio broadcasting stations
by providing regional and national services."

The FCC (1999b) discussed the three IBOC system proponents, especially their incompatibility. As with AM stereo, each of the systems accomplished DAB delivery differently. The FCC said that there were "significant
differences" and referred to CEMA's 1997 final report, which concluded
that "IBOC systems tested exhibited two major deficiencies: (1) poor digital audio performance under impaired signal conditions; and (2) incompatibility with analog FM service." The FCC also cited CEMA's preference for
Eureka-147. However, IBOC proponents "contend that they have made
substantial progress towards developing technically viable IBOC systems."
The FCC referred to USADR's October 7, 1998, petition and also to pro-

ponents' reported agreement to submit test results to NRSC by the December 15, 1999, deadline.

Comments and Replies to USADR's Petition. The FCC (1999b) received 23 comments and six reply comments about USADR's petition, and they overwhelmingly supported DAB. IBOC was the preferred delivery method if "its compatibility with existing analog service is demonstrated" during lab and field tests. Otherwise, an IBOC decision would be premature. CEMA and NPR asked for consideration of NB and Eureka-147, but other "commenters generally agreed with USADR that a single DAB transmission standard ultimately will be required to ensure a successful transition to digital." AM stereo was evoked by some commenters as evidence for needing a DAB transmission standard, arguing that "a single standard is necessary to provide the certainty that consumers, licensees and equipment manufacturers would need to justify their investment in DAB technology." Further, "a number of commenters cited the Commission's adoption of a DTV transmission standard as precedent for a similar action in this proceeding."

As it had been nine years since the FCC opened its initial DAB proceeding, the FCC (1999b) wanted "to set forth the public policy objectives that will guide our deliberations in this proceeding." First, the Commission cited its "settled determination that fostering the development and implementation of terrestrial DAB is in the public interest." It continued: "We believe that the principles advanced by the Commission in Docket No. 90-357 regarding the terrestrial radio broadcast service remain valid, and will look to them in developing our approach to a terrestrial DAB service." The overriding goals were "to provide vastly improved radio service to the public" and "to authorize a DAB service that permits broadcasters and listeners to realize fully the superior technical performance capabilities of this technology." The FCC (1999b) wanted existing broadcasters to introduce DAB and used DTV as an example of implementing new technology "within the existing framework of local television broadcasting." It was "the best way to preserve the unique benefits of the local television broadcast service," and "existing television broadcasters were the group best suited to introduce this new service to the public 'in the quickest and most efficacious manner.' We believe that the same reasoning applies here."

The FCC (1999b) wanted a DAB system to be "spectrum efficient" and "to foster a rapid and nondisruptive transition to DAB for broadcasters and listeners." The FCC said that it "will favor systems that do not require burdensome investments in new broadcast transmission equipment" and that "make it possible for manufacturers to produce reasonably-priced digital receivers." The Commission listed 10 evaluative criteria, listed in no particular order, and solicited comment: "(1) enhanced audio fidelity; (2) robustness to interference and other signal impairments; (3) compatibility with existing analog service; (4) spectrum efficiency; (5) flexibility; (6) auxiliary capacity; (7) extensibility; (8) accommodation for existing broadcasters; (9) coverage;

and (10) implementation costs/affordability of equipment." The Commission recognized the potential benefit of setting "a fixed analog 'sunset' date" for analog to cease as it had with DTV. However, differences between the LDR and USADR systems could impact its decision making. The FCC said that USADR's "all-digital mode transmissions could interfere with an adjacent channel station transmitting an analog signal." Therefore, a "system that permits stations to implement rapidly an all-digital radio service may serve the public interest better than one that delays the opportunity to fully realize the benefits of DAB until the end of what is likely to be an extended transition period."

IBOC would not require new spectrum, which would be "administratively efficient," but the FCC (1999b) was concerned about inefficient spectrum use of "current IBOC system designs . . . premised on doubling the bandwidth licensed to AM and FM stations to 20 kHz and 400 kHz, respectively, spectrum which is currently included under current 'emission masks.' " The Commission added: "A permanent expansion of the channel bandwidth might constitute a fundamental change in spectrum assignment principles." As an alternative, the FCC would consider allocating new spectrum: "Now, with the completion of the plan for the introduction of DTV, we believe that it may be possible to use a portion of the television spectrum for DAB." The Commission solicited "comment on whether the six megahertz of spectrum at 82-88 MHz, currently used for TV Channel 6, could be reallocated to DAB service at the end of the DTV transition" and "without adversely affecting the broadcast television service." Of course, Channel 6 allocation could significantly delay DAB because "the earliest this spectrum will be available in many areas is 2007." Interestingly, the FCC admitted that DTV's transition "could be significantly later." The FCC also noted that "IBOC and new-spectrum DAB options need not be mutually exclusive and, in fact, could be complementary." The FCC (1999b) used its DTV proceeding to explain its regulatory model:

In the DTV proceeding, we observed that the traditional rationale for mandating a standard arises when two conditions are met: first, there would be a substantial public benefit from a standard; second, private industry either will not, or cannot, achieve a standard because the private costs of participating in the standard-setting process outweigh the private benefits, or a number of different standards have been developed and private industry cannot reach consensus on a single standard. The Commission, in fact, did identify the same kind of considerations in support of adopting a mandatory DTV standard that commenters now argue support the adoption of a mandatory DAB transmission standard. We noted that mandated standards might provide needed certainty to consumers, licensees, and equipment manufacturers, particularly where the launch of a new technology is involved. Moreover, we reasoned that standard-setting would help obviate the "chicken and egg" dilemma that can impede the introduction and acceptance of new technology and impose additional costs on consumers. We also recognized, however, that mandatory standards can have drawbacks, including potential deterrence of technical innovation—particularly where a technology is new and further development can reasonably be anticipated to occur—and curtailment of some forms of competition.

Much of the FCC's (1999b) DAB NPRM focused on testing procedures. The Commission applauded NRSC and CEMA for their efforts and said that it would ask them for further assistance in facilitating and evaluating IBOC system development. The FCC asked "each proponent to submit a copy of its test reports to the Commission as part of the record in this proceeding" but also saw "merit in a second stage of comparative testing of IBOC systems on a common testing platform." The Commission reaffirmed "that it is necessary and appropriate to rely to some degree on the expertise of the private sector for DAB system evaluations and, ultimately, recommendations for a transmission standard." The FCC concluded with a call for comments and reply comments within 75 days of the NPRM's publication date.

USADR was more enthusiastic with the NPRM than was LDR. USADR's Struble said: "We're ecstatic. They clearly stated that digital audio broadcasting is in the public interest and laid out criteria for quickly evaluating the technology" (McConnell, 1999b, p. 20). LDR was concerned that the FCC's consideration of non-IBOC DAB would cause senseless delay of DAB (p. 20).

USADR and DRE Combine Forces

In a somewhat surprising turn of events, DRE announced on December 14, 1999, that it would cease development of its IBOC system to back USADR's cause. DRE received a percentage of USADR stock and would develop certain data applications for USADR's system. IBOC was one step, albeit a large one, from a Grand Alliance. NRSC chairperson Charles Morgan admitted that the deal would relieve some of NRSC's testing burden but cautioned against unfettered optimism. He stated: "My opinion was we should wait until both systems are fully developed, and put them both on the table, so that people can look at them. Then would be the right time for an alliance *if* an alliance is proper" (Stimson, 2000a, p. 1).

Harris Corporation was excited about the USADR and DRE alliance. Harris, as one of the five AM stereo system proponents, knew all too well the pitfalls of not setting standards. Jim Woods (2000), Harris VP, stated:

Most in the industry remember that AM stereo—a development that offered significant benefits to radio broadcasters and their listeners, ultimately was derailed by a battle of egos and dueling standards. If this happens to IBOC Digital Radio, everyone will lose, from radio suppliers to broadcasters themselves. We simply cannot afford to repeat the AM stereo debacle—a debacle that would put us at risk of relinquishing our right to define the future of over-the-air radio in a manner that benefits our listeners and extends the brand identity that local radio broadcasters have worked to develop. (p. 3)

Woods called for an IBOC Grand Alliance and suggested DTV as a model: "Working together, U.S. DTV proponents not only managed to reconcile technical differences, but they managed to do so quickly and effectively—together" (p. 3).

Only USADR met NRSC's December 15, 1999, deadline to submit IBOC field and lab test information. DRE submitted no data because of its alliance with USADR. As expected, LDR withheld data, presumably to make its point in favor of common system testing.

Meanwhile, on January 3, 2000, Canada finally began its long-predicted DAB broadcasts into the United States. Four stations in Windsor, Ontario, just across the border from Detroit, initiated DAB simulcasting. The stations, owned by CHUM Ltd., were CKLW-AM, CKWW-AM, CIMX-FM, and CIDR-FM. By June 2000 the stations were breaking even economically and combined for a 5.8 percent total share of the Detroit market (Careless, 2000).

On January 24, 2000, USADR and DRM (2000), a global broadcasting consortium, announced a working agreement to develop and promote an AM DAB standard. Peter Senger, DRM chairman, said: "Our aim is to ensure that a receiver bought anywhere in the world will work anywhere in the world. Just as important, is ensuring that the transition from analog to digital is as smooth and as low-cost as possible both for the industry and the billions of listeners around the globe. We warmly welcome the opportunity of working with USA Digital Radio. Developing a digital standard for the market worldwide has always been DRM's primary objective." Both Sirius and XM were preparing to deliver SDARS programming by the end of 2000. Sirius launched its first satellite on June 30, 2000 and sent up two more in September and October. XM's first satellite launch was scheduled for November 2000 with others to follow in early 2001. Both XM and Sirius pointed to consumers' dissatisfaction with traditional radio, particularly the overabundance of commercials, inferior signal quality, and lack of programming choices. The FCC required XM and Sirius to build an SDARS receiver capable of receiving both services, but it would not be ready until 2004. The companies had no plans to merge, and neither expected to earn anything for at least five years (Rathbun, 2000). A *Radio World* editorial stated SDARS's launch "should be a wake-up call for those who wonder whether terrestrial radio needs a digital system" (DAB: Radio gets iBiquitous, 2000, p. 62).

Apparently prompted by the growing threat to terrestrial IBOC DAB by SDARS, the on-again/off-again relationship between USADR and LDR took another turn. On August 23, 2000, USADR (2000) and LDR announced an agreement to join efforts in developing a single IBOC DAB system. The DOJ and FTC approved the merger. The system produced by the newly formed iBiquity Digital Corporation would include LDR's PAC audio compression technology. FCC Commissioner Kennard said his Commission would promote IBOC DAB. He explained: "It's very much in our plans. We need to make sure the broadcast industry moves from the analog to the digital age. We're going to do everything we can to facilitate that. It's not an easy question, though, because the IBOC technology is new. It's fair to say a lot of questions have not yet been resolved" (Stimson, 2000b, p. 7). Indeed, there appeared to be continuing doubt among some FCC engineers that IBOC DAB could work on AM and FM. Neither iBiquity nor the FCC offered a timetable for an IBOC DAB solution.

Do Broadcasters and Consumers Want DAB?

Neither broadcasters nor consumers seemed particularly disturbed over DAB's slow progress. As with other technologies, DAB would experience a transition period until saturation could be achieved, during which both analog and digital radio signals would be available. An analog-to-digital transition period was expected to last 10 to 15 years after DAB approval, but broadcasters could keep their listener base intact during the transition. DAB would initially cost more than analog. Depending on how much upgrading had been done over the years, station conversion could cost from $20,000 to $200,000.

Receivers would cost about 10–15 percent more, but consumers would not immediately discard old receivers for new ones. The automobile industry has typically embraced new radio technology, but it would take perhaps half a decade to get DAB receivers into new cars after the setting of a standard. It would take about two years to get DAB receivers to store shelves.

Of course, nothing would happen at all until the FCC made a decision on DAB. Despite USADR's request to set a DAB standard by September 2000, there was no clue as to what the FCC might do. As radio broadcasters waited for a decision, TV broadcasters moved ahead with DTV.

Chapter 6

❖ ❖

Advanced Television from HDTV to DTV

Since the 1980s there has been a movement to improve U.S. television. Various attempts have been called ATV, SDTV, IDTV, UDTV, EDTV, DTV, and HDTV.

Attempts to improve TV video and audio are not new. GE broadcast the first television programs at 30 lines of resolution in 1928. On January 14, 1935, Britain's Television Committee set its country's standard at a minimum of 240 lines of resolution (30 frames per second). The British postmaster general raised the standard to 405 lines (25 frames per second) on February 4, 1937. Europe has two incompatible terrestrial standards—PAL and SECAM—both with 625 lines and 50 cycles. Other than France, which uses SECAM, PAL is employed in Western Europe, China, and most of the world other than North and Central America, Japan, and South Korea. PAL was developed in the 1960s by Germany's Telefunken to eliminate color problems experienced in long transmission links. By 1939 U.S. broadcasts contained 441 lines (30 frames per second). The NTSC U.S. standard of 525 was set in 1941. Like the United States, Japan employs the NTSC system but uses a different stereo standard than the United States

DEVELOPMENT AND EVOLUTION OF U.S. HDTV

The new digital audio/video standard approved for United States TV is the third major enhancement since NTSC established its standard in 1941. The first was color in 1954, and the second was MTS in 1984.

Although DTV and HDTV are frequently used interchangeably, they are different. DTV means that video, audio, and other auxiliary services are in digital form. When the ATV process started in the late 1980s, broadcasters were excited at the prospect of an analog system with 1,125 lines of resolution—

more than double NTSC's 525 lines. However, the FCC's pursuit of digital delivery "retired the 1125 analog system, not by mandating a specific alternative production standard, but by effectively insisting on digital processing" (Fadden, 1998, p. 30).

In the beginning, the FCC preferred the term ATV, meaning that spectrum could be used to broadcast extra SDTV channels, HDTV, or other digital services. When digital technology was introduced, the FCC changed from ATV to DTV. DTV can be HDTV or SDTV, but not all DTV is HDTV. HDTV refers to six operating modes of the DTV system supporting CD-quality sound, higher resolution video with a wide-screen 16:9 aspect ratio image, and scanning at 1,080 or 720 lines. Twelve other DTV modes produce SDTV that, with its lower-resolution scanning at 480 lines, is comparable to NTSC video. SDTV is a subcategory of the ATSC's HDTV proposal. Broadcasters' interest was piqued because several SDTV programs can be broadcast in spectrum space used by a single HDTV program (Ranada, 1999).

Definition refers to the quantity of visible detail that one can see on the television screen and to the quality of audio working in concert with the picture. DTV's picture contains up to five times the detail and 10 times the color information of analog signals. McConnell (1995e) wrote: "If a 'standard definition' picture is worth a thousand words, a high definition picture is a Russian novel" (p. 36). Its 16:9 widescreen aspect ratio, a cinema-like format, is one-third wider than 4:3 screens. Audio is CD quality Dolby Digital. HDTV's picture has "the liveness or presence of video with the resolution and subtlety of 35-mm film" (Davies, 1990, p. 34), but some DTV experts claim that 35-mm film production quality cannot be replaced by video. Although each offers advantages, the medium of choice would depend on the result that one seeks to achieve.

FCC's ATV Rule-making Proceeding

At the request of broadcasters, the FCC (1990c) inaugurated its ATV rule-making proceeding in 1987, stating:

ATV refers to any television technology that provides improved audio and video quality or enhances the current television broadcast system known as NTSC. The generic term "ATV" includes High Definition Television (HDTV) systems. HDTV systems aim to offer approximately twice the vertical and horizontal resolution of NTSC receivers and to provide picture quality approaching that of 35 mm film and audio quality equal to that of compact discs. The Commission has previously decided that an ATV system that transmits the increased information of an ATV signal in a separate 6 MHz channel independent from an existing NTSC channel will allow for ATV introduction in the most non-disruptive and efficient manner.

FCC chairman Dennis Patrick preferred the term "higher resolution television" but cautioned: "There is no Holy Grail at the end of this search.

There is no definitive HDTV, high resolution TV, high-definition TV. We're talking about a series of tradeoffs. How clear is a clear picture? How good is good enough? It is an extraordinarily complex question that involves trade-offs not just for the body politic, but for broadcasters as well" (Classic Patrick, 1989, p. 32).

Patrick's marketplace approach to broadcast regulation was similar to that of his predecessor, Mark Fowler. Rather than pick a standard, leave it to the marketplace. If it works, it works; if it fails, it fails. The FCC accepted no responsibility for a technology's success or failure. By setting technical parameters, a better system could always emerge. Patrick formed the ACATS to research HDTV and to recommend a system. He appointed former FCC chair Richard Wiley as head. Patrick said that it was "absolutely essential" to pick an evolution-friendly HDTV standard and suggested that "win-win solutions are achievable by resorting to marketplace decision-making" (FCC's 'blue ribbon,' 1989, p. 75).

Obviously bowing to tremendous HDTV interest, the Commission was far more willing to work with industry toward a solution than it had with AM stereo. Commissioner Ervin Duggan, a marketplace supporter, said that AM stereo proved "that sometimes the marketplace needs our help with standard-setting" (Lambert, 1993c, p. 94). Duggan realized that both TV broadcasters and consumers needed time to evaluate HDTV and to implement it. He believed that consumers "deserve to be the ultimate arbiters" (p. 94).

Concerned about the United States lagging behind Japan and Europe, Congress considered several HDTV bills in 1989, but only one made it from committee. Congress considered suspending "industry antitrust regulations for cooperative efforts by companies on high technologies such as HDTV research and development" (Gatski, 1990a, p. 1), a consideration never given to AM stereo proponents. Legal threats and antitrust laws squelched efforts by broadcasters who wanted to establish an AM stereo consensus. Congress also focused on tax break incentives and seed money. Congress passed no part of the bill, and Congresswoman Helen Bentley (R-MD) claimed that Japan pressured the Bush administration to back off on HDTV. Others attributed Congress' vacillation to consumers' disinterest in HDTV.

NBC, Cablevision Systems Corp., Hughes Communications, the News Corp., and Rupert Murdoch joined forces in early 1990 to deliver HDTV via DBS. Although Japan and Europe had used DBS for HDTV delivery, United States plans were strictly terrestrial. DBS promised more than 100 channels of digital video and audio. Terrestrial HDTV proponents showed little concern, but it was evident that DBS sparked an urgency (Carter & Gatski, 1990). Richard Wiley said that ACATS would not be swayed to "have a rush to judgment," and his job was "to keep the spurs down" (Getting down, 1990, p. 8). Wiley said that there was no firm schedule for testing systems but believed that it would happen quickly. His committee was considering proposals by Zenith and an unnamed proponent to consider widening the screen but was uncertain if "that should be a part of the overall HDTV process" (p. 8). Wiley said that a hybrid system suggested by "the private sector" and utilizing positive aspects of various systems would be considered (p. 9).

ATRC

Motivated by the rapid pace of emerging technology, several major players announced on January 25, 1990, that they would join forces to establish an HDTV system standard. North American Philips agreed to work with ACTV systems cosponsors NBC, Thomson Consumer Electronics, and David Sarnoff Research Center. Known as ATRC, they sought to develop a simulcast system broadcasting two separate signals, as opposed to pursuing previous plans for an augmentation system. Simulcasting meant that one signal would be sent as HDTV, and the other as NTSC, allowing a transition period until such time that all signals would be HDTV. Augmentation meant that HDTV and NTSC would be broadcast over two channels, but the system did not allow for total HDTV conversion. Until their agreement, North American Philips and others had disagreed on augmentation and simulcasting. North American Philips preferred augmentation and had been captious of NBC and Sarnoff's predilection for a gradual transition to HDTV through simulcasting. North American Philips wanted immediate conversion to HDTV. The consortium was a major step toward making HDTV a reality, and it was hoped that other proponents would join them (Gerson, 1990; Struzzi, 1990).

The first step in selecting a standard was testing, but the proponents were not ready, and testing equipment was still under development (Stilson & Pagano, 1990). Proponents' lack of readiness hinged on GI's introduction of an all-digital system, which Wiley believed "caused many proponents to go back to the drawing board to review their plans and maybe find out that they also could go to a digital form" (HDTV transmission, 1990, p. 52). As the future would prove, waiting for the digital system was a good decision.

Wiley would attempt to meet the FCC's September 30, 1992, testing deadline but admitted that "the timetable has slipped quite a bit" (p. 54). From 23 ATV system proposals before the FCC in 1987, just six remained: ACTV/Sarnoff Research Center (analog EDTV system); Narrow-MUSE/ NJK/Japan Broadcasting Corp. (HDTV analog simulcast system); Digital Simulcast HDTV/ATRC (digital HDTV simulcast system); DigiCipher/GI Corp. (digital HDTV simulcast system); Spectrum Compatible HDTV/ Zenith Electronics (HDTV simulcast analog/digital hybrid system); Channel-Compatible HDTV/MIT Electronics (HDTV simulcast analog/digital hybrid system). Wiley cautioned:

Now, keep in mind, these proponents are fundamentally different. You know, the television set today is made up of 525 lines, and it's read every other line. So you're really getting about 260 lines out of the television set today. The theory of high-definition television is to double the lines of resolution, either by reading 525 progressively, or doubling the number of lines to 1,050, or maybe 1,250, or what have you. These systems have different formats. Some of them are, for example, 1,125 lines, and some of them are 787 lines; some of them are 525 with every line being read. Well, you're comparing apples, oranges and bananas, basically. That's not easy. (Stilson & Pagano, 1990, p. 54)

Wiley agreed that a standard would be necessary for successful HDTV, but even then success would not happen overnight. An indefinite transition period would be necessary. As Wiley put it: "We're not all going to suddenly go out and buy high-definition television sets" (p. 55).

Meanwhile, the ATTC proceeded with HDTV testing plans. The first step was to build a suitable testing plant. The facility was scheduled for completion in April 1990 and would be capable of testing one system while setting up or breaking down another. Each proponent would be assigned office space adjacent to the laboratories. Peter M. Fannon, ATTC executive director, said: "Until you test, frankly, everything else is PR" (Blinder, 1990a, p. 21).

DTV Spectrum

The FCC hoped to implement HDTV with minimal disruption to broadcasters. On September 6, 1990, the FCC (1990c) announced that it would "select a 'simulcast'" HDTV system employing "design principles independent of the existing NTSC technology." Simulcast meant that a program would be broadcast simultaneously on the original NTSC channel and the newly assigned HDTV channel. Chairman Al Sikes said that simulcasting was in consumers' best interest: "In part [simulcasting] developed because of the view that some years down the road broadcasters will put much higher value on what they are doing on their advanced television channel and might then cut back on their NTSC channel and prematurely leave consumers in a lurch. We are not intending to create a new service. We are intending to give broadcasters a channel transitionally and the aggregates of those channels should then be used for emerging technologies in the future" (Beacham, 1992, p. 3).

Prior to digitalization, HDTV required even more spectrum space than the gluttonous NTSC signal. Loaded with about 10 times the data of NTSC, HDTV required twice as much space as NTSC (Behrens, 1986). Eventually, researchers found a way to reduce spectrum requirements by compressing or squeezing "a huge amount of digital data (20 million bits of information per second into existing 6-MHZ slices of broadcast spectrum)" (Horowitz, 1996, p. 104). Digital compression created more channel space, and many broadcasters preferred "flexible use," using the space to transmit multiple channels simultaneously to generate additional revenue (Beacham, 1995). One HDTV signal would take up an entire channel, but several lower-resolution digital channels could be substituted. Unlike analog, digital channels do not interfere with adjacent channels. After a transition period, stations would return their analog channel for auction or assignment elsewhere.

In July 1992 the FCC (1992a) announced four major goals in establishing an allotment table. First, the Commission maintained its plan to allocate a separate HDTV channel to NTSC broadcasters. Second, the FCC planned to assign all channels on UHF. Third, all HDTV channels would cover a radius of at least 55 miles. Fourth, in case of interference to NTSC signals, priority would always be given to HDTV. The FCC hoped to finalize its table in 1993 and "to maintain a flexible position with respect to new ATV developments that offer important new benefits and which are in a sufficiently concrete state of development to be considered with existing systems." The FCC would consider "any new systems that are sufficiently developed to be tested."

The problem for broadcasters was that other public and private services wanted the spectrum, such as DAB and PCS (So many new, 1991). Many new technologies look to UHF for spectrum, and DAB proponents were no exception. However, the MSTV argued bitterly against DAB allotment.

Congress and the White House noted the financial bonanza to be gained from selling spectrum and attempted to withdraw the additional channel proposal. They wanted to sell spectrum to raise money toward the federal deficit. Broadcasters, satellite companies, cable operators, the computer industry, consumer electronics, and Hollywood all fought for control of DTV (Barry, 1997). Congress used spectrum as leverage to get broadcasters started on DTV plans. Both the House Telecommunications Subcommittee and FCC chairman Sikes warned broadcasters to "plan to invest in an expedient transition to full high-definition television or risk losing proposed additional spectrum" (HDTV spectrum, 1991, p. 14). If broadcasters hesitated, the spectrum would be assigned elsewhere.

The FCC (1990c) wanted to phase in DTV by allowing broadcasting to continue on existing transmitters and receivers. HDTV would begin on new channels. As a result, the FCC left "open the possibility of adopting an EDTV system" compatible with NTSC sets providing "some but not all of the enhancements of HDTV" (FCC to take, 1990, p. 38). Sikes believed that there would be no reason for EDTV if HDTV were approved. Proponents believed that EDTV could ease the transition for consumers by providing "an economical bridge" to HDTV (Refined HDTV, 1990, p. 40).

Should the FCC opt for EDTV, such a procedure would not be unprecedented. The Commission had taken a similar approach with AM radio when it implemented NRSC standards in two distinct phases. However, the FCC was not keen on EDTV. Sikes stated: "We have not completely foreclosed future assessment of all enhanced television options. But I do think that any objective review of the record will show that the simulcast HDTV option we have pointed toward has greater public interest promise" (Slim chance, 1990, p. 26). Only two EDTV systems were proposed: Faroudja Laboratories' Super NTSC EDTV system and the David Sarnoff Research Center's ACTV system.

Faroudja withdrew its system when it missed the September 1, 1990, deadline for paying its testing fee. By early 1992, ACTV/Sarnoff had all but dropped its EDTV efforts in order to work toward a digital system (Betting, 1992).

Compatibility with existing equipment was an important consideration in standards proceedings. For a system to be selected, it needed to accommodate consumers' existing receivers. Just because the FCC allowed color television, most consumers could not immediately dispose of their monochrome sets. A color signal must be capable of reception by a black-and-white set—not in color but in black-and-white. The CBS color TV system was not compatible and failed, forcing the FCC to change standards. Stereo radio or television transmissions have always needed compatibility with existing receivers, but DTV presented an entirely different problem. Analog TV could not receive digital signals, so DTV meant no compatibility without a converter or a new set, making analog sets obsolete.

Digital Technology

The analog signal is "a continuously variable and varying signal" (Mirabito, 1994, p. 26). A digital signal "is not a continuously variable and varying signal" and "assumes only a finite number of discrete values" (p. 27). Digital is a computer language in which any kind of information is converted to zeros and ones, which are binary digits, or bits, and are the smallest pieces of video or sound information in a digital system. Upon conversion, the information "can be fed to and stored in computers as long strings of bits," known as "digital information" (Gates, Myhrvold, & Rinearson, 1995, pp. 23–24). Mannes (1991) explained: "An uncompressed, digitized HDTV signal might require more than *a billion* bits per second," and "storing those billion bits would require more than 80 3½-inch floppy disks" (p. 30).

Digital information delivered digitally is virtually unlimited, and the family TV set may be operated more like a multimedia computer (Doyle, 1992). MIT's Michael Bove said: "High-definition is the least interesting thing about the next generation of TV. The interesting part is that it will put a computer into your TV" (Rogers, 1993, p. 30). Broadcasters were not pleased to hear that computers might save U.S. television. George Gilder (1990), a major proponent of TV deregulation and computer entry into TV, believed that the "death of television" as we have known it "would be the salvation of American competitiveness" (p. 75). Gilder expected "leaders of United States electronic firms would rejoice at the news," but his "friends in the computer industry" were no more optimistic than their TV counterparts (pp. 75–76). The computer industry relented, but broadcasters did not.

Digital Compression. Compression, a major advantage of digital delivery over analog, is "the method by which only a portion of a video signal is transmitted, allowing a decoder on the receive end to reconstruct the full image" (Cole, 1992a, p. 51). Weiss (1992) elaborated:

Compression, as the term is applied to video images, takes advantage of two facts: 1. There is much in the images that is redundant (repeated, repetitive, superfluous, duplicated, exceeding what is necessary, etc.). 2. The human eye/brain combination has limitations to what it can perceive. By making use of these factors, it is possible to greatly reduce the amount of information that must be transmitted from a picture source (such as a camera) to a display (such as a television monitor or receiver) in order to convince the eye/brain combination that it is seeing an image of what the camera saw. (p. 35)

Compression made it easier for the FCC to locate extra channels for broadcasters because stations with similar coverage areas could be spaced closer together, meaning less interference than with analog. Mannes (1991) explained: "In a digital signal, theoretically, as long as the interference is below a certain threshold, the TV receiver will be able to restore a noisy signal to its proper modulation level. Even so, error correction is a significant part of a digital signal" (p. 30). Digital channels take up less space on satellite transponders, allowing cable and DBS deliverers to distribute more channels at lower costs with more diverse programming (Compression: Changing, 1990). It remains to be seen whether programming diversity will happen. Vladimir Zworykin, who along with Philo Farnsworth is considered a "Father of Television," contended that television's best feature was the on/off switch.

Compression's importance to DTV "is to reduce the quantity of information that must be transmitted from a picture source to a display" allowing "many applications that are not otherwise possible, either for technical or economic reasons" (Weiss, 1992, p. 35). Although "the search for an international [digital] standard has been likened to that for the Holy Grail," there has been some success (Goldberg, 1993, p. 100). The JPEG developed a compression standard for still photography, and the MPEG proposed a video standard. In both instances, "the amount of compression applied is up to the people who encode the signal" and that video is "digitized," and the process "is analogous to a photograph being projected through a fine screen, and each tiny square in the resulting mosaic or bitmap being assigned a value of 1 or 0 for 'on' or 'off'" (pp. 100–101). Not all video is compressed equally, so "MPEG intelligently decides which parts of a moving picture need to be compressed and which ones don't" (p. 101). MPEG "goes beyond JPEG and applies temporal compression in addition to spatial compression, and "MPEG-1 is generally used to compress relatively low-resolution pictures" (Fibish, 1995, p. 33). MPEG-2 "was devised primarily for delivery of compressed television for home entertainment" and "can be used to record or transmit studio-quality video in a manner more efficient than Motion-JPEG," meaning "higher picture quality at the same bit rate or equivalent picture quality at a lower bit rate" (p. 33).

Wide-Screen Aspect Ratios. The Working Group on High-Definition Electronic Production, established by the SMPTE, determined that a wider screen ratio of 16:9 would result in less waste of image space. A 16:9 ratio, at "exactly one-third wider than the 4x3 aspect ratio currently in use," was "the best compromise when all the many film and video formats that would be transmitted through the HDTV system were considered" (Weiss, 1997a, p. 35).

Some broadcasters and many filmmakers were more interested in screen size than resolution. The average viewer watching a 27-inch screen from 10 feet away can probably see no advantage in DTV, so at typical viewing distances clarity of a picture is less noticeable than scope. Negative aspects of TV are not noticed due to the distance at which the picture is viewed, the TV production itself, and the small picture size. As screen size increases, "HDTV's advantages become much more apparent" (Thorpe, 1989, p. 92). Wide-screen sets became available in 1993 to consumers, who seemed more interested in the 16:9 ratio than resolution. Movie producers of the 1950s used wide-screen formats as an attractive alternative to the nearly square TV picture, but it took TV set designers four decades to respond (Heiss, 1993). With a widescreen, viewers get more than "the old squarish sets" and "more than just a rectangular screen"; they get a picture "that's closer to how filmmakers shoot" (Goldberg, 1994, p. 66). TV producers were planning ahead by shooting many programs in formats compatible with ATV developments. Programs shot in 16:9 ratio could more easily adapt to 4:3 in the present than to convert 4:3 to 16:9 in the future (Shooting with the future, 1992).

Japanese HDTV

Perhaps the most important nontechnical aspect of DTV is that the United States can regain the prominence that it lost to Japan in television technology. Japan had spent two decades working on the technology while the United States dragged its feet (Rogers, 1993). It is ironic that the United States "became the clear leader in HDTV by starting late" and that Japan "paid the price for being first" with analog HDTV (Husted, 1994). DTV is computer-driven, and the United States is far ahead of Japan and Europe in the computer industry (Elmer-Dewitt, 1992).

Responding to the United States' tremendous strides in DTV, Japan formed its Promotion Association for Research and Development of AIM, consisting of 122 corporate participants. AIM sought to develop its own digital imaging system by 2005, with further developments by 2015. Japan's UDTV would incorporate high-resolution still photography and motion picture images for business, industry, and consumer use. Some observers conceded that "the plan clearly shows the Japanese penchant for long-term planning and long-term strategies" (UDTV, 1993, p. 29). It may be better explained as Japan's attempt "to save face as it finally becomes clear the country's Herculean and costly efforts to develop the H-Vision HDTV system and promote it as a world standard have failed overseas" (p. 29). Critics did not believe that Japan's objectives were practical because AIM "tends to oversimplify digital imaging technology" (p. 32).

The IUEW and IBEW said that DTV would create an estimated 100,000 new U.S. jobs. IUEW posited: "If we had kept color TV in the United States instead of giving it to the Japanese and Taiwanese, half a million people would be working in color television" (Duston, 1992, p. 8B). The issue became "overtly political" in March 1993, when the Clinton administration and various congressmen said that DTV's standard should be based on generation of employment (Shotgun, 1993). Although its right to do so was questioned, the FCC directed ACATS to make jobs part of the equation. ACATS' Richard Wiley said: "That's not for me to question. The FCC told me to look into it, so I'll look into it" (Scully, 1993b, p. 60).

Some considered IBEW's contention hogwash. Dick (1997b) observed: "It's easy to see why the IBEW supports the adoption of DTV. After all, they want its members to be the ones who will build these supposed millions and millions of sets. While I'm all for American jobs, it's just too bad the unions aren't being honest with their members about where these new sets will really be manufactured" (p. 6). Thomson Consumer Electronics announced in February 1997 that it was eliminating at least 1,500 jobs at two United States factories by moving its operations to Mexico. Although "most TV sets are not made in America and the adoption of DTV won't change that," it was believed that DTV was created simply to make NTSC technology obsolete "because TV set makers need DTV to sell new sets" (p. 6).

ATV Systems

By 1990 GI developed an all-digital system, and other United States HDTV systems soon followed, giving the United States "a clear technical lead in HDTV development" (A short, 1993, p. 60). The number of proposed systems peaked at 23, but "through mergers and attrition" just six remained by June 1990: ACTV/Sarnoff Research Center; Narrow-MUSE/NJK/Japan Broadcasting Corp.; Digital Simulcast HDTV/ATRC; DigiCipher/GI; Spectrum Compatible HDTV/Zenith Electronics; Channel-Compatible HDTV/MIT (p. 60).

In January 1991 GI and MIT combined efforts to become American Television Alliance but would still submit two systems. MIT needed funding, and many of GI's engineers were MIT graduates. MIT gained economic support, and GI gained MIT's wealth of engineering expertise. GI admitted that discussions with other proponents had taken place. MIT wanted a digital system, but funding was insufficient until the merger (GI and MIT, 1991). By spring 1991, only Narrow-MUSE/NJK/Japan Broadcasting Corp. and ACTV/ Sarnoff Research Center system were analog (Time "to deliver," 1991).

HDTV testing began on July 12, 1991, at ATTC. The first examined was ACTV/Sarnoff's EDTV system. Those who remembered AM stereo hoped that the system standard would borrow from the best aspects of all competitors to avoid delays produced by legal wrangling over licensing and royalties. There was concern about consumer interest in HDTV (The long and winding, 1991).

On May 7, 1992, DigiCipher/GI, Channel-Compatible HDTV/MIT, Spectrum Compatible HDTV/Zenith Electronics, and AT&T agreed to share technology and to apportion royalties should one of those systems be chosen as the standard. Digital Simulcast HDTV/ATRC officials were considering a similar arrangement, but any decision would be postponed until all systems were tested. Dr. James E. Carnes, Sarnoff president and CEO, elaborated: "Everyone has designed what they think is the best system. It will take the tests to differentiate between the different systems, to show their strong points and weak points. After the testing, I think the atmosphere will be better for discussions of a hybrid system" (Cole, 1992c, p. 14). All proponents admitted to informal discussions about consortiums. Robert Rast, GI VP, said: "We have to figure out a way to turn the selection process from an adversarial to a cooperative phase" (p. 14). In 1992 the FCC tested four digital systems but experienced difficulty in determining a superior system. The FCC ultimately asked proponents to work jointly toward a solution (A short, 1993).

Broadcaster and consumer interest appeared to be waning, leaving much of the fascination to "a new generation of computer and film technologists who view the broadcaster's HDTV proposals as already obsolete and a dead-end for future expansion" (Beacham, 1991, p. 26). Film director Francis Ford Coppolla said that broadcasters were "powerful" and "greedy and want to stop progress" by "putting pressure on congressmen to give us less than something we have to have" (p. 26). Some broadcasters wanted "scalable video," which is "digitally encoded and decoded in such a way that it can be displayed on devices of varying screen resolution" (p. 26). That meant that "the consumer can buy the quality and resolution level of receiver he or she desires," with all sets capable of the same programming (p. 26). Scalable video made compatibility possible. Proponents of scalable wanted HDTV technology that could achieve widespread use and could evolve. Some believed that if broadcasters did not accept scalability the computer industry would. FCC chairman Sikes was very high on "dynamic scalability," that is, "a flexible" DTV system carrying "multiple scenes and camera angles, or even multiple programs" (The digits, 1992, p. 70). Sikes said that the consumer would dictate much of what he or she would see (p. 70).

HDTV's Cost

Broadcasters wanted time to digest and understand the rapidly moving digital push and its impact on broadcasting and localism (The digits, 1992). Economics were of utmost concern. On January 7, 1993, MSTV asked the FCC for scalable TV, meaning to use DTV to its best advantage economically and in the public interest. MSTV, citing the All-Channel Receiver Act of 1962 as precedent, also asked the Commission "to consider mandating all-channel, NTSC/ATV receivers, three years after setting an ATV standard" (Lambert, 1993b, p. 20). Only Congress, not the FCC, can set receiver standards.

To ease economic burdens of conversion, many broadcasters wanted an intermediate step such as EDTV. EDTV would save little money, as equipment would be no more compatible with HDTV than NTSC. Sikes preferred simulcasting: "The commission has outlined some deliberate and progressive steps to let the marketplace work and, at the same time, provide incentives to encourage HDTV development" (Sikes reaffirms, 1991, p. 27). A slow and deliberate transition would not necessarily lessen the financial shock, as obsolescence was a chief concern with quickly evolving technology. HDTV is expensive, but exact figures were difficult to determine because much cost would be determined by a conversion timetable. Some estimates for station conversion were as high as $40 million, but others were as little as $5 million (HDTV: Coming, 1990). CBS' Joe Flaherty believed that HDTV's cost would be similar to color conversion in the 1950s (Cole, 1991a). However, Jack Clifford, Providence Journal Broadcasting Group, said: "No one doubted color. Retail advertisers came to us and said they would begin advertising with us only after we had color. TV profits were going up then and money was available for color. But HDTV comes at a different time and I'm damned if I can find a significant return on the investment. And the subscriber discontent that it is bound to produce frightens me" (Is hi def worth, 1991, p. 8). In view of threats to traditional broadcasting by cable, DBS, and other new technologies, it was important for terrestrial broadcasters to plan for both the cost and quality of HDTV before losing more viewers to competition.

HDTV applications go beyond broadcasting and entertainment purposes, and detail is extremely beneficial for computer technology, medical images, military use, and other purposes requiring detailed video. Blinder (1990b) observed: "While the broadcast arena remains mired in a transmission standards war that should keep HDTV from American homes for years to come, the business world has long seemed to be the natural launching pad for this breakthrough in electronic imaging. As islands unto themselves, video departments are unshackled by FCC regulations, and free to concentrate on the technology's considerable benefits as a production and teleconferencing medium" (pp. 39–40). HDTV is important in medicine, "where you really need to see *exactly* what the surgeon is doing," and "a remote diagnostic system using HDTV . . . allows patients in rural areas to be seen by a specialist without traveling long distances to a hospital" (p. 43).

At an April 1992 meeting, the FCC decided that once an HDTV standard was established, broadcasters would have to implement HDTV broadcasting on their extra channel within five years. The decision was met with disdain by broadcasters who were unconvinced that HDTV would provide "a satisfactory return on investment" that quickly (HDTV: Too close, 1992, pp. 4, 14). Many cost-related concerns centered on stations in smaller markets. Some broadcasters believed that manufacturers would take advantage by driving up prices on conversion equipment. Broadcasters would have to invest in HDTV or lose their broadcast privileges and would be forced to make decisions without knowledge of consumer desire for HDTV. A *Broadcasting* editorial stated that "broadcasters must soon put up or shut up: $10 billion against $100 billion for the audience. Worse still, the broadcasters' 10 has to come first, before the audience shows its hand" (Hard call, 1992, p. 66). Further, "the priority of broadcasters has changed while all this invention was going on. They've become less interested with enhancement of their medium than with its survival" (p. 66).

With AM stereo fresh in many minds, broadcasters planned to appeal the FCC's decision (Lambert, 1992c). Some were less concerned about the timetable, believing that the FCC would be flexible. Broadcasters reacted strongly to the FCC in a joint filing signed by 101 parties, including CBS, ABC, NBC, Fox, PBS, NAB, AMST, the Association of Independent Television Stations, and others. They roundly opposed the 15-year plan for total HDTV conversion, mandating five years for construction and five years for equipment installation. More time was requested due to costs of transmission equipment and receivers. Broadcasters wanted HDTV channels to cover the same basic area as analog channels. Broadcasters also attacked the 100 percent simulcast plan, believing that the second channel should be used for experimentation. NCTA countered: "Any attempt to exploit ATV as a new programming service, rather than an improved technology, will be an enormous spectrum giveaway worth billions of dollars—all at little perceived benefit to today's television households" (Sukow, 1992b, p. 32). AT&T and LMCC supported the FCC's proposals. LMCC believed 15 years sufficient for conversion, especially since other interests were awaiting return of the borrowed channels. Most parties agreed that the FCC should review the deadline requirement in 1998 (pp. 31–32).

Undaunted, Sikes responded: "As Americans embraced color television, VCR's, compact discs and other major technologies, you will see a similar love affair with the next generation of television" (HDTV: Too close, 1992, p. 14). Sikes did not want digitally compressed HDTV channels used for multichannel NTSC signals but thought that some experimentation was acceptable. He mentioned interactive game shows as a possibility. Broadcasters were upbeat, believing that consumers needed extra incentive to adopt HDTV (What multichannel, 1992).

The FCC surrendered some ground on its HDTV implementation timetable, voting 5–0 to keep the overall 15-year limit for total conversion. The initial five-year limit was raised to six. The Commission shortened the simulcasting period from four years to three years, with no simulcast requirement the first year. Fifty percent simulcasting would be in effect the second year, and full simulcasting the third year. Broadcasters argued that there would be full-time HDTV channels at full cost playing to just 5-percent receiver saturation, but the FCC said that a short time period would provide consumers incentive to buy receivers (Flint, 1992).

THIS IS A TEST

On March 23, 1992, a 12-minute HDTV telecast was shown on Capitol Hill to enthusiastic representatives from broadcasting and government, including Al Sikes. The signal was sent from 10 miles away by noncommercial WETA-TV, Washington (Lambert, 1992a). By mid-1992, increasing speculation centered on a hybrid HDTV system standard. The hybrid question was more than technical; it was "a business and political question" (Cole, 1992b, p. 8). To study the hybrid question, the FCC attempted "to eliminate direct conflict of interest" in forming a 25-member ACATS subcommittee comprising TV consultants, industry representatives, network officials, and manufacturers (p. 8).

On August 26, 1992, the FCC (1992a) formally proposed a rule making on "policies, procedures and technical criteria to be used in allotting" stations extra channels for ATV. The FCC "intended to provide industry and other interested parties with the maximum opportunity to participate in the formulation of ATV allotment and assignment policy and to negotiate agreements for both allotments and assignments." The Commission proposed four general objectives with its allotment table: (1) to furnish all existing broadcasters with an ATV channel, guaranteeing equal opportunity for ATV access to existing broadcasters; (2) "to maximize the service areas of all ATV stations" by "using a process that would attempt to replicate the coverage areas of existing stations"; (3) "to allot all ATV channels to the UHF band"; and (4) "to prefer new ATV operations over NTSC operations in the allotment process," while taking into account protection of any affected existing NTSC service in actual ATV operations during the transition period.

The Commission would "consider information from the comments filed in response to this Further Notice and other sources, such as data from the testing of the proponents' technical systems, in finalizing its ATV allotment policies and preparing its proposal for a final ATV Table" (FCC, 1992a). The FCC invited "interested parties to submit specific proposals for . . . alternative approaches." The FCC (1992a, 1992b, 1992c) set deadlines for comments and reply comments and later granted two extensions to ensure as much participation as feasible.

Assigning another channel to each existing station created unique problems not experienced by the FCC in previous proceedings. How should the Commission handle a situation in which an existing station's license was being challenged? What about call letters for the second channel? Should manufacturers be required to produce sets that could simultaneously handle

NTSC and ATV? What would happen to the extra channel after HDTV market saturation? The FCC (1992d) posited many questions in its ongoing quest "to establish procedures that will result in a smooth, successful transmission to ATV."

On November 12, 1992, the FCC (1992e) issued a final rule instituting several ATV actions and preliminary decisions. The Commission extended the application process and construction period to six years and disagreed with MSTV's position on "costs, burdens, and risks" of HDTV's implementation. The FCC agreed that receiver penetration may begin slowly but believed that "such a delay would act against the public interest goals of accomplishing a swift ATV transition, and against broadcasters' goals of maximizing transitional revenues from their ATV channel." The FCC (1992f) also showed interest in "any new audio developments," "flexible use of audio and data," and "any analogous instances of extensibility that arise."

The Commission was criticized for its second channel allotment. Was it fair that existing broadcasters, for that reason alone, be given a new channel? Should not channels be made available to other applicants? The FCC (1992e) said that it "does not have the same responsibility to ensure spectrum efficiency with respect to these other industries. Nevertheless, it is expected that alternative media will participate early and fully in the transition to ATV. In this connection the Commission expects that alternative media (possibly including cable, VCR, DBS and computers) will begin ATV implementation promptly, thereby exerting additional competitive pressures on broadcasters to begin the transition to ATV." Receiver penetration would not be a factor in awarding extra channels, because "the Commission means to allay concerns that broadcasters will be forced to make investments that are premature and ill-suited to marketplace realities." The Commission refused to "adopt a staggered approach to initial ATV implementation, with large markets implementing first and small markets last, as some parties ask." Aware that stations in smaller markets would face more difficult economic constraints in converting to ATV, the FCC implemented a protracted filing deadline and a "'sliding scale' approach to construction periods" that "should provide such stations adequate relief." The FCC left room for further adjustments as deemed necessary. "Staggering" was not a viable option because it "might cause administrative delays and ultimately could impede the activation of ATV service."

The FCC (1992e) "tentatively" effected "a flexible approach that permits low power television service broadcasters to convert to ATV in response to local demand" and not be forced to convert by a deadline. As expected, the Commission set a period of 15 years from date of adoption as the deadline for total ATV conversion, because "[I]t appears that this period will allow equipment manufacturers, broadcasters and consumers sufficient time to accept conversion without significant market disruption or uncertainty." One respondent claimed that 15 years was too lengthy. The FCC disagreed but would not be "inflexible." It set 1999 as a reasonable time to check ATV's progress. In justifying its deadline, the FCC (1992e) "also expects that eliminating the need for both ATV and NTSC equipment will prove more convenient and less confusing to consumers. Moreover, our periodic reviews will take the extent of consumer acceptance into account before ratifying the important determination to eliminate NTSC broadcasting."

Second Channel Simulcasting

Despite Sony's urging, the Commission would not "adopt a production standard for broadcast ATV service" (FCC, 1992e). The FCC also decided to phase in simulcasting "to ensure as smooth a transition to full simulcasting as possible for both broadcasters and viewers." Fifty percent simulcasting would be required in the seventh year, but the Commission delayed setting a deadline for 100 percent simulcasting and full conversion to ATV. Reconsideration could occur in 1999 "should ATV penetration be higher than initially projected." The FCC (1992e) explained: "This approach will also afford broadcasters seven years of initial flexibility to explore the creative potential of the ATV mode and to attract viewers to ATV, as most commenters argue is needed. The Commission agrees with one party who suggests that the viability of ATV may hinge on consumers' ability to differentiate ATV from NTSC programming. Thus, broadcasters and program producers should be afforded sufficient time and flexibility to establish, as a technical matter, a distinctive ATV format in the marketplace."

The FCC (1992e) defined simulcasting as "the broadcast on the NTSC channel, within 24 hours, of the same basic material as that broadcast on the ATV channel, with the exclusion of commercials and promotions. The Commission will not permit the use of the ATV conversion channel of an ATV-NTSC pair for subscription services on a stand-alone basis. This restriction applies to the use of the ATV conversion channel throughout the 15-year transition period, not merely during the period in which simulcasting is required." The Commission made a distinction between commercials/promotions and programming.

As with previous standards, the Commission said that "any winning ATV system would have to be licensed to other manufacturing companies on reasonable terms" (FCC, 1992e). The FCC directed system proponents "to submit, prior to testing, a statement that any relevant patents they own would be made available either free of charge or on reasonable, nondiscriminatory terms." The decision was not universally accepted, but the Commission held "that this requirement adequately safeguards the consumer and competitive interests in reasonable availability of relevant patents, and thus, that greater regulatory involvement is not necessary at this time." The FCC reserved the right to revisit its decision. The FCC expected the prevailing company to disclose technical specifications of its system upon acceptance. Preferably, mass production of professional and consumer grade equipment would occur quickly. The FCC recognized compatibility's importance, particularly in regard to broadcast, cable, and computer and data utilization.

Chairman Sikes announced his resignation for January 19, 1993. As an appointee of Republican president George Bush, Sikes decided to end his term the day before Bill Clinton's inauguration. Sikes left a number of unfinished items other than HDTV, such as DAB and the congressionally mandated selection of an AM stereo. Sikes' successor would be left up to Clinton, who also faced the task of filling Commissioner Sherrie Marshall's seat (Gatski, 1993a).

The "Grand Alliance" System

Many advocates hoped that the remaining HDTV proponents would strike an agreement to form a hybrid system. In February 1993 Japan Broadcasting Company pulled its NJK/Narrow-Muse system from contention. It was the last analog system. Apparently, a "fatal flaw" (HDTV "Grand Alliance," 1993) was discovered, making it "vastly inferior to results" of other proponents. ACATS planned another round of testing, but with just four systems remaining from the original 23, Richard Wiley supported a "Grand Alliance" hybrid system. Wiley said that if the "best elements of the different systems" were combined, "the best possible HDTV system" would be produced (Sukow, 1993a, p. 54). Testing was to commence on April 1, 1993, and Wiley believed that an alliance should be formed beforehand. Time was needed to construct and test an alliance system, but the delay could be lessened by not testing four systems. There was some doubt that an alliance would be struck, but Wiley set an alliance deadline for May 24, 1993, because he wanted HDTV ready for the 1996 Atlanta Olympics. If there was no agreement by then, individual system testing would begin. The cable industry was especially interested in a Grand Alliance and wanted cable compatibility considered. No proponent had the capacity to send cable signals, but there would be little difficulty in adding features to a merged system (Scully, 1993c).

On May 24 the Grand Alliance became an actuality following "a week of intensive negotiations" in which "the three groups vying to develop the United States HDTV standard . . . agreed to merge their efforts and develop a single system" (Scully, 1993d, p. 59). They were given until the end of 1993 to work out details and construct the model. Although an FCC decision was expected to be delayed for a year or so, HDTV's United States introduction would ultimately be expedited. Congressman Ed Markey (D-MA), House Telecommunications Subcommittee chair, noted: "This is not the end of the road. This is a deal struck among private parties; the HDTV standard-setting decision remains a public process, subject to public scrutiny" (p. 60). Some critics believed that the alliance was a cop-out. Doherty (1996) complained: "A process that started out as a race designed to produce a single HDTV technology winner, a Darwinian style shoot-out of six systems with survival of the fittest, has wound up thwarting natural evolutionary forces. HDTV competition eroded into a pooling of all the patents, and no HDTV managers would go down with their weakened ship in this regatta. No, sir!" (p. 24).

At the 1993 International Television Symposium in Montreux, Switzerland, Europe's HDTV community begged the United States to consider one of its systems, which were all analog. Joseph Flaherty, Grand Alliance coordinator, said that a European system could be considered if one were ready, but "we can't delay forever" (Dickinson, 1993, p. 8). The alliance was expected to circumvent litigation.

TELEVISION AUDIO

"An old radio joke goes like this. *Question*: How does a radio engineer test an audio circuit? *Answer*: With lots of test gear and time. *Question*: And how does a television engineer test an audio circuit? *Answer*: 'Hello, can you hear me?'" (Fedele, 1998, p. 8). TV audio was virtually unnoticed until MTS. Even then, there was little respect for it. Paryzek (1998) noted: "There's only one thing worse than TV audio . . . stereo TV audio: It's twice as bad" (p. 94). Other than assuming that HDTV would include advanced audio, little was said or done about it. As with AM radio, consumers of TV audio prior to stereo "typically listened to their television's audio on a 2-inch speaker that had slightly more dynamic range than the proverbial cup and a string" (Fedele, 1998, p. 8). Hoffner (1991) observed that

all parties to the advanced television effort have espoused significantly improved audio systems to accompany improved video systems. There is, however, less clarity as to what constitutes an improved audio system. It would not be an overstatement to say that the proponents feel that the large screen presentation formats that will be spawned by a widescreen, improved definition picture will require expansion of the two-channel stereo paradigm to some form of "spatial sound" that employs, at the least, the four audio signals of surround sound. Some scenarios included more than four signals. (p. 28)

Grotticelli (1998c) added: "Throughout the history of NTSC, audio has been relegated to the back burner, where it has stewed and systematically improved to become the current state-of-the-art matrixed stereo. . . . The current reality, though, is that all of the HDTV demos I've seen did not include audio" (p. 6).

MTS

As with radio, crude attempts were made at TV stereocasting. One was simulcasting music events over radio. As with DTV, TV stereo was inspired out of the necessity to keep up with other technologies, such as VCRs, videodisc players, and cable. Each featured audio superior to that of broadcast television. Another incentive was to satisfy audiophiles spoiled by high-fidelity audio systems that had steadily grown prevalent and available since FM stereo's 1961 inception. Television broadcasters not only took notice but acted quickly. AM stereo's lessons were not forgotten. Although many saw the Grand Alliance's choice of Dolby AC-3 as something new and innovative, it was really just a further improvement on MTS, "which still defines the high-end of broadcast TV audio" (Starzynski, 1997, p. 24).

The FCC (1977) defined MTS as "[a]ny system of aural transmission that utilizes aural baseband operation between 15 kHz and 120 kHz to convey information or that encodes digital information in the video portion of the television that is intended to be decoded as audio information." The proceeding began with a July 1, 1977, NOI responding to BBI's petition requesting "amendment of Part 73 of the Commission's Rules to allow TV station licensees to use a TV aural baseband subcarrier for cueing and coordinating electronic news-gathering crews in the field" (p. 18100). Respondents "were enthusiastic about using the TV aural baseband for certain operational purposes" (p. 18100). An NPRM followed on November 20, 1979, which would "allow limited use of the TV aural baseband for electronic news gathering (ENG) and coordination and TV transmitter telemetry functions" (p. 18100). However, EIA's BTSC formed a MSS "to ascertain the practicality of various program-related uses of the TV aural baseband and to develop appropriate technical standards for consideration by the FCC" (p. 18100).

BTSC did not want MTS left in a fruitless marketplace predicament as AM stereo had been. In effect, BTSC launched a preemptive strike to help ensure MTS' successful launch by recommending a system to the FCC. Should the industry make a proposal after an FCC decision, BTSC could be in violation of antitrust laws.

MTS Systems. Just three systems competed to be MTS standard: Zenith, Inc., Electronic Industries Association of Japan, and Telesonics Systems Inc. BTSC tested each system and planned a September 25, 1982, vote. Once Telesonics recognized that it would not be chosen, it threatened BTSC with antitrust action if another system was endorsed. The NCTA was concerned about cable incompatibility. NAB and EIA, BTSC's parent group, cited potential problems associated with system changes made after testing was completed. Nonetheless, cable compatibility problems were ignored, and all systems were found to broadcast stereo satisfactorily (TV stereo concerns, 1982).

On December 22, 1984, BTSC recommended Zenith as standard and endorsed dbx, Inc.'s companding system, which complements MTS "by encoding the transmitted signals and decoding it at the receiver." It "can dramatically improve the signal-to-noise ratio of television sound" (TV stereo concerns, 1982, p. 30). Overwhelmingly, broadcasters wanted the FCC to forgo marketplace standard setting, which obviously destroyed both AM stereo and teletext. NAB wanted a standard to "foster confidence in receiver manufacturers that an active market will exist for their products" and to "encourage broadcasters to implement MTS transmissions" (Consensus forms, 1998, p. 126). Likewise, consumers "can purchase TV stereo receiving equipment with the confidence it will receive all TV stereo signals" (p. 126). Dolby president Bill Jasper commented: "We agree that a standard is needed to avoid the AM stereo fiasco. On the other hand, we don't want the government telling us how to run things" (p. 126).

The final MTS ruling came on March 29, 1984. In a 5–0 vote the FCC approved "use of subcarrier frequencies in aural basebands of TV transmitters" (Prentiss, 1985, p. 117). The authorization created MTS and approved the Zenith-dbx system as BTSC recommended. The Commission believed that technological advancements were inevitable so did not make Zenith-dbx the industry standard. Rather, it reserved a pilot subcarrier at 15,734 Hz for the exclusive use of the BTSC-recommended system. The pilot subcarrier "triggers receiver stereo circuits and alerts the operator to TV stereo reception" and "would protect BTSC receivers from operating on other formats, and allow other multichannel sound transmission systems to operate, based on marketplace demands" (pp. 117–118).

Feldman (1984) called MTS "the most significant step taken yet toward the final integration of audio and video" that "will have as profound an effect on the future of audio in the home as did the coming of stereo FM" (p. 39). MTS was available to stations, manufacturers, and consumers effective May 7, 1984 (FCC, 1984). Some observers hedged their bets about consumer acceptance, yet stereo became a desirable and viable aspect of the television experience. Its status was raised from TV's "stepchild" to preeminence (Hoffner, 1993, p. 28).

Digital Audio. Audio was featured prominently at HDTV World Conference 1992. An HDTV Audio and Ancillary Services panel was dedicated to audio and strongly recommended that HDTV include more than two-channel audio. It endorsed five-channel surround sound, allowing "for a wide range of reproduction of the coded bit stream, from mono on low-end TV sets, to stereo, all the way up to the five channels (plus bass), depending upon the hardware used in the receiver" (Gruszka, 1992, p. 43).

In 1961 the FCC denied TV stereo because experts believed that stereo's big sound would overwhelm TV's small screen. HDTV presented the opposite problem, as its big screen and vivid detail would overpower two-channel stereo. For many years, theatrical films have featured "at least four-channel surround sound (stereo, hard center, and mono surround)," and many "have five-channel surround sound (left and right surround channels) as well" (Hoffner, 1993, p. 28). Skelton (1996) said that "for those who found the stereo conversion daunting, the next change in TV sound that lurks on the horizon will be so drastic, so sweeping and so expensive, that the introduction of MTS will seem but a tiny and distant memory" (p. 88).

Spatial sound can be applied with analog or digital audio, but digital offers other advantages, such as noise immunity. Noah (1993) explained: "This advantage exists through the entire recording, production, transmission and reception process. Multiple-generation recording, perhaps the greatest source of noise in analog production, introduces no noise whatsoever to the audio carried by a digital signal. The nature of digital signals eliminates interference from adjacent channels or signals within a device. Print-through and crosstalk associated with the archival process are eliminated as well" (p. 20). With DTV, it is important that "digital audio systems are inherently compatible with computer-based editing systems, disk-based storage devices and optical (read digital) distribution systems" (p. 24). Audio is important to a full HDTV experience and is made even more important when one considers MTS' very recent and still evolving history. Consumers have come to expect high-quality TV audio, something that was an oxymoron in television's first three decades.

Grand Alliance audio was an area that needed to be resolved. Zenith and GI featured Dolby AC-3 audio, Sarnoff employed Musicam 5.1, and MIT utilized its own MIT-AC audio system. Proponents devised an arbitration process to settle on disputed features such as audio, scanning format, data transportation, and transmission. The FCC's HDTV advisory committee appointed five working groups for the task. A fifth group would study cost of receivers and transmission equipment, and it hoped to estimate the financial effect of new technology on broadcasters and consumers (Scully, 1993e).

By November 1993 the Grand Alliance settled on Dolby's AC-3 audio system (later known as Dolby Digital), the only competitor meeting all the alliance's requirements. Problems were exposed in competing audio systems during testing. Dolby AC-3 was created originally for surround sound accompanying 35-mm film produced for movie theaters. Dolby AC-3 utilizes up to 5.1 discrete audio channels: left, right, center, subwoofer, left surround, and right surround. Hoffner (1996) added: "Stereo surrounds facilitate the spatial localization of rear-field sounds as well as front-field sounds" (p. 32). The alliance decided on MPEG-2 for digital compression. MPEG-2 was on its way to becoming an ISO standard (Cole, 1993) and "encompasses more than just basic video compression" (Fibish, 1995, p. 58). Audio compression and all TV signal data formatting were also standardized.

From the beginning, the FCC wanted ATV video and audio introduced in tandem. However, digital audio seemed to receive little attention throughout the process. Grotticelli (1998c) noted: "Although DTV is being sold as improved pictures and sound, the audio portion has been given little if any attention among station engineers thus far. It seems that getting the video infrastructure in place is taking up everyone's time and leaving little room for audio concerns" (p. 6). It was unlikely that most stations would be prepared to broadcast the Dolby Digital standard (aka AC-3) with its 5.1 channel surround sound. Some had never upgraded from mono to stereo, so it was likely that many consumers would receive DTV video and mono audio. There were comparatively few program sources recorded with the Dolby Digital 5.1 surround sound, and most of those were feature films. There was hope in the industry that audio would begin to garner more attention. Larry Shenosky, KRON-TV, San Francisco, operations director, said that HDTV "will be an excellent opportunity for our industry to right that wrong" (Grotticelli, 1998c, p. 6).

The Final Piece of the Grand Alliance Puzzle

The last hurdle in finishing the model HDTV system was choosing a transmission system. Although important, it was not expected to be a major problem. In late February 1994 the FCC's HDTV advisory committee selected Zenith's 8-Level Vestigial Side-band (8-VSB) transmission technology as the first subsystem for the model system (Aversa, 1994). 8-VSB was selected over GI's, but as allies they would jointly reap the benefits. GI's engineers believed Zenith's system to be a little better. Bob Rast, GI VP, said that the companies "got together" to make "substantial improvements in" their technologies (High-definition TV moves, 1994, p. F2). ATSC's Robert Hopkins (1994) said: "When a technical decision is made, technical performance is the number one priority in making the decision" (p. 185).

Four subsystem standards were already decided: audio, picture scanning formats, data compression, and data packets. Despite 8-VSB's selection, many broadcasters preferred a modulation system called COFDM. COFDM offered acknowledged benefits such as alleviating ghosting, improving coverage, and facilitating subsidiary nonbroadcast services. Some believed that COFDM was motivated by broadcasters' seeking to delay HDTV. Because the Grand Alliance system had not been tested, the door was open for a challenge. Richard Wiley said: "If [COFDM] is demonstrably better, we would have to look at it. We would also have to look at the timing" (Green light, 1994, p. 18).

DTV Flexible Use

Clinton-appointee Reed Hundt succeeded Sikes as FCC chairman. Sikes left a folio of incomplete details, including HDTV. Like many of his predecessors, Sikes was criticized for his handling of regulatory matters, but his work toward digitizing TV earned him retrospective appreciation. Hundt, however, was known for his "cavalier attitude toward the regulated industries" as "a growing scandal" (Adding insult, 1994, p. 74). Although Sikes wanted the extra channel to be used exclusively for HDTV simulcasting, Hundt did not, believing that broadcasters could use the channel for other purposes as long as public interest was served. Broadcasters and Richard Wiley wanted flexible use if it did not "preclude HDTV or give us a lower standard than NTSC" (Multiple messages, 1994, p. 40).

Broadcasters decided to support COFDM, which through multiplexing could "substitute hundreds—even thousands—of low-frequency signals for the high-frequency signal currently employed" (Foisie, 1994, p. 40). However, $10 million was needed to produce the prototype, and no one knew where it would originate. A group consisting of Fox, NBC, ABC, CBS, PBS, MSTV, and NAB pledged $1.2 million, but it was possible that the Grand Alliance system would be approved long before a COFDM system was built (p. 40).

Congress was investigating both HDTV exclusivity and multiple use. A House committee supported the NII bill, H.R. 3636, which would allow broadcasters to utilize their channel for nonbroadcast uses. Bob Rast, GI VP, retorted: "We suggest that is not the intent of advanced television in the United States. We're looking at providing more than we ever had, not more of the same" (Sukow, 1994b, p. 20). Broadcasters would still be required to return their extra channel after 15 years. Conversely, the Senate was formulating bill S. 1822 to require channel utilization only for new programming (McAvoy & Stern, 1994). Sponsor Ernest Hollings (D-SC) later added spectrum flexibility as a criterion.

Flexible use frustrated Grand Alliance members, who planned to demonstrate HDTV before the Commission in April 1994. GI's Rast said: "Everybody has got to get back to the message that it's great pictures" (McConnell, 1994a, p. 41). The Grand Alliance received little feedback from the FCC, which in two years replaced a chairman and two commissioners. The Grand Alliance planned an ATTC, tour to orient FCC newcomers about HDTV and "to see some response from the commission" (McConnell, 1994b, p. 47).

The Grand Alliance wrote Senator Hollings complaining that his bill might allow broadcasters a second channel absent HDTV. NAB's Fritts advised Hollings: "The companies involved in the Grand Alliance apparently want you to tie the FCC's hands and mandate their technology. It's understandable why the Grand Alliance would want to remove both the FCC's discretion and the marketplace's role in this matter, but we can think of no reason why this would serve the public interest" (NAB, alliance, 1994, p. 40). The second channel was assigned for HDTV, and the alliance believed it should remain so. *Broadcasting & Cable* editors disagreed: "Had the FCC committed to an analog HDTV system when that appeared to be the shape of things to come, we might now be backpedaling from an HDTV system the equivalent of an eight-track player in a CD world" (Room to move, 1994, p. 58). Hollings withdrew the bill when Senate minority leader Bob Dole (R-KS) "demanded so many changes at the last minute, and threatened so many procedural roadblocks, that it became impossible to move S. 1822 to a Senate vote" (The end of the beginning, 1994, p. 78).

Remember AM Stereo

System testing was completed in August 1994, and the FCC was analyzing results. Preliminary reports indicated that the system passed muster (McConnell, 1994c). HDTV entered a critical phase in 1995. Broadcasters

wanted more time, money, spectrum, and flexibility. Others—from telephone companies to radio stations and more—wanted pieces of the spectrum. The Grand Alliance was to finish its prototype HDTV system by
January 31, 1995, but MPEG-2 compression element testing caused a
delay. ACATS' Wiley expressed "disappointment" and said that no testing
schedule would be set until the alliance reported to him (McConnell,
1995a, p. 18). The delay allowed more time for completion of the
COFDM multiplexing system, which developers believed would happen by
July 31, 1995.

Criticism of Hundt grew. Some observers feared that he was jeopardizing
"free, over-the-air broadcasting capable of reaching every American home,"
while tending to drift into a "Socratic mode" by asking more than answering
(Here comes tomorrow, 1995, p. 118). In a January 1995 address to CES in
Las Vegas, Hundt asked: "Is there a good reason to set a national standard for
digital broadcast transmission and reception?" (p. 118). *Broadcasting &
Cable* editors replied: "Yes, there's every reason to set a national standard.
Our slogan on this one is: 'Remember AM stereo.' That was the last time the
commission adopted a marketplace solution to spectrum management, and it
was a disaster. Not only should there be a standard but it should aim high—
essentially, to provide for HDTV at the top while allowing flexibility further
down" (p. 118).

Hundt wanted the 15-year DTV phase-in shortened: "After all, the
quicker broadcasters move from one place in the spectrum to another, the
faster we could recover the valuable public property of the airwaves" (Mc-
Connell, 1995c, p. 103). There was growing sentiment, particularly in
Congress, to charge broadcasters for spectrum. Others believed that broadcasters should meet minimal children's programming requirements. Commissioner James Quello, interim chairman between Sikes and Hundt,
opposed both proposals. Quello said First Amendment considerations
could prevent specific program rules, and he did not believe that broadcasters should pay for spectrum that would distribute free, over-the-air programming (Jessell, 1995a).

Meanwhile, MSTV and Broadcasters Caucus filed a channel allotment design with the FCC, assigning extra channels to 1,691 TV license holders.
Three objectives were considered. First, each existing NTSC channel would
get another. Second, the alternate channel would broadcast to an area as similar as possible to the original. Third, obstruction to other NTSC channels
should be insignificant. The FCC took the proposal under advisement. Industry reaction was mixed. Most complainants focused on high channel assignments considered undesirable for two reasons. First, low channel
numbers get more consumer use because they are easier to find. Second,
some believed that higher assignment meant lessened signal quality. Engineers believed that technological advancement made both points unimpor-
tant (McConnell, 1995d).

On July 28, 1995, the FCC opened its *Fourth FNPRM and Third NOI* on ATV spectrum and impact on existing TV broadcasters. The FCC (1995a) stated:

[We] will pursue and balance the following goals in this proceeding: 1) preserving a free, universal broadcasting service; 2) fostering an expeditious and orderly transition to digital technology that will allow the public to receive the benefits of digital television while taking account of consumer investment in NTSC television sets; 3) managing the spectrum to permit the recovery of contiguous blocks of spectrum, so as to promote spectrum efficiency and to allow the public the full benefit of its spectrum; and 4) ensuring that the spectrum—both ATV channels and recovered channels—will be used in a manner that best serves the public interest.

In 1995 Congress began to covet spectrum previously pledged to TV broadcasters in 1992, because it had seen the FCC raise $9 billion by auctioning spectrum for PCS during 1994 and 1995. Many in Congress did not understand why broadcasters should not have to bid on new spectrum (McAvoy, 1995).

As cable TV and telephone companies entered the picture, flexibility became a key issue with broadcasters, and HDTV became a secondary priority. West (1995a) observed:

For years it was assumed the second channel would come broadcasters' way, as a companion to high-definition television. . . . But a funny thing happened on the way to tomorrow. Satellite broadcasters, looking for a way to increase the number of channels they could carry, came up with compression. Suddenly, there was the possibility of broadcasting perhaps 10 signals where one had been before. But in digital television, not analog. Overnight, there was new life in HDTV, the chance to cram something like 27 megahertz into six. It wasn't long before someone realized that not only could the terrestrial broadcaster use digital to broadcast HDTV, but he could use it to compress more NTSC channels into the 6 MHz the FCC had been trying so hard to aggregate for HDTV. The serpent had entered paradise. (p. 22)

Congress' interest in billions of dollars that could be garnered from selling spectrum appeared to doom the second channel. Hundt wanted broadcasters to compete successfully against other video competition. He explained: "If we let the whole world go digital except broadcasters and give them no way to convert to digital, we would be dooming this industry" (Jessell, 1995b, p. 24). However, Hundt believed that broadcasters should ante up for spectrum with dollars or public interest commitments. Hundt, in his contradictory style, about-faced at the 1995 NAB meeting in Las Vegas. He stated: "There has to be the possibility to deliver full HDTV over the air, but I am wary of the wisdom of the government mandating how you should take advantage of the business opportunities that the digital revolution creates. I suspect you know better than the government what to send" (Jessell, 1995c, p. 8). Then he added that some programming should be required (p. 8). Commissioner Quello said that any programming stipulations presented "a First Amendment time bomb" (Quello: No quid, 1995, p. 8).

An unnamed lawyer said: "Nobody knows where he is coming from at any given moment. Consequently, no one can trust him. The situation is very, very serious for those trying to deal with the FCC" (Jessell, 1995d, p. 6). A cable industry spokesperson added: "There is zero credibility. He says one thing one day and another thing another day" (p. 6). Even longtime commissioner Quello would not support Hundt: "Somewhere down the road there has to be peaceful, respectful coexistence. But you can't get it where there is a credibility gap. . . . If I make an agreement with him today, I have to watch what comes down" (p. 7).

Glenn A. Reitmeier of the David Sarnoff Research Center said: "Flexible use has become a buzzword. Some mistakenly believe broadcasters have a choice between HDTV and flexible use. Nothing could be further from the truth. I believe HDTV will give broadcasters the greatest possible flexibility" (Beacham, 1995, p. 21). Reitmeier explained that the Grand Alliance system could transmit "virtually any combination of video, audio and data" within the sphere of HDTV and "should translate into new revenue streams for the broadcast industry" (p. 21). If broadcasters had readily embraced HDTV and the Grand Alliance instead of being greedy in their desire for optional flexibility, they may have had a much smoother road to the second channel and ultimately to broadcasting better audio and video. The point was confirmed by Hundt, who ordered the FCC's Mass Media Bureau to reconsider second channel allocation for HDTV.

Jack Fields, House Telecommunications Subcommittee chairman, admitted: "A lot of us are asking questions [about spectrum use] that have never been asked before" (McAvoy, 1995, p. 23). NAB's Fritts said that broadcasters "don't have the financial wherewithal for equipment upgrades, the new towers, extra personnel, engineering costs and legal costs to get HDTV done. We don't have the money to be able to do that on top of paying multibillion dollars for spectrum" (p. 23). Wiley responded: "If we had that kind of vision in the 1950s, I doubt this country would even have color television. The broadcasters need to realize the Grand Alliance is their ticket to the digital age" (Beacham, 1995, p. 21).

Multiple SDTV. With the introduction of digital compression, several NTSC signals could fit in a channel occupied by one analog channel. It was called SDTV, which ATSC defined as "a *digital* television system in which the quality is approximately equivalent to that of NTSC" (Weiss, 1995, p. 16). Richard Wiley called SDTV "the digital equivalent of current television" with data and CD sound quality (McConnell & West, 1995, p. 32). Flexible use forced ACATS to include the previously taboo subject of SDTV in its system proposals to the FCC so broadcasters would be appeased and fully support the Grand Alliance. Wiley favored SDTV's flexibility, calling it "a subset of digital" (p. 32). He "encouraged it right along" because through the Grand Alliance we get "the best of both worlds. We can have HD and we can have multiple SD—and that's great for broadcasters, by the way" (p. 34). Consumers would require digital receivers to decipher SDTV, so it was not certain that there would be any cost reduction as compared to HDTV receivers. In September 1995 Hitachi was developing an SDTV decoder to convert HDTV to NTSC. Hitachi said that the $300 decoder's necessity was based on a transitional period in which "there will be a mix of HD and SD broadcasting" (McConnell, 1995f, p. 51).

Enamored with SDTV, Hundt stated: "I can't imagine why anybody wants the government to limit the flexibility and capability of this new technology" (View from the top, 1995, p. 54). Dick Smith, FCC chief engineer, added: "There really is no option for broadcasters. They must go to the digital service—and, personally, I think to the high-definition service—or they don't have a future. Without digital, and without high definition, there's little future for the broadcasters" (West, 1995b, p. 38). Dick (1995) wrote: "Broadcasters now have a golden opportunity to reinvent their industry," and those who do not adapt "will find themselves trying to sell the electronic equivalent of black-and-white kinescope images in an era of multichannel broadcasting and HDTV" (p. 6). Many broadcasters, however, did not want to "be bothered by either the opportunity or the progress the millennium presents," and that "is an attitude that can cost them dearly, near term and long" (High cost of hesitancy, 1995, p. 62).

Grand Alliance DTV Standard

On November 28, 1995, at ACATS' ninth and final meeting, it issued its final report and recommendation to the FCC (1995b), heralding "the greatest advance in broadcast television technology since its inception" (FCC, 1995b). The committee noted that in 1987, "it was not certain . . . whether a complete ATV system could work in 6 MHz over-the-air channels." After eight years and "after countless public meetings involving hundreds of industry volunteers and a rigorous program of testing and analysis conducted on seven prototype ATV systems at three futuristic laboratories," ACATS recommended the system's adoption as DTV standard. ACATS believed that the system met "performance objectives and is better than any of the four original digital ATV systems," was superior to any known alternative system," and fulfilled "the requirements for the United States ATV broadcasting standard."

Having achieved its purpose, ACATS' ATTC subcommittee planned to disband on December 31, 1995, but Westinghouse's Group W and the major networks wanted it to continue. ATTC president Peter Fannon said: "The mission of this lab would lie in assisting broadcasters and manufacturers in the development of the equipment and the systems necessary for the wide scale deployment of digital HDTV and ATV systems" (Morris, 1995, p. 8).

Congress was interested in spectrum auctions to raise money to balance the federal budget by 2002. Money uncollected by 2002 would not count toward that budget. With a goal of $14.3 billion, Congress could get $3.8 billion by selling ENG spectrum used by broadcasters to produce remotes and sporting events. The balance could be raised by selling spectrum reserved for television. Broadcasters were faced with forgoing the DTV channel or returning the analog channel more quickly. NAB called it an "an either/or choice; would you like to be hung or would you like to be shot?" (Stern, 1995, p. 4). Critics of the extra channel believed that broadcasters were given "an unfair competitive advantage" to "reap an unearned and unconscionable windfall at the expense of American taxpayers" (McConnell, 1995h, p. 18). Others called it "nothing less than a national scandal" (p. 18).

In the 1996 election year, spectrum became an even hotter topic. With an estimated value of $5 billion to $15 billion (rising to $70 billion in 10 years), Republican presidential candidate Bob Dole wanted an auction immediately. Calling the second channel "corporate welfare," he stated: "Broadcast spectrum is a national resource, and as such belongs to every American. If someone wants to use [that] resource, [taxpayers] should be fairly compensated for it" (Space sales, 1996, p. 9). Linda Golodner, National Consumers League president, called Dole and Congress "shortsighted" because "holding auctions now presents a legitimate threat to free over-the-air broadcast television" (Horowitz, 1996, p. 104). Dr. James Carnes, David Sarnoff Research Center president, wanted "Congress to help accelerate the transition to ATV" (p. 104). He added: "We've created a miracle, but it's gotten bogged down by politics" (104). Doherty (1996) agreed, calling ATV "a political football" (p. 24).

Experimental HDTV. In May 1996 WRAL-TV, Raleigh, North Carolina, applied for a license to transmit experimental HDTV signals. WRAL-HD would simulcast original and CBS programming. Owner Capitol Broadcasting, Inc. believed HDTV necessary to contend with other competitors such as DBS and traditional and wireless cable (WRAL-TV files, 1996). The FCC granted the request in June. Applications by Washington, D.C.'s WRC-TV and WETA-TV and Maryland Public Television were pending.

Hoping to expedite HDTV, MSTV and EIA established the Model HDTV Station Project, transforming Washington's WRC-TV from analog to digital. Washington was chosen to promote lobbying for HDTV and the second channel. WHD-TV debuted in August 1996. PBS affiliate WETA was converting to DTV at a cost of $10 million to $14 million. James McKinney, former ATSC head, directed the model project, and several HDTV manufacturers pledged equipment donations. McKinney said $10 million or more was needed to produce programming, but just $1 million would be required to outfit a station for rebroadcasting HDTV programming (MSTV/EIA to build, 1996).

DTV's *Fifth FNPRM*

The FCC (1996a) opened its *Fifth FNPRM* on May 9, 1996, intending to standardize the Grand Alliance system. The Commission said the system was "successfully designed, built and tested" and "embodies the world's best digital television technology and promises to permit striking improvements to today's television pictures and sound; to permit the provision of additional services and programs; to permit integration of future substantial improvements while maintaining compatibility with initial receivers; and to permit interoperability with computers and other digital equipment associated with the national information initiative."

Using the Grand Alliance system, broadcasters could employ HDTV or other DTV such as transmission of text and data. Broadcasters could use DTV to transmit several lower-resolution programs simultaneously or to send just one high-resolution program. The Commission endorsed flexibility and, as with MTS, left room for future analysis and for other advanced technologies to emerge. Hundt said that DTV was "not just evolutionary, but revolutionary," and Commissioner Rachelle Chong called it "nothing short of remarkable" (HDTV rules, 1996, p. 10). Wheatley (1996) was skeptical: "Sure, HDTV is just 5 years away—problem is, it's been that way since 1985. The FCC has got to get off its collective ass and approve a standard" (p. 6).

Critics of flexible use believed that broadcasters were foolish to chase multiple program opportunities when the real goal should be transmitting the best possible pictures. Broadcasters were opening themselves for further congressional inquisition when they should have been moving toward HDTV.

Progressive versus Interlaced Scanning

Computer guru Bill Gates and movie mogul Steven Spielberg opposed a DTV standard. At issue for their Americans for Better Digital TV coalition were the progressive and interlaced scanning display monitors (Broadcast digital TV, 1996). Progressive scanning, the domain of computer monitors, transmits information to the screen in one pass. With progressive scanning, primarily preferred for data and text displays, all lines are scanned in progression from top to bottom, from 1 to 525 (Barry, 1998). NTSC video employs interlaced scanning in two passes, creating 525 lines of resolution and 60 cycles. An electron gun alternately scans every other line on its first pass, or lines 1, 3, 5, 7, 9, 11, and so on. On the second pass, every line is scanned, including those already scanned. Interlaced computer pictures flicker, but TV does not (Barry, 1998). Gates and associates wanted to block the interlaced Grand Alliance system, even though it was expected to be totally progressive within five years. Progressive scanning requires much more spectrum than interlace.

Until the entry of the computer industry and pixels, visual quality depended on the number of lines and number of fps, which is 30 in the United States and 25 in Europe. Pixels are picture elements representing the smallest detail that can be produced in an image. SDTV contains about 300,000 pixels per frame, but HDTV contains at least 2 million pixels (Ranada, 1999). Robin (1998) explained: "The computer industry uses the term *vertical resolution* when referring to the number of active lines per picture and *horizontal resolution* when referring to the number of active pixels per line. Resolution can be misleading, especially with several different computer resolution formats. Among them are: 640x480, 800x600, 1,024x768 and 1,280x1,024" (p. 46).

Gates and company found congressional support as Larry Pressler (R-SD), Senate Commerce Committee chair, sought to block the DTV standard. TV manufacturers wanted to proceed with production, an impossible objective without a standard (Stern, 1996). Computer hardware and software manufacturers were greatly concerned about "the tech flexibility of annual upgrades—and also selling us all new hardware and software every year, as they're used to. TV production equipment and consumer TV set makers know their products have always been built to last after substantial investment, even if they're not upgradeable" (Broadcast digital TV, 1996, p. 9). Dick (1996) said computer makers "don't want a mandated HDTV standard because then they couldn't obsolete your TV set every 18 months" (p. 4). His contention was credible. Epstein (1997) wrote:

Contained within the original Grand Alliance proposal was a list of image formats. The 18 formats contained in the list included both progressive and interlaced scanning at various line and field rates. The plan was for all sets to accommodate these image formats. As a result of last-minute lobbying by the computer industry, the standard accepted by the FCC does not contain this table of formats. Early sets will be able to receive and display the original formats, and it is expected that broadcasters will broadcast signals adhering to these formats. However, since they are not contained within the standard, there is nothing to stop further formats from being introduced. This leaves open the possibility that televisions may become obsolete every few years as new image formats come into play. (p. 9)

The 18 formats are detailed in the table on the next page.

As with AM stereo, the lack of a true standard DTV system created another "chicken and egg" or circular problem. Manufacturers could proceed at their own peril by developing sets capable of deciphering 18 digital formats, but since the standard was open, it remained to be seen how many would do so. Without a standard, there could be no full-scale production of consumer sets, which would bring costs down considerably. What if stations opted to transmit in some as yet unknown digital format? The likely scenario was that stations would employ one or more of the 18 formats, but there was no guarantee. *Advanced Imaging* added another possibility to the equation:

Somebody in the television market is likely to step forward with a stripped down, less expensive, digital TV set that may not handle every format a prosumer multi-thousand dollar "Grand Alliance 18-format baby" might—but be a baseline standard for every-man, even drive others out. Ask: Who can be most comfortable with the profit margins from such TVs—or PCs? How willing are consumers to update digital TVs or even "TV software" as they do with computers so regularly? What will the economics of broadcasting or narrowcasting in this situation really be? Can a PC videocast find a way to pay for itself? Are PC makers really willing to compete with TV makers or will TV makers take over the PC? These questions will now be asked for real. (Advanced TV fall-out, 1997, p. 8)

ATSC recommended 18 formats, but they were not standards. Broadcasters could employ whatever DTV format or format combination they wanted.

The computer industry was joined in its battle by cable. Although cable companies had favored setting an ATV standard and had participated for eight years in seeking one, they became concerned about limitations to future innovation and competition that may be imposed by a standard. Broadcasters argued that cable was more concerned with broadcasters getting a digital jump than about preserving technological progress. Other DTV opponents included the Directors Guild of America and the American Society of Cinematographers, which opposed interlace scanning and wanted a 2:1 screen ratio instead of 16:9. Conversely, the MPAA and set manufacturers favored 16:9 and both interlace and progressive scanning.

Lines of Vertical Resolution	Pixels	Aspect Ratio	Frames per second and Scanning Format	
1,080	1,920	16:9	60i	
1,080	1,920	16:9	30p	H
1,080	1,920	16:9	24p	D
720	1,280	16:9	60p	T
720	1,280	16:9	30p	V
720	1,280	16:9	24p	
480	704	16:9	60i	
480	704	16:9	60p	
480	704	16:9	30p	
480	704	16:9	24p	
480	704	4:3	60i	S
480	704	4:3	60p	D
480	704	4:3	30p	T
480	704	4:3	24p	V
480	640	4:3	60i	
480	640	4:3	60p	
480	640	4:3	30p	
480	640	4:3	24p	

Source: Broadcasting & Cable, November 16, 1998, p. S19.

The Grand Alliance claimed flexibility and scoffed at cable's flip-flop (No help, 1996).

A major DTV standard supporter was the Clinton administration, which raised AM stereo as a rallying point. Noting that no standard doomed AM stereo, a White House spokesperson said that implementation of a single DTV standard would ensure industry investment. Another Clinton aide added: "One need only look to America's experience with AM stereo to realize that the acceptance and likelihood of success of new broadcast technologies are greatly enhanced when a standard is adopted" (McConnell, 1996c, p. 18). Dick (1996) added: "It's no secret that FCC chairman Reed Hundt would like to avoid the issue and let the 'marketplace' decide the HDTV issue. Give me a break! Anyone remember AM stereo? While the FCC stood back and waited, Kahn and Motorola were busy beating each other to death trying for a 'marketplace' decision. The result was that AM radio almost died, and AM stereo is about as popular as former Arkansas governor, Jim Guy Tucker" (p. 4).

There was a congressional effort to delay assigning DTV licenses, which could have led to spectrum auctions. A bill introduced by Barney Frank (D-MA) to prohibit the FCC from assigning free licenses was defeated 408–16 (Rosen, 1996). There were rumors of similar ensuing legislation. Despite congressional rumblings, the FCC released its DTV channel allotment draft in August 1996. Hundt emphasized "draft" and said that the commission would seek to "improve on it" in cooperation with broadcasters (McConnell, 1996d, p. 17). A primary concern was eliminating interference among new channels and better facilitating reallocation to other services at the end of a grace period.

Hundt would not reach "any final decisions until we have a consensus among all the parties involved," such as broadcasters and computer interests (FCC's Hundt centered, 1996, p. 4). Hundt said that no standard "would be okay with" him: "I'm very easygoing on this as long as the computer industry and the TV manufacturers are both in sync and agree to the details" (p. 4).

Obviously, broadcasters and manufacturers wanted a DTV standard. The computer industry wanted to stop it or at least eliminate interlace scanning. The film industry wanted wide-screen TV. The White House modified its stand to reflect the conflicts, and the wavering was attributed to the impending election. The White House asked the three parties to recommend a compromise to the FCC, and Hundt replied: "If they can't find a compromise, then we should invent our own compromise. We've got the technical expertise to do it" (McConnell, 1996f, pp. 6–7).

Industry publications, such as *Broadcasting & Cable* and *TV Technology*, had steadfastly supported the Grand Alliance system but backed off some. A *Broadcasting & Cable* editorial stated: "The digital TV standard has been too long in coming. It is with great reluctance that we suggest taking time out for one more fix" (One more time, 1996, p. 78). Likewise, *TV Technology* asked for a compromise, saying that anything else "isn't realistic or practical" (A call for compromise, 1996, p. 6).

The parties agreed to talk and surprisingly hammered out an agreement. Known as "the Grand Compromise," interlace scanning was removed from the system, and picture formats were left to the marketplace to decide. Manufacturers figured to design sets capable of deciphering multiple formats as originally proposed by the Grand Alliance. In turn, computer companies agreed not to solicit a spectrum auction. Both sides asserted victory (McConnell, 1996h). Broadcasters remained uneasy because DTV was a political hot potato. Eventually, the White House gave up on an auction. Weiss (1997b) stated: "The AM stereo debacle was clearly in memory. . . . No one working on Advanced Television wanted to see a repetition of the AM stereo situation" (p. 32). Speaking for those frustrated over DTV's incessant delays, Pohlmann (1997a) lamented: "We've landed men on the moon, but my TV set is about as modern as an Edsel. . . . Where the hell is my HDTV?!" (p. 28).

Chapter 7

The Grand Alliance and the Introduction of DTV

On December 24, 1996, the FCC (1996c) officially adopted the DTV Grand Alliance standard complete with compromises, but the Commission did "not mandate a conversion to digital television, only requiring that digital television signals that are transmitted conform to certain standards." The *Fourth Report and Order* required DTV transmissions to comply with the Grand Alliance system, but the video format layer was not mandated, so future technological innovation could occur. There were no requirements for scanning, aspect ratios, or resolution lines.

The FCC used all but a page or so of ATSC's nearly 200 pages of recommendations made in September 1995. There were two notable omissions. Computer interests convinced the FCC to delete mandated implementation of interlaced scanning and 16:9 aspect ratio. The FCC was pleased that "competing industries, working together, can develop *de facto* industry selected standards that satisfy the interests of contending parties. We commend these industries for their efforts" (FCC, 1996c). The FCC believed that it had provided "a requisite level of certainty to broadcasters, equipment manufacturers and consumers [so] the benefits of digital broadcasting will be realized more rapidly." The Commission also believed that the standard permitted "interoperability with computers" and encouraged "innovation and competition."

In discussing reply comments to its NPRM, the FCC acknowledged what most observers seemed to know—that broadcasters wanted a standard system. Thanks to AM stereo, broadcasters strongly opposed the marketplace. Conversely, computer interests favored the marketplace. The FCC (1996c) reported: "Broadcasters, equipment manufacturers and some consumer groups contend that DTV has startup, coordination and splintering problems that are more severe than those of other network industries and that a DTV standard adopted by the Commission is needed to overcome these problems.

In contrast, cable and computer interests contend that all sectors of the broadcast industry have significant incentives to reach a consensus on transmission and reception standards without a government mandate."

The film industry was split, with MPAA supporting the standard and others opposing due to the "inclusion of interlaced scanning and other perceived deficiencies, particularly in its video and audio specifications" (FCC, 1996c). Cable opposed FCC intervention. The FCC (1996c) said that NCTA "is not critical of the specific ATSC DTV Standard, but questions whether any standard should be dictated by government. Nevertheless, it recognizes the need for performance standards for controlling interference."

The FCC was left to decide how to assign digital channels and how long stations could keep their analog channel. There would probably be programming restrictions, such as how much public service and children's programming would be expected. The Commission speculated that it would take at least until April 1997 for the rule-making proceedings to play out (Martin & Estevez, 1997).

The DTV decision continued the FCC's recent tradition of not setting a complete standard. The FCC approved the Grand Alliance and computer compromise, but broadcasters and others did the work. The reluctant regulators had done much as they had since AM stereo and MTS. Let the industry do the work and the FCC will endorse the decision and enforce technical parameters. Reber (1997a) called DTV the "'non-standard' standard," so "no one knows yet what digital TV will be" (p. 8).

Grand Alliance supporters, who had failed to convince the FCC to select a standard, faced the daunting task of convincing the marketplace not only that their system was the best but that the proposed ATSC formats are the best. Bob Myers, Hewlett-Packard engineer, concluded: "The path ahead is *no* more clearly defined than it was prior to the "Great Compromise"—if anything, it's quite a bit less clear! In reality, all this has done is to take the FCC out of the process of determining what the standard formats are going to be" (An *Advanced Imaging* roundtable, 1997).

In true political fashion, President Clinton appointed an advisory group in February 1997 to determine public interest requirements for broadcasters, which Hundt had long desired as a DTV license requirement. While ordering the FCC to move rapidly in assigning licenses, the Clinton administration believed that it would need a year for the committee to conduct its work (Fleming, 1997). So much for the FCC's April 1997 deadline. However, Antonoff (1997) did not think that the DTV delay would matter because "the viewing public doesn't care as much about the future as it does for its nostalgic past" (p. 104). He explained:

The public's fondness for the familiar is threatening HDTV's future. Women can start a letter-writing campaign when some of TCI's cable systems replace the Lifetime Channel with yet another macho-oriented sports network, but hardly anyone cares when the FCC drags its feet over approval of a high-definition TV standard. Despite its alleged women-oriented programming, the fact is that much of Lifetime's programming consists of off-network reruns. Encore performances of *Murder She Wrote* may not be hurting HDTV directly, but it's clear that a lot more people get upset over not being able to see what they're used to seeing at the expense of taking a chance on watching something entirely new. (p. 104)

Cable was beginning to understand that it must adapt to HDTV, but business was flat and considerable upgrading was necessary. It privately questioned consumers' willingness to support financially such audio and video improvements, yet some cable executives saw DTV "as an opportunity to get back into the game, and they're relieved that they didn't waste big bucks on some incompatible, interim technology" (Pohlmann, 1997b, p. 27).

The FCC set a January 10, 1997, channel allotment comment deadline, and there was obvious broadcaster dissension over the handling of DTV and channel allotments. *Broadcasting & Cable* chided broadcasters: "A curious phenomenon is manifesting itself in regard to digital television. The broadcasting industry that has been beating on the FCC's doors for nine years to get a standard and the necessary spectrum is now dragging its feet about getting on air. What's going on here?" (Stalled at the start, 1997, p. 110). The editors proposed: "We'd go back to Dick Wiley, who created digital HDTV in the first place, and ask him to mobilize a government/industry task force to implement the digital revolution as quickly as humanly possible" (p. 110). It was a surprising reaction for the preeminent broadcast trade to take. No one needed to look past AM stereo to see the problem; the FCC's DTV decision was really a nondecision. Beacham (1997a) criticized the press and compared HDTV with a war that no one knew about:

Back in the 1960s there was a popular Vietnam War protest poster that asked: "What if they gave a war and nobody came?" I'm beginning to think that slogan could be revived for the digital television wars that lie ahead. To read the popular press you'd think there will be only smooth sailing until we reach the picture-perfect world of digital television. The widely heralded "compromise" on the DTV transmission standard is now history, and the White House has chosen to avoid a nasty fight with broadcasters over spectrum auctions. All that's needed now is for the FCC to assign the new digital channels and for Circuit City to start hawking digital TV sets. So what's wrong with this "crisp, clear" DTV picture? Well, it's sort of like the Vietnam War days when the nation's leaders forgot to tell the people exactly what was going on. (p. 27)

On April 2, ATSC (1997) announced a program to certify television sets, computers, and other consumer video devices capable of receiving all ATSC video formats. Certification was aimed at avoiding consumer confusion. The program would not specify display types such as progressive or interlace scanning, HDTV, or SDTV. ATSC also considered certification of other types of devices serving different or limited functions. ATSC expected to finalize technical details at subsequent meetings.

DTV's *Fifth* and *Sixth Report and Order*

In regard to DTV, the FCC released both its *Fifth Report and Order* and *Sixth Report and Order* on April 3, 1997. For the *Fifth Report and Order*, the FCC (1997h) said that it wanted "to provide for the success of free, local" DTV by allowing "broadcasters to use their channels according to their best business judgment, as long as they continue to offer free programming on which the public has come to rely." Multiple SDTV channels would be acceptable. DTV would be free to consumers and would be "at least comparable in resolution to today's service and aired during the same time periods as today's analog service." HDTV would not be required, and broadcasters could program DTV "to put together whatever package of digital product they believe will best attract customers and to develop partnerships with others to help make the most productive and efficient use of their channels." Profit and flexibility were acceptable motives as long as broadcasters attracted "acceptance" of DTV and promoted sales of receivers.

In its *Sixth Report and Order* the FCC (1997h) said that DTV channel allotment "accommodates all eligible existing broadcasters, replicates existing service areas, and ensures sound and efficient spectrum management." The Commission believed that the table would "facilitate early recovery of 60 MHz of spectrum at channels 60-69 and recovery of additional 78 MHz of spectrum at the end of the transition period." Originally, the FCC sought to recover 72 MHz after the transition period. The FCC deferred a decision on spectrum use but mentioned "assigning 24 MHz for public safety uses" and 36 MHz for auction.

The FCC's (1997f) *Fifth Report and Order* emphasized spectrum economy. The Commission explained: "Only if DTV achieves broad acceptance can we be assured of the preservation of broadcast television's unique benefit: free, widely accessible programming that serves the public interest." The FCC wanted "robust competition in the video market" with "more choices at less cost," "to encourage broadcasters to offer digital television as soon as possible," and "to promote the viability" of DTV services. The FCC (1997f) believed that viewers would greatly impact services offered by stations:

Our decisions to adopt the DTV Standard and to use 6 MHz channels permit broadcasters to provide high definition television in response to viewer demand. If we do not mandate a minimum amount of high resolution television, we anticipate that stations may take a variety of paths: some may transmit all or mostly high resolution television programming, others a smaller amount of high resolution television, and yet others may present no HDTV, only SDTV, or SDTV and other services. We do not know what consumers may demand and support. Since broadcasters have incentives to discover the preferences of consumers and adapt their service offerings accordingly, we believe it is prudent to leave the choice up to broadcasters so that they may respond to the demands of the marketplace. A requirement now could stifle innovation as it would rest on *a priori* assumptions as to what services viewers would prefer. Broadcasters can best stimulate consumers' interest in digital services if able to offer the most attractive programs, whatever form those may take, and it is by attracting consumers to digital, away from analog, that the spectrum can be freed for additional uses.

The FCC (1997f) announced a nine-year DTV phase-in period for complete transition from analog by 2006. The FCC considered 15 years but decided it was too lengthy. The FCC concluded that transition "will cost significantly less than thought at the time of the *Third Report and Order*," so "conversion can occur more quickly and NTSC spectrum can be surrendered sooner than earlier anticipated." The Commission promised "thorough reviews of the progress of DTV every two years" and "to make adjustments to the 2006 target, if necessary." The FCC cited DBS, cable, and wireless cable competition as factors in lowering costs and as motivation to implement broadcast DTV quickly. In regard to evaluation, "key factors for consideration will include viewer acceptance," penetration of receivers and converter boxes, "availability of digital-to-analog conversion by retransmission media such as cable, DBS, and wireless cable, and generally the number of television households that continue to rely solely on over-the-air analog broadcasting."

Stations would hold two channels until 2006 and then return one channel. Viewers would need a DTV set or set-top converter, which is any of several types of decoders for cable TV, DTV, or Internet functions designed for hookup to TV sets. To jump-start DTV, 25 stations in the nation's top 10 TV markets (representing 30 percent of U.S. viewers) pledged to deliver DTV within 18 months, or by May 1, 1999. The markets were Atlanta, Boston, Chicago, Dallas/Fort Worth, Detroit, Los Angeles, New York, Philadelphia, San Francisco, and Washington, D.C. The FCC (1997f) chose the graduated method to "provide for a rapid construction of digital facilities by network-affiliated stations in the top markets, in order to expose a significant number of households, as early as possible, to the benefits of DTV." The Commission added: "We require those most able to bear the risks of introducing digital television to proceed most quickly." Stations owned by, or affiliated with, networks (ABC, CBS, NBC, and Fox) in markets 11 through 30, representing about 53 percent of all viewers, would broadcast DTV within 30 months, or by November 1, 1999. Markets 11–30 included Baltimore, Charlotte, Cincinnati, Cleveland, Denver, Hartford/New Haven, Houston, Indianapolis, Miami/Ft. Lauderdale, Minneapolis/St. Paul, Orlando/Daytona Beach/Melbourne, Phoenix, Pittsburgh, Portland (Oregon), Raleigh/Durham, Sacramento/Stockton/Modesto (California), San Diego, Seattle/Tacoma, St. Louis, and Tampa/St. Petersburg/Sarasota. Other commercial stations would have five years to convert. Noncommercial stations would have until 2003. That left three to four more years of the nine conversion years to make the transition easier for consumers.

The FCC (1997f) said that broadcasters and manufacturers universally accepted its 6 MHz channel assignment. For second channel license eligibility, the FCC cited the *Telecommunications Act of 1996.* "Congress specifically addressed the eligibility issue" and "provided that the Commission 'should limit the initial eligibility for [DTV] licenses to persons that, as of the date of such issuance, are licensed to operate a television broadcast station or hold a permit to construct a station (or both).' . . . Following Congress' direction, we determine that initial eligibility should be limited to those broadcasters who, as of the date of issuance of the initial licenses, hold a license to operate a television broadcast station or a permit to construct such a station, or both." The Commission concluded: "We will continue our previously adopted policy to limit initial eligibility for DTV licenses to existing full-power broadcasters."

About its Table of Allotments, the FCC (1997i) wrote: "While the Commission continued the secondary status of low power TV and TV translator stations, it adopted a number of administrative and technical measures to minimize the impact of DTV implementation on low power operations." The FCC (1997f) was sensitive to LPTV but said: "We have not been able to find a means of resolving this problem. However, we note that limiting initial eligibility to full-power broadcasters does not necessarily exclude LPTV stations from the conversion to digital television."

Some commenters were concerned about public interest requirements, but guidelines were established by the *Telecommunications Act of 1996.* The FCC (1997f) said: "Broadcasters have long been subject to the obligation to serve the 'public interest, convenience and necessity.' In the 1996 Act, Congress provided that broadcasters' public interest obligations extend into the digital environment," and "Congress clearly provided that broadcasters have public interest obligations on the program services they offer, regardless of whether they are offered using analog or digital technology."

The FCC (1997f) did not "adopt a simulcast requirement for the early years of the transition," but expected 50 percent program simulcasting by year six, 75 percent by year seven, and 100 percent by year eight. The Commission added: "We recognize that we will need to define clearly 'simulcasting' in the context of DTV and will do so as part of our two-year reviews or other appropriate proceeding."

Until saturation and until cable could catch up, it was expected that consumers would use old-fashioned rabbit-ear antennae to pick up DTV. Directional bowtie antennae, which adequately received DTV from about 25 miles, were recommended for indoors. Roof-mounted antennae, which could receive signals from nearly 75 miles, were best.

In its *Sixth Report and Order,* adopted simultaneously with the fifth, the FCC (1997a) revealed its allotment table, rules, and procedures for assigning frequencies recovering spectrum. The FCC accommodated eligible existing broadcasters, replicated existing service areas, ensured proper and efficient spectrum management, and provided for early recovery of 60 MHz of spectrum (channels 60–69) and an additional 78 MHz of spectrum at the end of transition. A total of 138 MHz of spectrum would be recovered. Commenters were supportive, but LPTV broadcaster Abundant Life Broadcasting, fearing displacement, argued that the FCC "should consider awarding temporary second channels to fewer than all full service TV licensees." Several parties recommended "modifications to" the "proposed eligibility criteria." Some argued that channel allotment consideration should go to entities other than broadcasters. The FCC disagreed, maintaining that its "primary allotment objective should be to develop a DTV Table that provides a channel for all eligible broadcasters." The FCC's decision was "consistent with the provisions" of the *Telecommunications Act of 1996* regarding DTV license eligibility. The FCC added: "We note that low power television and TV translator operations are authorized only on a secondary basis. We have consistently maintained this approach towards low power service. Our decisions with regard to this issue have, in fact, been upheld on judicial review in *Polar Broadcasting v. F.C.C.*" The Commission acknowledged LPTV's public interest benefits and was working to "mitigate the impact of DTV" but ultimately determined that "there is simply not enough available spectrum to preserve all existing translators and LPTV stations."

Commenters generally favored basic service replication, but some were opposed. The FCC (1997a) explained: "These parties, who represent primarily the interests of existing UHF stations, generally express concern that the service replication plan would perpetuate the existing competitive disparities between UHF and VHF stations." The Commission added: "Most of the broadcasters opposing the service replication approach ask that we ensure that stations in a market have comparable technical facilities."

Under its "core spectrum plan," the FCC (1997a) "would attempt to provide all existing broadcasters with access to a 6 MHz channel for digital broadcasting within the core digital TV spectrum, *i.e.*, channels 7 to 51." But, it was impossible to accomplish the goal in all cases. Channels assigned outside the core spectrum "would have to move their DTV operations to a channel in the core spectrum when one became available." Likewise, the Commission said: "Broadcasters whose existing NTSC channels were in the core spectrum could move their DTV operations to their NTSC channel at some time in the future. Broadcasters whose DTV transition channel and existing NTSC channel were both outside of the core area could obtain a new DTV channel when channels in the core spectrum are recovered."

Ultimately, the FCC (1997a) concluded: "We continue to believe that the most advantageous approach for assignment of DTV channels is to match stations with the channel that best replicates their existing service areas. We agree with the commenting parties that this approach will preserve both viewers' access to the existing stations in their market and stations' access to their existing populations of viewers, and thereby ensure an orderly transition to DTV service for both commercial and noncommercial stations." The FCC added: "We intend to consider in a future rule making whether to create a new class of low power television broadcast stations that would modify the secondary status of these stations and provide them some level of interference protection."

The FCC (1997a) did not assign both channels 3 and 4 in the same markets, because set-top boxes and VCRs normally use them for output signals and could be "vulnerable to interference if there were an off-the-air signal present on the same channel as their output signal." To avoid FM radio interference, Channel 6 was assigned "only where there is no other readily available allotment opportunity that would provide for adequate replication of an existing station's service area." The FCC's decision was generally supported, but some commenters were concerned about channel interference with LMS. Such situations would arise, but the FCC found it unnecessary "to prescribe a special DTV channel designation scheme at this time." The FCC added: "As indicated in the *Second Further Notice*, we have been coordinating for some time now with Canada and Mexico on the allotment of DTV channels in the border areas. We are working to complete interim agreements on DTV with both of these countries. We have also coordinated the DTV Table with the Canadian and Mexican administrations and believe that it will be generally acceptable to them. We therefore expect that only minor adjustments will be necessary to conform the Table to these agreements."

The Commissioners Respond. Hundt and each commissioner attached separate statements to both reports and orders. Hundt wrote: "Today's decision marks the culmination of a long and worthy effort in Congress and at the Commission to ensure that 21st century America has a free, universally available digital medium that not only entertains but that educates and informs children and adults" (FCC, 1997b). Hundt gave no credit to broadcasters and manufacturers. Hundt said that the proceeding was "a radical departure from earlier Commission decisions that were presented to this Commission with its current membership as of 1994" and was "a significant change from earlier policies." The departure and change were unknown given the FCC's course since the 1982 AM stereo marketplace decision. Apparently, Hundt was unaware of the Commission's marketplace history, as he listed "benefits of our changes in direction" that "can be measured in many ways." One was to recapture spectrum to "generate new services and economic growth for the economy." The "early return can also be measured in lives saved, as 24 MHz can now, and should be, reallocated to the critical needs identified in the report of the Public Safety Advisory Committee." A second benefit, Hundt determined, was "the accelerated provision" of DTV services to the public. Hundt exclaimed: "This Commission can justly be proud of these many improvements in its policies for the digital television service. We even changed the name from the misleading 'high definition' to the apt 'digital.'" Dick (1997c) believed that Hundt's DTV timetable "wouldn't hold up to real-world scrutiny":

Articles from the Dow Jones news service, the Associated Press and others are pointing out the holes in Mr. Hundt's "trust me" plan to trash every analog television in

American—primarily to balance his boss's budget. We've been tilting at Reed's wind-mill for years. But now, the mainstream media and elected politicos are finally awaking from their Potomac naps and discovering the same thing. As viewers begin to wake up to the realities (read that as costs) of the FCC's fast-track schedule, the wisdom of cramming digital television down the throats of American consumers on a bent-for-hell pace will be questioned. (p. 6)

Hundt concluded as he started—by congratulating the FCC: "Thanks to the Commission's actions today, the future is now. And the future for Digital Television, while not guaranteed, is much brighter for the changes we have made" (FCC, 1997b). There was little doubt why broadcasters were not en-amored with Hundt.

Commissioner Quello called the DTV proceeding "an historic moment for all of us" (FCC, 1997d). Unlike Hundt, Quello acknowledged "the hard work of the broadcasting, manufacturing and computer industries," which "have developed the best, most innovative plan for digital broadcasting in the world." He added: "Engineers and executives alike have devoted years of their lives to bring us to this point, and for them, the work has only begun." As a veteran broadcaster himself, Quello said that he was "proud of what the television industry and the other industries involved have accomplished thus far, and I am excited about the future."

Quello lauded efforts to maximize spectrum use. Although acknowledging the intent of taking back "138 MHz of spectrum at the end of the transition period" (FCC, 1997d), Quello emphasized that the "decision here in no way prejudges what any recovered spectrum will be allocated for, and does not foreclose the possibility of its use for full power" or LPTV services. Quello cited attempts "to balance the need for a smooth transition to digital televi-sion with the continued operation of low power television."

Commissioner Chong submitted separate attachments for each proceeding (FCC, 1997c, 1997g). Chong (1997g) wrote a statement "concurring in part" with the *Fifth Report and Order*. She declared: "Today, we complete the Digital TV trilogy of decisions. With the issuance of this decision, its companion DTV Allotment decision, and the DTV Standards decision we adopted last December, the industry finally will have the regulatory certainty and confidence to move ahead to bring state-of-the-art digital television to American households." Chong reiterated many of Hundt's points but added: "I respectfully disagree with those that argue that this is a 'free giveaway' of spectrum to broadcasters. This is a technology transition. Congress and the Commission have agreed that a temporary loan of a second channel is war-ranted to smooth the transition from analog technology to digital technology for consumers."

Chong (FCC, 1997g) focused on an "expeditious and orderly" DTV tran-sition, and believed "that as audiences begin to see and experience for them-selves the improved DTV service, they will begin buying up digital TVs, just as they embraced other innovations in technology, such as color TVs, VCRs and CD players." Chong stated: "It is critical that consumer acceptance remains the driving force of this transition." She added: "Converting to digital television is a costly and complicated undertaking for broadcasters. While I too would like to drive this transition swiftly, we must stay within the realm of reason." Chong applauded large market broadcasters for committing to a rapid implementation of DTV, hoping "it will help drive a speedy transition."

Chong (FCC, 1997c) was "pleased to support" the second channel allotments, rules, frequency assignments, and plans for spectrum recovery. Chong declared: "This was a difficult task, but I believe we have generally succeeded in ensuring that all eligible existing broadcasters are accommodated, and that existing service areas are generally replicated." Chong wanted to investigate "the possibility of using part of the spectrum for public safety needs," because "many parties to this proceeding made compelling arguments that spectrum in the channels 60–69 range would go a long way towards solving some of the pressing spectrum need of public safety users." Chong called it "a worthy goal and one that I believe we ought to pursue." Chong also acknowledged that "there is not enough spectrum during the transition period to accommodate every low power service."

Commissioner Susan Ness (FCC, 1997e) called the proceeding "the momentous result of an extraordinary industry–government partnership." Ness proclaimed: "The landscape of television will be forever changed." Ness resurrected AM stereo's infamous chicken-and-egg analogy: "Broadcasters are not eager to invest significant sums to broadcast a signal that no one can receive. Manufacturers are reluctant to build—and consumers will be reluctant to buy—receivers for which there is no programming. The only solution is for both industries to move forward in tandem, sharing the commitment and the risk." Although mentioning the top 10 broadcasters' commitment to rapid DTV transition, Ness stopped short of crediting broadcasters for their work. Ness understood that there could be "extenuating circumstances that are outside the broadcasters' control, such as inability to secure tower locations for new antennas." Ness said: "In short, the deployment schedule is rapid, rigorous, and yet reasonable. It is practical and achievable. It enjoys the strong support of the broadcasters and receiver manufacturers upon whom we depend to roll out service to the public."

Ness (FCC, 1997e) noted HDTV's "potential to provide a theatrical viewing experience" but added: "We permit, but do not require, the use of digital channels to offer HDTV." Ness elaborated: "While we do not require broadcasting in high definition, we carefully avoid any policies that would inhibit its emergence. The consumer marketplace—not the government—should determine the success or failure of HDTV."

Ness called the allotment schedule "a masterpiece of engineering" (FCC, 1997e): "Many said it couldn't be done, but this plan accommodates all existing broadcast stations during the transition in a manner that avoids loss of

free, over-the-air broadcast service to consumers." Ness also favored allocation of 24 MHz of spectrum for public safety. Ness concluded with some
praise for the industry: "I urge them to proceed with the same vigor and
commitment they have so ably demonstrated in recent weeks." Although her
appreciative attempt was overdue, there was little consolation in acknowledging "weeks" when there had indeed been many years of hard work put in by
broadcast and electronics industries.

The Commission precipitated uneasiness among broadcasters due to its
support of the computer industry's entry into DTV. Many broadcasters believed that Hundt used his position as a "bully pulpit" to promote "a far different vision of DTV than what the broadcasters had in mind a decade ago
when they asked the FCC to give them a second channel to augment existing broadcasts, to deliver HDTV" (Birkmaier, 1997a, p. 16).

DTV's Coming-Out Party

The FCC adopted its *Fifth and Sixth Reports and Orders* days prior to
NAB's 1997 Las Vegas meeting. Hot topics were conversion costs and
HDTV versus multiple-channel-SDTV. Microsoft, Compaq, and Intel lobbied broadcasters to use a computer-compatible 720-P format, meaning 720
lines with progressive scanning. HDTV supporters preferred the 1080-I format with 1,080 lines of interlaced scanning and 16:9 screen ratio. Multichannel SDTV proponents targeted the 480-P format using 480 lines,
progressive scanning, and 16:9 ratio. ATSC's Robert Graves said that computer interests were "trying to confuse broadcasters and delay HDTV while
they get their own act in order" (McClellan, Dickson, & Rathbun, 1997,
p. 4). Robert Stearns, Compaq VP, calling the Grand Alliance standard "extremely expensive and silly," stated: "Let me edit down for you. We are going
into the TV business" (Beacham, 1997b, p. 44). Microsoft's Windows NT
Version 5.0 incorporated broadcast reception capabilities that supported "a
variety of film and video resolutions" (Grotticelli, 1997, p. 21).

By the end of 1999, Intel broke from the ranks because of broadcasters'
negative reactions to the computer industry. Originally believing that 18
DTV formats were too complicated and costly, Intel changed its stance after
testing a software-based, all-format decoder from Hitachi America Ltd. Intel
realized that it would be productive to remove barriers between the computer
industry and broadcasters. Because each was interested in accelerating DTV
integration with personal computing platforms, Intel did not believe that its
change of direction would put it at odds with Microsoft and Compaq. Intel
hoped that ordinary philosophical disagreements would not be interpreted as
a computer industry rift (Beacham, 1998a).

At NAB, a transcontinental HDTV broadcast was made from WHD-TV in
Washington, D.C., to Las Vegas' Convention Center. ATSC did not plan for
the demonstration to follow the April 3 DTV reports and orders so closely,

but the timing was impeccable. ATSC's Mark Richer said: "We hoped the FCC would make a decision, but now there is such excitement in the broadcast industry about moving to digital television and high-definition television that it is really starting to turn into a big celebration. It is really exciting" (Suydam, 1997, p. 36). Birkmaier (1997b) observed: "It appears that the decade-long effort to develop an advanced television standard is finally over. Or is it? Based on the high degree of flexibility given to broadcasters, it is more likely that this is just the beginning of the DTV story" (p. 27).

It was expected that manufacturers would be producing DTV sets by 1999, albeit at substantially higher prices than analog sets. Reber (1997b) observed: "In short, the transition from analog to digital means a complete overhaul of the American television broadcasting infrastructure. The transition will be costly with every participant—from television producer to broadcaster to home viewer—having to replace their current NTSC equipment with new DTV digital gear. In the face of our television system overhaul the American public still has not spoken on the issue. No one knows if DTV will sell" (p. 13). Reber (1997b) also broached the interlaced and progressive scanning issue:

Whoever wins this looming battle over incompatible DTV receivers and wins the biggest audiences will have an impact on how broadcasters choose to transmit their new digital signals—progressive or interlaced. If the broadcasters choose solely interlace DTV production equipment, their transmissions cannot be received on the computer industry's progressive-scan display devices. The issue also is divided by differences of opinion between the broadcast and computer industries as to whether interlaced scanning at 1,080 lines or progressive at 720 lines provides the best high-definition video. Soon it will be our turn, the American public, to decide which of the industries vision of DTV will prevail. (p. 13)

It was believed that most local TV stations would broadcast the more economically efficient 480-I, using a Grand Alliance encoder to convert video produced by 525-line interlace NTSC cameras and VTRs. Even then pictures would be 4:3, meaning that black side panels would border viewers' home screens similarly to top and bottom letter boxes. Network programming would be 16:9 without letter boxes. Inconsistencies were expected for DTV's first few years. Cameras with switchable 4:3/16:9 digital were available, making the transition easier. Consumers could force local stations to employ 16:9 after seeing network feeds.

Producing DTV. An often overlooked DTV effect is its impact on on-screen talent, set designers, and photographers. The 16:9 screen ratio impacts DTV production. Producers discovered early the difference between 4:3 and 16:9 ratios in the heights and widths on all aspects of scenery. There will be a 16:9 learning curve for photographers used to shooting 4:3 video, resulting in "an unlearning and a relearning" period for "every level of the production community: producers, directors, cameramen, graphics and technicians" (Dickson, 1997b, p. 66).

TV is an optical illusion created by lighting, camera angles, and effects. On-screen talent will be affected because ordinary makeup techniques will need altering. With HDTV, the viewer can see more clearly five o'clock shadows and other hair-related areas on a performer's person. My grandfather, a veteran horseman, bought the first color TV in our community in the early 1960s. He was most impressed that he could see the frothy sweat on the horses used on *Bonanza*. There may be no connection, but *Bonanza* is credited as the show that brought color TV into the mainstream.

Most HDTV viewers will probably see more detail than ever imagined, and much of it may be unwelcome. Paulsen (1997) noted: "[W]e are being warned that some on-air personnel will need the picture 'fuzzed' or they will look sort of, well, ugly—with warts, moles, spaces between their teeth. Has any of us had a professional portrait that wasn't 'touched up'?" (p. 82). Do we really want to see Peter Jennings' perspiration and/or possible epidermis-related flaws? Many stage sets look very nice via NTSC, but anyone who has seen sets in person realizes that they are not particularly impressive. HDTV gives viewers a similar perspective, so more money will be spent on set design and props. Mark Viola of Showman Fabricators, a film, TV, and industrial scenery builder, said: "In our experience, the biggest change was the use of high-end laminates and veneers to replace the painted wood grains, and the replacement of vacuum form brick [plastic sheets of brick surface stapled on the walls] with handmade bricks of split homosote [a compressed wood fiber product]" (Cudworth, 2000, p. 17). Such changes certainly would cost more in both time and dollars, forcing new methods of creating faux realism. Certainly, digital effects, lighting, and camera angles will play more prominent roles than ever. With DTV, there is no business as usual.

ABC, NBC, CBS, and Fox planned to use different DTV formats. As with local stations, networks wrestled between broadcasting HDTV or multiple SDTV. Should interlace or progressive be employed and at what resolution? Based on manufacturers' plans, DTV receivers would decode all 18 approved formats. The problems lay with viewers' deciding between progressive or interlace screens. CBS, consumer-friendlier than its counterparts, was first to announce its decision to employ HDTV using both interlace and progressive scanning. NBC considered using prime-time HDTV but SDTV at other times. Fox leaned to multichannel SDTV. Bob Seidel, CBS engineer, said: "If you do HDTV part of the day, then multichannel part of the day, how are people going to find you? That's going to be very confusing to consumers and very difficult to market" (Dickson, 1997a, p. 54). Cable operators were forced to wait until there were answers—especially regarding HDTV versus multichannels.

ABC president Preston Padden believed that stations and networks should commit to 480-P to move forward with DTV. Sinclair Broadcasting Group had similar plans. Some called Padden's suggestion "AM Stereo II" (AM stereo II, 1997, p. 74). He countered: "The technology is getting so good that we can contemplate multiple channels without any difference in picture quality that the consumer is going to see" (Ratnesar, 1997, p. 60). Hundt was incensed over broadcasters' multichannel SDTV preference, despite his statement supporting DTV flexible use. Although it reaffirmed his wishy-washiness, Hundt said: "The great myth here is that this was all about HDTV. HDTV has been a fraud by the broadcasters all these years" (p. 60). Why, then, did he not stop the "fraud" when he had the chance? Hundt then explained that he was most upset because broadcasters did not pay for spectrum (Some parting shots, 1997).

Broadcasters, an insecure lot, were nervous and unsure of how to implement DTV. In the 1920s they begged the federal government to regulate them. Although much rhetoric is given to their rights and freedoms, there is still an underlying need to have a standard and to be told what to do. Broadcasters are slow to change, as evidenced by time taken to accept new technologies. Neither FM, FM stereo, nor color TV was an overnight success. Even 10 years after color TV's advent, just 3–5 percent of homes had TVs on which to watch color programming. It took 25 years until about half of American homes had color sets.

Congressional Intervention. Senator John McCain's (R-AZ) Senate Commerce Committee called broadcasters to testify on Capitol Hill in September 1997. Hundt was also called, with senators expressing their displeasure about his handling of DTV and the marketplace approach. Senator Ernest Hollings (D-SC) said: "Here we have a chairman who doesn't even want to go along with the law. . . . If you are trying to change the rules, you are going to have to get a whole new Congress" (Albiniak, 1997d, p. 18).

Billy Tauzin (R-LA), House Telecommunications Subcommittee chair, said: "The intent of Congress was for broadcasters to use their channels for HDTV. If broadcasters don't use those channels [to offer some] HDTV, they can expect serious new obligations—both financial and public interest" (Albiniak, 1997c, p. 11). Tauzin was not opposed to multichannel SDTV but wanted HDTV implemented. Some believed that broadcasters would "carry as much HDTV as the market demands," which did not "mean every broadcaster will broadcast every program in HDTV, or that every broadcaster will broadcast some HDTV" (Room in the tent, 1997, p. 82). The debate raised the question: "What is HDTV?" (Silbergleid, 1997, p. 5). Did it even matter? Could most viewers tell the difference between various formats? Perhaps it would be up to consumers to define HDTV.

At first glance, it appeared that some congresspeople wanted to protect consumers, but in reality they wanted to ensure rapid spectrum return. The spectrum could then be auctioned for billions of dollars. Some congresspeople wanted warning labels on new sets and VCRs telling consumers that their equipment would become obsolete after 2006, and others wanted all sets and VCRs to be DTV-ready after 2001. Congressmen John Dingell of Michigan and Edward Markey of Massachusetts, sponsors of the legislation, denied that their motive was money. Markey called it "pure fantasy" (Albiniak, 1997a, p. 7).

The House Commerce Committee sponsored legislation to allow broadcasters to keep their extra channels beyond 2006. Tauzin recognized a potentially major logistical problem in DTV conversion. Just eight companies and 21 crews in the United States had "the experience and knowledge to erect towers exceeding 1,200 feet" (Miotto, 1997, p. 86). NAB figured that approximately 70–90 percent of 1,400 broadcast towers required replacement. Could that be done by the deadlines? Owen Ulmer, Stainless Inc. towers, did not believe it so: "You have to recognize that these guys are trained on the job. You don't just go out and start erecting a 2,000-foot tower tomorrow" (p. 86). Tauzin wanted stations to keep analog channels until 95 percent of viewers in their respective markets acquired DTV sets or converters. Building towers is "a massive undertaking," and the "strategy is to give broadcasters a little breathing room to make this work" (Albiniak, 1997b, p. 14).

Hundt Resigns. FCC chair Hundt, expected to serve at least until June 1998, tendered his resignation to President Clinton in May 1997. Broadcasters did not try to change Hundt's mind. Polon (1997b) explained:

[L]ike the departure of Richard Nixon, the bureaucratic demise of Hundt would leave a void that could not be easily filled for editorial cartoonists, technical magazine editorialists, and professional cynics of all kinds. The Commission under Hundt became exactly what the drafters of the enabling legislation for the FCC some 60-odd years ago abhorred—a tool of the White House directly responsible to the President in practice. The Commission, like the similarly established FBI and the SEC, were supposed to be, in theory, above partisan politics. What many fear most after Hundt's departure is what will happen to the Commission if it continues to travel farther down the same road. (p. 16)

Clinton had just appointed William E. Kennard and Harold W. Furchtgott-Roth to replace James Quello and Andrew Barrett. By fall 1997 Kennard replaced Hundt, and Gloria Tristani and Michael Powell were appointed Commissioners. Susan Ness was the lone holdover. Enigmatic Furchtgott-Roth did not own a television set. Never before had the FCC appointed so many new members at one time. No one knew what to expect.

Reaction to DTV Channel Allotment

Reaction to the FCC's DTV channel assignments was mixed. Coverage areas for most DTV channels were on par with the analog channel, and some were better. However, some coverage areas were smaller than counterpart analog channels. By June 1997 the FCC received about 200 petitions asking for reconsideration of DTV allotments. Some threatened legal action. The Commission and NAB expected some complaints because of the enormous task, but Los Angeles County had a different concern. Six Los Angeles licenses were placed on channels 60-69, precluding "public safety use of the 746-806 MHz band until the end of the DTV transition" (McConnell, 1997b, p. 18).

The FCC (1997j) addressed concerns about channels 60–69 with a July 9 NPRM. The Commission would protect the 15 stations on channels 60–69 until the end of the transition period, then move them elsewhere. Then it would allocate 24 megahertz (764-776 MHz and 794-806 MHz) to fixed and mobile services and designate it for public safety use. It would "allocate the remaining 36 megahertz at 746–764 MHz and 776–794 MHz to the fixed, mobile, and broadcasting services." The FCC planned to assign the 36 MHz "through competitive bidding." The spectrum was considered appropriate for public safety because of light TV use adjacent "to existing public safety operations in the 806–824 MHz band."

Consumers became reluctant to buy new sets—digital or analog—so Zenith Electronics Corporation promised buyers that it would accept trade-ins of Zenith sets on new DTV sets, giving full credit for the old set toward the newer one. The offer was good only on 32- to 60-inch screen sizes purchased from authorized Zenith dealers (Zenith addresses obsolescence, 1997).

Canada adopted ATSC's DTV standard on November 8, 1997. Careless (1997) reported that "they're not adopting a new digital standard out of a desire to radically improve over-the-air TV. Instead, they're trying to keep up with their neighbors to the south: neighbors who generate most of Canada's primetime content, and who support the country's production industry through international co-productions" (p. 14). On November 21 South Korea followed suit because ATSC's standard fitted Korea technologically and economically. Canada's reason for adoption was interesting in light of its decision to initiate a new terrestrial DAB system (Eureka-147).

On December 31, 1997, the FCC (1997l) adopted its *Report and Order* regarding reallocation of channels 60–69 (746–806 MHz). NPRM proposals "were in part an outgrowth" of the *Sixth Report and Order* and allotment table. The FCC received 67 comments and 17 reply comments, and feedback was mixed. The FCC said that there was strong support from "public safety agencies, radio equipment manufacturers, and many states, counties, and municipalities" for "reallocating 24 megahertz of channels 60–69 for public safety use." However, MSTV and NAB, "in joint comments, disagree with our proposal to allocate channels 63, 64, 68, and 69 to public safety and recommend allocating channels 66–69 as an alternative." One reason was adjacent-channel interference to existing LMS at 806–824 MHz. There was support for the proposal, and the FCC ultimately denied opposition to stick with its original plan.

As for allocating 746–806 MHz for new services, the FCC (1997l) said that there was concern that full-power DTV transmitters could interfere with adjacent, lower-powered LMS. CBA believed that "there is no reason to preclude low power broadcasters from competing for non-public safety spectrum in the 746-806 MHz band." The Commission denied the requests because the

"Budget Act requires that we allocate the remaining 36 megahertz of spectrum from channels 60–69 for commercial services that will be assigned by competitive bidding." The Commission would allow broadcasters to remain on the spectrum and disagreed with commenters that "including full power broadcasting in this spectrum is likely to cause interference problems with other commercial applications, especially low-power mobile applications." The FCC was "not persuaded that such sharing" of spectrum was "not feasible."

The FCC (1997l) said: "Several parties filed comments objecting generally to the DTV transition plan and the allocation of Channels 60–69 to other services. Broadcasters argue that we should retain TV channels 60–69 to provide spectrum for TV licensees who may encounter difficulties with the transition from analog TV to DTV, and to provide a 'safe haven' into which displaced LPTV and TV translator licensees could move during the DTV transition period." Other commenters wanted all TV operations cleared from the band immediately, "citing the critical need for more public safety spectrum and the difficulties in spectrum sharing between TV and other services."

The FCC (1997l) did not "retain this spectrum as a 'safe haven'" because there were "limited potential benefits." Limited benefits, the Commission believed, "are outweighed by the costs of delaying much needed public safety services and opportunities for new services." The FCC added: "We also find no merit in the argument that we should remove immediately all TV broadcasting operations from TV channels 60–69. The operation of some TV and DTV stations in this spectrum is clearly required to facilitate the DTV transition; and the Budget Act provides for this." The FCC said: "Commenters were sharply divided as to whether any further actions should be taken to accommodate LPTV and TV translators in channels 60–69." Again, the Budget Act "leaves us no latitude in clearing LPTV and TV translator stations from the band at the end of the DTV transition period." LPTV and TV translators would operate on channels 60–69 until the end of DTV transition "as long as they do not cause harmful interference to primary services." Although unspecified, the FCC said that DTV transition could "be extended in some markets for several reasons."

The FCC (1997l) declared that 764–776 MHz and 794–806 MHz (channels 63–64 and 68–69) would primarily be allocated to fixed and mobile public safety radio services. Also, "commercial portions of the band at 746–764 MHz and 776–794 MHz bands (TV channels 60–62 and 65–67) will be allocated to the fixed, mobile, and broadcasting services, and licenses in these bands will be assigned by competitive bidding." Stations with licenses for channels 60–69 could keep them until the end of transition.

The top 10 market stations were preparing to introduce DTV in November 1998. The stations were volunteers and were not obligated by law or regulation to be first. Several obstacles hindered them, including channel allotment complaints, tower status, and transmitter delivery/installation. Some border stations were delayed while the United States and Canada solved coverage and interference problems. Chief engineer Mike Dobach, WWJ Detroit, said: "We have the tower, have the space, have commitments by the manufacturers, but until the FCC issues a construction permit we are at a standstill" (Anderson, 1998a, p. 19).

The *Fifth Report and Order*

In its long-awaited *Memorandum Opinion and Order on Reconsideration of the Fifth Report and Order* adopted February 17, 1998, the FCC (1998a) responded "to petitions for reconsideration from various parties" and took the "opportunity to reaffirm, revise, or clarify certain" of their actions. The FCC (1998c) "affirmed the principles of its April 3, 1997, DTV *Sixth Report and Order* that assigns each broadcaster a new channel for DTV operations and allows TV broadcasters to replicate their existing NTSC service with their new DTV channels." The Commission also released a *Reconsideration Order*, in which it "finalized the core spectrum to be used for DTV, made adjustments to UHF DTV power levels, took steps to avoid adjacent channel interference and made administrative and technical changes to minimize the impact of DTV implementation on low power operations." The FCC did not address must-carry and retransmission but would do so in a separate notice.

Much of the proceeding corrected oversights or mistakes. Two stations were erroneously omitted from DTV channel allotment. Others argued that they had pending applications for an analog channel so should have received a DTV channel. The FCC refused those requests but granted permission for new licensees to build DTV stations if certain requirements were met. Analog licensees would have to convert to DTV by the 2006 deadline. Any broadcaster not completing construction by the deadline could file for an extension.

The FCC (1998a) considered the effect of allotments on radio stations and considered NPR's petition to alter the construction schedule. NPR contended that "a significant number of educational FM stations will have to relinquish their tower space and pay for a costly relocation of their transmitting antennas." The FCC said that NPR's conclusions were "speculative" and "has not demonstrated at this time that the construction schedule will have any undue negative impact on a significant number of public radio stations."

The FCC (1998a) addressed noncommercial TV issues. It denied petitions asking for construction schedule modifications because "determining the specific nature of whatever special relief may be needed for noncommercial educational broadcasters is best considered during our periodic reviews." Los Angeles County wanted earlier spectrum recovery for channels 60–69 in southern California "to alleviate the severe spectrum shortages facing Los Angeles area public safety agencies." San Bernardino objected to early recovery, "maintaining that too early a reversion date may hurt viewers in rural areas dependent on traditional translator services." The FCC (1998a) denied both requests but would designate some spectrum for public safety in southern California.

The *Sixth Report and Order*

The FCC's (1998b) *Memorandum Opinion and Order on Reconsideration of the Sixth Report and Order* was more complicated than the *Fifth Report and Order*, because it dealt with 231 petitions about its allotment table. The FCC was "generally maintaining the DTV allotment principles and policies set forth in the Sixth Report and Order." Methodically and categorically, the FCC addressed the petitions and rendered its decision for each. The FCC (1998c) summarized its responses to the 231 petitions, focusing primarily on minor table adjustments.

Kennard, Furtchgott-Roth, and Ness issued individual statements. Kennard said: "The FCC has just passed another milestone on the road to bringing the benefits of digital television (DTV) to the American public" (FCC, 1998e). Kennard believed that broadcasters were given "the regulatory certainty" needed "to proceed expeditiously" to DTV. He was "pleased" with volunteers initiating the conversion, because consumers would soon see DTV. Kennard concluded: "The FCC must continue to move expeditiously on the remaining DTV issues, such as must carry coverage, public service obligations and fees for ancillary services. However, the structure and framework for digital television is now in place that will enable broadcasters and TV set manufacturers alike in 1998 to go from the planning stage into the building and manufacturing stage. This is great news for consumers and television viewers across the country" (FCC, 1998e).

Commissioner Ness (1998f) was brief and generally supportive of the FCC's process, but Furchtgott-Roth issued a lengthy statement. He was also supportive "with one exception" (FCC, 1998d). Furchtgott-Roth was particularly concerned about a "spectrum grab" and its impact on LPTV. The FCC's "decision to expand the post-transition core will do little to ease the technical burdens of the transition on full power broadcasters and will do nothing to save existing LPTV stations that are displaced during the transition." Furchtgott-Roth concluded: "We seem to say that as long as there are benefits to a decision, the costs do not matter, and that such decisions are particularly easy if consumers never know what services they are missing or how the federal budget is affected. This unwillingness to conduct straightforward cost-benefit analyses and provide consumers all the information they deserve is becoming a shameful hallmark of this agency" (FCC, 1998d).

Cable and DTV

Expensive prototype DTV sets were displayed at the 1998 winter CES in Las Vegas with costs ranging from $5,000 to $10,000. Set-top converters averaged $700. Sets were expected on the market by fall 1998. About 14 companies developed DTV sets, including Ampro, Hitachi, JVC, Mitsubishi, Panasonic, Philips, Pioneer, Runco, Samsung, Sharp, Sony, Thomson,

Vidikron, and Zenith. Thomson's "forecast for DTV sales in the first year is more than 20,000 and less than 100,000" (Garber, 1998, p. 19).

Cable vendors were not enamored with DTV. TCI, the nation's largest cable company, announced in January 1998 that it would "downconvert broadcaster transmission of 1,080 interlace (1,080-I) HDTV and then pass it on to its subscribers in a lower resolution, 480 progressive (480-P) format" (Bloomfield, 1998, p. 14). Note: AT&T merged with TCI in June 1998 and was cleared to acquire TCI in March 1999. On August 3, 1999, TCI officially became AT&T. TCI's customers would receive signals with less than 20 percent of the resolution offered by 1080-I. CEMA president Gary Shapiro stated: "Manufacturers and broadcasters have committed to bringing Americans the astounding picture resolution of HDTV, but now TCI's 14 million customers may never have the chance to see it. This is a huge tragedy for the American consumer" (p. 14). Shapiro added: "The FCC must ensure that if broadcasters transmit programming in high-definition, cable companies are required to pass the programming through to the consumer in the same manner. Otherwise, cable subscribers will be involuntarily downconverted to a picture resolution no better than today's TV" (p. 14). Although 480-P is a digital format, it is not HDTV. Shapiro continued: "Any effort to label 480-P as true HDTV is an attempt to fool American consumers, who want the highest level of resolution they can get" (p. 14).

A similar situation occurred with MTS. Many stations transmitted stereo, but cable passed it to the consumer as mono. Some consumers cannot be convinced that all FM is not stereo, as the two have become almost synonymous, but all audio is not stereo, and all digital video is not high-definition. Leo Hindery, TCI president, said that CEMA was incorrect and misleading consumers. Hindery said: "The technology in TCI's advanced digital set-top devices allows a TV signal in any HDTV format to be transmitted to a customer's high-definition TV set. Second, customers who do not own a high-definition TV set can receive 480-P HDTV signals, translated into a standard-definition format, with the set-top device as currently configured. As the market for HDTV evolves, TCI will continue to respond to the needs of its customers. Any accusation that we are impeding this process is dead wrong" (p. 14). Hindery called 480-P HDTV but later acknowledged that only 720-P and 1080-I are HDTV (p. 18). The situation illustrated a major problem faced by DTV and other new technologies. Abbreviations caused considerable problems, because anyone wanting to cloud an issue could spit out a slew of letters and numbers. Colman (1998) observed: "The current furor over HDTV is like the cooking class from hell. Mix equal parts semantics, bureaucracy and economics; blend thoroughly, then pressure cook until too hot to handle" (p. 44).

In March 1998 Fox revealed that it would primarily broadcast SDTV at 480-P but would broadcast 780-P in prime time. Larry Jacobson, Fox president, said: "The marketplace is going to guide us from there" (McClellan & Dickson, 1998, p. 6). CBS and NBC would broadcast 1080-I in prime time, but ABC chose 720-P. ABC president Preston Padden said 720-P offered better picture quality than 1080i and believed that "second-generation of HDTV displays" would employ 720-P (Grotticelli, 1998b, p. 15). Padden said progressive formats made more creative video possible. He added that ABC's decision would have come sooner, but there was no manufacturer commitment to produce 720-P equipment until Panasonic supplied enough equipment to support the format. ABC's "continued, persistent pursuit of 720p equipment is what led to Panasonic's decision" (p. 16). Padden believed that differing formats would not deter DTV. He explained: "All of the receivers are being made with chips that will decode all of the different formats, so the consumer won't have to worry about which set to buy. And, there's no added cost related to our decision, because the most expensive format to decode is the 1080i. Interlace signals are not susceptible to digital manipulation in as elegant a fashion as progressive signals" (p. 16).

Cable and Congress. Billy Tauzin, House Telecommunications Subcommittee chair, summoned ABC, CBS, NBC, and Fox to explain and demonstrate format choices to his subcommittee. Tauzin explained: "My concern from the beginning has been that there is a reason why we picked 6 [MHz]— because that's what it took to deliver a HDTV signal" (Albiniak, 1998a, p. 42). He added: "Congress meant for them to show that signal to Americans. Give them a chance to see it, and give them a chance to accept it or reject it. After that, whether they broadcast it just in prime time or broadcast HDTV signal that is compressed has less relevance. In the end there may be some consequences to the broadcasters; there may be some quid pro quos we have to talk about" (p. 42). Sharing Tauzin's concern, Senator Jesse Helms (R-NC) sent a letter to Kennard stating: "I did not envision that networks or television stations would use the digital spectrum solely to increase the number of channels they could offer. A multitude of standard definition programs may line the networks' pockets, but it will not attract viewers nor will it promote the use or distribution of high definition wide-screen receivers; it will drastically slow the transition . . . and delay the recovery of the analog spectrum for auction" (Helms advocates, 1998, p. 110). Helms added: "Those networks and stations that do not choose to participate in the highest quality of HDTV do not deserve the newly assigned digital channels" (p. 110).

At the April 23, 1998, hearing, Tauzin focused almost solely on cable. TCI's Hindery said that despite information to the contrary, set-top cable boxes "can pass through any format—480 progressive, 720 progressive, 1080 interlace and, ultimately, 1080 progressive" (Albiniak, 1998b, p. 4). Boxes would down-convert digital signals to analog but could not pass high-definition formats higher than 720-P at 24 frames. TCI would "simply design a device that can handle the other formats" (p. 6). NBC planned to broadcast about 10 hours weekly of prime-time HDTV by fall 1998, and CBS planned five hours. NBC's first 1080-I broadcast would be *The Tonight Show with Jay Leno*. Plans of ABC, Fox, and PBS were unknown (Grotticelli, 1998a).

Cable was concerned about the touchy subject of DTV must-carry rules. Networks' format differences added fuel to the fire. *TV Broadcast* reported: "The broadcast industry has tried to paint a picture of urgency, claiming that if cable—which controls over 60 percent of United States viewing households—does not pass along its high definition channels, the result will be a domino effect: HDTV (1980i and 720p) receivers won't sell, producers won't make HDTV programs, and the new digital TV world will stall" (Must-carry debated, 1998, pp. 1, 104). Scott Sassa, NBC Television Stations president, acknowledged the importance of cable to DTV's transition. He commented: "If cable passes through the advantages of DTV to consumers with as little disruption to viewing habits as practicable, it will go a long way toward the mass acceptance of DTV" (p. 104). Cable could be detrimental if it passed lower-quality signals, which seemed likely given its limited bandwidth.

DTV's Cost

Kovacs (1999) observed: "[HDTV] seems to be cloaked in stealth at the moment. Many in the television industry believe that HDTV is too expensive, too undefined and too new to justify time spent studying the equipment and its use. Buying HD gear is simply out of the question for most people. After all, where can you display it? Who uses it? How can you justify the expense? It's not even a blip on many of our equipment-buying radar screens" (p. 28). A lot was said about DTV conversion's high cost, but there were few realistic estimates. Graham (1998) developed "a conservative estimate of what HDTV is going to cost" (p. 27). Graham said: "$157 billion dollars or $1,570 for each of the 100 million households in the United States, and four out of five of those households will have the 'set-top box' on one of their present NTSC 'old' TVs (so they will actually lose ground since their other TVs won't pick up signals any more)" (p. 27). He added: "Only one out of five households will actually have HDTV, and none of their older NTSC TVs will pick up signals anymore. These dollar estimates are extremely conservative and could easily double" (p. 27). Graham assigned $3,000 for each new DTV set (20 million sets), $250 each for 80 million set-top boxes (not including multiple-TV households), $1,000 each for 20 million HD VCRs, and 100 million households times 1.5 wasted TVs times average cost of $250. Graham did not calculate costs for wasted analog VCRs. Station cost estimates were based on an average conversion of $20 million each. Graham said that consumers, who will shoulder the greatest economic burden, have not exactly "been clamoring for" DTV (p. 27).

Deadly DTV Interference

A February 1998 interference problem between Dallas' WFAA-DT and medical telemetry devices prompted the FCC to freeze DTV permits. Fenton and Livingstone (1998) reported: "When Dallas station WFAA began testing its DTV equipment, nearby hospitals found that their telemetry monitoring systems, which transmit data on patients' vital signs to doctors and nurses, stopped working. Fortunately, no one was hurt, and WFAA ceased testing as soon as it was made aware of the problem. How did it happen? Medical telemetry devices are 'secondary users' of the TV band and have been free to use unoccupied portions of the spectrum. However, all TV stations have been assigned new digital channels in those same 'unoccupied' portions" (p. 6). In a joint statement, the FCC (1998g) and FDA explained the interference problem and what was being done to correct it: "Medical telemetry devices have long shared the TV broadcast spectrum on a secondary basis. This sharing can continue during the implementation of digital television. However, it is important to ensure that broadcasters, the health care community and manufacturers of medical devices have adequate information and take appropriate steps to avoid radio frequency interference." The FCC (1998h) produced a "Fact Sheet" to explain terms and how it would deal with interference and said that users of telemetry devices can call TV stations in their market to learn what channels each station will use for DTV. Information for every market was listed at http://www.fcc.gov/healthnet/.

The WFAA situation raised two important questions. First, would DTV licensees be legally liable for harm caused by interference from their DTV signals? What would happen if signal interference were to be blamed for an injury or fatality? Second, what would the implications be in allowing the medical industry to override broadcast interests in licensing matters? The questions were tough but needed to be answered by the FCC.

By May 1998 at least nine lawsuits and 32 petitions were filed with the FCC in regard to DTV rules and channel allotments. Except for two California suits, most were filed with the United States Court of Appeals in Washington, D.C. The FCC wanted all suits consolidated into one, but Mountain Broadcasting objected because delaying the process would prevent fewer solutions to rectify problems. Many complainants focused on reductions in broadcast coverage areas between analog and digital channels (McConnell, 1998).

DTV Progress in the United States and the World

There was positive news as 38 of 42 stations met the May 1, 1998, deadline to file DTV construction applications. Three of four delinquent stations filed for extensions, and the fourth planned to do so. Forty stations represented major network affiliates in the top 10 United States markets (Digital TV deadlines, 1998). By July, 16 stations had broadcast DTV. Broadcasters were dismayed that there were no DTV receivers, without which stations could not test reception. Indoor antenna DTV reception remained a big question mark (Dickson, 1998).

There was DTV progress in other countries. Canada, Mexico, South Korea, Japan, and Taiwan employed ATSC's system. Like the United States,

Canada and Mexico planned to phase out analog broadcasting by 2006. Australia and New Zealand chose European DVB's system produced by EBU (Freed, 1998).

Must-Carry Consideration. Broadcasters and cable debated DTV's must-carry rules, and the FCC (1998i) opened an NPRM on July 9. The FCC (1998j) said: "The Notice addresses the need for compatibility between digital systems, seeks comment on possible changes to the mandatory carriage rules, and explores the impact carriage of digital television signals may have on other Commission rules." The Commission added: "The broadcast signal carriage rules discussed in the Notice originate from the Cable Television Consumer Protection and Competition Act of 1992. This statute amended the Communications Act of 1934 to provide television stations with certain carriage rights on local market cable television systems." The FCC (1998i) sought comment on resolving digital equipment compatibility issues, DTV transition from full must-carry to no must-carry requirements, DTV signal carriage by small cable operators, DTV picture quality degradation on cable, defining duplication during transition, DTV channel positioning options, and other definitions and criteria. The FCC (1998i) explained why must-carry regulations should be revisited for DTV:

Under the mandatory carriage provisions, cable operators, subject to certain capacity based limitations, are generally required to carry local television stations on their cable systems. The Act states that systems with more than 12 usable activated channels must carry local commercial television stations, "up to one-third of the aggregate number of usable activated channels of such system[s]." Beyond this requirement, the carriage of additional broadcast television stations is at the discretion of the cable operator. In addition, cable systems are obliged to carry local noncommercial educational television stations according to a different formula and based upon a cable system's number of usable activated channels. Low power television stations may request carriage if they meet six statutory criteria. A cable operator, however, cannot carry a low power station in lieu of a full power station.

The FCC (1998i) offered seven possible must-carry solutions: (1) to require that all cable systems carry all commercial DTV and analog stations up to the one-third capacity limit; (2) require cable systems to add DTV stations as they begin to broadcast; (3) require immediate carriage of DTV signals with a limit of three to five channels per year; (4) require broadcasters to pick which channel would be carried—analog or digital; (5) require DTV must-carry when a certain, but not yet specified, percentage of consumers own DTV receivers; (6) require DTV must-carry after a specified date; and/or (7) require no DTV must-carry until total transition is made from analog to digital. The FCC said: "The most difficult carriage issues arise during the transition period when the digital and analog signals are operating simultaneously. In the NPRM the Commission tentatively finds that the Communications Act and its legislative history has given it the discretion to manage carriage issues during the transition period. Recognizing the complexities that will arise during this time, and the possibility of cable service disruptions, the Commission believes it has the ability to develop rules to facilitate the transition process to achieve the goals underlying the mandatory carriage requirements of the statute." The FCC's deadline for comments was September 17, 1998, and for reply comments was October 30, 1998.

The FCC took no position on must-carry, and some were unhappy with the noncommittal approach. *Broadcast Engineering* summed up the opinion of many broadcasters:

Nobody likes to be told what to do, but this may be the case after the FCC gets finished with the must-carry issues as they relate to the new digital TV channels. The commission is walking a tightrope, trying to stay neutral. The FCC has some of the best technical minds in the country, but these are not the good old days back when the commission did what *they* thought best for all concerned. As a result of that kind of thinking and action, we ended up with a very fine, technically superior, broadcast industry. The commission has, however, slowly drifted into a wishy-washy, let the non-technically, uninformed consumer, swayed by flashy layouts from Madison avenue [*sic*] ad agencies, make the decision for them. With that in mind, it appears that the commissioners are steering clear, as usual, of any broadcast/cable industry face-off over digital must-carry rules. The time-proven contest of the clash of differing opinions in a public form [*sic*] has always been the best way to ascertain the better way of doing things. Why should it be any different for this issue? (Must carry, 1998, p. 20)

Some pundits predicted DTV must-carry would end up where analog must-carry did, in the United States Supreme Court. In 1992 the Court upheld analog must-carry's constitutionality.

A day before the FCC's NPRM, broadcast, cable, and electronics representatives appeared before Congress to complain about the FCC, its DTV timetable, and its hesitance to act on must-carry. Libin (1998) concluded: "The future of digital television (DTV) portends consumer confusion, expensive equipment, reception problems and cable incompatibility" (p. 26). Senator John McCain lamented: "It hardly qualifies as a success story in the making" (p. 26). McCain added: "It is long past time for the American public to hear about the problems they will experience in the rollout of digital TV" (p. 26). *Broadcasting & Cable* editors wrote: "Let's admit it: digital television is in danger of being declared dead on arrival" (Grand Alliance II, 1998, p. 74). They added: "If former FCC chairman Reed Hundt wanted a marketplace solution, he got one. He also brought us AM Stereo II" (p. 74).

DTV for Sale

On August 7, 1998, a San Diego audio/video dealer sold the first DTV sets. About 8,000 people lined up to see the new $5,499 sets, but no one could see a broadcast because San Diego had no DTV station. The sets were capable of receiving NTSC signals. Panasonic scheduled the debut of DTV set-top converter boxes in October for $1,500 (Birkmaier, 1998). FCC chair Kennard was not pleased that IEEE-1394 (aka Apple Computers' "Firewire") and Sony's i.Link had not been adopted as the standard digital component connection more rapidly. He wanted developers to accelerate the schedule (Must carry, 1998). "Firewire" was a device to drive set-top boxes and DTV system audio and video components, computers, and peripherals. In a September 1998 speech to the IRTS, Kennard said that the Commission did its part to implement DTV and would do no more. He said: "I resist that; I reject that. . . . The role of government is not to supply business plans . . . or put artificial limits on the business plans you come up with" (Jessell, 1998, p. 22). The FCC would support an "aggressive" DTV schedule and would act on must-carry.

Commissioner Powell opposed rapid DTV rollout, believing the 2006 deadline "far too aggressive" (McConnell, 1998, p. 14). Powell said: "We're facing a potential train wreck" (p. 14). He said that consumers could reject DTV, resulting in indefinite analog broadcasting. He added: "With a product this expensive, I'm not sure we'll get two or three shots at this. I think it will be extraordinarily difficult to achieve the ubiquitous customer acceptance that is necessary for success" (p. 14).

Set-top converters were important to DTV. Consumers have typically kept TV sets for about 12 years, so it was unlikely that one would dump sets to advance DTV. A similar cycle has affected audio. Listeners did not discard AM receivers because FM was introduced. Many who owned records, cassettes, and players did not dispose of them upon introduction of compact discs. As Dick (1998b) pointed out: "New technology seldom exists in a vacuum. Rather, it usually has to work with legacy (that means old) equipment" (p. 10). Consumers will continue to use VCRs and VHS videotapes for a long time. It is not economically viable to discard old for new—especially in such an expensive endeavor as audio/video.

DTV's Official Debut

DTV officially debuted over 42 U.S. stations on November 1, 1998. But, the first broadcast occurred days earlier on October 29, when 24 stations broadcast John Glenn's return to space. A problem for consumers was finding DTV stations and sets. The problem would be compounded should a station opt for multiple SDTV channels rather than one HDTV channel. It would work this way. The traditional analog channel for Atlanta's WSB-TV is Channel 2. WSB-DT was assigned Channel 39. Rather than tune DTV receivers to Channel 2 or Channel 39, viewers would tune to Channel 2-0 for analog, but would dial Channel 2-1 for the first DTV channel. If WSB employed multicasting, subsequent channels would be listed as Channel 2-2, Channel 2-3, and on through as many as six channels, or 2-6. Without DTV sets or converters, consumers would receive analog Channel 2 until phase-out. For the record, ABC affiliate WSB-DT's first broadcast was a 7 P.M. network broadcast of Disney's *101 Dalmatians*. Disney-owned ABC planned to air five other movies during DTV's first year.

On November 19, 1998, the FCC voted unanimously to impose fees on stations using multiple channels as subscription services. Many companies hoped to form miniversions of over-the-air, cable-type services. Because spectrum was free to broadcasters, the Commission believed that there should be compensation for charging customers. Fees were set at 5 percent of the gross revenue generated by such channels aside from money gained by advertising. Payment by DTV licensees would be due each year on December 1 for services running from September to September. Network ratings declined in 1998 as they had for several years, and affiliates and other over-the-air stations were considering subscription services to offset that trend.

In December 1998 Time Warner Cable struck an agreement to carry CBS programming voluntarily and not by must-carry rules. It was hoped that the deal would lead to many more. Many observers believed that DTV was doomed without cable. Within a year, Fox and NBC struck cable carriage deals with AT&T.

By January 1999 about 13,000 DTV sets were sold in the United States—although they were not necessarily HDTV-capable. Importantly, products were available in stores rather than just on convention floors. For the first time, CES demonstrated sets that retailers could stock and sell. Prices remained expensive, ranging from $3,000 to $17,000. In November 1998 manufacturers and cable adopted "Firewire" (aka IEEE-1394) as the standard digital component connection. "Firewire" allowed broadcast signals to communicate with cable boxes (Ashworth, 1999a). As pessimistic as 1998 had seemed until DTV's November debut, 1999 was starting out positively. Previous technologies had followed similar patterns.

As broadcasters and cable wrangled over must-carry, DBS companies moved forward with DTV. DBS threatened cable, and companies such as RCA, DirectTV, Dish Network, Primestar, and USSB were turning up the heat. Some employed DTV test channels, and others were soon to follow. If cable balked at carrying DTV, it seemed certain that DBS providers would carry it. Numerous consumers subscribed to DBS services, but reluctant ones cited local channel unavailability as the primary reason for not subscribing. A second reason was that each set needed a dedicated DBS receiver. Both problems were being addressed.

Progress was made in June 1999, when NAB agreed to allow DirecTV to carry local stations. Other DBS companies had not struck such deals (Albiniak, 1999). Cable was initially created to give customers better local TV reception without the inconvenience of adjusting antennae. As cable caught on, some broadcasters in other geographic locations beamed signals to cable companies in other locales. Superstations WTBS and WGN are examples.

Cable-only stations and subscription services began to appear. Bills were introduced in Congress by Senator John McCain (R-AZ) and Representative Billy Tauzin (R-LA) to allow DBS operators to carry local stations. Without local channels, DBS subscribers were forced to use basic cable or antennae to receive them. Switching between DBS and cable/antennae was inconvenient, especially for American viewers accustomed to clicking remotes to get programs instantaneously.

A DTV Business Model. In broadcasting's history, such a sweeping change had never been attempted. There was no DTV business model. One strategy was to establish industry partnerships. To that end, Mitsubishi agreed to underwrite CBS' filmed HDTV productions during the 1999–2000 season. CBS broadcast 80 percent of its schedule in 1080-I. Fourteen CBS-owned and -operated stations were converted to DTV, and 40 more were to be ready by November 1, 1999 (Ashworth, 1999b). A similar arrangement was made between ABC and Panasonic. Panasonic built a 720-P mobile production truck and provided other equipment for ABC's 1999 *Monday Night Football.* Home Box Office, Fox, and PBS provided their own HDTV programming. Most of the programming debuted in fall 1999. Few local stations planned DTV programming beyond passing through network feeds. ABC and Panasonic were also expected to end their *Monday Night Football* partnership. The arrangement between CBS and Mitsubishi was not renewed, but both companies vowed to continue some kind of relationship. However, for the 2000–2001 TV season CBS made a deal with Panasonic to deliver 17 of its 18 prime time programs. Only CBS's *Walker, Texas Ranger* was excluded from the deal because it was shot with 16mm film (Kerschbaumer, 2000). CBS also formed a partnership with Thomson Consumer Electronics, which would sponsor CBS's HDTV Super Bowl XXXV broadcast on January 28, 2001, and four NFL playoff games. Thomson had previously underwritten CBS's HDTV broadcast of NCAA basketball's Final Four in March 2000 (Dickson, 2000a).

On April 26, 1999, NBC's *The Tonight Show* became the first regularly scheduled network program produced and transmitted in HDTV. Host Jay Leno poked fun at HDTV in his monologue and jabbed at competitors. He humorously cautioned viewers not to misinterpret HDTV as "Fox's HDT&A format." He also mentioned there are about as many people with capability to watch HDTV as there are UPN viewers. He joked: "I remember the old days of television, when shows would be made sharper because of the writing." Otherwise, the May 1 deadline for top 10 market network stations passed unceremoniously.

The Tonight Show sponsor Procter & Gamble produced HDTV commercials for the debut. The commercials were never seen, as NBC's facility was incapable of playing the spots. Procter & Gamble's Jim Gosney said: "But they weren't alone. At the time, none of the three networks [ABC, CBS, and NBC] had a procedure for airing HD commercials. They all assumed they were going to upconvert 4:3 commercials, and for the most part that's exactly what they were asked to do" (Holt, 1999, p. 26). Nothing had changed seven months later.

FCC chair Kennard was frustrated with DTV's slow progress. As early as September 1998, Kennard complained that more was not being done to develop cooperation among DTV players. At a May 20, 1999, roundtable discussion, Kennard met with representatives of consumer electronics, filmmaking, cable, retailing, broadcasting, program production, and high technology. Kennard set a July 1 deadline for establishing a timetable to resolve disputes and compatibility issues. There had been little progress since manufacturers and cable adopted IEEE-1394 ("Firewire") as the standard digital component connection. Some manufacturers did not think "Firewire" was necessary on all DTV sets. Critics called the deadline meaningless without provision to enforce it. Kennard, a staunch marketplace supporter, was reluctant to impose government mandates. He preferred that businesses produce their own solutions.

Kennard's deadline was met, and two problems were addressed. One was a dispute over copy protection for DTV programming, and MPAA wanted an agreement by August 1, 1999. MPAA, opposing CEMA over copy protection, wanted final authority over what could be copied and how frequently. CEMA believed that MPAA was violating fair use recording rights. NCTA believed that "Firewire" would alleviate MPAA's apprehension with its built-in copy protection. The second issue was set-top boxes. NCTA wanted manufacturers to build DTV sets to receive signals without a box. NCTA wanted a solution by October 31 (McConnell, 1999a). By July 1999 Sony was marketing DTV set-top boxes for a suggested retail price of $1,599.

In February 2000 Kennard expressed his continued displeasure with the lack of progress in making DTV sets cable-compatible. Kennard was unhappy with "cable-ready" labels on DTV sets. He wanted all units built with "Firewire" and to be labeled as to interoperability.

By the end of April about 60 stations in 24 markets were broadcasting DTV, but the digital/analog issue confused consumers. Upset retailers saw themselves doing the bulk of DTV marketing and education and wanted manufacturers and broadcasters to do more (Veilleux, 1999).

As of mid-July, 41 stations in the top 10 television markets were broadcasting DTV. Some New York and Chicago stations were not broadcasting DTV due to problems with antenna space. DTV broadcasts primarily comprised SDTV programming. There were retailer unawareness and a lack of programming. Viewers wanted to know when they would get HDTV (Bowser, 1999).

Audio continued to get short shrift. DTV stations were using MTS instead of Dolby Digital 5.1 surround sound. The major networks were serious about the audio standard, but affiliates were converting signals to stereo or into discrete audio pairs. Grotticelli (1999) observed: "At this point, one year after the first digital broadcasts began, multichannel audio is still a good idea whose time has yet to come. I'm waiting for the time when that captivating DTV audio comes crashing through the glass ceiling of budgetary constraints" (p. 6).

COFDM and 8-VSB Revisited

Broadcasters were never satisfied with Zenith's 8-VSB transmission technology. ACATS selected 8-VSB in 1994 despite broadcasters' preference for COFDM, which alleviated ghosting, improved coverage, and facilitated subsidiary nonbroadcast services. At the time, ACATS' Richard Wiley said that if COFDM "is demonstrably better, we would have to look at it." In 1999 Sinclair Broadcast Group questioned 8-VSB's viability, favoring COFDM because it enhanced over-the-air DTV reception. Indoor reception, presenting the harshest multipath conditions, was a problem for 8-VSB. Bow-tie antennae and rabbit ears were insufficient in picking up DTV signals indoors. Consumers needed outdoor antennae, but many balked at the prospect. David Smith, Sinclair president and CEO, said: "Today, it does not work. Period and end of sentence" (Dickson, 1999, p. 22). Sinclair solicited further tests and comparisons and wanted an organization other than ATSC to do it. A major question was whether the problem was transmission and/or reception. In 1994 some believed that support for COFDM was motivated by broadcasters seeking to delay DTV, so Sinclair's objections drew criticism. Harris Corporation and Thomson Consumer Electronics, believing that antennae and receivers would improve indoor reception, defended 8-VSB as efficient and cost-effective.

Changing modulation schemes would hurt DTV and override any potential improvement. It was generally accepted that COFDM experienced better reception, but it cost more to implement. However, its signal was more than twice as strong as 8-VSB, with only equal coverage area, meaning higher costs to broadcasters for electricity and equipment. COFDM also carried less data than 8-VSB. NBC admitted that 8-VSB was a less than perfect system but stood behind it because COFDM was an unacceptable alternative. Philips and the Fox network believed that 8-VSB could be improved, but CBS saw no problem with it.

8-VSB development was not stagnant, with chips improving as the debate raged. Motorola, Philips, and Sarnoff Labs' NxtWave developed receiver chips to enhance 8-VSB reception by fighting static and multipath problems while delivering error-free indoor and mobile reception. Dynamic multipath is caused when signals reflect off moving objects, such as vehicles or windblown tree limbs. Each chip would cost $20 to $22.

At Commissioner Ness' request and based on "issues raised in result of indoor reception demonstrations by the Sinclair Broadcasting Group, Inc.," the FCC's (1999a) OET independently assessed COFDM and 8-VSB. OET found that "DTV service availability approaches that of NTSC service in most instances and with expected receiver improvements will exceed it in the near future." OET reported: "In general, with the exception of Sinclair, other parties continued to support the 8-VSB system as the DTV transmission standard. They generally stated that all of the factors that have been identified regarding COFDM performance in the Sinclair demonstrations were well understood and considered at the time the DTV transmission system decision was made." OET decided that "the ATSC 8-VSB standard should be retained," because "the relative benefits of changing the DTV transmission to COFDM are unclear and would not outweigh the costs of making such a revision."

Sinclair believed that OET's report was meant to discourage further challenges. On October 8, 1999, Sinclair filed a *Petition for Expedited Rulemaking*, asking the FCC to allow DTV transmission using COFDM or 8-VSB modulation. Via letter, the FCC (2000a) denied Sinclair's petition on February 4, 2000.

The FCC (2000b) cited Sinclair's 8-VSB objections, but said CEMA's October 14, 1999, response claimed Sinclair's "petition fails to assert any valid basis for re-opening the DTV standards proceeding at this late date, and presents only arguments that are repetitive of those previously considered." CEMA said "re-opening the DTV standards proceeding would create uncertainty and benefit only those seeking to delay the transition to digital broadcasting." Sinclair refuted CEMA's assertions on October 29, 1999.

The FCC (2000b) concluded that Sinclair's petition was unwarranted. It added: "We continue to believe that NTSC service replication is achievable by DTV operations using the 8-VSB standard. We note that field test data taken to date supports this conclusion. Sinclair has presented no persuasive evidence to indicate that NTSC service replication cannot be achieved with the 8-VSB standard." The Commission said Sinclair presented no "valid technical information to refute OET's assessment of these 8-VSB advantages or to refute the recommendation in its report that the ATSC 8-VSB standard be retained." The FCC adopted the Grand Alliance standard to "ensure that all affected parties, i.e., broadcasters, equipment manufacturers, and the public, have sufficient confidence and certainty to promote the introduction of DTV service." Further, "allowing more than one standard could result in compatibility problems and increase the risk that consumer DTV equipment purchased in one city would not work well in another city; or that a digital television set purchased one year might not work several years later." The Commission wanted to protect consumers and "to preserve a universally available television service." The FCC also cited the circularity, or chicken-and-egg, problem of multiple standards resulting in consumer and manufacturer reluctance to purchase DTV equipment "because they would not wish to take the risk of investing in what may soon be an obsolete technology, or because they believe better technologies would soon be available."

Despite denying the petition, the FCC (2000b) recognized the importance of Sinclair's issues. The Commission commended Sinclair "for its leadership efforts in identifying certain DTV receiver performance concerns and for providing information and data that will be useful to consumer electronics manufacturers in building receivers that meet the expectations of broadcasters and consumers." The FCC would continue to test 8-VSB and COFDM, with primary attention placed on DTV receivers.

CEA (2000), formerly CEMA, was pleased with the decision. CEO Gary Shapiro said: "I hope this ruling will close the door on this issue. As demonstrated by more than ten years of laboratory and field tests, 8-VSB is clearly the best system for broadcasting digital television in the United States. And retailers report that consumers who are viewing over-the-air digital television love what they're seeing."

Nat Ostroff (2000), Sinclair VP, said that the dismissal "did not end the debate over the performance of the DTV transmission system." He added: "We believe that it is only a matter of time before the industry and the consumer come to Sinclair's position."

Indeed, the debate continued. Some critics heavily criticized the FCC for not doing more to investigate Sinclair's claims and to determine beyond a shadow of a doubt that 8-VSB was more viable than COFDM. However, in a surprising turn of events, ATSC announced that it would not continue its adamant opposition to COFDM. ATSC formed a task force to begin meeting March 31, 2000, in Washington. Robert Graves, ATSC chair, said: "We want to reach out to people who remain unsatisfied with the performance of the system—and in some sense we all are—and make ATSC the place where this kind of analysis can be done in as scientifically sound a manner as possible" (McConnell, 2000, p. 10). Sinclair appeared vindicated. Sinclair's Mark Hyman declared: "A year ago, many people thought we were the crazy aunt in the basement. Today, there appears to be a widespread acknowledgement that we've been right all along" (p. 10). MSTV, NAB, and NBC had questioned 8-VSB's performance. NAB called ATSC's action "long overdue" (p. 10). In June 2000, ABC and NBC jointly filed a letter with the FCC rebuffing 8-VSB and supporting COFDM. The networks stopped short of dropping their support for the Grand Alliance system, but did say that 8-VSB must improve its operation in environments containing multipath interference. Nat Ostroff, Sinclair VP, said: "NBC and ABC confirmed everything we've been saying for a year" (LeSueur, 2000a, p. 12). At a June 30, 2000, press conference, FCC Chair Kennard stated:

I'm concerned that if we make this change to COFDM at this particular time it's going to introduce visual delay in the rollout of DTV, because it will involve fundamentally changing the table of allocation for the television services. Remember the broadcast industry virtually unanimously embraced 8-VSB just a few years ago. This was exhaustively looked at in the FCC proceedings. Now I understand that COFDM is a better technology for transmissions and local communications, but when we designed the process of converting to digital this service was optimized for a fixed broadcast service. And 8-VSB, broadcasters told us, is what we needed in order to make this transition. (LeSueur, 2000a, p. 12)

Kennard chastised broadcasters: "This is the biggest opportunity that the television industry has had in eight years. And you ought to be racing to go digital. We don't want to do anything to interrupt the procedure by delaying the process" (LeSueur, 2000a, p. 12). *Broadcasting & Cable* editors were critical of Chairman Kennard's position, and wrote: "Lack of FCC resolve in bringing the competing industries together has cost the public three years of digital progress. The COFDM diversion has cost another. For, free, over-the-air digital broadcasters, there aren't many more to lose" (First things first, 2000, p. 78). Brad Dick (2000), *Broadcast Engineering* editor, added: "8-VSB has had almost six years to make itself work and it still doesn't. We should not gamble on promised future fixes that *might* make tomorrow's 8-VSB as good as COFDM is today. The solution is to kill 8-VSB now" (p. 8).

Meanwhile, Congress again called broadcasters to task about HDTV. At a July 2000 hearing, Billy Tauzin (R-LA), House Telecommunications Subcommittee chair, warned: "Let me be abundantly clear to the broadcast community: You asked that Congress provide you with an opportunity to offer HDTV. We did that. Now some of you are getting cold feet. There has been talk of broadcasters trying to leverage timing of their exit from the old analog portion of their licenses for financial benefit. This is pure nonsense" (LeSueur, 2000b, p. 14). Tauzin threatened broadcasters with penalties for failing to implement HDTV.

DTV's First Anniversary. In DTV's first year, there was much potential of which little was realized. Ashworth (2000) believed: "Though no one wants federal agencies and special interest groups to lay down stifling rules, it is clear that the industry needs more leaders—broadcasters willing to go out on a limb and provide the HD content, cable willing to negotiate on must-carry, manufacturers offering reasonably priced sets without indoor reception difficulties, and a government willing to set standards and enforce deadlines" (p. 6).

By November 4, 1999, 60 of 122 top 30 market stations were broadcasting DTV. Some were given construction extensions. The number increased to 126 DTV stations in April 2000, leaving nearly 1,600 stations to go. By September 2000, just 151 DTV stations were broadcasting. Must-carry remained a key issue with DTV. Bob Rini, a broadcast attorney, said: "If the FCC fails to act in a timely way, it will not move forward on the timetable they envisioned" (Bowser, 2000, p. 43). Others took a more optimistic view, believing 151 DTV stations a good number because just 120 stations were mandated to be on air. Still, it was believed a vast majority of stations facing a 2002 conversion deadline would not meet it. Stephen Flanagan, engineering

VP for Post-Newsweek Stations Inc., stated: "Whatever enthusiasm station managers once had for DTV seems to be gone. It is very difficult getting anyone excited about the transition right now" (Bowser, 2000, p. 43). There were those in the industry who believed the FCC's reluctance to address the must-carry issue was only adding fuel to the modulation debate between 8-VSB and COFDM. Dickson (2000b) reported: "One broadcast source believes that Kennard's 2006 deadline will actually 'stoke the fires on the modulation debate' because some broadcasters will use the controversy over 8-VSB modulation as a stalling tactic. But he thinks the FCC has already made up its mind and 'we're stuck with 8-VSB," (p. 14). There were few DTV sets and few DTV programs. CEMA reported 50,000 DTV sets sold to dealers in 1999, but no consumer sales statistics were given. Reportedly, 13,000 DTV sets were sold in 1998, but as few as 5,000 may have been shipped to dealers. The sets were not HDTV but DTV-ready, meaning that they needed—at added cost—two outboard tuners/decoders to display not only full-resolution, wide-screen HDTV but also basic DTV. Most set-top boxes were for DTV and not for HDTV. Indeed, combination HDTV/DTV compatible set-top boxes were not expected on the market until at least the end of 2000. True HDTV sets displaying 1,080 lines by 1920 pixels cost $25,000 in mid-2000 (Utz, 2000).

Do Consumers Want DTV and/or HDTV?

An unanswered question concerns the consumer's role in the DTV process. When prototype sets were introduced in 1998 at CES in Las Vegas, manufacturers were cautiously optimistic about consumer acceptance. Sony's John Briesch viewed set-top converters as important to gradual acceptance and believed that color TV's acceptance record could serve as a barometer: "The new marketing revolution for HDTV could easily span 10 years before consumers have these sets in their homes. We want to set the right expectations for this technology and not create too much confusion" (Garber, 1998, p. 19).

Prior to the Grand Alliance, critics suggested that "a wider, bigger, clearer picture at significantly higher cost would not bring a consumer stampede to high definition TV set retailers" (Shotgun, 1993, p. 36). Reber (1997b) wrote:

History does not support the contention that the public, other than a niche segment, will pay a significant premium for even dramatic improvement to picture and sound quality as was the disappointing scenario with VHS vs. LaserDisc (or VHS vs. Super VHS, or 8mm vs. Super 8, or VHS vs. CD Video). The jury is still out on DVD. Further, most Americans do not receive their television programming over-the-air anyway, but via cable system or several DBS services. Then too, the broadcasters will have new competition from the well financed computer industry who has its own agenda for capturing the new spectrum digital content market. From every perspective, the world we know is eventually going digital. The question is what will be the outcome? (p. 13)

Indeed, some consumers seek out innovations. Although computers and TVs are drawing nearer to each other, we are yet a long way from a happy marriage of the two that will suit most consumers. Pohlmann (1996) observed: "Techie types are impressed by computers and peripherals with wires hanging all over the place, but most people get more of a rise out of washing machines. Most people aren't hackers" (pp. 19–20). Paulsen (1997) sarcastically noted: "Just sit my Digital HDTV receiver over there beside my quadraphonic sound receiver, SVHS tapes, electric potato peeler, Edsel automobile, quarter-keg home beer container, TV with a phone built in, tele-text receiver, cans of New Coke, no-money down real estate program, chinchilla ranch plans, and Yugo automobile" (p. 82).

Schneider (1994) stated: "I constantly read about all the sources of information, news, movies, and other forms of entertainment that will someday be coming over our phone lines by way of HDTV. This is all well and good, but who can afford it?" (p. 8). Many experts are skeptical about DTV's acceptance at any cost. The first sets are very expensive, but as more people buy DTV sets and more broadcasters transmit DTV programming, the cost and variety should become more attractive to consumers (Scully, 1993c). Estimates in early 1997 had DTV sets costing $1,000–$2,000 more than analog sets. By the end of the year, estimated DTV set prices ballooned to $7,000 or $8,000. Were manufacturers using scare tactics to sell conventional sets? Brinkley (1997) observed: "Some industry pundits said they believed these companies are simply trying to scare people by telling them HDTVs will be so expensive that it makes no sense to wait for them. Could there be any better demonstration of the industry's desperate need to get HDTVs into the stores as quickly as possible?" (p. 54). Leo Hindery, TCI president, believed it "reprehensible that the CEMA wants to sell $500 million worth of TV sets. We should ask the customers what they want, what they'll pay for and then give it to them" (Petrozzello, 1997, p. 67). Hindery added: "If we cram HDTV down customers' throats, we'll lose. If HDTV changes things to the detriment of my customers because they won't pay for enhanced programs, why do we need it? The push for HDTV should come from the consumer, not from technology" (p. 67).

Most of the $7,000 to $10,000 prices were for big-screen DTV sets, but even portables cost about $3,000. Experts cautioned against buying anything other than large-screen sets. Utz (2000) explained:

The average United States consumer views his TV receiver from a distance of about seven picture heights, which calculates to 10 feet for a 27-inch diagonal picture tube. The TV picture takes up about 10 percent of the viewer's field of vision. At this distance, viewers can't see the scanning lines and most of the NTSC fuzziness that HDTV is supposed to fix. In other words, if you replaced your NTSC TV with an HDTV with the same picture height and viewed it from the nominal 10 feet, you'd see hardly any difference in the picture, except for the screen being a wider shape. . . .

If you want to appreciate the beauty of HDTV (and having seen it, I can attest that it is gorgeous), you have to move closer to the set or get a bigger screen. Three picture heights is the magic number; a 75-inch (diagonal) screen viewed from 10 feet has been shown to display all the glory of HDTV. At this range, your eyes can perceive the added sharpness, and the larger screen will add to the viewing experience, because now 30 percent of your viewing angle is taken up by the screen. (p. 88)

A widely held view is that forecasts of potential consumer acceptance are overblown. Polon (1997a) believed that DTV set size would impact consumer acceptance as much as cost:

[T]he size of consumer electronic appliances has become an issue in the home in the 1990s that did not exist previously. Research tells us that American's [*sic*] frequently live in smaller spaces, utilize the living space that they have differently and the decor of the home is much more important. Women have assumed a much greater role in the purchase of consumer electronic items for the home and have forced the consumer audio industry, for example, to downsize and repackage home audio systems. How well the large TV sets envisioned for DTV will fit into this scheme remains to be seen. (And how well DTV widescreen models fit in entertainment centers really remains to be seen.) (p. 19)

Meigs (1989) said that "almost no one has bothered to ask the one key question: What do viewers want?" (p. 4). There is evidence to support two suppositions. First, consumers may not want DTV. Second, consumers may be confused and seeking answers about DTV. Johnson (1997) accused broadcasters of employing "hysterical stratagems . . . as it maneuvers for the best position from which to exploit the watershed of digital broadcast" (p. 56). Johnson added:

I sympathize with consumers who are bewildered, daunted, and paralyzed. The industry is hyperventilating over this issue. Reluctant broadcasters are talking out of both sides of their mouths as they evade a clear commitment to digital service, to say nothing of high-definition service. Television makers, mortified at the prospect of a crash in analog sales are refashioning their own rhetoric to suit the occasion. For the consumer, the digital issue doesn't appear to be all that pressing. It's hardly a cultural crisis. In any case, compatible broadcasts will continue for many years, probably longer than anyone has suggested. (p. 56)

CBO Report on DTV's Deadline. Reber (1998), while attending the 1998 NAB meeting in Las Vegas, "realized that there were no *true* experts on what at this point is largely a theoretical environment" (p. 12). He heard many varying opinions about "formats, operating systems, pixels, aspect ratios, and compression schemes," which "added up to a bunch of mixed signals that didn't match," yet "virtually everyone I spoke to agreed that as soon as HDTV was made a voluntary step it was questionable whether or not it was going to happen" (p. 12). Congress' Balanced Budget Act of 1997 dictated that significant portions of the spectrum occupied by the channels be auctioned no later than 2002. CBO (1999) conducted a study in regard to broadcasters' deadline to return their second channel and analyzed factors affecting the transition's timing and "whether the transition is likely to continue beyond the currently scheduled end date of December 31, 2006." CBO said that its mandate for the study was to offer objective, impartial analysis and to make no recommendations.

Based on the report, it seemed evident that stations would not return the channels by 2006. Due to a legislative loophole, it was possible that stations might keep both channels permanently. Congress' magic number for DTV penetration was based on 85 percent of a market's TV households subscribing to MVPD. Consumers satisfied with over-the-air TV would not subscribe to MVPD, prohibiting 85 percent penetration. However, broadcasters could outsmart themselves by employing multiple-channel SDTV. They could be considered MVPD, and DTV's penetration point would be achieved. As specified by the Balanced Budget Act, CBO (1999) said "that so-called market penetration test is to be applied at the level of the television market. However, the law does not define a television market." The FCC has no standard definition for market but adapts an appropriate definition case by case.

CBO cited other factors weighing against 85 percent penetration. Lack of antenna towers for broadcasters and rooftop antennae for consumers figured into the equation. Another factor was consumers not buying DTV sets, causing low set sales and a slower rate of set price reductions. Another was insufficient DTV programming on cable. Just four of 200-plus United States cable markets have ever reached 85 percent penetration. Nationwide, 95 percent of all homes are passed by cable, but subscriptions reach just 67 percent.

Cable must-carry of DTV signals was a primary issue, and the FCC was trying to determine how to resolve the matter. CBO (1999) noted: "At some point, the DTV programming delivered by a cable service must be translated into a format that can be displayed by a digital TV set or converted for display on an analog TV set."

CBO (1999) said that DTV's success or failure lay with broadcasters, MVPD (such as cable and satellite), and set manufacturers, but "consumers will be the ultimate arbiters of the value of the new technology and the speed of its adoption," making them "the so-called wild card in the transition." CBO cited a circular, chicken-and-egg model, making "it hard to say which step comes first." CBO surmised:

On the one hand, all of the elements of the transition could mesh smoothly with a high level of consumer desire for digital TV, thus creating the conditions for its rapid adoption. On the other hand, problems with the transition–delays in getting stations on the air, lack of cable carriage, or less of a decline than expected in equipment prices, to name a few–could cause the transition to be prolonged. Ultimately, the transition will take place only if consumers decide that the benefits offered by the new service outweigh the costs of adopting the new technology.

CBO believed "the transition to digital television is likely to continue beyond the tentative ending date of 2006 set out in the Balanced Budget Act."

Will DTV's 18 Formats Impact Consumer Acceptance?

One need only to look to AM stereo to understand the pitfalls of multiple formats. Just because the FCC adopted a DTV "technical standard" does not mean that the transition will be smooth. TV set manufacturers promised multidecoding receivers capable of receiving all the formats, but AM stereo multidecoders flopped in the marketplace. AM stereo multidecoders needed to sort out five formats, while DTV multidecoders were faced with deciphering 18 different transmission formats. Manufacturers implemented a tagging system for DTV-compatible sets, but a similar strategy failed with AM stereo.

What about those broadcasters who forgo HDTV in favor of multiple-channel SDTV? While they see dollar signs, have they thought about the negative consequences? Paulsen (1997) submitted: "The broadcasters hope that big money is to be made selling the additional inventory created by the second channel, or the four additional channels. But what about the possibility that their stations may be lost in the sea of channels that could develop when all five stations in the market go multiple channel operation and there are 25 channels to split the audience? Are you ready for 'dollar-a-holler spots'? It seems we are left with the equipment manufacturer as the only one that stands to make some big money out of this without the risk" (p. 82).

Consumer DTV interest appears conditional, and there is confusion over several important issues. Consumers and broadcasters want to know exactly what high-definition/digital means and how much it will cost. Another nagging question concerns the learning curve, or how to use equipment more complex than in the past—particularly with the entry of the computer industry. Beacham (1997c) observed: "A daunting maze of complex technical issues still surrounds the installation of the most basic personal computer in the home or office. Despite claims to the contrary, these are not yet simple appliances average people can easily set up and productively use" (p. 24). Beacham (1997c) added: "Today's TV set, if anything, is simple and reliable. Turn it on, flip the channels, and it works. . . . So far, the DTV revolution seems to be more about a few companies racing each other to find the pot of gold at the end of the rainbow than about building a next-generation television system whose goal is to serve the needs of people" (p. 24). Pensinger (1997) asked: "Once we've built it, will they come?" (p. 18). In an age in which many consumers have trouble operating the clock and programming functions on their VCRs, how is the average consumer supposed to learn to use DTV?

Costs always factor into manufacturing and marketing, and undoubtedly some manufacturers will offer cut-rate models that decode just part of the spectrum of formats. What, then, will a consumer do when a new TV set cannot decode favorite channels? Thomas A. Jordan, Leitch Inc. VP, stated: "It always costs more to design and manufacture a product that does more. Had the networks settled on a single standard, all equipment would be a single standard. Now, standards-sensitive equipment must deal with two or more formats, and this translates to higher costs" (The battle over formats, 1998, p. 40). Nat Ostroff, Sinclair Broadcast Group VP, compared the format war to the *Titanic*, saying that "we seem to be steaming at full speed toward an iceberg and no one is on watch" (p. 40). Dick (1998a) concluded: "It seems to me that all of this talk about different platforms will do nothing but confuse the viewers. I guess that wouldn't be so bad if the intent was to provide the best service possible, but I suspect the format selection was a lot more political than it was analytical" (p. 10).

DTV has thus far shown similarities and differences with color TV, MTS, and AM stereo. Powers stated: "I think there are more similarities than non-similarities. The similarities in the battle before the FCC are striking. While there were only two major United States companies fighting for the lead in color development at that time compared to today's free-for-all, there was still a lot of international action then. There were major debates over the NTSC system for several years after color" (Powers, 1991, p. 68). Powers said that "the technology is ready [but] the market is far from it" because there are so many marketing angles presented by cable, broadcasting, satellites, and video (p. 68). Powers agreed that there may be no overwhelming demand or desire for DTV, but "it was a 'keep-up-with-your-neighbor' mentality that pushed CDs along, and that will probably be true of high definition" (p. 68).

DTV does not ensure that a broadcast station will be more successful than it was with analog transmission. Another AM stereo parallel may be drawn. Consumers really did not see a need when they already had FM stereo. MIT's Andy Littman agreed: "Home television is not driven by technological issues; it's driven by consumers. They have to buy it. HDTV can't skyrocket the way CDs did because there isn't an immediate need" (Webster, 1990, p. 66).

The Program's the Thing. Have consumers been dissatisfied with the NTSC standard? With HDTV, all stations will presumably be on a level playing field, but will there be a rush to convert? Beacham (1997a) suggested that we take notice of history beyond even the AM stereo fiasco: "[I]t should be remembered that home viewers have not yet spoken on the issue. No one knows if DTV will sell. It could be a big-time consumer electronics flop. To assume that the American viewing public will automatically pay a significant premium for a TV set that receives a slightly better over-the-air picture flies in the face of recent history. (Remember the VHS vs. laserdisc video-quality battle and who won?)" (p. 27).

Doyle (1992) argued that DTV is "much to do about nothing" and concluded: "If you walk down the street and ask somebody what's wrong with television, you're not going to find anybody who says: Resolution" (p. 165). DTV acceptance hinges greatly on programming. The average consumer may not be able to tell much difference between NTSC and DTV. In television's early days, picture quality did not matter as much as having a picture. It was intriguing enough to consumers that their radio had pictures. Color TV was also exciting, but consumers are past all that. Many more entertainment sources exist today, giving consumers more options. Today's viewers are more sophisticated, and DTV's picture quality probably will not matter without programming. An ABC engineer observed: "I don't care what the technology is . . . the program is the thing" (Seeing the future, 1991, p. 5).

Nick Trigony, Cox Broadcasting president, said: "I think the picture is pretty good right now. When you hear people complain about what's going on TV, they complain more about product than picture" (Husted, 1998, p. C-1). Krantz (1997) wondered: "Will the shows themselves get better when HDTV takes over?" He answered: "Dream on. There are certain things in life that even computers cannot be expected to accomplish" (p. 69).

Dick (1998a) agreed: "TV viewing always comes down to *programming*, not technology. I don't care how much resolution you add to 'Roseanne' or 'NYPD Blue,' I won't watch it. And, it doesn't matter how little resolution is used to transmit 'Ally McBeal' or 'Married with Children.' Some people will still tune in. To borrow a phrase, 'It's the programming, stupid!'" (p. 10). Dick's prediction appeared to be proven during the 1999–2000 TV season. Antonoff (2000) noted: "Last season some high-def proponents thought that prime-time sitcoms like *The King of Queens* and dramas like *Nash Bridges* would be so compelling in the 1080i format that viewers would rush out and buy expensive new sets. It turned out that *The King of Queens* was no funnier in HD, and Don Johnson's jackets simply looked more rumpled when he climbed out of this Mustang" (p. 164). Antonoff (2000) added that sports programming was also disappointing: "Two years ago everyone thought the killer app would be sports. It turned out that in the case of the NFL, the real drama was off screen as competing camera crews jockeyed for the best positions. A shortage of high-def equipment sometimes left the HDTV team taking wide-angle pictures from above while NTSC squad was better positioned to cover more of the field up close" (p. 164). Pensinger (1997) opined: "I personally think there will always be a need for good storytellers and there will be an increasing demand for professional editors to select and arrange information from the ever-growing maze. But then, if you and I knew what the consumer really wanted, I wouldn't be writing this and you wouldn't be reading it—we'd both be running to our broker to get in on the ground floor" (p. 18).

Chapter 8

The FCC's Changing Regulatory Role

FCC PROCEDURE AND POLICY

The major overriding issue in broadcast transmission standards proceedings is not necessarily technological but how the FCC handles procedure and policy. Although there were similarities, FCC policy and procedure caused the greatest differences between the developments of color TV, FM stereo, AM stereo, MTS, DAB, and DTV. AM stereo, caught in the middle of the FCC's controversial deregulation of radio proceeding from 1979 to 1981, was an unfortunate victim of timing. The FCC emphasized that deregulation was about eliminating unneeded rules and reducing paperwork burdens on broadcasters. No broadcaster minded the paperwork reductions, but the FCC's reluctance to set transmission standards was unacceptable. Who is to say FM stereo, MTS, and DTV would not have suffered similar destinies under similar circumstances? As broadcasters learned from AM stereo, they must shape their own fates. The lesson was heeded, as evidenced by both MTS and the DTV Grand Alliance, which, in effect, resulted in marketplace standards.

Since 1982 the FCC has maintained its traffic cop policy of policing only technical parameters. Except when Congress forced it to pick an AM stereo standard in 1993, the Commission has selected no standard that is not a hybrid of more than one system (MTS) or that has not had the consensus of broadcasters (MTS and DTV). A new regulatory model emerged, called Amstereoization by some.

Marketplace Lessons

Although it has been much maligned, the AM stereo marketplace had its benefits. If AM stereo as a technology never succeeds, at least we can use the previously unknown marketplace as a measuring stick for future standards proceedings. Prior to AM stereo, we had no idea what to expect if the FCC failed to set a standard. Now, we know. We also know that the marketplace can work to a point but has trouble bringing about a conclusion. Within two years, just the systems of Motorola and Kahn were left from the original five. After 1984, however, more harm than good was done. By spending too little time on promotion and entirely too much time on trying to stop Motorola, all Kahn did was hurt AM stereo. There is nothing wrong with fighting for a cause, but after years of infighting broadcasters grew weary and uninterested.

AM stereo has made a lasting impact on the study of policy. What happened to AM stereo because of the marketplace decision may indeed be more important than AM stereo itself. The FCC and broadcasters are well advised to study AM stereo history as new technologies such as DAB and DTV are introduced (Huff, 1992a, 1992b). So far, the Commission does not appear to have paid much attention to AM stereo's lessons, as evidenced by the slow development of innovations. Broadcasters have learned never again to expect anything but the unexpected from the FCC. MTS was the first major test, and the industry responded quickly and decisively. If the FCC was not going to set a standard, then the industry would do it. The strategy worked, as evidenced by the overwhelming support of Zenith as MTS standard. Unlike AM stereo, MTS was initiated more smoothly and with little difficulty.

Another marketplace benefit is AM radio's quality improvement. As broadcasters waited for an AM stereo solution, NRSC-1 and NRSC-2 offered rays of hope to AM. Nonetheless, the delay in selecting a system standard negatively impacted AM stereo. The circularity, or chicken-and-egg, situation ensued. Without a standard, most stations would not convert, and most manufacturers hesitated to build receivers. Without widespread equipment availability, consumer education and promotion were nearly impossible. It was not so much that AM stereo was rejected by the marketplace; it was that the public never knew enough about it to reject it. About 13 percent of United States AM stations transmitted stereo in 1991, but most listeners were unaware. Lack of promotion was problematic, but it is difficult to promote something not readily available to consumers. If someone at "Stereos Are Us" wanted to demonstrate AM stereo receivers, would there be an AM stereo station nearby to which one could listen? If a station transmitted stereo, but there were no receivers, how would one hear it? In effect, AM stereo cannot be the problem. Having never had a chance to succeed, it was victimized.

Could AM stereo have succeeded with a standard? As stated in its marketplace proceeding, the FCC feared lengthy litigation in setting a standard. Despite congressional intervention in 1992, it maintained that apprehension. For AM stereo to have had a chance, it needed stations to upgrade with all available improvements including stereo, NRSC-1, and NRSC-2. Receivers incorporating improved AM technology needed to be developed and marketed. At that point, stations and receiver companies needed to educate all consumers about AM stereo, including dealers, sales personnel, and retail customers. Promotion and education are equal partners. Finally, AM audio quality would have had to compare favorably with FM. Sufficient programming was necessary to hold listeners when they tuned in to try AM stereo.

Convincing AM managers to install systems was a formidable task. Suffering through tough economic times, many owners were not financially able to install AM stereo equipment. There was also tremendous apathy to overcome. The uncertainty caused by DAB did not help. Although DAB will not be a reality for some time, it threatened AM broadcasters already on the verge of quitting the fight.

MTS in the Marketplace. Twenty-three years after postponing TV stereo, the Commission finally approved it in 1984. Proceedings for AM stereo and MTS began in 1977. Broadcasters, witnessing the AM stereo fiasco, were compelled to seek their own resolution. TV broadcasters quickly formed a consensus of support for one system much as it later did with DTV's "Grand Alliance." The FCC did not pick a specific system but created a hybrid from multiple proposals, allowing broadcasters to deliver MTS via any method as long as it did not cause interference. The FCC did not officially call BTSC's system a standard, but broadcasters convinced the FCC to give it pilot protection, which was refused Motorola's AM stereo system in 1988. Other MTS systems would be relegated to nonprotected frequencies. MTS could just as easily have been victimized like AM stereo. It was overdue, and although high costs caused some initial hesitation, there was soon a steady conversion. Similarly to FM stereo, TV broadcasters were free to advance a new service for broadcasters and consumers.

The Commissioners. The FCC incarnations presiding over color TV and FM stereo were much different from those determining the fates of AM stereo, MTS, DTV, and DAB. In addition to the FCC's continued deregulatory trend, there has been considerable turnover of chairs and commissioners since the 1982 AM stereo decision. A string of marketplace proponents has served as chair, including Mark Fowler, Dennis Patrick, Al Sikes, Reed Hundt, and William Kennard. Longtime commissioner James Quello was interim FCC chairman for 11 months in 1993, between Sikes and Hundt.

Fowler, a "classic free marketeer," presided over the AM stereo decision (From public interest, 1985, p. 38). AM stereo and MTS were initiated by his predecessor, Charles Ferris, so he inherited the proceedings. Patrick succeeded Fowler and was chair when the FCC opened its HDTV proceeding in 1987. Patrick's marketplace approach was similar to Fowler's, so his intent with HDTV was similar to that with AM stereo. Rather than the FCC's picking a standard, let broadcasters do it. If it works, it works; if it fails, it fails. The FCC did not accept responsibility for a technology's success or failure. By setting technical parameters, not standards, better systems could be designed and introduced. Patrick said that it was imperative to pick an HDTV standard that could evolve, because it "may turn out that win-win solutions are achievable by resorting to marketplace decision-making" (FCC's 'blue ribbon,' 1989, p. 75).

Sikes changed the direction of HDTV from analog to digital but was succeeded by Hundt, who was notorious for changing his position on a subject from the beginning of a speech to the end. Hundt left DTV without a single system or format standard. His Commission recommended ATSC's 18 formats but mandated standard parameters only for transmission, transport, and digital compression. Hundt also opened the door for the computer industry.

Kennard replaced Hundt before the DTV proceeding was completed, but he opposed standard setting as did his predecessors. Kennard did not believe that DTV would turn out like AM stereo but acknowledged that anything is possible in the marketplace. He stated: "For 20 years, policymakers have been moving towards more of a market-based approach to regulation. And it's worked. Why, suddenly, should we reverse course because we have this digital broadcast technology? It's just sort of curious to me" (Steady as she goes, 1998, pp. S9-S10).

Certainly, the sheer volume of new technologies has frustrated the FCC to the point that it may never set standards as it once did, especially in view of ever-present threats of litigation when the "wrong" standard is selected. The FCC's AM stereo marketplace decision eliminated the possibility of having its decision challenged in a lengthy legal battle. Leonard Kahn frequently threatened the FCC with litigation, but it is difficult to believe that a lawsuit would have harmed AM stereo more than the marketplace. The Commission apparently believed otherwise.

The Proceedings. For color TV, stereo FM/AM/TV, DTV, and DAB, the FCC opened formal inquiries to determine necessity and feasibility. The FCC selected the wrong color TV system in 1950, but it corrected the error four years later. FM stereo's approval took just three years (1958–61), but five years was required for AM stereo approval (1977–82)—without a standard. MTS took seven years (1977–84). The FCC's DTV process lasted for 12 years (1987–98), and even now there are loose ends remaining. DAB's proceeding began in 1990, but there is still no end in sight. What caused these increasing time discrepancies for FCC proceedings?

Stereo system testing for AM, FM, and TV consumed about the same amount of time. It took much longer for DAB and DTV, which can partially be attributed to the digital element. There were nearly three times the FM stereo systems to test than there were for AM stereo and almost five times more FM stereo systems than for MTS, yet, the Commission and its adjunct agencies of the 1950s rapidly filtered out an FM stereo standard in three years. The FCC did all its preliminary research on FM stereo feasibility and delegated technical study to NSRC. The number of systems was narrowed from 14 to a final choice of the two-system hybrid. The FCC made a decision and stood by it, and all loose ends were tied together when FM stereo went on the air in 1961.

The FCC did not help AM stereo but boosted FM further by establishing duopoly rules in the 1960s. AM operators, who frequently simulcast programming on FM, owned many FMs. Most FMs were neglected, so the FCC initiated rules making it illegal for station owners to devote more than a certain percentage of time to simulcasting. The rules, in combination with stereo, became invaluable for FM in its competition with AM. Yet in the 1980s, the Commission not only refused to set an AM stereo standard, it eliminated the simulcasting rules. AM was relegated to the situation from which FM had been rescued. The Commission argued that both the marketplace and the reinstatement of simulcasting would be good for AM. The Commission's actions were puzzling. Why were totally opposite stances taken for FM and AM?

In 1961 FM was totally dominated by AM's audience shares. Even after stereo, FM took nearly 18 years to draw even with AM. Through patience, determination, programming, and promotion, FM raised itself from the grave to become AM's worst nightmare. FM sneaked up on AM, and by the time AM operators responded, the damage was done.

With DTV, it is apparent that the lessons learned from the FCC's AM stereo debacle were not lost on broadcasters. However, the process was greatly affected by the computer industry. Legitimate fears arose that TV equipment, like computer hardware and software, may regularly and rapidly become obsolete. Because DTV is incompatible with NTSC, major costs have been placed on broadcasters and consumers to convert to digital. Unlike previous standards, such as color TV, FM stereo, MTS, and AM stereo, DTV was not an enhancement but departed totally from the norm. The lack of a true, unadulterated DTV standard is a problem, as the marketplace has not been effective in technical standard setting. Tied directly to these factors is the unanswered question of whether consumers want DTV. DTV has caused tremendous confusion among consumers, manufacturers, and broadcasters. Consumers may play the most important role in determining DTV's success or failure. The FCC (2000c) took a major step to aid consumers in understanding TV. In a September 14, 2000 action, the Commission adopted rules for the labeling of DTV receivers "to insure that consumers will be fully informed about the capabilities of digital TV receivers to operate with cable television systems." As reported in a press release, the FCC (2000c) specified "labels for three categories of DTV receivers":

1. "Digital Cable Ready 1": a consumer electronics TV receiving device capable of receiving analog basic, digital basic and digital premium cable television programming by direct connection to a cable system providing digital programming. A security card or Point of Deployment (POD) module provided by the cable operator is required to view encrypted programming. There is no 1394 digital connector or other digital interface. This device does not have two-way capability using cable facilities.

2. "Digital Cable Ready 2": A consumer electronics TV receiving device that in addition to the features of the Digital Cable Ready 1 sets also includes the 1394 digital interface connector that may be used for attaching the receiving device to various other consumer appliances. Connection of a Digital Cable Ready 2 receiver to a digital set-top box may support advanced and interactive digital services and programming delivered by the cable system to the set-top box.

3. "Digital Cable Ready 3": A consumer electronics TV receiving device that in addition to the features of the Digital Cable Ready 1 sets is capable of receiving advanced and interactive digital services by direct connection to a cable system providing digital programming and advanced and interactive digital services. The Commission said additional industry work was still required for design specifications for the Digital Cable Ready 3 category of receivers, and that it would therefore keep the record open in this proceeding, giving the Commission the option of incorporating these specifications into its rules at a later date.

The FCC (2000c) believed "the labeling scheme being adopted will permit consumers to make well-informed decisions about DTV equipment puchases based on a clear understanding of the capabilities of receivers with different labels."

BROADCAST TECHNOLOGY

With the exception of the first color TV decision and DTV, compatibility has been an important consideration in FCC proceedings. For a system to be selected, it needed to accommodate existing receivers. Just because the FCC allowed color TV, consumers could not or would not immediately discard their monochrome sets. The color signal needed to be received by monochrome sets—not in color, but in black and white. Likewise, stereo needed compatibility with monophonic receivers. Digital broadcasting made compatibility virtually moot. New concepts such as convergence and interoperability have become objectives, meaning that new technologies are expected to communicate between each other and to work together.

HDTV was originally analog, but it was not long until it became digital. In 1990 the FCC began a proceeding for DAB to give radio an opportunity to achieve CD-quality audio. There may not be an overwhelming consumer demand or desire for DAB or DTV, but they could succeed because of "a 'keep-up-with-your-neighbor' mentality that pushed CDs along" (Powers offers, 1991, p. 68). DAB can be delivered via IBOC on AM and/or FM, by satellite, or though both methods. With its pictures, TV itself was enough of a challenge to radio, but the introductions of color in the 1950s, MTS in the 1980s, and digital technology in the 1990s have made radio less of an FCC priority.

DTV has experienced Amstereoization during a lengthy, ongoing proceeding delayed by digitalization, computers, and the FCC's indecision. With DTV, the FCC continued its marketplace approach of not setting a complete standard. Broadcasters and other organizations did the work. The FCC approved the Grand Alliance and computer compromise but did not set a standard. The FCC standardized no scanning formats and no aspect ratio for DTV, meaning that it did not select one combination of pixel count, line count, frame rate, aspect ratio, and progressive or interlace scanning. The Commission wanted flexibility and left it to the marketplace to choose which format to employ. An editorial stated: "As soon as Bill Gates whined that the 18 standards they'd set might not fit into his plans for world domination, the FCC threw out the standards entirely!" (Highly dubious TV, 1997, p. 134). Beacham (1997a) added: "Right now, traditional over-the-air broadcasters are headed into the future on a wing and a prayer. There is no guarantee their current business model will survive in a digital era. How they fare against an energetic new group of competitors from the computer industry will be one of the most interesting stories to watch" (p. 27).

When approved, DAB will undergo a transition period like DTV during which both analog and digital signals will be transmitted. Unlike DTV, DAB's signal would need to be received by existing analog receivers until saturation of DAB receivers could be achieved. That could take many years. The automobile industry has typically embraced new radio technology, as it did AM stereo, but it could take half a decade to get DAB receivers into new cars after a standard is set. If no DAB standard is set, the process could take much longer. Europe has been far ahead of the United States in DAB development, but receivers are difficult to find. Despite their de facto Eureka-147 system standard, Europeans are experiencing Amstereoization—lack of consumer acceptance or understanding. There is uncertainty over how to interest consumers in DAB. Thomas Rohde of receiver manufacturer Fujitsu Ten Europe, said: "We need to find an easy way to market and explain the product so that the consumer is not intimidated and seeks more information" (Clark, 1997, p. 6). Rohde's words could easily be applied to AM stereo or DTV.

Two years after approval, there is renewed wrangling over the DTV transmission system. The COFDM multiplexing system is believed by many broadcasters to be better than the Grand Alliance's 8-VSB transmission system. Unlike previous regimes, Clinton's administration supported a DTV standard. Noting AM stereo's failure, a White House spokesperson said that the implementation of a single DTV standard would ensure industry investment in the cause. The FCC acknowledged that broadcasters wanted a standard. Unsurprisingly, computer interests and FCC chairman Reed Hundt favored the marketplace. The FCC (1996c) reported: "Broadcasters, equipment manufacturers and some consumer groups contend that DTV has startup, coordination and splintering problems that are more severe than those of other network industries and that a DTV standard adopted by the Commission is needed to overcome these problems. In contrast, cable and computer interests contend that all sectors of the broadcast industry have significant incentives to reach a consensus on transmission and reception standards without a government mandate."

CONSUMER ACCEPTANCE

One major difference between DTV and previous standards is the FCC-mandated conversion deadline. CBO (1999) observed: "The rate at which consumers adopt new electronics products derives from the interaction of the quality and price of the new product on the supply side and the general desirability of the new product on the demand side. All consumer electronics products are unique, and their adoption rates differ. Considering the rates of adoption of other such products highlights the ambitiousness of the goal of completing the DTV transition by 2006."

No audio/visual technology has ever saturated the market in as short a time. A conversion deadline was never set for color TV or stereo AM/FM/TV, but it could happen with DAB. Few observers are convinced that DTV's will be met. Just five consumer electronics technologies have reached or exceeded 85 percent penetration: radios, monochrome TVs, color TVs, VCRs, and telephones. In 1995 VCRs became the quickest technology to reach 85 percent—after nearly 20 years on the market. If DTV's acceptance rate is similar to that of VCRs, it will reach 85 percent penetration about 2017 (Schubin, 1998). CD players have not reached the plateau. Cable TV has yet to pass 70 percent penetration and reached 67 percent only in 1998—50 years following its introduction and after 20 years of rapid growth.

After eight years, monochrome television reached 50 percent penetration in 1954. Television offered one benefit that radio could not, and that was a picture. Even so, acceptance was relatively slow. By 1978 about 98 percent of all U.S. homes had TV, but only 83 percent of them had color television 25 years after its introduction. The NTSC color TV system was introduced in 1954 but surpassed 50 percent penetration in 1971. Garvey (1980) wrote: "Perhaps the real question is not why color developed so slowly, but why it developed at all. There was a peculiarly circular problem to be solved if color was to become established—there was little incentive to buy a color set until there was adequate color programming, but broadcasters and advertisers had little incentive to invest in color programming until a reasonable percentage of the audience had color sets. The problem was exacerbated by the high price of color sets, equipment, and programming" (p. 515).

The Comparative Cost of Color and DTV. Although the difference between monochrome and color is obvious, it was not enough to get consumers to pay exorbitant prices for it to get the same programming. Using NASA's GDP Deflator Inflation Calculator to adjust costs from one year to another, it is possible to estimate how much early TV sets would cost in year 2000 dollars. (The year 2000 price equivalent is in parentheses.) At the time of TV's debut at the 1939 New York World's Fair, RCA's least expensive receiver featured a five-inch screen and cost $199.95 ($2,174.90). By 1940 the set was half price at $99.95 ($1,087.18). No sets were produced during World War II, but when production resumed in 1946, RCA's least expensive receiver was $250 ($2003.60).

By 1948 Pilot Radio television sets with three-inch screens sold for $99.50 ($658.81). In 1954 a consumer could spend $150 on a 21-inch set ($858.09). The first color television sets were introduced by Westinghouse in 1954. The set with a 12.5-inch screen sold for $1,295 ($7,408.18). Just 30 sets were sold in a month and the price dropped to $1,100 ($6,292.66). RCA responded with its own 12.5-inch set in 1954 for $1,000 ($5,720.60), which it reduced to $495 ($2,831.70) by year's end. By 1955 RCA sold a 19-inch color model for $795 ($4,501.69). The price was lowered to $499.95 ($2,754.93) in 1956. Color set prices fell approximately 70 percent in three years but did not fall again until 1963 (Garvey, 1980, p. 518), when RCA lowered its least expensive model to $450 ($2,423.66). In 1964 the price decreased to $400 ($1,912.96). GE sold an 11-inch color model in 1965 for $250 ($1,175.88). That same year, 21-inch monochrome sets sold for $90 ($423.32). By 1963 the average price for a color TV set was $308 ($1,046.34). The sale of color TV sets surpassed monochrome sales for the first time in 1972 (p. 518).

How do prices of the first color TV sets compare to those of the first DTV sets? (The 1954 price calculation is in parentheses.) DTV sets displayed in 1998 ranged from $5,000 ($903) to $7,000 ($1,264.20) for smaller sets to $10,000 ($1,806) for big-screen models, making them unaffordable for most consumers. Set-top converter boxes averaged about $700 ($126.42), and although the prices were certain to drop, there was little reason to believe that they would drop exponentially. Portable sets cost about $3,000 ($541.80). *Atlanta Journal-Constitution* newspaper advertisements in February 2000 for Mitsubishi and Toshiba DTV sets listed prices from $2,999.99 to $3,999.99. All sets were upgradable to HDTV (cost unknown) and featured 16:9 aspect ratios. Mitsubishi's 46-inch tabletop model cost $2,999.99 ($555.60), and its 55-inch projection set cost $3,999.99 ($740.80). Toshiba's Cinema Series 34-inch set was priced at $3,999.99 ($740.80). In two years, big-screen models had dropped about $6,000.

It should be understood that DTV sets are competing in a retail market in which the average analog TV set price at the end of 1999 was $340. CBO (1999) said that costs of DTV sets and converters would need to drop significantly for broad acceptance. However, CBO observed: "No one knows how far the prices of sets must decline before they become a mass market item, but one analyst believes that $500 is the price point that elevates a consumer electronics product to mass market status." There was no evidence available to indicate that prices would fall drastically enough to ensure the 2006 transition, but "as with other consumer electronics devices, the costs of producing displays should come down as manufacturing techniques advance."

Without doing an elaborate comparison, there is little difference between the adjusted set prices of early color TV and early DTV. Cost was prohibitive for sets then, and it appears to be a problem now. DTV might break the record of VCRs, but it could meet the fates of CBS' color TV system or AM stereo. The FCC and Congress want to auction off TV's analog spectrum in 2002, but those who purchase that spectrum cannot claim it until DTV reaches 85 percent penetration. Based on the histories of other broadcast technologies—especially color TV—the new owners may have a long wait to take control of their spectrum. Compare the progress of color TV to predictions for DTV, and the 2006 deadline for total conversion from analog to digital TV does not seem doable. CBO (1999), however, issued a caveat:

Although the history of the introduction of other products seems to bode poorly for the adoption of digital TV, such comparisons should not be given too much weight. For example, comparing digital TV with color TV is complicated by the fact that when color broadcasts were first introduced, they could be viewed, at a lesser quality but without additional expense, on existing black-and-white sets—which reduced the incentive to buy a new color one. Perhaps the largest difference between the introduction of digital TV and other consumer electronics devices is that digital TV is being introduced into the marketplace as a public policy, enjoying government mandates such as technology standards (absent in the introduction of VCRs) and required broadcasting (absent in the introduction of color TV). Those mandates should help speed the new technology's adoption compared with a product whose introduction is completely driven by the market.

Broadcast Stereo. Stereo was considered essential for the survival of FM in the 1960s and later for AM in the 1980s. As color TV was motivated by the popularity of Technicolor movies, radio listeners wanted to hear stereo recordings on the air. TV did not need stereo to survive, but consumers spoiled by FM's quality and stereo VCRs demanded better TV sound. As technology progressed, CD-quality became desirable. AM stereo presented yet another problem. Unlike television's visual advantage over radio, what could AM offer that did not already exist with FM and FM stereo? Perhaps nothing for pure audiophiles, but AM offered at least one benefit not afforded by FM. AM could be heard hundreds of miles away, while FM was limited to less than 100 miles of quality coverage area.

Unlike stereo and color, few consumers have complained about TV's picture. Very early in the HDTV process, Meigs (1989) pointed out that little emphasis was placed on consumers' desires. From the beginning all the focus was placed on "those with the least connection to reality," from optimistic politicians and futurists to pessimists "led by our nation's vision-impaired broadcast executives" (p. 4). Seldom has anyone "bothered to ask the one key question: What do viewers want?" (p. 4).

Retailers and distributors are key in consumer acceptance, but they did little to promote AM stereo and to educate consumers—either what it was or how it sounded. Had there been a system standard selected, the industry could have rallied around it, and AM stereo would at least have had an opportunity to succeed. Leonard Kahn's "chicken and egg" situation for receivers applies not only to AM stereo but also to all other technologies. Without receivers there is no DAB, MTS, or DTV. Why should manufacturers produce receivers if consumers don't want them? Why would a broadcaster transmit AM stereo, MTS, DAB, DTV, and so on if consumers do not care and if there are no receivers? Although the FCC did not select a standard, MTS turned out differently than AM because certain aspects of one system were protected. TV broadcasters understood what happened to AM stereo and decided to support one system. When MTS was launched in 1984, it had an opportunity to succeed, and broadcasters capitalized on it. DTV's Grand Alliance was also a reaction to AM stereo, but the FCC's failure to protect formats has jeopardized it.

A major difference between color and DTV was David Sarnoff, who personally took charge of color TV and spent millions on "program production, network infrastructure, station upgrades, and receiver design" (Whitaker, 1998a, p. 68). Even with Sarnoff's tenacity color TV's success was not easily realized. Without consumer interest or a Sarnoff to drive DTV, cost becomes key. Whitaker called it the "*Sarnoff* factor" and explained: "In 1953, RCA was in a unique position: It could influence program production, distribution, and reception. It owned NBC, which owned programs, and it made television sets. In those days, RCA could afford to lose tens of millions of dollars on its color TV ventures because Sarnoff believed that he would make the money back a hundred-fold, which he probably did. Sarnoff also had the power to stay-the-course in the face of a business line that was an embarrassing loss center" (p. 68). With Sarnoff gone a similar situation appears unattainable by today's standards.

DTV has been hindered like AM stereo in many ways. It is not certain that consumers desire DTV, because a satisfactory product is already available. Computer advocates want DTV, but for different reasons. Although it is inevitable that computers and TVs are drawing nearer to each other, we are a long way from a happy marriage of the two that will suit most consumers. Whitaker (1998a) observed: "United States consumers have demonstrated an insatiable appetite for new electronic gadgets. Television broadcasters have, in the past, been the benefactors of this growth market. Now, as consumers branch out from traditional, over-the-air entertainment sources to other media, broadcasters are playing a whole new ball game" (p. 68).

AM stereo had but five different transmission standards with which consumers had to contend. DTV is even more complicated. FCC chairman Reed Hundt boasted: "What we've done here is guarantee there will be dozens of different kinds of digital television receivers of many, many different prices. Some with software, some with big screens, some suitable for your wristwatch" (Reber, 1997, p. 8). Reber (1997) responded: "But what this says really is that consumers will be faced with confusion and worry about the ability to receive ALL digital signals or the obsolescence of the equipment they must purchase. Significantly, there is no provision in the standard that assures their new digital widescreen sets will be compatible with all video format transmissions or that HDTV programming will be offered and assured over time to justify set prices at least $1,000 to $1,500 higher than the cost of sets today" (p. 8).

DTV does not ensure that a broadcast station will experience more success using digital transmission than it did with analog. NBC took the lead with color TV but gained little advantage over other networks. Garvey (1980) stated: "While this expansion of color programming eventually built an audience with color sets, there is no evidence that NBC gained much from its considerable investment" (p. 521). NBC was at the forefront due to RCA, its parent corporation, which "held most of the patents on the newly approved color system and was a major manufacturer of equipment both for home and for the television industry" (p. 521). Because the FCC changed the color standard once, RCA feared that it could happen again. Therefore, it was imperative "not only to get the system *approved*, but also to get it *established*" (p. 522). But, as has been emphasized, RCA had Sarnoff, who understood the "chicken and egg" scenario, which Garvey called a "circular problem" (p. 523). Garvey explained: "The solution to the circular problem of programming and audience lay in the ability of RCA to benefit from color even though it was of dubious value to NBC itself. Color made economic sense if it was viewed in the broader context of programming, audience, *and* manufacturing" (p. 523). By waiting out the market, however, ABC and CBS have prospered and "suffered no economic loss by delaying their entrance into color" (p. 523).

Until questions about the introduction, cost, and consumer acceptance of DTV and DAB are answered, the "circular problem" makes their futures uncertain at best. The FCC, broadcasters, manufacturers, and consumers are all keys to the success or failure of new technologies. No one yet knows whether the average consumer desires digital broadcasting and, just as importantly, whether that consumer is willing to support it. However, we can learn much about regulating the future of broadcasting technology by looking at the past.

Bibliography

Abramson, D. (1982, May 3). Long delay predicted for AM stereo solution. *Television/ Radio Age*, pp. 33–35, 75–76.

Adding insult to injury. (1994, March 7). *Broadcasting & Cable*, p. 74.

An *Advanced Imaging* roundtable: Advanced television & digital HDTV: What happens now? (1997, January). *Advanced Imaging*, pp. 49–54.

Advanced Television Systems Committee (ATSC). (1997, April 2). ATSC announces certification program for digital television [Press Release] [WWW document]. URL http://www.atsc.org/Press/PR-Certi.html

Advanced TV fall-out. (1997, January). *Advanced Imaging*, p. 8.

Albiniak, P. (1997a, June 9). Planned obsolescence. *Broadcasting & Cable*, p. 7.

Albiniak, P. (1997b, June 16). House would give more time for DTV transition. *Broadcasting & Cable*, p. 14.

Albiniak, P. (1997c, August 25). Tauzin warns against abandoning HDTV. *Broadcasting & Cable*, p. 11.

Albiniak, P. (1997d, September 22). Broadcasters ease fears over HDTV. *Broadcasting & Cable*, pp. 18–19.

Albiniak, P. (1998a, April 6). Tauzin asks for network HDTV plans. *Broadcasting & Cable*, p. 42.

Albiniak, P. (1998b, April 27). HDTV no problem, says cable. *Broadcasting & Cable*, p. 4.

Albiniak, P. (1999, July 5). NAB, DirecTV minds meet. *Broadcasting & Cable*, p. 7.

AM: Band on the run. (1985, November 11). *Broadcasting*, pp. 35, 46, 48, 50, 52.

AM broadcasters: Anxious for stereo. (1985, April 22). *Broadcasting*, pp. 95–96.

AMRC closer to launching DARS. (1998, April 15). *Radio World*, p. 3.

AM stereo battle nears end. (1985, May 15). *Radio World*, p. 5.

AM stereo: Big deal in Big D. (1982, April 5). *Broadcasting*, p. 41.

The AM stereo fight continues. (1986, April 21). *Broadcasting*, pp. 68, 70.

AM stereo gets another hearing. (1981, February 16). *Broadcasting*, pp. 84–85.

AM stereo goes on the air: Fighting for equality between the radio bands. (1982, August 2). *Broadcasting*, pp. 23–24.

AM stereo makers tout their wares. (1984, September 24). *Broadcasting*, pp. 56, 58.

The AM stereo marketplace struggles for a standard. (1984, March 19). *Broadcasting*, pp. 84–86.

AM stereo on parade at CES. (1983, January 17). *Broadcasting*, pp. 116, 118.

The AM stereo question: Motorola or multisystem? (1984, May 7). *Broadcasting*, pp. 95–97.

AM stereo standard overdue. (1986, November 1). *Radio World*, p. 5.

AM stereo support eroding. (1986, August 1). *Radio World*, p. 5.

AM stereo: The solution still eludes. (1982, April 12). *Broadcasting*, pp. 35–36.

AM stereo II. (1997, August 18). *Broadcasting & Cable*, p. 74.

AM uniformity. (1987, July 27). *Broadcasting*, p. 85.

Anderson, K. (1998a, January). Volunteer stations prep for November deadline. *Television Broadcast*, pp. 19, 30.

Anderson, K. (1998b, October 26). USDR asks FCC for DAB standard. *Broadcasting & Cable*, p. 62.

Antonoff, M. (1997, February/March). Off the Air: Monkey Wrench. *Video*, p. 104.

Antonoff, M. (2000, September). Killer apps and HDTV. *Stereo Review's Sound & Vision*, p. 164.

Armstrong, D.F. (1948, March). What to look for in FM. *Scientific American*, pp. 115–118.

Arnold, J. (1999, January 6). All-digital discussion [Letter to the Editor]. *Radio World*, p. 5.

Ashworth, S. (1999a, February 10). CES upbeat about DTV sales in 1999. *TV Technology*, pp. 1, 10.

Ashworth, S. (1999b, June 2). Mitsubishi, CBS partner to produce HD programming. *TV Technology*, p. 16.

Ashworth, S. (2000, January 12). Who among us will lead? *TV Technology*, p. 6.

Aversa, J. (1994, February 17). Futuristic TV moves step closer [Associated Press report]. *Mobile Press Register*, p. 7D.

Bad vibes for AM stereo. (1980, April 21). *Broadcasting*, pp. 80–81.

Baraff, B.J., & Peltzman, L.J. (1986, September 26). Petition for rulemaking of Texar Inc.: In re request for amendment of section 73.128 of the commission's rules and regulations (AM stereophonic broadcasting) to establish a uniform technical standard for AM stereophonic broadcasting. (Available from Baraff, Koerner, Olender, & Hochberg, P.C., 2033 M St. N.W., Washington, DC 20036).

Barnouw, E. (1968). *The golden web: A history of broadcasting in the United States, 1933–1953*. New York: Oxford University Press.

Barry, J. (1997, April). HDTV gets closer. *Stereo Review*, pp. 18, 20.

Barry, J. (1998, July). Digital TV demystified. *Stereo Review*, pp. 29–31.

The battle over formats. (1998, May). *Broadcast Engineering*, p. 40.

Beacham, F. (1991, December). HDTV at a turning point. *TV Technology*, pp. 25–26.

Beacham, F. (1992, May). Sikes: A new ballgame for HDTV. *TV Technology*, p. 3.

Beacham, F. (1994a, March 9). DCR to begin satellite DAR service. *Radio World*, pp. 1, 8.

Beacham, F. (1994b, March 23). WBBR is first audio superstation. *Radio World*, pp. 1, 3.

Beacham, F. (1995, April). Alliance touts HDTV's flexibility. *TV Technology NAB Extra*, p. 21.

Beacham, F. (1996, August 23). Digital TV airs "grand" soap opera. *TV Technology*, pp. 1, 8.

Beacham, F. (1997a, March 13). DTV War: What is it good for? *TV Technology*, p. 27.

Beacham, F. (1997b, April 24). Compaq rejects DTV standard. *TV Technology*, p. 44.

Beacham, F. (1997c, July 3). In praise of democratic design. *TV Technology*, pp. 22, 24.

Beacham, F. (1998a, January 5). Intel to support all DTV formats. *TV Technology*, pp. 1, 22.

Beacham, F. (1998b, November 2). Back to TV's future. *TV Technology*, pp. 43–44.

Behrens, S. (1986, May). The fight for high-def. *Channels*, pp. 42–47.

Betting on the future. (1992, February 10). *Broadcasting*, p. 82.

Birkmaier, C. (1997a, May). Big M little TV. *Television Broadcast*, pp. 16, 92.

Birkmaier, C. (1997b, May). FCC launches DTV era. *Television Broadcast*, pp. 1, 27.

Birkmaier, C. (1998, September). Out-of-the-box thinking. *Television Broadcast*, pp. 11, 38.

Black, Jay, Bryant, Jennings, & Thompson, Susan. (1998) (5th ed.). *Introduction to media communication*. Boston: McGraw-Hill.

Blinder, E.J. (1990a, February). Poised to test, ATTC builds its laboratory. *Television Engineering*, pp. 21–22.

Blinder, E.J. (1990b, July). HDTV: The corporate video waiting game. *Corporate Video Decisions*, pp. 38–43.

Bloomfield, L. (1998, February). TCI has "different" HDTV. *Broadcast Engineering*, pp. 14, 18.

Botik, B. (1992, August 19). DAB reality check [Letter to the Editor]. *Radio World*, p. 5.

Bowser, A. (1999, August 2). Up and running in the top 10. *Broadcasting & Cable*, pp. 30, 32.

Bowser, A. (2000, September 2000). The DTV waiting game. *Broadcasting & Cable*, pp. 42–44, 48, 50.

Brazil chooses C-QUAM. (1986, March 1). *Radio World*, p. 1.

Brenner, D. (1992). No, but I read the magazine article. *Media Studies Journal*, 6, 93–103.

Brinkley, J. (1997, Winter). Good things come to those who wait. *Stereophile Guide to Home Theater*, pp. 50, 52, 54, 56.

Broadcast digital TV: A new star war? (1996, August). *Advanced Imaging*, p. 9.

Broadcasters, military at odds over DAB as WARC approaches. (1991, October 7). *Broadcasting*, pp. 60–61.

Brown, R. (1993, February 8). Time Warner takes stake in cable radio. *Broadcasting*, p. 31.

Bruun, R.J. (1961, November 24). F-M stereo sales rise. *Electronics*, pp. 22–23.

Bunzel, R.E. (1991, November 18). In-band systems gain from S-band DAB. *Broadcasting*, pp. 50, 52.

Butler, A. (1992, August 19). Technical seminar to examine DAB, EBS. *Radio World*, pp. 51, 53.

CAB advises government pick C-QUAM. (1986, November 1). *Radio World*, p. 1.

A call for compromise. (1996, October 25). *TV Technology*, p. 6.

Canada: Avoid U.S. mistakes. (1986, April 1). *Radio World*, p. 5.

Careless, J. (1990, July 11). Canada launches DAB tests. *Radio World*, pp. 1, 14.

Careless, J. (1992, January 22). Canada pursues L-band DAB. *Radio World*, p. 1.

Careless, J. (1994, January 12). Pioneer commits to DAB. *Radio World*, pp. 3, 9.

Careless, J. (1995, November 29). Canada DAB on track. *Radio World*, pp. 1, 8.

Careless, J. (1996a, March 20). Canadians have doubts about DAB roll out. *Radio World*, p. 14.

Careless, J. (1996b, September 4). DAB allocation begins in Canada. *Radio World*, pp. 8, 15.

Careless, J. (1997, December 4). Canada to adopt ATSC standard. *TV Technology*, p. 14.

Careless, J. (1999, July 21). Slow Canadian DAB irks pioneer. *Radio World*, pp. 3, 7.

Careless, J. (2000, June 7). Canadian DAB reaches into U.S. *Radio World*, pp. 1, 12.

Carey, J. (1989, July/August). Adopting new technologies. *Society*, pp. 10–16.

Carroll, J. (1961, June 24). Stereo comes to FM: Part II. *Saturday Review*, pp. 31–32.

Carroll, J. & Kolodin, I. (1961, May 27). Stereo comes to FM. *Saturday Review*, p. 38.

Carroll, J.M. (1960, November 4). FCC studies broadcast report. *Electronics*, pp. 32–33.

Carter, A. (1988, February 1). NRSC proceeds with AM goals. *Radio World*, p. 7.

Carter, A. (1990a, March 28). AMs asked to air NRSC radio ads. *Radio World*, p. 3.

Carter, A. (1990b, July 25). NAB's stand on DAB. *Radio World*, pp. 1, 8.

Carter, A. (1992, June 24). Experts debate future of DAB. *Radio World*, p. 1.

Carter, A. (1993, March 24). Japan embraces C-QUAM. *Radio World*, p. 9.

Carter, A. (1995, October 4). AT&T demos IBAC DAB in Big Easy. *Radio World*, pp. 1, 14.

Carter, A., & Gatski, J. (1990, March). HDTV by satellite coming to U.S. *TV Technology*, pp. 1, 20.

Chris Payne to Motorola. (1982, August 14). *Billboard*, p. 70.

Clark, M. (1997, November 12). DAB makes European commercial debut. *Radio World*, pp. 1, 6.

Classic Patrick. (1989, July 24). *Broadcasting*, pp. 32–33.

Cobo, L. (1995, September 20). In-band slammed by EIA testing process. *Radio World*, pp. 1, 3.

Cohen, J. (1997, April 2). WorldDAB, WorldSpace wrangle. *Radio World*, pp. 8, 13.

Cole, A. (1991a, May). Nothing cheap about HDTV. *TV Technology NAB Extra*, p. 8.

Cole, A. (1991b, September 11). Cheney opposes L-band use. *Radio World*, p. 3.

Cole, A. (1992a, March). Compression race heating up. *Computer Video Technology*, pp. 51, 53.

Cole, A. (1992b, May). Special HD panel chosen. *TV Technology*, p. 8.

Cole, A. (1992c, June). Zenith, GI to divide HD profits. *TV Technology*, pp. 1, 14.

Cole, A. (1993, December). HD alliance gets to work on specifics. *TV Technology*, pp. 1, 8.

Cole, H. (1996, July). Stop DARS with best local shot. *Tuned In*, pp. 42–43.

Colman, P. (1998, February 9). Lines drawn on HDTV. *Broadcasting & Cable*, pp. 44–46.

Compressing business awaits. (1993, May 26). *Radio World*, p. 5.

Compression: Changing the world of television? (1990, June 11). *Broadcasting*, pp. 68, 70–71.

Congressional Budget Office. (1999, September). Completing the transition to digital television. [WWW document]. URL http://www.cbo.gov/showdoc.cfm?index=1544&sequence=0&from=1

Connecticut weighs AM stereo ad law. (1985, August 12). *Broadcasting*, pp. 56–57.

Consensus forms on MTS. (1984, January 9). *Broadcasting*, pp. 126–128.

Consumer Electronics Association. (2000, February 4). CEA Applauds FCC's Unanimous Decision to Dismiss Sinclair DTV Proposal. [WWW document].

C-QUAM violations alleged. (1986, May 1). *Radio World*, p. 1.

Cripps, D. (1997a, March). HDTV: Nothing as it appears. *Widescreen Review*, pp. 56, 58.

Cripps, D. (1997b, December). The story on HDTV. *Widescreen Review*, pp. 44–48.

Crowley, S. (1991, July 24). USA Digital hopes for in-band fit. *Radio World*, p. 12.

Cudworth, A.L. (2000, January 26). HD presents new challenges for set designers. *TV Technology*, p. 17.

Czitrom, D.J. (1982). *Media and the American mind from Morse to McLuhan*. Chapel Hill: University of North Carolina Press.

DAB in-band wagon. (1992, August 31). *Broadcasting*, pp. 30–32.

DAB launched by Germany in Bavaria. (1995, November 1). *Radio World*, pp. 1, 9.

DAB looks for a home. (1990, September 3). *Broadcasting*, pp. 48–49.

DAB: Radio gets iBiquitous [Editorial]. (2000, August 2). *Radio World*, p. 62.

DAB: Radio's salvation or destruction? (1990, July 16). *Broadcasting*, p. 79.

DAB receivers delayed in Europe. (1996, March 20). *Radio World*, p. 17.

DAB: Stay the course. (1992, September 9). *Radio World*, p. 5.

DAB strategy. (1991, January 28). *Broadcasting*, p. 53.

DAB tests get L-band. (1996, January 10). *Radio World*, pp. 1, 6.

DAB truce is welcome progress. (1993, April 14). *Radio World*, p. 5.

Davies, J.C. (1990, March). The lowdown on high def. *Audio*, pp. 30, 34, 36.

Debriefing Chairman Sikes on the eve of NAB'92. (1992, April 13). *Broadcasting*, pp. 50–51, 54–55.

Delco AM stereo tests near end. (1982, October 2). *Billboard*, p. 22.

Diamond, A., & Sneegas, J. (1992, October 26). Monday memo. *Broadcasting*, p. 20.

Dick, B. (1995, July). Broadcaster's golden opportunity. *Broadcast Engineering*, p. 6.

Dick, B. (1996, August). Buy this baby, and it'll last you a lifetime. *Broadcast Engineering*, p. 4.

Dick, B. (1997a, February). Regarding "Frankenstein TV." *Broadcast Engineering*, p. 8.

Dick, B. (1997b, March). DTV: A new saddle on an old horse. *Broadcast Engineering*, p. 6.

Dick, B. (1997c, May). The granny factor. *Broadcast Engineering*, p. 6.

Dick, B. (1998a, May). My digital is better than your digital. *Broadcast Engineering*, p. 10.

Dick, B. (1998b, September). One size doesn't fit all. *Broadcast Engineering*, p. 10.

Dick, B. (2000, August). Kill the 8-VSB Frankenstein. *Broadcast Engineering*, p. 8.

Dickinson, C. (1993, July). U.S. can't wait for European HDTV. *TV Technology*, p. 8.

Dickson, G. (1997a, May 12). Networks have different views of DTV. *Broadcasting & Cable*, pp. 52, 54, 56.

Dickson, G. (1997b, June 23). DTV: A sports revolution. *Broadcasting & Cable*, p. 66.

Dickson, G. (1998, July 20). Counting down to DTV. *Broadcasting & Cable*, pp. 22–24.

Dickson, G. (1999, August 2). Back to the future. *Broadcasting & Cable*, pp. 22–24.

Dickson, G. (2000a, August 21). Thomson huddles with CBS on hi-def. *Broadcasting & Cable*, p. 14.

Dickson, G. (2000b, October 16). Kennard's DTV smokescreen? *Broadcasting & Cable*, p. 14.

Digital Radio Research Inc. (1995, August 22). EIA/NRSC DAB System Lab Test Results: An Assessment. [WWW document].

Digital TV deadlines. (1998, May 11). *Broadcasting & Cable*, p. 23.

The digits have it. (1992, October 5). *Broadcasting*, p. 70.

Doherty, R. (1996, February). The decade of HDTV . . . eh, SDTV? *Advanced Imaging*, p. 24.

Dorsey, S. (1992, September 23). Put music first, not DAB [Letter to the Editor]. *Radio World*, p. 5.

Doyle, M. (1992). *The future of television: A global overview of programming, advertising, technology and growth*. Lincolnwood, IL: NTC Publishing Group.

Dreyfack, M. (1984, March). Who's ready for AM stereo? *Marketing and Media Decisions*, pp. 114, 116, 118.

Duston, D. (1992, October 7). High-definition TV coming to U.S.; venture may mean 100,000 jobs [Associated Press report]. *Mobile Press*, p. 8B.

Electonics newsletter: Stereo standards group files field-test report. (1960, October 21). *Electronics*, p. 11.

Electronics newsletter: The question now: When stereo standards? (1960, November 4). *Electronics*, pp. 9–10.

Elmer-Dewitt, P. (1992, March 30). The picture suddenly gets clearer. *Time*, pp. 54–55.

Emma, T., & Wolff, M.F. (1960, March 4). Future developments in engineering. *Electronics*, pp. 159–163.

The end of the beginning. (1994, September 26). *Broadcasting & Cable*, p. 78.

Epstein, S. (1997, January). The new HDTV standard. *Video Systems*, p. 9.

Eureka's Plenge discusses DAB. (1991, November 20). *Radio World*, pp. 3, 11.

Fadden, J. (1998, January). 2006: A camera odyssey. *Video Systems*, pp. 30–32.

Fall RADAR study finds FM continuing to grow. (1982, December 18). *Billboard*, p. 11.

FCC. (1955, March 25). Part 3—Radio broadcast services: Miscellaneous amendments (Docket No. 10832; FCC 55-340). Washington, DC: Federal Register, pp. 1821–1826.

FCC. (1958, July 11). FM broadcast stations: Notice of inquiry regarding specified non-broadcast activities on a multiplex basis (Docket No. 12517; FCC 58-636). Washington, DC: Federal Register, pp. 5284–5285.

FCC. (1959, March 18). Standards of good engineering practice concerning certain FM broadcast stations: Further notice of inquiry (Docket No. 12517; FCC 59-211). Washington, DC: Federal Register, p. 1997.

FCC. (1960a, May 12). FM broadcast stations: Transmission of stereophonic programs on multiplex basis (Docket No. 13506; FCC 60-498). Washington, DC: Federal Register, pp. 4240–4243.

FCC. (1960b, November 8). Kahn Research Laboratories, Inc.: Order extending time for filing comments (Docket No. 13596). Washington, DC: Federal Register, pp. 10667–10668.

FCC. (1961, April 25). Part 3—Radio broadcast services: Permission of FM broadcast stations to transmit stereophonic programs on a multiplex basis (Docket No. 13506; FCC 61-524). Washington, DC: Federal Register, pp. 3529–3534.

FCC. (1976). *Broadcast operator handbook* (1st ed.). Washington, DC: Author.

FCC. (1977a, July 7). AM Stereophonic broadcasting: Inquiry (Docket No. 21313; FCC 77-445). Washington, DC: Federal Register, pp. 34910–34913.

FCC. (1977b, December 12). AM and FM broadcast financial data, 1976. Washington, DC: Author.

FCC. (1978a, October 19). In the matter of AM stereophonic broadcasting: Notice of proposed rule making (Docket No. 21313; FCC 78-638). Washington, DC: Author, pp. 1–29.

FCC. (1978b, December 11). AM and FM broadcast financial data, 1977. Washington, DC: Author.

FCC. (1979, October 5). Inquiry and proposed rulemaking: Deregulation of radio (Docket No. 79-219; FCC 79-518). Washington, DC: Federal Register, pp. 57635–57723.

FCC. (1980, September 11). In the matter of stereophonic broadcasting: Memorandum opinion and order and further notice of proposed rulemaking (Docket No. 21313; FCC 80-477). Washington, DC: Author, pp. 1–32.

FCC. (1981, February 24). Deregulation of radio (Docket No. 79-219; FCC 81-17). Washington, DC: Federal Register, pp. 13888–13955.

FCC. (1982, March 18). In the matter of AM stereophonic broadcasting: Report and order (proceeding terminated) (Docket No. 21313; FCC 82-111). Washington, DC: Author, pp. 1–32.

FCC. (1984, April 27). The use of subcarrier frequencies in the aural baseband of television transmitters (Docket No. 21323; FCC 84-116). Washington, DC: Federal Register.

FCC. (1988a, January 28). In the matter of AM stereophonic broadcasting: Memorandum opinion and order. (FCC Record 3, (2) FCC 88-16). Washington, DC: U.S. Government Printing Office, pp. 403–406.

FCC. (1988b, September 22). Improvement in the quality of the AM broadcast service by reducing adjacent channel interference and by eliminating restrictions pertaining to the protected daytime contour (Docket No. MM-88-376; FCC 88-252). Washington, DC: Federal Communications Commission Record, pp. 5687–5694.

FCC. (1989, May 8). AM broadcast service; improvement of quality by reducing adjacent channel interference and by eliminating restrictions pertaining to the protected daytime contour (Docket MM 88-376; FCC 89-118). Washington, DC: Federal Register, pp. 19572–19575.

FCC. (1990a, July 18). In the matter of review of the technical assignment criteria for the AM broadcasting service (Docket MM-87-267; FCC 90-136). Washington, DC: Federal Communications Commission Record, pp. 4381–4481.

FCC. (1990b, August 21). In the matter of amendment of the commission's rules with regard to the establishment and regulations of new digital audio radio services (Docket No. 90-357; FCC 90-281). Washington, DC: Federal Communications Commission Record, pp. 5237–5240.

FCC. (1990c, September 26). Advanced Television Systems and Their Impact on the Existing Television Broadcast Service: Policy Decision (Docket No. 87-268; FCC 90-295). Washington, DC: Federal Register 55 FR 39275.

FCC. (1992a, August 26). Advanced Television Systems and Their Impact on the Existing Television Service: Proposed Rule (Docket No. 87-268; FCC 92-332). Washington, DC: Federal Register.

FCC. (1992b, October 8). Advanced Television Systems and Their Effect on the Existing Television Service: Proposed rule; extension of comment period. (Docket No. 87-268; DA 92-1344). Washington, DC: Federal Register 55 FR 39275.

FCC. (1992c, October 26). Advanced Television Systems and Their Effect on the Existing Television Service: Proposed rule; extension of comment period (Docket No. 87-268; DA 92-1445). Washington, DC: Federal Register.

FCC. (1992d, November 12). Broadcast Services; Advanced Television Systems: Proposed Rule (Docket No. 87-268, FCC 92-438). Washington, DC: Federal Register 57 FR 53679.

FCC. (1992e, November 12). Broadcast Services; Advanced Television Systems: Final Rule (Docket No. 87-268, FCC 92-438). Washington, DC: Federal Register 57 FR 53588.

FCC. (1992f, December 28). Broadcast Service; Advanced Television Systems: Proposed rule; extension of comment period. (Docket No. 87-268, DA 92-1714). Washington, DC: Federal Register 57 FR 61591.

FCC. (1993, December 20). Radio broadcasting; Establishment of a single AM radio stereophonic transmitting standard: Final rule. (Docket No. 92-298; FCC 93-485). Washington, DC: Federal Register.

FCC. (1995a, July 28). In the Matter of Advanced Television Systems and Their Impact upon the Existing Television Broadcast Service: Fourth Further Notice of Proposed Rule Making and Third Notice of Inquiry (MM Docket No. 87-268/FCC 95-315).

FCC. (1995b, November 28). Advisory Committee on Advanced Television Service: Advisory Committee Final Report and Recommendation (Advanced Television Test Center, 1330 Braddock Place, Suite 200, Alexandria, VA 22314-1650).

FCC. (1996a, May 9). In the Matter of Advanced Television Systems and Their Impact upon the Existing Television Broadcast Service: Fifth Further Notice of Proposed Rule Making (MM Docket No. 87-68/FCC 96-207).

FCC. (1996b, July 25). In the Matter of Advanced Television Systems and Their Impact upon the Existing Television Broadcast Service: Sixth Further Notice of Proposed Rule Making (MM Docket No. 87-268/FCC 96-317).

FCC. (1996c, December 24). In the matter of Advanced Television Systems and Their Impact upon the Existing Television Broadcast Service: Fourth Report and Order (MM Docket No. 87-268/FCC 96-493).

FCC. (1997a, April 3). Advanced Television Systems and Their Impact upon the Existing Television Broadcast Service: Sixth Report and Order (MM Docket No. 87-268; FCC 97-115). [WWW document]. URL http://www.fcc.gov/Bureaus/Engineering_Technology/Orders/1997/fcc97115.html

FCC. (1997b, April 3). Re: Adoption of Digital Television Allotment and Service Rules Reports and Orders: Separate Statement of Chairman Reed E. Hundt

(MM Docket No. 87-268; FCC 97-115). [WWW document]. URL http://www.fcc.gov/Speeches/Hundt/huntdtv.html

FCC. (1997c, April 3). Re: Advanced Television Systems and Their Impact upon the Existing Television Broadcast Service, Sixth Report and Order (MM Docket No. 87-268; FCC 97-115): Separate Statement of Commissioner Rachelle B. Chong. [WWW document]. URL http://www.fcc.gov/Speeches/Chong/separate_statements/chngdtv.html

FCC. (1997d, April 3). Re: Adoption of a New Table of Allotments. Advanced Television Systems and Their Impact upon the Existing Television Broadcast Service (MM Docket No. 87-268, FCC 97-115, Sixth Report and Order): Press Statement of Commissioner James H. Quello. [WWW document]. URL http://www.fcc.gov/Speeches/Quello/states/quelodtv.html

FCC. (1997e, April 3). Re: Advanced Television Systems and Their Impact upon the Existing Television Broadcast Service (MM Docket No. 87-268; FCC 97-115/FCC 97-116): Separate Statement of Commissioner Susan Ness. [WWW document]. URL http://www.fcc.gov/Speeches/Ness/States/nessdtv.html

FCC. (1997f, April 3). Advanced Television Systems and Their Impact upon the Existing Television Broadcast Service: Fifth Report and Order on (MM Docket No. 87-268; FCC 97-116). [WWW document]. URL http://www.fcc.gov/Bureaus/Mass_Media/Orders/1997/fcc97116.html

FCC. (1997g, April 3). Re: Advanced Television Systems and Their Impact upon the Existing Television Broadcast Service, Fifth Report and Order (MM Docket No. 87-268; 97-116): Separate Statement of Commissioner Rachelle B. Chong, Concurring in Part. [WWW document]. URL http://www.fcc.gov/Speeches/Chong/separate_statements/chngdtv5.html

FCC. (1997h, April 3). Commission Adopts Rules for Digital Television Service: Report No. MM 97-8 [Press Release]. (MM Docket No. 87-268). [WWW document]. URL http://www.fcc.gov/Bureaus/Mass_Media/News_Releases/1997/nrmm7005.html

FCC. (1997i, April 3). Commission Adopts Table of Allotments for DTV; Establishes Policies and Rules: Report No. MM 97-9 [Press Release]. (MM Docket No. 87-268). [WWW document]. URL http://www.fcc.gov/Bureaus/Mass_Media/News_Releases/1997/nrmm7006.html

FCC. (1997j, July 9). In the Matter of Reallocation of Television Channels 60–69, the 746–806 MHz Band: Notice of Proposed Rule Making (ET Docket No. 97-157; FCC 97-245). [WWW document]. URL http://www.fcc.gov/Bureaus/Engineering_Technology/Notices/1997/fcc97245.txt

FCC. (1997k, September 4). Commission terminates pioneer's preference program; Dismisses all pending pioneer's preference requests (Docket Nos. CC 92-297, ET 94-124, GEN 90-314, GEN 90-357, IB 97-95, ET 93-266) Report No. ET 97-7 OET Action. [WWW document]. URL http://www.fcc.gov/Bureaus/Engineering_Technology/News_Releases/1997/nret7012.html

FCC. (1997l, December 31). In the Matter of Reallocation of Television Channels 60–69, the 746–806 MHz Band: Report and Order (ET Docket No. 97-157; FCC 97-451). [WWW document]. URL http://www.fcc.gov/Bureaus/Engineering_Technology/Orders/1997/fcc97421.txt

FCC. (1998a, February 17). Advanced Television Systems and Their Impact upon the Existing Television Broadcast Service: Memorandum Opinion and Order on

Reconsideration of the Fifth Report and Order (MM Docket No. 87-268; FCC 98-23). [WWW document]. URL http://www.fcc.gov/Bureaus/ Mass_Media/Orders/1998/fcc98023.html

FCC. (1998b, February 17). Advanced Television Systems and Their Impact upon the Existing Television Broadcast Service: Memorandum Opinion and Order on Reconsideration of the Sixth Report and Order (MM Docket No. 87-268; FCC 98-24). [WWW document]. URL http://www.fcc.gov/Bureaus/ Engineering_Technology/Orders/1998/fcc98024.html

FCC. (1998c, February 18). Advanced Television Systems and Their Impact upon the Existing Television Broadcast Service: FCC Adopts Final DTV Allotment Table Policies and Rules (Report ET 98-2MM Docket No. 87-268; FCC 98-23/FCC 98-24). [WWW document]. URL http://www.fcc.gov/Bureaus/ Engineering_Technology/News_Releases/1998/nret8002.html

FCC. (1998d, February 18). Re: Advanced Television Systems and Their Impact upon the Existing Television Broadcast Service—Memorandum Opinion and Order on Reconsideration of the Fifth and Sixth Report and Order: Separate Statement of Commissioner Harold W. Furchtgott-Roth Dissenting in Part (MM Docket No. 87-268; FCC 98-23/FCC 98-24). [WWW document]. URL http://www.fcc.gov/Speeches/Furchtgott_Roth/Statements/ sthfr804. html

FCC. (1998e, February 18). Re: Advanced Television Systems and Their Impact upon the Existing Television Broadcast Service—Memorandum Opinion and Order on Reconsideration of the Fifth and Sixth Report and Order: Statement of FCC Chairman William Kennard on Adopting Final DTV Allotments and Rules (MM Docket No. 87-268; FCC 98-23/98-24). [WWW document]. URL http://www.fcc.gov/Speeches/Kennard/Statements/stwek808.html

FCC. (1998f, February 18). Re: Advanced Television Systems and Their Impact upon the Existing Television Broadcast Service—Memorandum Opinion and Order on Reconsideration of the Fifth and Sixth Report and Order: Separate Statement of Commissioner Susan Ness (MM Docket No. 87-268; FCC 98-23/FCC 98-24). [WWW document]. URL http://www.fcc.gov/Speeches/ Ness/States/stsn805.html

FCC. (1998g, March 25). Joint Statement of the Federal Communications Commission and the Food and Drug Administration regarding Avoidance of Interference between Digital Television and Medical Telemetry Devices. [Press Release] [WWW document]. URL http://www.fcc.gov/Bureaus/Engineering_ Technology/News_Releases/1998/nret8003.txt

FCC. (1998h, March). Office Of Engineering and Technology Fact Sheet: Sharing of Analog and Digital Television Spectrum by Medical Telemetry Devices [WWW document]. URL http://www.fcc.gov/oet/faqs/medical.html

FCC. (1998i, July 9). In the Matter of Carriage of the Transmissions of Digital Television Broadcast Stations Amendments to Part 76 of the Commission's Rules: Notice of Proposed Rule Making (CS Docket No. 98-120). [WWW document]. URL http://www.fcc.gov/Bureaus/Cable/Notices/1998/fcc98153.txt

FCC. (1998j, July 9). Commission Adopts Notice Seeking Comment on Digital Broadcast Signal Carriage Issues (CS DOCKET NO. 98-120; Report No. CS 98-12 Cable Services Action). [Press Release] [WWW document]. URL http://www.fcc.gov/Bureaus/Cable/News_Releases/1998/nrcb8017.txt

FCC. (1999a, September 30). DTV Report on COFDM and 8-VSB Performance (OET Report FCC/OET 99-2). [WWW document]. URL http://www.fcc. gov/Bureaus/Engineering_Technology/Documents/reports/ dtvreprt.txt

FCC. (1999b, November 1). In the Matter of Digital Audio Broadcasting Systems and Their Impact on the Terrestrial Radio Broadcast Service: Notice of Proposed Rule Making (MM Docket No. 99-325). [WWW document]. URL http://www.fcc.gov/Bureaus/Mass_Media/Notices/1999/fcc99327.txt

FCC. (2000a, February 4). FCC Denies Sinclair Petition for Rulemaking on COFDM Standard. [Press Release] [WWW document]. URL http://www.fcc.gov/ Daily_Releases/Daily_Business/2000/db0204/nret0002.html

FCC. (2000b, February 4). Letter to Martin R. Leader of Fisher, Wayland, Cooper, Leader & Zaragoza, L.L.P., re: FCC Denies Sinclair Petition for Rulemaking on COFDM Standard. [WWW document]. URL http://www.fcc.gov/ Daily_Releases/Daily_Business/2000/db0204/fcc00035.txt

FCC. (2000c, September 14). FCC adopts rules for labeling of DTV receivers [Press Release] [WWW document]. URL http://www.fcc.gov/Bureaus/OPP/ News_Releases/2000/nrop0001.html

FCC acquits C-QUAM. (1986, August 1). *Radio World*, pp. 1, 10.

FCC acts on NRSC. (1988, August 15). *Radio World*, pp. 1, 10.

FCC asked to choose AM stereo standard. (1986, September 29). *Broadcasting*, pp. 35–36.

FCC brings AM stereo back to the barn. (1980, June 30). *Broadcasting*, pp. 19–20.

FCC chairman wants to reopen DARS spectrum to new applicants. (1995, September 11). *Broadcasting & Cable*, p. 8.

FCC dismisses Kahn complaint. (1986, August 15). *Radio World*, pp. 1,7.

FCC gives up on AM stereo choice, will leave it to marketplace. (1982, March 8). *Broadcasting*, pp. 36–37.

FCC holds the line on AM stereo. (1988, January 18). *Broadcasting*, p. 49.

FCC makes it Magnavox for AM stereo. (1980, April 14). *Broadcasting*, pp. 27–28.

FCC offers three spectrum options for DAB. (1990, October 1). *Broadcasting*, pp. 62–63.

The FCC on the firing line in Las Vegas. (1980, April 21). *Broadcasting*, pp. 42, 44.

FCC pulls plug on Harris AM stereo. (1983, August 29). *Broadcasting*, pp. 35, 36.

FCC's 'blue ribbon' HDTV committee extended to 1991. (1989, July 24). *Broadcasting*, p. 75.

FCC seeks comments on DARS. (1995, July 12). *Radio World*, p. 2.

FCC's Hundt centered in the eye of the storm. (1996, September 27). *TV Technology*, pp. 4, 7.

FCC takes action to close AM-FM fidelity gap. (1989, April 17). *Broadcasting*, pp. 54–55.

FCC to include mask. (1988, May 15). *Radio World*, pp. 1, 3.

FCC to take simulcast route to HDTV. (1990, March 26). *Broadcasting*, pp. 38–40.

Fedele, J. (1998, April 20). 5.1 audio channels—the final frontier? *TV Technology*, pp. 8, 10.

Feldman, L. (1984, July). Stereo TV here at last. *Stereo Review*, pp. 37–39.

Feldman, L. (1992, October 21). Tuner tests out "Super." *Radio World*, pp. 1, 14–15, 29.

Fenton, B., & Livingstone, W. (1998, June). Stay tuned. *Stereo Review*, p. 6.

Few visitors at booths: AM stereo developments get limited CES interest. (1983, January 22). *Billboard*, p. 19.

Fibish, D.K. (1995, December). Video compression overview. *Video Systems*, pp. 32–33, 58.

Fields, H. (1985, October 28). Inside the FCC: James McKinney. *Television/Radio Age*, pp. 95–96.

The final days. (1980, August 4). *Broadcasting*, pp. 23, 26–27.

First things first [Editorial]. (2000, July 31). *Broadcasting & Cable*, p. 78.

Fleming, H. (1997, February 10). White House calls for "expediting" digital TV licenses. *Broadcasting & Cable*, p. 7.

Flint, J. (1992, September 21). FCC gives on HDTV timetable. *Broadcasting*, pp. 5–6.

Flint, J. (1993, March 15). Electronics group, NAB team for in-band digital radio. *Broadcasting & Cable*, p. 51.

FM share up to 70%. (1985, June 14). *Radio and Records*, p. 1.

FM: The great leaps forward. (1979, January 22). *Broadcasting*, pp. 32–34, 36, 39.

Fogarty: Favors rapid approval for DBS petitions. (1982, April 5). *Television/Radio Age*, pp. 68–69.

Foisie, G. (1994, March 28). Road to digital HDTV takes detour. *Broadcasting & Cable*, p. 40.

Format experimentation on the AM band. (1985, November 11). *Broadcasting*, p. 50.

Forrest, J. (1994, March). World satellite market driven by compression. *TV Technology*, p. 5.

Four sides of the AM stereo coin. (1982, August 9). *Broadcasting*, pp. 50–51.

Fowler, M.S. (1982, January 13). Getting the government out of programming: FCC chief calls it "unregulation." *Variety*, pp. 145, 182.

Fowler, M.S. (1984, June). The boom goes bust, the bust goes boom. *Communications and the Law*, 6 (3), 23–29.

Freed, K. (1998, November 2). The world adapts to digital. *TV Technology*, pp. 1, 34.

From public interest to marketplace: Changing point of view at the FCC. (1985, June 17). *Broadcasting*, pp. 38, 40–41.

FTC said to be investigating Motorola on antitrust grounds. (1985, March 11). *Broadcasting*, p. 42.

Garber, I. (1998, February). CES shows reality of DTV for consumers. *Television Broadcast*, p. 19.

Garvey, D.E. (1980, Fall). Introducing color television: The audience and programming problem. *Journal of Broadcasting*, 24 (4), 515–525.

Gates, B., Myhrvold, N., & Rinearson, P. (1995). *The road ahead*. New York: Viking Penguin.

Gatski, J. (1990a, January). HDTV legislation loses momentum. *TV Technology*, pp. 1, 10.

Gatski, J. (1990b, May 9). DAB shows future of radio. *Radio World*, p. 15.

Gatski, J. (1992a, January 8). Strother, Schober Boycott DAB Group. *Radio World*, p. 3.

Gatski, J. (1992b, August 19). Digital radio standard talks planned. *Radio World*, p. 52.

Gatski, J. (1992c, October 21). DAB mark in dispute. *Radio World*, pp. 1, 10.

Gatski, J. (1992d, October 21). Canada skeptical about in-band DAB. *Radio World*, pp. 8, 10.

Gatski, J. (1992e, November 4). EIA faces difficult timetable. *Radio World*, pp. 1, 3.

Gatski, J. (1993a, January 6). FCC chairman to resign January 19. *Radio World*, p. 3.

Gatski, J. (1993b, January 20). NAB DAB task force endorses in-band. *Radio World*, p. 6.

Gatski, J. (1993c, April 14). NRSC to guide in-band DAB testing. *Radio World*, pp. 1, 12.

Gatski, J. (1993d, June 9). Cost estimates for DAB. *Radio World*, pp. 1, 22.

Gatski, J. (1993e, June 9). Germany delays Eureka evaluations. *Radio World*, p. 3.

Gatski, J. (1993f, June 23). Compression standard not easy to implement. *Radio World*, pp. 1, 7.

Gatski, J. (1994, September 7). USA Digital on-air in Chicago. *Radio World*, p. 1.

Gerson, R. (1990, April). Rival HDTV makers join forces. *Video Review*, p. 20.

Getting down to business. (1990, March). *TV Technology*, pp. 8–9.

GI and MIT form HDTV alliance. (1991, February 4). *Broadcasting*, p. 42.

Gilder, G. (1990). *Life after television: The coming transformation of media and American life*. Knoxville, TN: Whittle Direct Books.

Goldberg, R. (1993, November). The big squeeze. *Popular Science*, pp. 100–103.

Goldberg, R. (1994, March). TV for the 21st century. *Home*, pp. 64, 66.

Graham, C. (1979, April). Soundwise: Stereo broadcasting likely in '79. *American Record Guide*, p. 53.

Graham, W. (1998, April). Is high definition TV worth the cost? *Television Broadcast*, p. 27.

Grand Alliance II. (1998, August 31). *Broadcasting & Cable*, p. 74.

Greenleaf, C. (1984, June). The first AM stereo road test. *Stereo Review*, pp. 18, 20.

Greenleaf, C. (1985, May). Evaluate your car stereo system. *Stereo Review*, pp. 57–60, 62.

Green light to testing of HDTV prototype. (1994, February 28). *Broadcasting & Cable*, p. 14.

Gross, J. (1991a, July 10). FCC vacillates on L-band. *Radio World*, pp. 1, 9.

Gross, J. (1991b, July 10). NAB DAB stand fuels battle. *Radio World*, p. 14.

Gross, J. (1992, January 8). Sat CD Radio waits for FCC action. *Radio World*, p. 7.

Grotticelli, M. (1997, May 8). Digital TV according to Microsoft. *TV Technology*, pp. 21–22.

Grotticelli, M. (1998a, May). Digital TV plans revealed. *TV Broadcast*, pp. 1, 110.

Grotticelli, M. (1998b, May). The ABCs of HDTV. *TV Broadcast*, pp. 15–16.

Grotticelli, M. (1998c, September). Is anybody listening? *TV Broadcast*, p. 6.

Grotticelli, M. (1999, September). Breaking the sound barrier. *TV Broadcast*, p. 6.

Gruszka, M. (1992, June). HDTV World tackles audio. *TV Technology*, pp. 13, 43.

Haber, A. (1995a, February 8). FCC lays groundwork for satellite radio. *Radio World*, pp. 1, 12–13.

Haber, A. (1995b, February 8). NAB nixes sat DARS. *Radio World*, p. 12.

Haber, A. (1996, September 4). Transmitter manufacturers eye DAB progress. *Radio World*, pp. 19, 63.

Hahn, K. (1994, February). What defines "digital" products? *TV Technology*, pp. 27, 54.

Hall, D.E. (1982, December 18). Motorola wins AM stereo test: But marketplace may not go with Delco's choice. *Billboard*, pp. 11, 62.

Hard call. (1992, April 20). *Broadcasting*, p. 66.

Harris Corporation. (1984, December 17). Harris signs AM stereo licensing agreement with Motorola. (Available from Harris Corporation, P.O. Box 4290, Quincy, IL 62305).

Harris Corporation. (n.d.). AM stereo position. (Available from Harris Corporation, P.O. Box 4290, Quincy, IL 62305).

Harris throws its weight behind Motorola. (1984, December 31). *Broadcasting*, p. 109.

Hartup, D.C., Alley, D.M., & Goldston, D.R. (1998, March 18). AM hybrid IBOC DAB system. *Radio World*, pp. 64–65.

Hawkins, W.J. (1980, July). AM stereo—FCC approves a system. *Popular Science*, p. 47.

HDTV, DAB interests wage war of words over UHF. (1990, December 3). *Broadcasting*, pp. 66–67.

HDTV: Coming "sooner than people expected." (1990, October 15). *Broadcasting*, pp. 43–44, 47.

HDTV "Grand Alliance" endorsed by Wiley. (1993, February 22). *Broadcasting*, p. 68.

HDTV rules. (1996, July/August). *Video*, p. 10.

HDTV spectrum: "Use it or lose it." (1991, November 11). *Broadcasting*, p. 14.

HDTV: Too close for comfort? (1992, April 13). *Broadcasting*, pp. 4, 14.

HDTV transmission tests set to begin next April. (1990, November 19). *Broadcasting*, pp. 52–53.

Head, S.W., & Sterling, C.H. (1982). *Broadcasting in America: A survey of television, radio, and new technologies* (4th ed.). Boston: Houghton Mifflin.

Heiss, M. (1993, February). Aspect aspects. *Video Systems*, pp. 10, 12.

Helms advocates "highest quality" HDTV. (1998, May). *Television Broadcast*, p. 110.

Here comes tomorrow. (1995, January 16). *Broadcasting & Cable*, p. 118.

Herwitz, T.R. (1985, December 9). Inside the FCC. *Television/Radio Age*, pp. 185–186.

High cost of hesitancy. (1995, August 21). *Broadcasting & Cable*, p. 62.

High-definition TV moves closer to consumer use [Associated Press report]. (1994, February 20). *Mobile Register*, pp. F1–F2.

Highly dubious TV. (1997, November/December). *Digital Home Entertainment*, p. 134.

Hirsch, J. (1992, October). The quest for audio perfection. *Stereo Review*, p. 26.

Hoffner, R. (1991, January). Digital audio's brave new world. *TV Technology*, pp. 28–29.

Hoffner, R. (1993, July). More and better audio for HDTV. *TV Technology*, p. 28.

Hoffner, R. (1994, February). Examining digital audio broadcast. *TV Technology*, p. 31.

Hoffner, R. (1996, October). Television sound comes of age. *TV Technology*, p. 32.

Holland, B. (1982, December 11). Study: AMers stereo bound. *Billboard*, pp. 1, 11.

Holland, B. (1983, September 3). Discrepancies cited: FCC tells Harris to withdraw its AM stereo system. *Billboard*, p. 14.

Holland, B. (1993, April 3). Digital b'casting applicant Space Systems drops out. *Billboard*, p. 87.

Holt, C. (1999, November). Commercial appeal. *Video Systems*, pp. 26–30, 140.

Homer, S. (1994, September 26). Europe looks skyward to DAB. *Broadcasting & Cable*, p. 59.

Hopkins, R. (1994, June). Digital terrestrial HDTV for North America: The Grand Alliance HDTV system. *IEEE Transactions on Broadcasting*, *40*(3), 185–198.

Horowitz, M. (1996, June). Off the air: The citizens for HDTV coalition joins the lobbying effort for advanced TV high fidelity. *Video*, p. 104.

Huff, W.A.K. (1992a). AM stereo in the marketplace: The solution still eludes. *Journal of Radio Studies*, *1*, 15–30.

Huff, W.A.K. (1992b, Fall). Radio's latest challenge: A report on the first two years of digital audio broadcasting. *Feedback, 33,* (4), 24–27.

Huff, W.A.K., & Rosene, J.M. (1993–94). Station managers and the status of AM broadcasting. *Journal of Radio Studies, 2,* 11–19.

Hughes, D. (1985a, October 15). All-stereo law eyed. *Radio World,* pp. 1–6.

Hughes, D. (1985b, November 15). State drops receiver tagging. *Radio World,* p. 2.

Hughes, D. (1985c, December 15). RAC unveils AM "wish list." *Radio World,* pp. 1, 6.

Hughes, D. (1986a, January 1). FCC: AM improvement on track. *Radio World,* pp. 3, 8.

Hughes, D. (1986b, February 15). Receiver tagging rejected. *Radio World,* p. 1.

Hughes, D. (1986c, August 1). Marketplace ruling sought. *Radio World,* pp. 1, 4.

Hughes, D. (1986d, September 1). Kahn seeks FCC test results. *Radio World,* p. 3.

Hughes, D. (1986e, October 1). FCC reveals AM stereo data. *Radio World,* pp. 3, 6.

Hughes, D. (1986f, October 15). Group W AMs to go C-QUAM. *Radio World,* p. 3.

Hughes, D. (1986g, November 1). Texar file awaits action. *Radio World,* pp. 1, 7.

Hughes, D. (1986h, December 15). Multimode petition is filed. *Radio World,* pp. 1, 8–9.

Hughes, D. (1987, February 15). AM stereo action awaits NTIA study. *Radio World,* p. 8.

Husted, B. (1994, February 27). Stay tuned for magic of high-definition TV. *Atlanta Journal/Atlanta Constitution,* pp. R1, R9.

Husted, B. (1998, January 11). Fine-tuning HDTV. *Atlanta Journal-Constitution,* p. C-1.

In-band: The only choice. (1995, September 20). *Radio World,* p. 5.

Industry has AM stereo and car CD on "hold." (1985, June). *Sight and Sound Marketing.* (Reprint available from Kahn Communications, Inc., 425 Merrick Avenue, Westburg, NY 11590.

In wake of TV deregulation action, FCC's Fowler reviews his regime, picks the coming issues. (1983, August 1). *Television/Radio Age,* pp. 27–29, 68–70.

Is hi def worth the investment return? (1991, May). *TV Technology NAB Extra,* p. 8.

It's official: Motorola is spotted lead in AM stereo race. (1980, September 22). *Broadcasting,* p. 40.

Japan testing five AM stereo systems. (1987, January 1). *Radio World,* p. 7.

Jessell, H.A. (1992a, May 9). WARC moves DAB step closer to reality. *Broadcasting,* p. 40.

Jessell, H.A. (1992b, October 5). FCC to make room for satellite DAB. *Broadcasting,* p. 15.

Jessell, H.A. (1992c, October 12). Satellite DAB moves ahead. *Broadcasting,* p. 12.

Jessell, H.A. (1995a, January 30). Quello says second channel should be free. *Broadcasting & Cable,* pp. 30–31.

Jessell, H.A. (1995b, April 10). Hundt: No free (digital) lunch. *Broadcasting & Cable,* p. 24.

Jessell, H.A. (1995c, April 17). Hundt proposes 2nd-channel freedom. *Broadcasting & Cable,* p. 8.

Jessell, H.A. (1995d, November 27). Uncertain Reed: Hundt's credibility gap. *Broadcasting & Cable,* pp. 6–7.

Jessell, H.A. (1998, September 21). DTV or bust, says Kennard. *Broadcasting & Cable,* p. 22.

Johnson, L.B. (1997, Winter). He who hesitates is lost. *Stereophile Guide to Home Theater*, pp. 51–52, 54, 56.

Jones: Staunchly backs marketplace philosophy. (1982, April 5). *Television/Radio Age*, pp. 70–71.

Josephson, S. (1982, December 13). Future strategy for successful AM stations: Programming experimentation to fill market voids. *Television/Radio Age*, pp. 44–45, 119–120.

Kahn, L.R. (1984, December 17). In the running [Letter to the Editor]. *Broadcasting*, p. 26.

Kahn, L.R. (1985, July 3). [Letter to] The best AM stereo stations in the world "the eagles." (Available from Kahn Communications, Inc., 425 Merrick Ave., Westbury, NY 11590).

Kahn Communications, Inc. (1985a). AM stereo: An "eagle and egg" situation. (Available from Kahn Communications, Inc., 425 Merrick Ave., Westbury, NY 11590).

Kahn Communications, Inc. (1985b). AM stereo decision "D Day." (Available from Kahn Communications, Inc., 425 Merrick Ave., Westbury, NY 11590).

Kahn Communications, Inc. (1985c). Get rid of the ionosphere, no skywave. (Available from Kahn Communications, Inc., 425 Merrick Ave., Westbury, NY 11590).

Kahn fights for stereo AM. (1985, August 5). *Television/Radio Age*, pp. 30–31.

Kahn files lawsuit against GM. (1988, June 1). *Radio World*, p. 7.

Kerschbaumer, K. (2000, October 2). An eyeful of HDTV. *Broadcasting & Cable*, p. 14.

Kirkeby, M. (1980, September 18). Broadcasters worried about AM's future. *Rolling Stone*, p. 28.

Kovacs, B. (1999, July/August). Producing HDTV. *Pro Video Review*, pp. 28, 36.

Krantz, M. (1997, April 14). A tube for tomorrow. *Time*, p. 69.

Lambert, P. (1992a, March 30). By HDTV's early light. *Broadcasting*, pp. 10–11.

Lambert, P. (1992b, April 20). In-band DAB makes design leaps. *Broadcasting*, pp. 32–33.

Lambert, P. (1992c, June 8). Broadcasters appeal for more HDTV time. *Broadcasting*, p. 23.

Lambert, P. (1993a, January 4). NAB and EIA forge separate DAB paths. *Broadcasting*, pp. 58–59.

Lambert, P. (1993b, January 11). MSTV calls for scalable ATV, all-channel tuner study. *Broadcasting*, p. 20.

Lambert, P. (1993c, January 18). Duggan on HDTV: Respect marketplace. *Broadcasting*, p. 94.

Leinwoll, S. (1993). RF spectrum prepped for next century. *Radio Craft 93*, pp. 101–103, 108.

LeSueur, C. (2000a, July 26). NBC, ABC repudiate 8-VSB. *TV Technology*, pp. 1, 12.

LeSueur, C. (2000b, August 23). Congress warns on HDTV. *TV Technology*, pp. 1, 14.

Libin, L. (1998, August). Washington gets the jitters. *Broadcast Engineering*, p. 26.

Lichty, L.W., & Topping, M.C. (1975). *American broadcasting: A source book on the history of radio and television.* New York: Hastings House.

Likely candidates for AM stereo. (1987, September 7). *Broadcasting*, pp. 75–76.

The long and winding road. (1991, August). *TV Technology*, p. 5.

Looking good. (1990, July 30). *Broadcasting*, pp. 6–7.

Looking into radio's crystal ball. (1992, September 7). *Broadcasting*, pp. 42, 47–48, 50.

Lucent Digital Radio. (1998a, May 11). New Lucent Technologies Venture Will Create Digital Radio Broadcast Systems [Press Release] [WWW document]. URL http://Lucent_pr_news.htm

Lucent Digital Radio. (1998b, May 15). Lucent Technologies' Perceptual Audio Coder receives highest rating in independent test [Press Release] [WWW document]. URL http://Lucent.PACven051598.htm

Lucent Digital Radio. (1998c). LDR Mission. [WWW document]. URL http://Lucent.ldrmission.htm

Mannes, G. (1991, March). TV-by-numbers. *Video Review*, pp. 28–31.

Martin, H.C., & Estevez, R. (1997, January). FCC adopts DTV standard. *Broadcast Engineering*, p. 12.

Masters, I.G. (1997). The future of radio. *Stereo Review*, pp. 83–86.

McAvoy, K. (1995, April 10). Congress sees gold in them thar channels. *Broadcasting & Cable*, p. 23.

McAvoy, K., & Stern, C. (1994, March 21). Flexibility: Broadcasters gaining more spectrum opportunities. *Broadcasting & Cable*, pp. 6, 8.

McClellan, S. & Dickson, G. (1998, March 30). Fox embraces 480 P, not HDTV. *Broadcasting & Cable*, pp. 6, 10.

McClellan, S., Dickson, G., & Rathbun, L. (1997, April 14). DTV for pain and profit. *Broadcasting & Cable*, pp. 4, 6.

McConnell, B. (1998, September 14). Powell raises red flag over DTV switch. *Broadcasting & Cable*, pp. 14, 16.

McConnell, B. (1999a, July 5). Rollout goals for DTV. *Broadcasting & Cable*, p. 7.

McConnell, B. (1999b, November 8). First step for digital radio. *Broadcasting & Cable*, p. 20.

McConnell, B. (2000, March 27). DTV standard in play. *Broadcasting & Cable*, p. 10.

McConnell, C. (1994a, April 18). HDTV proponents to show their stuff to FCC. *Broadcasting & Cable*, p. 41.

McConnell, C. (1994b, August 1). FCC commissioners to get HDTV eyeful. *Broadcasting & Cable*, p. 47.

McConnell, C. (1994c, August 8). HDTV field testing wraps up. *Broadcasting & Cable*, p. 40.

McConnell, C. (1995a, January 9). HDTV developers need more time. *Broadcasting & Cable*, p. 18.

McConnell, C. (1995b, January 16). FCC OKs satellite radio spectrum. *Broadcasting & Cable*, p. 28.

McConnell, C. (1995c, January 16). More, not less, time needed for HDTV switch. *Broadcasting & Cable*, p. 103.

McConnell, C. (1995d, January 23). To every thing there is a season, and to every station a digital channel. *Broadcasting & Cable*, p. 165.

McConnell, C. (1995e, April 10). Viewers will demand HDTV, say backers. *Broadcasting & Cable*, p. 36.

McConnell, C. (1995f, September 11). Hitachi unveils SDTV decoder. *Broadcasting & Cable*, p. 51.

McConnell, C. (1995g, September 25). Battle lines drawn over DARS. *Broadcasting & Cable*, p. 54.

McConnell, C. (1995h, December 11). Critics to take aim at ATV channels. *Broadcasting & Cable*, p. 18.

McConnell, C. (1996a, April 22). DARS runs into problems at FCC. *Broadcasting & Cable*, pp. 24, 26.

McConnell, C. (1996b, April 29). Plan would divide DARS into 3 slots. *Broadcasting & Cable*, p. 18.

McConnell, C. (1996c, July 22). White House calls for digital TV standard. *Broadcasting & Cable*, p. 18.

McConnell, C. (1996d, August 19). FCC enumerates TV's future. *Broadcasting & Cable*, pp. 17–18, 20, 22.

McConnell, C. (1996e, September 16). A stroll down FCC's memory lane. . . . *Broadcasting & Cable*, pp. 22, 24.

McConnell, C. (1996f, October 21). Broadcasters arm for ATV fight. *Broadcasting & Cable*, pp. 6–7, 12.

McConnell, C. (1996g, November 25). CD Radio loses bid for pioneer's preference. *Broadcasting & Cable*, p. 18.

McConnell, C. (1996h, December 2). Removing the offending interlace. *Broadcasting & Cable*, p. 6.

McConnell, C. (1997a, March 10). Satellite quest nears end. *Broadcasting & Cable*, pp. 20–21.

McConnell, C. (1997b, June 23). Broadcasters complain to FCC about digital assignments. *Broadcasting & Cable*, p. 18.

McConnell, C. (1998, May 11). Digital disagreements go to court. *Broadcasting & Cable*, pp. 22–23.

McConnell, C., & West, D. (1995, December 4). Dick Wiley: Delivering on digital. *Broadcasting & Cable*, pp. 32, 34, 36, 40.

McGinley, T. (1999, March 17). A peek into DRE's DAB research. *Radio World*, pp. 3, 10.

McKinney's insight on AM report. (1986, April 17). *Broadcasting*, p. 37.

McLane, P.J. (1998, November 25). Will radio ever be all-digital? *Radio World*, p. 4.

McLane, P.J. (2000, February 16). A digital radio status report. *Radio World*, p. 4.

McLeod, N. (1994, February). DAB—delivery, delay or debacle? *Electronics World + Wireless World*, pp. 160–165.

McVicker, D. (1992, December 9). Broadcast interests guide digital compression tests. *Radio World*, pp. 8–9.

Meadows, L. (1996a, June 12). Tests to start regardless. *Radio World*, pp. 1, 11.

Meadows, L. (1996b, August 7). Tests begin in San Francisco. *Radio World*, pp. 1, 13.

Meadows, L. (1996c, August 21). DARS: Broadcast pioneers. *Radio World*, p. 6.

Meadows, L. (1997, January 8). NAB waits while IBOC readied. *Radio World*, pp. 1, 6.

Meadows, L. (1998, April 15). Expanded-band CPs come to life. *Radio World*, pp. 1, 8.

Meigs, J.B. (1989, September). Now it's our turn. *Video Review*, p. 4.

Miotto, A. (1997, June 5). Stainless foresees boom in DTV. *TV Technology*, p. 86.

Mirabito, M.A.M. (1994) (2nd ed.). *The new communications technologies*. Boston: Focal Press.

Mitchell, P.W. (1993, November). Digital on the air. *Stereo Review*, pp. 103–106, 108, 110.

Montgomery, E. (1999, March 17). AM radio fights its own success. *Radio World*, pp. 16, 26.

More hope from McKinney. (1985, December 9). *Broadcasting*, pp. 41–42.

Morris, A. (1995, December). ATTC completes mission. *TV Technology*, p. 8.

Motorola appears to be leading in AM stereo race. (1984, April 2). *Television/Radio Age*, pp. 44, 94–95.

Motorola files for AM stereo court action. (1988, July 1). *Radio World*, p. 14.

Motorola gets Australian boost. (1984, October 15). *Broadcasting*, p. 68.

Motorola Inc. (1986a). Motorola C-QUAM AM stereo bulletin. (Available from Motorola Inc., 1216 Remington Road, Schaumberg, IL 60195).

Motorola Inc. (1986b, March). C-QUAM AM stereo: Questions and answers for the consumer. (Available from Motorola Inc., 1216 Remington Road, Schaumberg, IL 60195).

Motorola Inc. (1986c, August). C-QUAM AM stereo receivers on the market as of August 1986. (Available from Motorola Inc., 1216 Remington Road, Schaumberg, IL 60195).

Motorola Inc. (1986d, August). C-QUAM AM stereo listing as of August 1986. (Available from Motorola Inc., 1216 Remington Road, Schaumberg, IL 60195).

MSTV/EIA to build HDTV station. (1996, April 8). *Broadcasting & Cable*, p. 10.

Multiple messages on multicasting at MSTV. (1994, March 28). *Broadcasting & Cable*, p. 40.

Multisystem AM stereo receivers: A solution to the marketplace problem? (1983, April 18). *Broadcasting*, pp. 95–96.

MUSICAM USA-CCS Europe. (2000). MUSICAM USE-CCS Europe [WWW document]. URL http://www.britton2000.com/isdn/musicam.htm

Must carry. (1998, September). *Broadcast Engineering*, pp. 20, 22.

Must-carry debated. (1998, May). *Television Broadcast*, pp. 1, 104.

NAB, alliance at odds over flexibility. (1994, August 8). *Broadcasting & Cable*, p. 40.

NAB '85: Getting technical in Las Vegas. (1985, April 29). *Broadcasting*, pp. 42, 44, 46, 48, 50, 52, 54, 56, 58, 60.

NAB goes for the brass ring with DAB. (1991, February 4). *Broadcasting*, pp. 15–17.

NAB poised to push IBOC. (1996, October 2). *Radio World*, pp. 1, 55.

NAB radio. (1988, April 18). *Broadcasting*, pp. 80–86.

NAB's preemptive strike. (1991, February 4). *Broadcasting*, p. 66.

National Association of Broadcasters. (1984, August). Radio technology report: The status of satellite programming and AM stereo. (Available from National Association of Broadcasters, 1771 N Street, N.W., Washington, DC 20036).

Nelson, R. (1993, November). Swept away by the digital age. *Popular Science*, pp. 92–94, 96–97, 107, 110.

New name for CD Radio. (1999, December 22). *Radio World*, p. 8.

Noah, J. (1993, August). Adios analog: Better get ready for better digital audio. *Video Systems*, pp. 20, 24, 26–27.

No help. (1996, July 15). *Broadcasting & Cable*, p. 82.

No perfect place in spectrum for digital audio. (1990, December 10). *Broadcasting*, pp. 110, 112, 114.

Norberg, E. (1984, March 5). What broadcasters must do to make sure AM stereo flies. *Broadcasting*, p. 30.

Norman, B. (1986, April 1). WZKY creates AM stereo craze. *Radio World*, p. 12.

Not whether, but when for AM stereo. (1979, May 28). *Broadcasting*, pp. 75–76.

NTIA likes NRSC-2. (1989, January 9). *Broadcasting*, p. 77.

NTIA wants C-QUAM protected. (1987, August 17). *Broadcasting*, pp. 70, 74.

One more time. (1996, October 21). *Broadcasting & Cable*, p. 78.

On the road to NAB. (1990, February 5). *Broadcasting*, pp. 65–66.

Operators endorse NAB's DAB objectives. (1991, February 18). *Broadcasting*, pp. 43–44.

Ostroff, Nat. (2000). Sinclair Broadcast Group response, re: FCC Denies Sinclair Petition for Rulemaking on COFDM Standard. [WWW document]. URL http://www.sbgi.net/dtv/fcc/fcc.htm

Outside the law. (1990, May 28). *Broadcasting*, p. 10.

Pai, S. (1997, November 26). IBOC: Two takes on digital radio effort. *Radio World*, pp. 14, 16.

Paryzek, J.A. (1998, November 2). TV audio [Letter to the Editor]. *TV Technology*, p. 94.

Paulsen, W.B. (1997, July). The DTV emperor has no clothes. *Television Broadcast*, p. 82.

Pear, T. (1994, October 19). Chairman chides industry. *Radio World*, p. 3.

Pensinger, G. (1997, July). DTV broadcaster: The transition. *Television Broadcast*, p. 18.

Peterson, A.R. (1997, December 24). IBOC team advances U.S. DAB research. *Radio World*, pp. 1, 6.

Petras, F. (1982, September). Car stereo: Coming attractions. *Stereo Review*, p. 22.

Petrozzello, D. (1997, July 28). Hindery takes aim at HDTV. *Broadcasting & Cable*, p. 67.

Plata, G.S. (1995, April 19). Mexico DAB: Waiting for results. *Radio World*, p. 6.

Plata, G.S. (1999, May 26). United States, Mexico seek S-band pact. *Radio World*, pp. 12, 14.

Pohlmann, K.C. (1992a, October). The sound of things to come. *Stereo Review*, pp. 62–64, 66, 68.

Pohlmann, K.C. (1992b, October). The sound of speed. *Stereo Review*, p. 33.

Pohlmann, K.C. (1996, July/August). Surf's up. *Video*, pp. 18–20.

Pohlmann, K.C. (1997a, January). Rant-TV. *Video*, pp. 28–30.

Pohlmann, K.C. (1997b, February/March). Cable guys. *Video*, pp. 26–29.

Pohlmann, K.C. (1997c, April). Unplugged. *Stereo Review*, p. 26.

Pohlmann, K.C. (1999, April). Digital radio. *Stereo Review's Sound & Vision*, p. 16.

Polon, M. (1997a, February). Who will buy a $2,000 television? *Television Broadcast*, p. 19.

Polon, M. (1997b, July). Farewell to Reed E. Hundt. *Television Broadcast*, p. 16.

Powers offers HD views. (1991, March). *TV Technology*, p. 68.

Prentiss, S. (1985). *AM stereo & TV stereo: New sound dimensions*. Blue Ridge Summit, PA: Tab Books.

Promote AM stereo on-air. (1985, November 15). *Radio World*, p. 5.

Quello: No quid pro quo. (1995, April 17). *Broadcasting & Cable*, p. 8.

Quello: Worried about future "glut" in TV services. (1982, April 5). *Television/Radio Age*, pp. 64–65, 124.

Quello: You cannot stop progress. (1995, March 22). *Radio World*, pp. 60, 62.

Radio 1979: Revving up for the 1980's. (1979, September 10). *Broadcasting*, pp. 36, 38, 40, 42.

Radio should look ahead. (1996, September 18). *Radio World*, pp. 1, 14–15, 67.

Radio survey shows AM stereo to grow. (1985, July). *Broadcast Management/ Engineering*, p. 12.

Radio technology coming of age. (1985, July 22). *Broadcasting*, pp. 76–79.

Ranada, D. (1999, May). Survival guide: Deciphering the technobabble. *Stereo Review's Sound & Vision*, pp. 92–94.

Rathbun, E.A. (2000, June 5). Radio flyer. *Broadcasting & Cable*, pp. 18–19, 22, 24, 26.

Ratnesar, R. (1997, September 1). A bandwidth bonanza. *Time*, p. 60.

Rau, M.C. (1985, April). Charting a course for AM improvement. *Broadcasting Engineering*, pp. 80, 84, 86.

Ray, W.B. (1990). *FCC: The ups and downs of radio-TV regulation*. Ames: Iowa State University Press.

Reber, G. (1997a, March). Without a HDTV standard. *Widescreen Review*, pp. 8–14.

Reber, G. (1997b, May). FCC approves digital TV license plan. *Widescreen Review*, pp. 8–9, 13.

Reber, G. (1998, June). H/DTV's mixed signals. *Widescreen Review*, pp. 12–27.

Refined HDTV cost estimates less daunting. (1990, April 9). *Broadcasting*, pp. 40–41.

Regulation by marketplace: How practical can it be? (1980, April 7). *Television/Radio Age*, pp. 54–57, 110, 112, 114, 116.

Reviving AM. (1985, January 14). *Broadcasting*, pp. 186, 188.

Rivera: Pessimistic about increasing minority ownership. (1982, April 5). *Television/ Radio Age*, pp. 74–75, 120.

Robin, M. (1998, April). Digital resolution. *Broadcast Engineering*, pp. 44–46, 48.

Rogers, M. (1993, January 23). Brave new TV: A simple guide to the television technology of the future. *TV Guide*, pp. 26–30.

Ronaldi, L.P. (1985, May 1). AM stations convert to C-QUAM. *Radio World*, pp. 1, 4.

Room in the tent. (1997, August 25). *Broadcasting & Cable*, p. 82.

Room to move. (1994, August 8). *Broadcasting & Cable*, p. 58.

Rosen, N. (1996, October). TV nation. Video, pp. 32–34, 36, 38.

Salsberg, A. (1982, June). Copping out. *Popular Electronics*, p. 6.

Satellite radio. (1994, January). *Satellite Communications*, p. 42.

Schneider, A. (1994 February). Who has the $? [Letter to the Editor]. *TV Technology*, p. 8.

Schubin, M. (1998, November). Forget November '98; Check out March '54. *Television Broadcast*, p. 47.

Scratch one. (1986, January 27). *Broadcasting*, p. 7.

Scully, S. (1993a, April 19). FCC told it's too soon to act on DARS. *Broadcasting & Cable*, pp. 54, 56.

Scully, S. (1993b, May 3). HDTV advisory committee to consider job creation. *Broadcasting & Cable*, p. 60.

Scully, S. (1993c, May 17). Cable, broadcast make HDTV recommendations. *Broadcasting & Cable*, pp. 57–58.

Scully, S. (1993d, May 31). The "Grand Alliance" becomes reality. *Broadcasting & Cable*, pp. 59–60.

Scully, S. (1993e, July 12). Grand Alliance lays out its battle plan. *Broadcasting & Cable*, p. 69.

Scully, S. (1993f, September 6). FCC told it's too soon to act on DARS. *Broadcasting & Cable*, p. 46.

Seeing the future. (1991, April). *TV Technology*, p. 5.

Shapiro, G.J. (1993, November 10). EIA on DAR: We need it, we will have it. *Radio World*, p. 42.

Shepler, J. (1985, July/August). Stereo vs. stereo—How AM compares to FM. *The Electron*, pp. 7–8.

Shooting with the future in mind. (1992, October 5). *Broadcasting*, p. 42.

A short history of HDTV. (1993, May 31). *Broadcasting & Cable*, p. 60.

Shotgun wedding. (1993, June). *International Broadcasting*, pp. 35–36.

Sikes, A. (1986, October 1). Sikes says NTIA to enter AM stereo arena. *Radio World*, pp. 10, 24.

Sikes reaffirms preference for simulcast HDTV. (1991, October 28). *Broadcasting*, p. 27.

Silbergleid, M. (1997, November). Defining HDTV. *Television Broadcast*, pp. 5, 87.

Single standard needed. (1986, December 15). *Radio World*, p. 5.

Skelton, T. (1996, February). Audio for wide-screen: ATV sound has got you surrounded. *Broadcast Engineering*, pp. 88, 90, 92–93.

Slim chance for EDTV appears to get slimmer. (1990, September 10). *Broadcasting*, pp. 26–27.

"Smitty": A radio career. (1999, March 31). *Radio World*, pp. 1, 14, 16, 18–19, 21, 23–24.

So many new technologies, so little space. (1991, May 6). *Broadcasting*, pp. 51–52.

Some parting shots from Reed Hundt. (1997, October 9). *TV Technology*, p. 86.

Space sales. (1996, April). *Video*, p. 9.

Spangler, M. (1997a, February 5). NAB supports FCC allocation of spectrum to wireless, though still concerned about DARS. *Radio World*, p. 11.

Spangler, M. (1997b, March 5). CEMA maneuvers on DAR, takes on DAB. *Radio World*, pp. 1, 6.

Spangler, M. (1997c, May 14). DARS hits the streets—in a few years. *Radio World*, pp. 1, 6.

Spangler, M. (1997d, August 6). DARS proponents want gaps filled. *Radio World*, p. 14.

Stalled at the start. (1997, March). *Broadcasting & Cable*, p. 110.

Stanley, T.P. (1986, July 18). [Letter to] Kahn Communications, Inc. (Available from Federal Communications Commission, Washington, DC 20554).

Starzynski, J. (1997, January). Handling 5.1-channel audio. *Broadcast Engineering*, pp. 24, 26.

Staying up. (1984, December 17). *Broadcasting*, p. 7.

Stay the course. (1998, July 22). *Radio World*, p. 5.

Steady as she goes. (1998, November 16). *Broadcasting & Cable*, pp. S8–S11.

Stereo broadcasting: What does it mean to advertising? (1958, October 24). *Printer's Ink*, pp. 21–24.

Stereocasting at crossroads. (1960, January 1). *Electronics*, p. 37.

Stereo decision creates new F-M market. (1961, May 5). *Electronics*, p. 32.

Stereo record standards set. (1959, January 30). *Electronics*, p. 39.

Stereo specs due this year. (1959, January 30). *Electronics*. pp. 26–27.

Stereo stimulates FM broadcasters. (1960, April 22). *Electronics*, pp. 30–31.

Stereo tests on the way. (1960, June 3). *Electronics*, pp. 48–49.

Sterling, C.H. (1970). Second service: A history of commercial FM broadcasting to 1969. *Dissertation Abstracts International*, 70, 03716. (University Microfilms No. 70-3716).

Sterling, C.H. (1982, Autumn). The FCC and changing technological standards. *Journal of Communication, 32* (1), 137–147.

Stern, C. (1994, July). Satellite radio plays waiting game. *Broadcasting & Cable*, p. 47.

Stern, C. (1995, September 11). TV spectrum under attack. *Broadcasting & Cable*, p. 4.

Stern, C. (1996, June 24). Dispute over HDTV standard. *Broadcasting & Cable*, pp. 16, 18.

Stern, C., & McConnell, C. (1995, January 9). FCC to advance telco TV, satellite radio. *Broadcasting & Cable*, pp. 6, 10.

Stilson, J., & Pagano, P. (1990, August 13). May the best HDTV system win. *Channels*, pp. 54–55.

Stimson, L. (1998a, May 13). NRSC group meets new DAB player. *Radio World*, pp. 1, 8.

Stimson, L. (1998b, May 13). Lucent enters IBOC fray alone. *Radio World*, pp. 1, 6.

Stimson, L. (1999a, January 20). Top radio groups invest in USADR. *Radio World*, pp. 1, 3.

Stimson, L. (1999b, February 17). No consensus on USADR and IBOC DAB. *Radio World*, pp. 3, 14–15.

Stimson, L. (1999c, March 3). The car receivers of the future. *Radio World*, pp. 1, 8, 12.

Stimson, L. (1999d, March 31). DAB, poised for 2000. *Radio World*, pp. 1, 8, 12.

Stimson, L. (1999e, April 14). Lucent to start IBOC field tests. *Radio World*, pp. 1, 10–12.

Stimson, L. (1999f, May 12). IBOC alliance called for at NAB99. *Radio World*, pp. 1, 8.

Stimson, L. (1999g, July 7). GM, Ford, Clear Channel boost satellite efforts. *Radio World*, pp. 1, 10, 15.

Stimson, L. (1999h, September 29). FCC speaks out on IBOC, sort of. *Radio World*, p. 3.

Stimson, L. (2000a, January 5). USADR, DRE combine DAB efforts. *Radio World*, pp. 1,6.

Stimson, L. (2000b, August 2). NRSC praises merger. *Radio World*, p. 7.

Stimson, L., & Barnes, R. (1998, July 8). USADR facility is unveiled. *Radio World*, pp. 1, 19.

Strother, R. (1990, December 31). Digital audio broadcasting: Choosing a terrestrial or satellite-based system? *Broadcasting*, pp. 61–62.

Struzzi, D. (1990, March). Philips joins ACTV team. *Millimeter*, p. 13.

Sukow, R. (1991, November 11). Scrambling in wake of S-band selection. *Broadcasting*, pp. 60–61.

Sukow, R. (1992a, April 20). Looking forward at NAB '92. *Broadcasting*, p. 20.

Sukow, R. (1992b, July 27). HDTV timetable gets support. *Broadcasting*, pp. 31–32.

Sukow, R. (1992c, September 14). Keeping tabs on new technologies. *Broadcasting*, p. 15.

Sukow, R. (1992d, November 23). Broadcasters blast satellite DAB, again. *Broadcasting*, p. 42.

Sukow, R. (1993a, March 1). Could HDTV's answer be a "Grand Alliance"? *Broadcasting*, p. 54.

Sukow, R. (1993b, May 12). An interim chairman with a radio agenda. *Radio World*, p. 8.

Sukow, R. (1993c, August 25). DAB testing schedule delayed. *Radio World*, pp. 1, 29.

Sukow, R. (1994a, February 23). DAB testing begins a little behind schedule. *Radio World*, p. 7.

Sukow, R. (1994b, April 20). Industry has role in NII. *Radio World*, pp. 1, 18, 20.

Sukow, R. (1994c, April 20). DAR proponents progress. *Radio World*, pp. 38, 45.

Sunier, J. (1960). *The story of stereo, 1881–*. New York: Gernsback Library.

Suydam, M. (1997, May 8). ATSC demos public HDTV broadcast. *TV Technology*, p. 36.

Sweeney, D. (1984, October). What's new. *Stereo Review*, pp. 71–75, 115.

Tait, T. (1995, November 1). BBC switches on national DAB service. *Radio World*, p. 7.

Take care of business. (1995, August 23). *Radio World*, p. 5.

Taylor, C. (1990a, June 27). Stations scramble to meet NRSC deadline. *Radio World*, pp. 1, 3.

Taylor, C. (1990b, August 8). DAB task force off to a fast start. *Radio World*, pp. 1, 10.

Taylor, C. (1993, May 12). Today's milestones etch radio's future. *Radio World*, p. 15.

Taylor, C. (1994, April 20). Receiver makers will propel consumer acceptance of DAR. *Radio World*, p. 14.

Taylor, C. (1995, May). NAB '95: Digital becomes reality at world's largest broadcasting convention. *The Radio World Magazine*, pp. 58, 60, 62.

Techweek. (1999, March 14). *Atlanta Journal-Constitution*, p. G-1.

Texar Inc. (1987, January). Hi-fidelity AM standard approved by NAB and EIA. (Available from Texar Inc., 616 Beatty Road, Monroeville, PA 15146-1502).

There's only one happy manufacturer. (1980, April 14). *Broadcasting*, pp. 27, 29–30.

Thorpe, L. (1989, August). HDTV: It's the size that counts. *Video Review*, p. 92.

Three's a crowd in AM stereo? FCC may opt for several systems. (1980, March 31). *Broadcasting*, p. 30.

Time 'to deliver' on promise of HDTV system is near, says Sikes. (1991, April 8). *Broadcasting* pp. 64–65.

Too many vested interests. (1995, November 29). *Radio World*, p. 5.

Trautmann, C. (1991, April 24). AM: And the band plays on. *Radio World*, p. 29.

Treasure or terror? (1992, December 9). *Radio World*, p. 5.

TV stereo concerns. (1982, November 1). *Broadcasting*, p. 30.

Twenty-five years of FCC chairmen. (1978, August 28). *Television/Radio Age*, p. 10.

Two left in AM stereo battle royal. (1984, December 17). *Broadcasting*, pp. 40–41.

UDTV: One step beyond. (1993, June). *International Broadcasting*, pp. 29, 32.

USA Digital Radio, Inc. (1998a, May 11). USA Digital Radio Responds to New Lucent Proposal. [Press Release] [WWW document]. URL http://www.USADR.press051198.htm

USA Digital Radio, Inc. (1998b, October 7). In the Matter of Amendment of Part 73 of the Commission's Rules to Permit the Introduction of Digital Audio Broadcasting in the AM and FM Broadcast Services (RM-9395 Petition for Rulemaking) [WWW document]. URL http://www.fcc.gov/Bureaus/Mass_Media/Filings/rm9395.pdf

USA Digital Radio, Inc. (1998c, October 7). USA Digital Radio takes historic Step: Files petition for rulemaking with FCC readies broadcasting industry for IBOC DAB Digital Radio. [Press Release] [WWW document]. URL http://www.USADR.press100798.htm

USA Digital Radio, Inc. (1998d, November 6). IBOC DAB regulatory process moves forward: FCC requests comment on USA Digital Radio Petition for Rulemaking [Press Release] [WWW document]. URL http://www.USADR. press110698.htm

USA Digital Radio, Inc. (1999a, January 7). Nation's largest radio broadcasters invest in USA Digital Radio [Press Release] [WWW document]. URL http://www. USADR.press010799.htm

USA Digital Radio, Inc. (1999b, March 11). USA Digital Radio announces board of directors [Press Release] [WWW document]. URL http://www.USADR. press031199.htm

USA Digital Radio, Inc. (1999c, April 19). USA Digital Radio Announces "EASE." [Press Release] [WWW document]. URL http://www.USADR. press0419992.htm

USA Digital Radio, Inc. (2000, August 23). Ibiquity digital takes flight. [Press Release] [WWW document]. URL http://www.ibiquity1.www_usadr_com.htm

USA Digital Radio, Inc. & Digital Radio Mondiale. (2000, January 24). USA Digital Radio and Digital Radio Mondiale to collaborate on a worldwide standard for digital AM radio. [Press Release] [WWW document]. URL http:// www.drm.org/drm_globpressrelase.htm

USADR proceeds with DAB plans. (1996, November 13). *Radio World*, p. 12.

Utz, P. (2000, April). HDTV for the hobbyist. *Camcorder & Computer Video*, pp. 84–89.

Veilleux, C.T. (1999, June). DTV sets now on sale. *Television Broadcast*, p. 36.

View from the top: Reed Hundt. (1995, December). *Broadcast Engineering*, pp. 54, 56–57.

Viles, P. (1992, December 21). New DAB system would beam 500 channels. *Broadcasting*, p. 33.

Waiting for full AM improvement. (1990, July 9). *Broadcasting*, pp. 74–75.

Walker, F. (1983, December 5). AM's salvation: Multi-system stereo receivers. *Broadcasting*, p. 31.

Waller, J.C. (1946). *Radio: The fifth estate.* Boston: Houghton Mifflin.

Washburn: Proud of role in dish size reduction. (1982, April 5). *Television/Radio Age*, pp. 66–67. 120.

Webster, J. (1990, October). HDTV and computer graphics. *Video Systems*, pp. 65–66, 68, 70, 72.

Weiss, S.M. (1992, October). Examining compression techniques. *TV Technology*, pp. 13–14.

Weiss, S.M. (1995, June). SDTV from an ATV point of view. *TV Technology*, pp. 16–18.

Weiss, S.M. (1997a, February 27). DTV standard: The grand compromise. *TV Technology*, pp. 35, 38.

Weiss, S.M. (1997b, March 13). The grand compromise. *TV Technology*, pp. 32, 36, 41.

West, D. (1993, January 25). NAB board sees future and it's digital. *Broadcasting*, pp. 112–113.

West, D. (1995a, April 10). The fateful battle for the second channel. *Broadcasting & Cable*, p. 22.

West, D. (1995b, June 19). FCC to mandate HDTV capability in receivers. *Broadcasting & Cable*, pp. 37–38.

What multichannel means to Sikes. (1992, August 24). *Broadcasting*, p. 12.

What's all this about multiplex? (1961, July). *Consumer Reports*, pp. 422–423.

Wheatley, J.J. (1996, July/August). Video, 2196 A.D. *Video*, p. 6.

Whitaker, J. (1998a, March). The new definition of TV. *Video Systems*, pp. 65–66, 68.

Whitaker, J. (1998b, March). TV's tested history. *Broadcast Engineering*, pp. 156, 158.

Willis, Peter. (1992, July). DSR or DAB—worlds of difference. *Electronics World + Wireless World*, pp. 544–545.

Woods, J. (2000). A supplier's view of DAB alliance. *Radio World*, p. 3.

Working group suggests using L-band for DAB. (1991, June). *TV Technology*, p. 3.

WorldDAB Forum. (1997, January). These are the statutes of the World DAB Forum for digital audio broadcasting. [WWW document]. URL http://www. WorldDAB.statutes.htm

WorldDAB Forum. (n.d. a). WorldDAB Forum—working towards the future of radio. [WWW document]. URL http://www.WorldDAB.about_home.htm

WorldDAB Forum. (n.d. b). Why does DAB sound better than today's conventional radio? [WWW document]. URL http://www.WorldDAB.whatis.htm

WRAL-TV files for HDTV license. (1996, June 14). *TV Technology*, p. 5.

Wright, S. (1997). *The Broadcaster's Guide to RDS*. Boston: Focal Press.

Wytkind, E. (1986a, April 1). Canada delays AM stereo rule. *Radio World*, pp. 1, 6.

Wytkind, E. (1986b, April 1). Marketing plans for Brazil set. *Radio World*, p. 8.

Wytkind, E. (1986c, May 15). FCC explores Kahn allegations. *Radio World*, pp. 1, 4.

Wytkind, E. (1986d, June 15). Kahn, Tohtsu sign. *Radio World*, p. 11.

Zavistovich, A. (1987a, March 1). NTIA study urges multimode. *Radio World*, pp. 1, 3.

Zavistovich, A. (1987b, December 1). NAB files petition on NRSC. *Radio World*, pp. 1, 7.

Zavistovich, A. (1987c, December 15). Hi-fi AM radios: On the way? *Radio World*, pp. 3, 6.

Zavistovich, A. (1988, January 1). NRSC radios: Are they coming? *Radio World*, pp. 11, 18.

Zavistovich, A. (1992a, July 22). Radio board to seek progress reports on in-band DAB. *Radio World*, p. 3.

Zavistovich, A. (1992b, July 22). It takes time to build a flying car. *Radio World*, p. 4.

Zavistovich, A. (1992c, September 23). DAB and the race run. *Radio World*, p. 4.

Zavistovich, A. (1992d, November 4). Alphabet soup and DAB. *Radio World*, p. 4.

Zenith addresses obsolescence. (1997, September/October). *Widescreen Review*, p. 13.

Index

ABC (American Broadcasting Company): radio, 6, 22–23, 27–28, 73; television, 123, 133, 149, 157, 165, 171–72, 176, 184, 196
Abel, John, 77, 84
Abrams, Lee, 102
ACATS (Advisory Committee on Advanced Television Service), 113, 120, 127, 133, 137, 174
ACTV (Advanced Compatible Television), 114, 116–17, 120–21
Advanced Imaging, 140–41
AES (Audio Engineering Society), 81
Aiwa, 63
All-Channel Receiver Act of 1962, 122
Allen, Gracie, 12
Ally McBeal, 184
Amati Communications Corp., 79, 82–83, 93
American Digital Radio, 72, 76–78
American Society of Cinematographers, 141
Amos and Andy, 12
Ampro, 163
AM radio: 7–9, 21, 67–68, 70, 72–75, 79, 81, 84, 92, 99, 101, 104, 128, 142, 170, 189; AM radio/FM radio simulcasting/duplication of programming, 14–15; audience

shares, 14–16, 19, 21–23, 25, 32, 34, 38, 41; broadcasters, 6–7, 15, 18, 65, 85, 109, 185, 187, 189; expanded band, 46–47, 77; Great Depression, 8; improvement of, 6–7, 40–47, 84, 116, 186; monophonic broadcasting, 17; programming/format, 6–7, 14, 42, 103, 187, 189; receivers, 14–15, 186, 191; World War II, 8, 46
AMRC (American Mobile Radio Corporation), 90, 94, 102. *See also* XM Satellite Radio
AMSC (American Mobile Satellite Corporation), 73
AM stereo, 6, 17–18, 70–71, 83–84, 92, 96–97, 100–101, 103, 105, 107, 113, 121, 123, 127, 130, 133–34, 140, 142, 143, 147, 154, 157, 169, 183, 185, 188–89, 191–92, 194–95; debut of, 32; marketplace decision, 1, 6–7, 27, 74, 129, 145–46, 152, 182, 185–86, 188–89; multidecoding receivers, 7, 20, 24–25, 27, 31, 34–36, 38–39, 43, 49–51, 53, 60–62, 182; multisystem transmission approach, 23, 30; origins, 17; petition to FCC, 18; receivers, 2,

6–7, 170, 186, 190, 195; superficial, 17; systems, 1–2, 5, 7, 17–18, 195; systems, incompatibility of, 2, 6, 20, 29, 43, 50, 104, 190
Amstereoization, 2–3, 82, , 92, 96, 103, 185, 191
analog audio, 68–71
Apple Computers, 170
Arbitron, 100
Armstrong, Edwin H., 8
ASPEC (Adaptive Spectral Perceptual Entropy Coding) algorithm, 80. *See also* digital compression of audio
Association of Independent Television Stations, 123
AT&T (American Telephone & Telegraph), 72, 79–80, 82–83, 88, 96–97, 121, 123, 164
Atlanta Journal-Constitution, 193
ATRC (Advanced Television Research Consortium). *See* Grand Alliance or ATRC
ATSC (Advanced Television Systems Committee), 112, 136, 138, 141, 145–47, 155–56, 160, 174, 176, 188
ATTC (Advanced Television Test Center), 115, 121, 133, 137. *See also* ACATS
ATV (advanced television), 111–112, 116, 119, 122–26, 131, 135, 137–38, 141, 143. *See also* DTV; HDTV
ATV simulcasting, 126, 150
ATV systems, 114, 137
ATV television receivers/sets, 125
Australian Department of Communications, 36
Aware System, 80. *See also* digital compression of audio

Baird, John Logie, 12
Ball, Lucille, 12
Barrett, Andrew, 86, 159
BBC (British Broadcasting Corporation), 85
BBI (Boston Broadcasters, Inc.), 129

Belar Electronics Laboratory, Inc. AM stereo system, 1, 5, 24–25, 27, 35–36, 100
Bell Laboratories Record, 12
Bell Labs, 72, 79–80, 82
Benny, Jack, 12
Bergen, Edgar, 12
Berle, Milton, 12
BittWare Research Systems, 67
Bliley, Thomas, 90
Bloomberg, Michael, 84
Boeing, 87
Bonanza, 157
Bonneville International Corp., 100
Bosch, 103
Briskman, Robert, 78
Broadcast Electronics, 38–39, 53
Broadcast Engineering, 169, 177
Broadcasters Caucus, 134
Broadcasting, 23, 33, 42, 74, 123. *See also Broadcasting & Cable*
Broadcasting & Cable, 133–34, 142, 147, 169, 177
Brown, Tyrone, 23–24
BTSC (Broadcast Television Systems Committee), 129–30, 187
Buick, 36
Burns, George, 12
Bush, George, 81, 113, 127

CAB (Canadian Association of Broadcasters), 51, 59, 77
cable television, 71, 125, 127–128, 135, 141, 146–47, 149–150, 157, 163–64, 166, 171–73, 181, 189–92
Cable Television Consumer Protection and Competition Act of 1992, 168
cable television must-carry rules, 166, 168–69, 181
cable television superstations, 72–73, 171
Cablevision Systems Corp., 113
Capital Broadcasting, Inc., 138
Carey, John, 3
CBC (Canadian Broadcasting Company), 74

CBO (Congressional Budget Office), 180–82, 192–94

CBS (Columbia Broadcasting System), 6, 13

CBS color wheel system, 6, 12–13, 194

CBS radio, 12, 23, 59, 67, 76–77, 94

CBS television, 122–23, 133, 138, 149, 157, 164–65, 171–72, 196; news, 12

CCIR (International Radio Consultative Committee), 80; TG–10/2, 80–81

CD (compact disc), 4, 67–69, 73, 80, 101–102, 112, 123, 133, 154, 170, 183, 190, 192

CD Radio, Inc., 72–74, 77–79, 84, 90–91, 94–95, 102. *See also* Sirius Satellite Radio

CEA (Consumer Electronics Association), 176. *See also* CEMA

CEMA (Consumer Electronics Manufacturers Association), 82, 94, 98, 101, 104–105, 107, 164, 173, 175–76, 178–79

CES (consumer electronics show), 101, 133, 163, 171, 178

Chancellor Media, 100

Channel-Compatible HDTV, 114, 120–21

Chase Capital Partners, 100

Cheney, Dick, 74

Chong, Rachelle, 86, 94, 139, 153–54

Chrysler Motor Company, 35–36, 62

CIDR-FM, Windsor, Ontario, 108

CIMX-FM, Windsor, Ontario, 108

CIRT (Mexico's Commission for New Radio and Television Technologies), 87

Citadel Communications, 100

CKLW-AM, Windsor, Ontario, 108

CKWW-AM, Windsor, Ontario, 108

Clarion, 63

Clark, Glen, 54, 57, 59

Clear Channel Communications Inc., 100, 102

Clifford, Jack, 122

Clinton, Bill, 81, 91, 120, 127, 132, 141, 146, 159

COFDM (coded orthogonal frequency division multiplexing), 132–34, 174–78

Columbia, 63

Communications Act of 1934, 6, 21, 26, 168

Compaq, 155

Congress, 1, 63–64, 91, 113, 116, 122, 124, 127, 133, 135–36, 138, 140, 142, 150, 152, 158–59, 165, 169, 177, 180, 185–86

Connecticut Department of Consumer Protection, 49–50

Consumer Electronics Group, 27

Consumer Electronics Show, 48

Continental, 39

Coppolla, Francis Ford, 121

Cox Broadcasting, 184

Cox Radio, 100

CRTC (Canadian Radio-Television and Telecommunications Commission), 51, 92

Cumulus Media, 100

DAB (digital audio broadcasting), 2–4, 48, 63, 67–68, 71–73, 76–77, 80, 83–85, 87, 92–93, 95–99, 103, 109, 116, 127, 185–88, 190–92, 195–96; IBAC delivery of, 68, 70, 82–83, 88, 90, 94; IBOC delivery of, 67–68, 70, 72–76, 80–84, 87, 89–91, 93–94, 96–102, 104–106, 108–109, 190; receivers, 83, 92, 101, 103, 191, 195; satellite delivery of, 68, 72–75, 78; system compatibility, 105; systems, 72, 78–80, 82–83, 104–105; terrestrial delivery of, 67, 70–75, 78, 100–101. *See also* DARS; DRB; DSB; SDARS

DARS (digital audio radio services), 86, 88, 90–91, 101, 104. *See also* DAB

DBS (direct broadcast satellite), 86; radio, 84, 86; television, 113, 118, 122, 125, 135, 149, 171–72, 178, 181

DCR (Digital Cable Radio), 71–72, 84; Music Choice, 84

DeForest, Lee, 7
Delco, 32–36, 43, 58, 83; Delphi-Delco
    division of, 102
Delta Electronics, 38–39, 53
Denon, 47–48, 81
DigiCipher, 114, 120–21
digital audio, 69, 130–31
Digital Communications, 72
digital compression of audio, 80–81. *See
    also* MPEG; MUSICAM algorithm;
    PAC algorithm
digital compression of video, 115,
    117–18
Digital Planet, 72, 79
Digital Simulcast HDTV, 114, 120–121
Dingell, John, 90–91, 158
Directors Guild of America, 141
DirecTV, 84, 103, 171
Dish Network, 171
Disney, 171
DOJ (Department of Justice), 51
Dolby AC-3, 129, 131. *See also* Dolby
    Digital
Dolby Digital, 131, 173
Dole, Bob, 133, 138
Dragnet, 12
DRB (digital radio broadcasting),
    92–93. *See also* DAB
DRE (Digital Radio Express Inc.),
    96–97, 99, 101, 103, 107–108
DRM (Digital Radio Mondiale), 108
DSB (digital satellite broadcasting), 86,
    95. *See also* DAB; satellite delivery
    of
DSBC (Digital Satellite Broadcasting
    Corp.), 79, 90, 94. *See also* DAB,
    satellite delivery of
DSP (digital signal processing), 80. *See
    also* digital compression of audio
DSR (digital satellite radio), 71. *See also*
    DAB, satellite delivery of
DTV (digital television), 2–4, 70, 80,
    98–99, 105–109, 116, 119–20,
    128, 134, 137, 141–143, 145, 150,
    153–56, 172, 185–89, 192, 195;
    audio, 130–31; flexible/multiple
    use, 132–133, 135–36, 139, 157;
    pixels, 139–140, 191; production of,

156–157; programming, 136,
    146–47, 149, 156, 164–66, 172,
    181, 184, 196; progressive and in-
    terlaced scanning, 139–141, 143,
    145, 147, 155–156, 164–65, 178,
    191; scalable video, 121; second
    channel, 134–36, 138, 142,
    147–52, 154–55, 159, 165, 180;
    set-top boxes/converters, 117, 149,
    159, 163, 170–71, 173, 178, 190,
    193; system compatibility, 117; tele-
    vision receivers/sets, 117, 140–41,
    147–49, 153, 155, 158, 160, 163–
    67, 169–71, 173, 176, 178–83,
    189–90, 193–96; transmission sys-
    tems, 132, 140, 175. *See also* HDTV
Duggan, Ervin, 113
DVD (digital versatile discs), 101, 178

EBU (European Broadcasting Union),
    67, 74, 83, 88, 168. *See also*
    WorldDAB
EBU EuroDab Forum, 88
EDTV (enhanced-definition television),
    111, 114, 116–17, 121–22
EIA (Electronic Industries Association),
    27, 48, 76, 78–84, 89, 91–94, 97,
    129, 138
Electronic Industries Association of
    Japan, 129
Emmis Communications, 100
Empire State Building, 8, 11
ENG (electronic news gathering), 138
Entercomm Communications, 100
ETSI (European Telecommunication
    Standards Institute), 85
Eureka-147, 67, 70, 72, 74–78, 80,
    82–83, 85–89, 92–96, 100–101,
    104–105, 191

FAA (Federal Aviation Administration),
    75
Farnsworth, Philo, 10, 118
Faroudja Laboratories, 116–17
FBI (Federal Bureau of Investigation),
    159
FCC (Federal Communications Com-
    mission):

AM stereo marketplace approach, 2, 7, 27
AM stereo system ratings matrices, 24–28
commissioners, 23, 30–31, 87
Deregulation of Radio, 3, 20–21, 26, 41, 185
IWG–2 (Informal Working Group 2) of, 75
NOI, 5
NPRM, 5
OET (Office of Engineering and Technology) of the, 174–75
pioneer's preference, 90–91
procedure and policy, 185–89
proceedings: 1955 FM stereo NOI, 10; 1977 AM stereo NOI, 1, 18; 1977 MTS NOI, 129; 1978 AM stereo NPRM, 19; 1979 MTS NPRM, 129; 1980 AM stereo FNPRM, 24–25; 1982 AM stereo Report and Order, 27, 31; 1984 MTS Final Rule, 130; 1988 NRSC NPRM, 43; 1990 ATV NPRM, 112; 1990 DAB NOI, 67; 1992 ATV FNPRM, 124; 1992 SDARS spectrum allocation NPRM, 78–79; 1992 terrestrial DAB FNOI, 78; 1993 AM stereo Report and Order, 1, 63; 1995 DARS NPRM, 88, 90, 94; 1995 Fourth ATV FNPRM and Third NOI, 135, 145; 1996 ATV Fifth FNPRM, 139; 1996 ATV Fourth Report and Order, 145; 1997 ATV Fifth report and Order, 148–50, 152–55; 1997 ATV Sixth report and Order, 148, 150–55; 1997 Reallocation of Television Channels 60–69 NPRM, 160; 1997 Reallocation of Television Channels 60–69 Report and Order, 160–62; 1997 SDARS Report and Order, 94–95; 1998 ATV Memorandum Opinion and Order on Reconsideration of the Fifth Report and Order, 162; 1998 ATV Memorandum Opinion and Order on Reconsideration of the Sixth Report and Order, 163; 1998 DTV Must–carry, NPRM, 168–69; 1999 DAB NPRM, 103–107
public interest and the, 21, 26, 46, 135, 150
Report and Order, 5
standards proceedings, 3
"tentative" AM stereo system decision by the, 23–24, 27
FDA (Food and Drug Administration), 167
Ferris, Charles, 23, 187
Fessenden, Reginald, 7
fiber optics, 86
Firewire IEEE-1394, 170–71, 173, 189–90
Flaherty, Joe, 122, 128
FM radio, 5, 6, 8, 21, 67–68, 70, 72, 74–76, 79, 81, 92, 99, 101, 104, 152, 158, 162, 164, 170, 189, 194; audience shares, 14–16, 19, 21–23, 25, 32, 34, 38, 41; broadcasters, 10, 109; FM radio/AM radio simulcasting/duplication of programming, 14–15; monophonic broadcasting, 17; programming/format, 6, 14, 103, 189; receivers, 15
FM stereo, 3, 6, 17, 68, 71, 158, 183, 185, 187–89, 192, 194; cost of, 10; FCC approval of, 10, 15, 129; multiplex, 9–10, 17–18; receivers, 10; superficial, 17; systems, 10, 18 , 188
Fogarty, Joseph, 23, 31
Ford Motor Company, 36, 62, 71, 102
Fortune, 13
Fowler, Mark, 34–35, 42–43, 56, 81, 113, 187; "print model" of broadcast regulation, 42–43
Fox Television Network, 123, 133, 149, 157, 164–65, 171–72
Frank, Barney, 142
Fritts, Eddie, 46, 70–71, 76, 86, 91, 93–94, 136
FTC (Federal Trade Commission), 39, 51, 54, 108
Fujitsu Ten Europe, 96, 191

Furchtgott-Roth, Harold, 159, 163

Gannett Co., 67, 76–77, 100
Gates, Bill, 139–40, 191
GE (General Electric), 10, 13, 27,
    111
GI (General Instrument), 72, 79–80,
    82, 114, 120–21, 132
Gilder, George, 117
Gleason, Jackie, 12
GM (General Motors), 32, 34, 36, 58,
    62, 72–73, 84, 102. See also Delco
Goldmark, Peter, Dr., 12–13
Gone with the Wind, 13
Grand Alliance or ATRC (Advanced
    Television Research Consortium),
    99, 101, 108, 111–12, 114–15,
    117, 120–21; 127–29, 132–34,
    136–37, 139–43, 145–46, 155–56,
    175–76, 178, 185, 187, 191, 195;
    audio, 131
Grundig, 83–84, 103
Gunsmoke, 12

Harris Corporation, 53, 107, 174; AM
    stereo system, 1, 5, 23–27, 33–37,
    39, 49, 65, 100, 107
HDTV (high definition television), 4,
    67, 74–77, 79, 86, 101, 111–16,
    119–23, 127–28, 131–36, 138–40,
    146, 148, 152, 154–56, 158, 164,
    170, 182–83, 187–88, 190, 194;
    production of, 156–57; program-
    ming, 138, 146–47, 157, 165–66,
    172–73, 177, 184, 196; second
    channel, 123, 125, 133; simulcast-
    ing, 114–16, 122–24, 132; televi-
    sion receivers/sets, 124, 137,
    164–66, 171, 178–80, 196; terres-
    trial delivery of, 113; World Con-
    ference, 130. See also DTV
Heftel Broadcasting, 100
Helms, Jesse, 165
Hindery, Leo, 164–65, 179
Hitachi, 63, 95, 137, 155, 163
Hollings, Ernest, 133, 158
Hughes Communications, 113

Hughes Electronics, 84
Hughes Space and Communications In-
    ternational, 95
Hundt, Reed, 81, 85, 87–88, 94, 132,
    134–37, 139, 142, 146, 152–53,
    155, 158–59, 169, 187–88, 191,
    195

IBEW (International Brotherhood of
    Electrical Workers), 120
iBiquity Digital Corporation, 108–109
IDTV (improved-definition television),
    111
IIS (Germany's Fraunhofer Institut für
    Integrierte Schaltungen), 67
Infinity Broadcasting, 94, 100
Intel, 155
IRTS (International Radio and Televi-
    sion Society), 170
ISO (International Standards Organiza-
    tion), 80–81
ITU (International Telecommunications
    Union), 85
IUEW (International Union of Elec-
    tronics Workers), 120

Jacor Communications, 100
Japan Broadcasting Corp., 114, 120,
    127
Jensen, 102
Jones, Anne, 23–24, 31, 34
JPEG (Joint Photographic Experts
    Group), 118. See also digital com-
    pression of video
JVC, 95, 163

Kahn, Leonard, 4, 18–19, 24–25, 27,
    33–34, 36, 39, 48–50, 51–53,
    58–60, 195
Kahn (Kahn Communications, Inc.) AM
    stereo system, 1–2, 5, 7, 17, 23, 27,
    35–37, 39, 49, 52–55, 60, 62, 63,
    97, 100, 142, 185
Kahn AM stereo petition to FCC, 18
Kahn/Hazeltine Corporation, 1
KDKA-AM, Pittsburgh, 32
KDKA-FM, Pittsburgh, 10

Kennard, William, 108, 159, 163, 165, 170, 173, 176–78, 187–88
Kenwood Corp., 63, 83, 102–103
The King of Queens, 184
Kintel Technologies, 72, 79
KNX-AM, Los Angeles, 59
KRON-TV, San Francisco, 132
KTSA-AM, San Antonio, 32
KUNV-FM, Las Vegas, 87

L-band, 67, 70, 74–77, 82–83, 87–88, 92, 94, 102
LDR (Lucent Digital Radio), 80, 93, 96–97, 99–103, 106
Lee, Robert, 23
Leno, Jay, 165, 172
Lifetime Channel, 146–47
Lincom, 72, 79
LMCC (Land Mobile Communications Council), 123
LMS (Land Mobile Services), 152, 160
Lone Ranger, 12
Loral Aerospace Holdings, 79, 95
LP (long playing record), 12
LPTV (low power television), 150–51, 153–54
Lukasik, Stephen, 24

Magnavox Electronics Company AM stereo system 1, 5, 19, 23–25, 27, 33–36, 100
Marconi, Guglielmo, 7
Markey, Ed, 127, 158–59
Married With Children, 184
Marshall, Sherrie, 127
Maryland Public Television, 138
Matsushita, 27
McCain, John, 158, 169, 172
McKinney, James (Jim), 41–42, 51, 55, 57, 59, 138
Meyer, Arno, 25
Mercury Digital Communications, 72, 79
Microsoft, 155
Minnesota Public Radio, 79
MIT (Massachusetts Institute of Technology), 79, 114, 117, 120, 131, 183

Mitsubishi, 163, 172
Monday Night Football, 172
Motorola, Inc., 97, 100, 142, 174; AM stereo (C–QUAM) system, 1–2, 4–5, 7, 17, 23–25, 27, 33, 35, 37–40, 48–49, 51–55, 58–65, 185, 187
Mountain Broadcasting, 167
MPAA (Motion Picture Association of America), 141, 146, 173
MPEG (Moving Picture Experts Group), 80–81, 118
MPEG-1, 118
MPEG-2, 118, 133
MPEG-2 AAC, 97
MSTV (Association for Maximum Service Television), 116, 121–122, 125, 133–134, 138, 160, 175
MTS (multichannel television sound or TV stereo), 2–4, 18, 76, 78, 82, 92, 99, 111, 128–31, 139, 146, 164, 183, 185–90, 192, 195; receivers, 195; superficial stereo, 17, 128; systems, 129–30
MTV, 7
Murdoch, Rupert, 113
MUSICAM (Masking pattern Universal Sub-band Integrated Coding And Multiplexing) algorithm, 80, 97, 131. *See also* digital compression of audio
MVPD (multichannel video programming distributors), 181

NAB (National Association of Broadcasters), 23, 31, 40–41, 46, 50, 67, 70–71, 73–75, 77–79, 81–82, 85–87, 91–96, 123, 129, 133, 135–36, 138, 155, 159–60, 171, 176, 180; super radio featuring AMAX, 47–48
Narrow-Muse, 114, 120, 27
NASA (National Aeronautics and Space Administration), 75, 78–80, 82–83, 192
Nash Bridges, 184
National Semiconductor, 27, 96
NB (new band), 82, 89, 104

NBC (National Broadcasting Company), 6, 113, 195–96; color programming, 13–14, 195–96; radio, 12, 27–28; television, 114, 132, 149, 157, 164–65, 171–72, 174, 176; television news, 12
NBMC (National Black Media Coalition), 51
NCTA (National Cable Television Association), 123, 146, 173
Ness, Susan, 86, 154–55, 159, 163, 174
News Corp., 113
NII (National Information Infrastructure), 133
Nippon, 63
Nixon, Richard, 159
NJK, 114, 120, 127
North American Philips, 114. *See also* Philips
NPR (National Public Radio), 77, 79, 100, 104, 162
NRBA (National Radio Broadcasters Association), 23, 32, 40, 50
NRSC (National Radio Systems Committee), 7, 41, 43–48, 79, 81, 84, 89, 92–93, 97, 99, 101, 103–104, 107–108, 116, 186
NSRC (National Stereophonic Radio Committee), 10, 188
NTIA (National Telecommunications Information Agency), 43, 58, 60–62, 75
NTSC (National Television System Committee) audio, 128; scanning, 139; video, 11, 35, 111–12, 114–16, 120, 122–26, 132, 134–35, 137, 149, 151, 155–57, 166, 170, 175, 179, 183–84, 189, 192. *See also* SDTV
NYPD Blue, 184

Onkyo, 63
Ostroff, Nat, 175, 183

PAC algorithm, 80, 97, 102. *See also* digital compression of audio
Padden, Preston, 157–58, 65
Pai, Suren, 99, 101

PAL (phase alternation line), 111
Panasonic, 95, 163, 165, 170, 172
Panero, Hugh, 102
Patrick, Dennis, 81, 112–13, 187
Payne, Chris, 33–34, 50, 53
PBS (Public Broadcasting System), 123, 133, 138, 165
PCS (personal communications services), 116, 135
Philips, 83, 163, 174. *See also* North American Philips
Pilot Radio Television Sets, 193
Pioneer Electronics, 54, 63, 83, 103, 163
Pohlmann, Ken, 1, 95
Powell, Michael, 159, 170
Press Broadcasting, 60–62
Pressler, Larry, 140
Primestar, 171
Primosphere, 79, 90, 94
Procter & Gamble, 172
Providence Journal Broadcasting Group, 122

Quello, James, 23, 30–31, 81–82, 86, 134, 136, 153, 159, 187

Radio Act of 1912, 21
Radio news, 12
Radio One, 100
RadioSat (Radio Satellite Corp.), 72–73
Radio World, 7, 67, 71, 89, 96, 108
Rau, Michael, 50, 76, 78
RCA (Radio Corporation of America), 8, 171, 193, 196; color TV system, 13, 195–96; experimental television station W2XBS, 11; television experimentation, 11
Reagan, Ronald, 81
Recoton, 102
Rivera, Henry, 31
RMA (Radio Manufacturers Association), 11, 13
Roseanne, 184
Rothblatt, Martin, 72, 77
Runco, 163

Samsung, 163
Sansui, 31, 34–35, 43, 49, 53, 63

Sanyo, 43, 63, 95
Sarnoff, David, 7, 11–12, 195–96
Sarnoff Research Center, 114, 116–17, 120–21, 131, 136, 138; NxtWave, 174
SB-ADPCM, 80. *See also* digital compression of audio
S-band, 70, 75–76, 79, 82–84, 90–91, 94–95, 102
SBE (Society of Broadcast Engineers), 79
SCI (Strother Communications Inc.), 71–72, 74, 76, 79
SDARS (satellite digital audio radio services), 68, 70–71, 73, 77, 79, 83–86, 88, 90–91, 94–95, 101–103, 108, 190. *See also* DAB, satellite delivery of
SDTV (standard definition television), 111–112, 147, 164; multiple channel delivery, 123, 136–37, 139, 148, 155, 157–58, 170, 182; pixels, 140
SEC (Securities Exchange Commission), 159
SECAM (séquential colour avec memorie, or sequential color with memory), 111
Shapiro, Gary, 81, 93, 164, 176
Sharp, 63, 163
Shively Labs, 67
SILK-FM, British Columbia, 92
Sikes, Al, 58, 76, 81, 115–16, 121–24, 127, 132, 134, 187–88
Sinclair Broadcast Group, 100, 157, 174–76, 183
Sirius Satellite Radio, 102–103, 108. *See also* CD Radio, Inc.
Skelton, Red, 12
Sklar, Rick, 25
Sky-Highway Radio Corp., 79
SMPTE (Society of Motion Picture and Television Engineers), 119
Sony, 27, 31, 34–35, 43, 49, 53–54, 63, 83, 103, 125, 163, 170, 173; iLink, 170; Software Corporation/Warner Music Group, 72
Space Systems, 95

Spectrum Compatible HDTV, 114, 120–21
Spielberg, Steven, 139
Sterling, Christopher, 29
Streeter, Bill, 24
Strother, Ron, 71, 74
Struble, Robert J., 98–101, 107
Super Bowl XXV, 172
Susan and God, 11

Tauzin, Billy, 158–59, 165, 172, 177
TCI (Tele-Communications Inc.), 146, 164–65, 179
Telecommunications Act of 1996, 150–51
Telecommunications Authorization Act of 1992, 1, 7, 63
Telefunken, 83, 111
Telesonics Systems Inc., 129
teletext, 129
television:
    black-and-white (monochrome), 12–13, 71, 137, 190, 192; programming, 3, 11–12; receivers/sets, 11, 117, 135, 120, 140, 143, 166, 191–93; transmission systems, 11
    broadcasters, 129, 136–39, 141, 143, 145, 153–54, 158, 182, 187, 189
    challenge to radio by, 9
    color, 4, 6, 70–71, 111, 120, 122–23, 154, 158, 178, 183–85, 187–90, 192, 195; during Korean War, 13; FCC approval of, 12, 35; programming, 3, 12–14, 157–58, 192; receiver incompatibility, 6, 13, 117, 190; receivers/sets, 6, 13–14, 49, 98–99, 114, 120, 135, 140, 143, 157, 166, 192–94, 196; systems, 12
    debut at 1939 New York World's Fair, 11, 193
    during World War II, 11
    Golden Age of, 11–12
    license freeze, 11
    monophonic audio, 17
    Television/Radio Age, 34
    television screen aspect ratio, 145, 191; (4:3), 119, 141, 156, 173; (16:9)

widescreen, 112–113, 119,
    141–42, 155–156, 165, 178, 180
Telos Systems, 97
Texar, Inc., 54, 57–62
TFT, 38–39, 53
Thomson Consumer Electronics, 72,
    79, 83, 114, 120, 163–64, 172,
    174
Time Warner Cable, 72, 171
Tohtsu Co., 53
The Tonight Show with Jay Leno, 165,
    172
Toshiba, 193
trade magazines, 5–6
transistors, 14
Tristani, Gloria, 159
TriTech Microelectronics, 97
TV Broadcast, 166
TV Technology, 142–43

UDTV (ultra-definition television), 111,
    119
UHF (ultra high frequency), 50, 60, 75,
    85, 116, 124, 148, 150–51, 154,
    160–62
United States Air Force, 74
United States Court of Appeals, 167
United States Supreme Court, 169
UPN (United Paramount Network),
    172
USADR (USA Digital Radio), 67–68,
    72–73, 76–81, 83, 85, 87–88,
    91–94, 96–109; iDAB, 98; Project
    Acorn, 72–73, 77
USSB (U.S. Satellite Broadcasting),
    171
Utah's Division of Consumer Protec-
    tion, 50

Van Allen, Dave, 54–57
Vaudeville, 12
VCR (videocassette recorder), 6, 101,
    123, 125, 128, 152, 154, 158,
    166, 170, 182, 192, 194. *See also*
    VTR
VHF (very high frequency), 50, 60, 85,
    151

videodisc players, 128
Vidikron, 163
VOA (Voice of America), 78–80, 82–83
Voron, Abe, 23
VTR (video tape recorder), 156. *See also*
    VCR

Walker, Texas Ranger, 172
WARC (World Administrative Radio
    Conference), 74–75, 77, 86
Washburn, Abbott, 23–24, 30
WBBM-FM, Chicago, 77
WBBR-AM, New York, 84
WBJB-FM, Lincroft, New Jersey, 101
WCMZ-AM, Miami, 47
Westinghouse, 10, 13, 59, 67, 94, 100,
    137, 193
WETA-TV, Washington, DC, 124,
    138
WFFA-DT, Dallas, 166–67
WGCI-AM, Chicago, 77
WGFM, Schenectady, NY, 10
WGN-TV, Chicago, 72–73, 171
WHD-TV Model HDTV Station Pro-
    ject, 138, 155
Wiley, Richard, 113–15, 120, 127, 132,
    134, 136, 147, 174
WILL-FM, University of Illinois, 77
WJLK-AM, Asbury Park, New Jersey,
    60
WNOE-AM, New Orleans, 77
WorldDAB, 88, 95
WorldSpace, 95
WPAY, New Haven, CT, 17
WPST-FM, Trenton, New Jersey,
    101
WRAL-HD, Raleigh, North Carolina,
    138
WRAL-TV, Raleigh, North Carolina,
    138
WRC-TV, Washington, DC, 138
Wright, Scott, 5–6
WSB-DT, Atlanta, 170–71
WSB-TV, Atlanta, 170
WTBS-TV, Atlanta, 72–73, 171
WWJ-TV, Detroit, 162
WWNO-FM, New Orleans, 77

WZKY-AM, Albemarle, North Carolina, 52

Xetron Corporation, 67
XM Satellite Radio, 102–103, 108. *See also* AMRC

Your Show of Shows, 12

Zenith Electronics Corporation, 10, 113, 120–21, 129–31, 160, 163, 186; 8-Level Vestigial Side-band (8–VSB) transmission system, 132, 174–78
Zworykin, Vladimir, 10, 118

About the Author

W. A. KELLY HUFF is Professor of Communication in the Department of Communication at Truett-McConnell College. He is the author of more than 70 publications and papers on communication, electronic media, and journalism.